THE
SOCIALIST REGISTER 1974

THE
SOCIALIST REGISTER
1974

EDITED BY
RALPH MILIBAND
and
JOHN SAVILLE

Merlin Book Club

THE MERLIN PRESS
LONDON

First published in 1974
by The Merlin Press Ltd
2–4 West Ferry Road,
Sufferance Wharf, Isle of Dogs,
London E.14

Printed in Great Britain by
Western Printing Services Ltd
Bristol

© The Merlin Press 1974

SBN 85036 187–7 (cloth)

SBN 85036 188–5 (paperback)

TABLE OF CONTENTS

ACKNOWLEDGEMENTS

This is the eleventh issue of *The Socialist Register* and we wish to express our warm thanks to our contributors and to our translators, Ben Brewster and Brian Pearce; and also to Martin Eve, our publisher. Once again, we should like to stress that the views expressed by any of our contributors are not necessarily shared by the others, or by the Editors. This must be taken as being particularly true of Leszek Kolakowski's "Rejoinder" to E. P. Thompson, which we regard in some ways as a tragic document. In a different perspective, we reject Walter Goldstein's formulations as to what a socialist government can or cannot do about multi-national corporations and nationalization. But it is obvious that his essay raises critical issues for the left, which we hope to see pursued in future volumes of the *Register*.

June 1974

R.M.
J.S.

MY CORRECT VIEWS ON EVERYTHING

A Rejoinder to Edward Thompson's "Open Letter to Leszek Kolakowski"

Leszek Kolakowski

Dear Edward Thompson,

Why I am not very happy about this public correspondence is because your letter deals as much (at least) with personal attitudes as with ideas. However I have no personal accounts to settle either with Communist ideology or with the year 1956; this was settled long ago. But if you insist,

> Let us begin and carry up this corpse
> Singing together. . . .

In a review of the last issue of *Socialist Register* by Raymond Williams, I read that your letter is one of the best pieces of Left writings in the last decade, which implies directly that all or nearly all the rest was worse. He knows better and I take his word. I should be proud to having occasioned, to a certain degree, this text, even if I happen to be its target. And so, my first reaction is one of gratitude.

My second reaction is of *embarras de richesses*. You will excuse me if I make a fair choice of topics in my reply to your 100 pages of the Open Letter (not well segmentated, as you will admit). I will try to take up the most controversial ones. I do not think I should comment on the autobiographical pages, interesting though they are. When you say, e.g. that you do not go to Spain for holidays, that you never attend a conference of Socialists without paying a part of the costs out of your own pocket, that you do not participate in meetings funded by the Ford Foundation, that you are like Quakers of old who refused to take off their hats before authorities, etc., I do not think it advisable to reply with a virtue-list of my own; this list would probably be less impressive. Neither am I going to exchange the story of your dismissal from the *New Left Review* for all the stories of my expulsions from different editorial committees of different journals; these stories would be rather trivial.

My third reaction is of sadness and I mean it. Incompetent though I am in your field of studies, I know your reputation as a scholar and

1

historian and I found it regrettable to see in your Letter so many Leftist clichés which survive in speech and print owing to three devices: first, the refusal to analyse words and the use of verbal hybrids purposely designed to confound the issues; second, the use of moral or sentimental standards in some cases and of political and historical standards in other similar cases; third, the refusal to accept historical facts as they are. I will try to say more precisely what I mean.

Your letter contains some personal grievances and some arguments on general questions. I will start with a minor personal grievance. Oddly enough, you seem to feel offended by not having been invited to the Reading conference and you state that if you had been invited you would have refused to attend anyway, on serious moral grounds. I presume, consequently, that if you had been invited, you would have felt offended as well and so, no way out of hurting you was open to the organizers. Now, the moral ground you cite is the fact that in the organizing Committee you found the name of Robert Cecil. And what is sinister about Robert Cecil is that he once worked in the British diplomatic service. And so, your integrity does not allow you to sit at the same table with someone who used to work in British diplomacy. O, blessed Innocence! You and I, we were both active in our respective Communist Parties in the 40s and 50s which means that, whatever our noble intentions and our charming ignorance (or refusal to get rid of ignorance) were, we supported, within our modest means, a regime based on mass slave labour and police terror of the worst kind in human history. Do you not think that there are many people who could refuse to sit at the same table with us on this ground? No, you are innocent, while I do not feel, as you put it, the "sense of the politics of those years" when so many Western intellectuals were converted to Stalinism.

Your "sense of politics of those years" is obviously subtler and more differentiated than mine, I gather this from your casual comments on Stalinism. First, you say, that a part (a part, I do not omit that) of responsibility for Stalinism lies upon the Western powers. You say, second, that "to a historian, fifty years is too short a time in which to judge a new social system, if such a system is arising". Third, we know, as you say, "times when communism has shown a most human face, between 1917 and the early 1920s and again from the battle of Stalingrad to 1946".

Everything is right on some additional assumptions. Obviously, in the world in which we live, important events in one country are usually to be credited in part to what happened in other countries. You will certainly not deny that a part of the responsibility for German Nazism lay upon the Soviet Union; I wonder how this affects your judgement on German Nazism?

Your second comment is revealing, indeed. What is fifty years "to a historian"? The same day as I am writing this, I happen to have read a book by Anatol Marchenko, relating his experiences in Soviet prisons and concentration camps in the early 1960s (not 1930s). The book was published in Russian in Frankfurt in 1973. The author, a Russian worker, was caught when he tried to cross the Soviet border to Iran. He was lucky to have done it in Khrushchev's time, when the regrettable errors of J. V. Stalin were over (yes, regrettable, let us face it, even if in part accounted for by the Western powers), and so, he got only six years of hard labour in a concentration camp. One of his stories is about three Lithuanian prisoners who tried to escape from the convoy in a forest. Two of them were quickly caught, then shot many times in the legs, then ordered to get up which they could not do, then kicked and trampled by guards, then bitten and torn up by police dogs (such an amusement, survival of capitalism) and only then stabbed to death with bayonets. All this with witty remarks by the officer, of the kind "Now, free Lithuania, crawl, you'll get your independence straight off!" The third prisoner was shot and, reputed to be dead, was thrown under corpses in the cart; discovered later to be alive he was not killed (de-stalinization!) but left for several days in a dark cell with his festering wound and he survived after his arm was cut off.

This is one of thousand stories you can read in many now available books. Such books are rather reluctantly read by the enlightened Leftist elite, both because they are largely irrelevant, they supply us only with small details (and, after all, we agree that some errors were committed) and because many of them have not been translated (did you notice that if you meet a Westerner who learnt Russian you have at least 90% chance of meeting a bloody reactionary? Progressive people do not enjoy this painful effort of learning Russian, they know better anyway).

And so, what is fifty years to a historian? Fifty years covering the life of an obscure Russian worker Marchenko or of a still more obscure Lithuanian student who has not even written a book? Let us not hurry with judging a "new social system". Certainly I could ask you how many years you needed to assess the merits of the new military regime in Chile or in Greece, but I know your answer: no analogy, Chile and Greece remain within capitalism (factories are privately owned) while Russia started a new "alternative society" (factories are state owned and so is land and so are all its inhabitants). As genuine historians we can wait for another century and keep our slightly melancholic but cautiously optimistic historical wisdom.

Not so, of course, with "that beast", "that old bitch, consumer capitalism" (your words). Wherever we look, our blood is boiling. Here we may afford to be ardent moralists again and we can prove—as you do—that the capitalist system has a "logic" of its own that all reforms are unable to cancel. The national health service, you say, is impoverished by the existence of private practice, equality in education is spoilt because people are trained for private industry etc. You do not say that all reforms are doomed to failure, you only explain that as long as reforms do not destroy capitalism, capitalism is not destroyed, which is certainly true. And you propose "a peaceful revolutionary transition to an alternative socialist logic". You think apparently that this makes perfectly clear what you mean; I think, on the contrary, that it is perfectly obscure unless, again, you imagine that once the total state ownership of factories is granted, there remain only minor technical problems on the road to your utopia. But this is precisely what remains to be proved and the *onus probandi* lies on those who maintain that these (insignificant "to a historian") fifty years of experience may be discarded by the authors of the new blueprint for the socialist society (In Russia there were "exceptional circumstances", weren't there? But there is nothing exceptional about Western Europe).

Your way of interpreting these modest fifty years (fifty-seven now) of the new alternative society is revealed as well in your occasional remarks about the "most human face of communism" between 1917 and the early '20s and between Stalingrad and 1946. What do you mean by "human face" in the first case? The attempt to rule the entire economy by police and army, resulting in mass hunger with uncountable victims, in several hundred peasants' revolts, all drowned in blood (a total economic disaster, as Lenin would admit later, after having killed and imprisoned an indefinite number of Mensheviks and SRs for predicting precisely that)? Or do you mean the armed invasion of seven non-Russian countries which had formed their independent governments, some socialist, some not (Georgia, Armenia, Azerbaijan, Ukraine, Lithuania, Latvia, Estonia; O God, where are all these curious tribes living?)? Or do you mean the dispersion by soldiers of the only democratically elected Parliament in Russian history, before it could utter one single word? The suppression by violence of all political parties, including socialist ones, the abolition of the non-Bolshevik press and, above all, the replacement of law with the absolute power of the party and its police in killing, torturing and imprisoning anybody they wanted? The mass repression of the Church? The Kronstadt uprising? And what is the most human face in 1942–46? Do you mean the deportation of eight entire nationalities of the Soviet Union with hundreds of thousands of victims (let us say seven, not eight, one was deported shortly before Stalingrad)? Do you mean sending to concentration camps hundreds of thousands of Soviet prisoners of war handed over by the Allies? Do you mean the so-called collectivization of the Baltic countries if you have an idea about the reality of this word?

I have three possible explanations of your statement. First, that you are simply ignorant of these facts; this I find incredible, considering your profession of historian. Second, that you use the word "human face" in a very Thompsonian sense which I do not grasp. Third, that you, not unlike most of both orthodox and critical communists, believe that everything is all right in the Communist system as long as the leaders of the party are not murdered. This is, in fact, the standard way of how communists become "critical": when they realize that the new alternative socialist logic does not spare the communists themselves and in particular party leaders. Did you notice that the only victims Khrushchev mentioned by name in his speech of 1956 (whose importance I am far from underestimating) were the Stalinists *pur sang* like himself, most of them (like Postychev) hangmen of merit with uncountable crimes committed before they became victims themselves? Did you notice, in memoirs or critical analyses written by many ex-communists (I will not quote names, excuse me) that their horror only suddenly emerged when they saw communists being slaughtered? They always are pleading the innocence of the victims by saying "but these people were communists"! (Which, incidentally, is a self-defeating way of defence, for it suggests that there is nothing wrong in slaughtering non-communists, and this implies that there is an authority to decide who is and who is not a communist, and this authority can be only the same rulers who keep the gun; consequently, the slaughtered are by definition non-communists and everything is all right.)

Well, Thompson, I really do not attribute to you this way of thinking. Still I cannot help noticing your use of double standards of evaluation. And when I say "double standards" I do not mean indulgence for the justifiable inexperience of the "new society" in coping with new problems. I mean the use, alternatively, of political or moral standards to similar situations and this I find unjustifiable. We must not be fervent moralists in some cases and Real-politikers or philosophers of world history in others, depending on political circumstances. This is a point I would like to make clear to you if we are to understand each other. I will quote to you (from memory) a talk with a Latin-American revolutionary who told me about torture in Brazil. I asked: "What is wrong with torture?" and he said: "What do you mean? Do you suggest it is all right? Are you justifying torture?" And I said: "On the contrary, I simply ask you if you think that torture is a morally inadmissible monstrosity." "Of course," he replied. "And so is torture in Cuba?", I asked. "Well, he answered, this is another thing. Cuba is a small country under the constant threat of American imperialists. They have to use all means of self-defence, however regrettable."

Then I said: "Now, you cannot have it both ways. If you believe, as I do, that torture is abominable and inadmissible on moral grounds, it is such, by definition, in all circumstances. If however there are circumstances where it can be tolerated, you can condemn no regime for the very fact of applying torture, since you assume that there is nothing essentially wrong with torture itself. Either you condemn torture in Cuba in exactly the same way you do for Brazil, or you prevent yourself from condemning the Brazilian police for the very fact of torturing people. In fact, you cannot condemn torture on political grounds, because in most cases it is perfectly efficient and the torturers get what they want. You can condemn it only on moral grounds and then, necessarily, everywhere in the same way, in Batista's Cuba or in Castro's Cuba, in North Vietnam and in South Vietnam."

This is a banal but important point which I hope is clear to you. I simply refuse to join people who show how their hearts are bleeding to death when they hear about any, big or minor (and rightly condemnable) injustice in the US and suddenly become wise historiosophists or cool rationalists when told about worse horrors of the new alternative society.

This is one, but not the only one, reason of the spontaneous and almost universal mistrust people from Eastern Europe nourish towards the Western New Left. By a strange coincidence the majority of these ungrateful people, once they come to or settle in Western Europe or in the US, pass for reactionaries. These narrow empiricists and egoists extrapolate a poor few decades of their petty personal experience (logically inadmissible, as you rightly notice) and find in it pretexts to cast doubts on the radiant socialist future elaborated on the best Marxist-Leninist grounds by ideologists of the New Left for the Western countries.

This is a topic I will pursue somewhat further. I assume that we do not differ in accepting facts as they are and that we do not get knowledge of the existing societies by the deduction from a general theory. (Again, I will quote my talk with a Maoist from India. He said: "The cultural revolution in China was a class struggle of poor peasants against kulaks." I asked: "How do you know that?", and he replied: "From Marxist-Leninist theory." I commented: "Yes, that is what I guessed." He did not understand, but you do.) This is not enough, however, for, as you know, any properly vague ideology is always able to absorb (meaning: to discard) all facts without giving up any of its ingredients. And the trouble is that most people are not dedicated ideologists. Their shallow minds work in such a way as if they believed that nobody has ever seen capitalism or socialism but only sets of small facts they are incapable of interpreting theoretically. They simply notice that people in some countries are better off than in others, that in some of them production, distribution and services are much more efficient than in others, that here people enjoy civil and human rights and freedom and there they do not. (I should rather say "freedom" in quotation marks, as you do; I do realize that this is a part of the absolutely obligatory Leftist spelling, to use the word "freedom" in quotation marks when applied to Western Europe; what a "freedom", indeed, enough to burst one's sides with laughter. And we, people without sense of humour, do not laugh.)

I do not try to make you believe that you live in paradise and we in hell. In my country, Poland, we do not suffer hunger, people are not being tortured in prisons, we have no concentration camps (in contrast to Russia), in the last couple of years we have had only few political prisoners (in contrast to Russia), and many people go abroad relatively easily (again, in contrast to Russia). Still, we are a country deprived of sovereignty, and this not in the sense Mr Foot and Mr Powell fear that Britain could lose her sovereignty because of joining the Common Market, but in a sadly direct and palpable sense: in that all key sectors of our life, including the army, foreign policy, foreign trade, important industries and ideology, are under tight control of a foreign empire which exerts its power with a considerable meticulousness (e.g. preventing specific books from being published or specific information from being divulged, not to speak of more serious matters). Still, we appreciate immensely our margins of freedom when we compare our position with that of entirely liberated countries like the Ukraine or Lithuania which, as far as their right to self-government is concerned, are in a much worse situation than the old colonies of the British empire were. And the point is that these margins, important though they are (we can still say and publish significantly more than people elsewhere in the rouble zone, except for Hungary), are not supported by any legal guarantees at all and can be (as they used to be) cancelled over-night by a decision taken by party rulers in Warsaw or in Moscow. And this is simply because we got rid of this fraudulent bourgeois device of the division of powers and we achieved the socialist dream of unity, which means that the same apparatus has all legislative, executive and judicial power in addition to its power of controlling all means of production; the same people make law, interpret it and enforce it; king, Parliament, army chief, judge, prosecutor, policeman and (new socialist invention) owner of all national wealth and the only employer at one and the same desk—what better social unity can you imagine?

You are proud of not going to Spain for political reasons. Un-principled as I am, I was there twice. It is unpleasant to say that this regime, oppressive and undemocratic though it is, gives its citizens more freedom than any socialist country (except, perhaps, for Yugoslavia). I am not saying this with *Schadenfreude*, but with shame, keeping in mind the pathos of the civil war. The Spaniards have the frontiers open (never mind the reason which is, in this case, thirty million tourists each year) and no totalitarian system can work with open frontiers. They have censorship after, and not before, publication (my own book was published in Spain and then confiscated, but after one thousand copies had been sold; we all should like to have the same conditions in Poland) and you find in Spanish bookshops Marx, Trotsky, Freud, Marcuse etc. Like us, they have no elections and no legal political parties but, unlike us, they have many forms of organization which are independent of the state and the ruling party. They are sovereign as a state.

You will probably say that I am talking in vain because you clearly stated that you are far from seeing your ideal in the existing socialist states and that you were thinking in terms of a democratic socialism. You did, indeed, and I am not accusing you of being an admirer of the socialist secret police. Still, what I am trying to say is very relevant to your article for two reasons. First, you consider the existing socialist states as (imperfect, to be sure) beginnings of a new and better social order, as transitional forms which went beyond capitalism and are heading towards utopia. I do not deny that this form is new but I do deny that it is in any respect superior to the democratic countries of Europe and I defy you to prove the opposite, i.e. to show a point in which the existing socialism may claim its superiority, except for the notorious advantages all despotic systems have over democratic ones (less trouble with people). The second, and equally important, point is that you pretend to know what democratic socialism means to you and you do not know. You write: "My own utopia, two hundred years ahead, would not be like Morris's 'epoch of rest'. It would be a world (as D. H. Lawrence would have it) where the 'money values' give way before the 'life values', or (as Blake would have it) 'corporeal' will give way to 'mental' war. With sources of power easily available, some men and women might choose to live in unified communities, sited, like Cistercian monasteries, in centres of great natural beauty, where agricultural, industrial and intellectual pursuits might be combined. Others might prefer the variety and pace of an urban life which redis-covers some of the qualities of the city-state. Others will prefer a life of seclusion, and many will pass between all three. Scholars would follow the disputes of different schools, in Paris, Jakarta or Bogota."

This is a very good sample of socialist writing. It amounts to saying that the world should be good, and not bad, and I am entirely on your side on this issue. I share without restrictions your (and Marx's, and Shakespeare's, and many others') analysis to the effect that it is very deplorable that people's minds are occupied with the endless pursuit of money, that needs have a magic power of infinite growth, and that the profit motive, instead of use-value, is ruling production. Your superiority consists in that you know exactly how to get rid of all this and I do not.

Why the problems of the real and the only existing communism which Leftist ideologists put aside so easily ("all right, this was done in exceptional circumstances, we won't imitate these patterns, we will do better" etc) are crucial for socialist thought is because the experiences of the "new alternative society" have shown very convincingly that the only universal medicine these people have for social evils—state ownership of the means of production—is not only perfectly compatible with all disasters of the capitalist world, with exploitation, imperialism, pollution, misery, economic waste, national hatred and national oppression, but that it adds to them a series of disasters of its own: inefficiency, lack of economic incentives and, above all, the unrestricted role of the omnipotent bureaucracy, a concentration of power never known before in human history. Just a stroke of bad luck? No, you do not say exactly so, you simply prefer to ignore the problem and rightly so, because all attempts to examine this experience lead us back not only to contingent historical circumstances but to the very idea of socialism and the discovery of incompatible demands hidden in this idea (or at least demands whose compatibility remains to be proved). We want a society with a large autonomy of small communities, do we not? And we want central planning in the economy. Let us try to think now how both work together. We want technical progress and we want perfect security for people; let us look closer how both could be combined. We want industrial democracy and we want efficient management: do they work well together? Of course they do, in the leftist heaven everything is compatible and everything settled, lamb and lion sleep in the same bed. Look at the horrors of the world and see how easily we can get rid of them once we make a peaceful revolution toward the new socialist logic. The Middle East war and Palestinian grievances? Of course, this is the result of capitalism, just let us make the revolution and the question is settled. Pollution? Of course, no problem at all, just let the new proletarian state take over the factories and no pollution any more. Traffic jams? This is because capitalists do not care a damn about human comfort, just give us power (in fact, this is a rather good point, in socialism we have far fewer cars and correspondingly fewer traffic jams). People die from hunger in India? Of course, American imperialists eat their food, but once we make the revolution, etc. Northern Ireland? Demographic problems in Mexico? Racial hatred? Tribal wars? Inflation? Criminality? Corruption? Degradation of educational systems? There is such a simple answer to everything and, moreover, the same answer to everything!

This is not a caricature, not in the slightest. This is a standard pattern of thought of those who have overcome the miserable illusions of reformism and invented the beneficial device for solving all problems of mankind, and this device consists in a few words which, when repeated often enough, start looking as if they had a content: revolution, alternative society, etc. And we have in addition a number of negative words to provoke horror, for instance "anti-communism" or "liberal". You use these words as well, Edward, without explanation, aware though you must be that the purpose of these words is to mingle many different things and to produce vague negative associations. What is, in fact, the anti-communism you do not profess? Certainly, we know people who believe that there are no serious social problems in the Western world except for the communist danger, that all social conflicts here are to be explained by a communist plot, that the world would be a paradise if only sinister communist forces did not interfere, and that the most hideous military dictatorships deserve support if only they suppress communist movements. You are not anti-communist in that sense? Neither am I. But you will be called anti-communist if you do not strongly believe that the actual Soviet (resp. Chinese) system is the most perfect society the human mind has invented so far, or if you wrote a piece of purely scholarly work on the history of communism without lies. And there is a great number of other possibilities in between. The convenience of the word "anti-communism", the bogeyman of the leftist jargon, is precisely to put all of them in the same sack and never to explain the meaning of the word. The same with the word "liberal". Who is a "liberal"? Perhaps a 19th-century free-trader who proclaimed that the state should forbear from interfering in the "free contract" between workers and employers and that workers' unions were contrary to the free contract principle? Do you suggest that you are not "liberal" in this sense? This is very much to your credit. But according to the unwritten revolutionary OED you are "liberal" if you imagine in general that freedom is better than slavery (I do not mean the genuine, profound freedom people enjoy in socialist countries, but the miserable formal freedom invented by the bourgeoisie to deceive the toiling masses). And the word "liberal" has the easy task of amalgamating these and other things. And so, let us proclaim loudly that we spurn liberal illusions, but let us never explain what we exactly mean.

Should I go on with this progressive vocabulary? Just one more word which, I emphasize, you do not use in this sound sense, the word "fascist" or "fascism". This is an ingenious discovery, with a fair range of applications. Sometimes fascist is a person I disagree with but, because of my ignorance, I am unable to discuss with, so I will better kick him. When I collect my experiences, I notice that fascist is a person who holds one of the following beliefs (by way of example): 1) That people should wash themselves, rather than go dirty; 2) that freedom of the press in America is preferable to the ownership of the whole press by one ruling party; 3) that people should not be jailed for their opinions, both communist and anti-communist; 4) that racial criteria, in favour of either whites or blacks, are inadvisable in admission to Universities; 5) that torture is condemnable, no matter who applies it. (Roughly speaking "fascist" was the same as "liberal".) Fascist was, by definition, a person who happened to have been in jail in a communist country. The refugees from Czechoslovakia in 1968 were sometimes met in Germany by very progressive and absolutely revolutionary leftists with placards saying "fascism will not pass".

And you blame me for making a caricature of the New Left. I wonder what such a caricature would be. Still, your irritation (this is one of the few points where your pen flares up) is understandable. You quote an interview I gave to the German Radio (and later translated from German into English and published in *Encounter*) where I said two or three general sentences expressing my disgust with New Leftist movements, as I knew them in America and Germany and—this is the point—I did not specify which movements I meant and I said instead vaguely "some people" etc. This means, I did not specifically exclude the *New Left Review* in 1960–3 when you were associated with it or even I tacitly included you in my statement. Here you got me. I did not specifically exclude the *New Left Review* in 1960–3 and, I admit, I did not even keep it in mind when I was talking to the German journalist. I thought that to say "some new leftists" etc. is rather like saying, e.g., "some British academics are drunkards". Do you think that many academics would be offended by such a (admittedly not very ingenious) statement, and if so, which ones? My comfort is that if I happen to say publicly such things on the New Left, my socialist friends somehow never feel that they could be included even if they are not specifically excluded.

But I cannot delay any longer. I hereby solemnly declare that in an interview to the German Radio in 1971, when I was talking about leftist obscurantism, I was not thinking of the *New Left Review* in 1960–63, with which Edward Thompson was involved. Will that be all right?

You are right, Edward, that we, people from Eastern Europe, have a tendency to underestimate the gravity of the social issues democratic societies face and we may be blamed for that. But we cannot be blamed for not taking seriously people who, unable though they are to remember correctly any single fact from our history or to say which barbaric dialect we speak, are perfectly able instead to teach us how liberated we are in the East and who have a rigorously scientific solution for humanity's illness and this solution consists in repeating a few phrases we could hear for thirty years on each celebration of the 1 May and read in any party propaganda brochure. (I am talking about the attitude of progressive radicals; the conservative attitude to the problems of the East is different and may be summarized briefly:

"This would be awful in our country, but for these tribes it is good enough.")

When I was leaving Poland at the end of 1968 (I had not been in any Western country for at least six previous years), I had a somewhat vague idea of what the radical student movement and different leftist groups or parties might be. What I saw and read I found pathetic and disgusting in nearly all (still: not all) cases. I do not shed tears for a few windows smashed in demonstrations, that old bitch, consumer capitalism, will survive it. Neither do I find scandalous the rather natural ignorance of young people. What impressed me was mental degradation of a kind I had never seen before in any leftist movement. I saw young people trying to "reconstitute" universities and to liberate them from horrifying, savage, monstrous, fascist oppression. The list of demands, with variations, was very similar all over the world of campuses. These fascist pigs of the Establishment want us to pass examinations while we are making the revolution; let them give all of us A grades without examinations; curiously enough, the anti-fascist warriors wanted to get their degrees and diplomas in such fields as mathematics, sociology or law, and not in such as carrying posters, distributing leaflets or destroying offices. And sometimes they got what they wanted, the fascist pigs of the establishment gave them grades without examinations. Very often there were demands for abolishing altogether some subjects of teaching as irrelevant, e.g. foreign languages (these fascists want us, internationalist revolutionaries, to waste time in learning languages, why? To prevent us from making world revolution!) In one place revolutionary philosophers went on strike because they got a reading list including Plato, Descartes and other bourgeois idiots, instead of relevant great philosophers like Che Guevara and Mao. In another, revolutionary mathematicians pass a motion that the department should organize courses on the social tasks of mathematics and (this is the point) each student should be able to attend this course as many times as he wanted and each time get credit for it, which meant that he could get the diploma in mathematics exactly for nothing. In still another place, the noble martyrs of the world revolution demanded to be examined only by other students they would choose themselves, and not by these old reactionary pseudo-scholars. Professors should be appointed (by students, of course) according to their political views, students admitted on the same grounds. In several cases in the US, the vanguard of the oppressed toiling masses set fire to University libraries (irrelevant pseudo-knowledge of the Establishment). Needless to say, you could hear that there is no difference, no difference at all, between the life in a California campus and a Nazi concentration camp. And all were Marxists, of course, which meant they knew three or four sentences written by Marx or Lenin, in particular the sentence "the philosophers have only interpreted the world, in various ways; the point, however, is to change it" (what Marx wanted to say in this sentence, it is obvious to them, was that it made no sense to learn).

I could carry on this list for pages but this may suffice, the patterns are always the same: the great socialist revolution consists, first of all, in giving us privileges, titles and power for our political opinions and in destroying the old reactionary academic values like knowledge and logical abilities (but these fascist pigs should give us money, money, money).

And what about the workers? There are two rival views. One (pseudo-Marcusian) says that these bastards were bribed by the bourgeoisie and one cannot expect anything more from them, now the students are the most oppressed and the most revolutionary class of society. Another (Leninist) says that workers have a false consciousness and do not understand their alienation, because the capitalists give them wrong papers to read, but we, revolutionaries, store in our heads the correct consciousness of the proletariat, we know what the workers should think and, in fact, do think without knowing it; consequently we deserve to take power (but not in this stupid electoral play which, as has been scientifically proved, is just for deceiving the people).

You say complacently "revolutionary farce". All right, it is. But to say this is not enough. This is not a farce capable of turning upside down the society but it is capable of destroying the university and this is a performance worth worrying about (some German universities look already rather like party schools).

And let us go back to the more general question we discussed earlier in private letters. You defend the movement I just described by saying "but there was a Vietnam war". Very much so, indeed, to put it elegantly. And many other things, no doubt. Traditional German universities had some intolerable features. Italian and French universities had others of their own. There are many things in any society and in any university to justify protest. And—this is my point—you will find no political movement in the world which has no good and well justified claims. If you look at mutual accusations of parties vying for power you always find some well chosen and well grounded points in their claims and attacks, and you do not take it as a reason to support all of them. Nobody is altogether wrong and you are right, of course, in saying that those who joined the communist parties were not altogether wrong. When you look at Nazi propaganda against the Weimar republic, you will find a great number of well justified points: they said that the Versailles Treaty was a shame, and it was; that the democracy was corrupted, and it was; they attacked aristocracy, plutocracy, the power of bankers and, incidentally, the pseudo-freedom, irrelevant to the real needs of the people and serving dirty Jewish newspapers. And this was not a good reason to say "all right, they do not behave very decently and some points in their ideas are rather silly, but they are not wrong in many questions, so let us give them a qualified support". At least, many people refused to say so. And in fact, had the Nazis not had many good points in attacking the existing regime, they would not have won, there would not have been such a phenomenon as the ranks of *Rotfront* passing with unfolded colours over to the SA. This is the reason why, when I saw movements imitating the same patterns of behaviour and imitating a part of the same ideology (viz. in all points concerning "formal" freedom and all democratic institutions, tolerance and academic values) I could not be strongly impressed by the saying: "but there was a Vietnam war".

You say that we should help the blind to recover their sight. I accept this advice with a slight restriction: it is difficult to apply when you have to do with people who are omniscient and all-seeing anyway. I do not remember having ever refused a discussion with people who were ready to have it, the trouble is that some were not, and this precisely because of their omniscience, which I lacked. True, I was almost omniscient (yet not entirely) when I was 20 years old but, as you know, people grow stupid when they grow older, and so, I was much less omniscient when I was 28 and still less now. Nor am I capable of satisfying those who look for perfect certainty and for immediate global solutions to all the world's calamities and misery. Still, I believe that in approaching other people we should, as far as we are able to do so, follow the Jesuit, rather than the Calvinist, method; this means, we ought to presuppose that nobody is totally and hopelessly corrupted, that everybody, no matter how perverted and limited, has some good points and some good intentions we can catch hold of. This is admittedly easier to say than to practise and I do not think that either of us is a perfect master in this maieutic art.

* * *

Your proposal to define yourself (and myself) by the allegiance to the "Marxist tradition" (as opposed to the system, the method, the heritage) seems to me elusive and vague. I am not sure of the meaning you confer on this attachment unless you simply find it important to be called "Marxist"; but you say you do not. Neither do I. I am not interested at all in being "a Marxist" or in being called so. There are certainly only few people working in the human sciences who would not acknowledge their debt to Marx and I am not one of them. I readily admit that without Marx our thinking about history would be different and in many respects worse than it is. To say this is rather trivial. Still, I think that many important tenets of Marx's doctrine are either false or meaningless or else true only in a very restricted sense. I think that the labour theory of value is a normative device without any explanatory power whatsoever; that none of the well known general formulae of the historical materialism to be found in Marx's writings is admissible and that this doctrine is valid only in a strongly qualified sense; that his theory of class consciousness is false and that most of his predictions proved to be erroneous (this is admittedly a general description of what I feel, I am not trying to justify here my conclusions). If I admit nevertheless to keep thinking, in historical (yet not in philosophical) matters, in terms inherited in part from the Marxian legacy, do I accept an allegiance to the Marxist tradition? Only in such a loose sense that the same statement would be equally true when I substitute for "Marxist"—"Christian", "sceptical", "empiricist". Without belonging to any political party or sect, to any Church, to any philosophical school, I do not deny my debt to Marxism, to Christianity, to sceptical philosophy, to empiricist thought and to a few other traditions (more specifically Eastern and less interesting to you) I have in my background. Neither do I share the horror of "eclecticism" if the opposite of eclecticism is philosophical or political bigotry (as it usually is in the minds of those who terrify us with the label of eclecticism). In such a poor sense, I admit to belong to the Marxist tradition, among others. But you seem to imply more. You seem to imply the existence of a "Marxist family" defined by the spiritual descendance from Marx and to invite me to join it. Do you mean that all people who in one way or another call themselves Marxists form a family (never mind that they have been killing each other for half a century and still do) opposed as such to the rest of the world? And that this family is for you (and ought to be for me) a place of identification? If this is what you mean, I cannot even say that I refuse to join this family; it simply does not exist in a world where the great Apocalypse can most likely be triggered off by the war between two empires both claiming to be perfect embodiments of Marxism.

*   *   *

There are in your letter several points which I should broach not because of their importance but because of the unpleasantly demagogic way you discuss them. I will take up two of them. You quote an article of mine containing a remark which I thought was rather a trivial platitude: that exploited classes have not been allowed to participate in the development of spiritual culture. And then you appear as a spokesman of the insulted working class and you explain to me, with indignation, that the working class developed a sense of solidarity, loyalty etc. In other words: I said this rather to deplore than to exalt the fact that the exploited were denied access to education— and you show disgust at the fact that, in my view, the working class has no moral! This is not a misreading but a sort of absurd "Hineinlesen" which makes any discussion impossible. And then, when I stigmatized as obscurantist the idea of a new, socialist logic or science (again, a truism, as I saw it), you explain that the point is not to change logic but that Marx did want to change the property relations. Did he, really? Well, what can I say except that you opened my eyes? And if you think that the question of a "new logic" or "new science" as opposed to "bourgeois logic" and "bourgeois science" was not at issue, you are entirely wrong. This was not an extravagance but a current pattern of thinking and talking among the Marxist-Leninist-Stalinists and these patterns were inherited intact by dozens of Lenins, Trotskys and Robespierres you could find in any American or German campus.

The second point is your comment on one sentence I uttered in the same interview you quoted; it said that "men have no fuller means of self-identification than through religious symbols" and that "religious consciousness . . . is an irreplaceable part of human culture". Here, you explode. "By what right (you say), what study of its tradition and sensibility, may you assume this as a universal in the heart of an ancient Protestant Island, doggedly resistant to the magic of religious symbolism. . . ." I am sorry for many reasons. First, that I gave my interview to the German journalist in the heart of the ancient Protestant Island instead of doing this on German soil. Second, that I failed to explain—which I assumed, wrongly, to be known—that "religious symbol" is not necessarily, contrary to what you obviously believe, a picture, a sculpture, a rosary etc., but everything people believe gives them a way of communicating with the Supernatural or conveys its energy (Jesus Christ himself is a symbol, not only a crucifix). I did not invent this use of the word but, since I did not explain it in my interview, I offended your iconoclastic English tradition. Does this lexical explanation appease somewhat your Protestant conscience hurt by a superstitious Ultramontanist? And you accuse me—that beats everything—of not proving, in this interview, my belief in the permanence of the religious phenomenon. I was really reckless in not quoting entirely, in this interview, all the books and articles I have written on the subject to support this view. You had no reason whatsoever to read these books (one of them, over eight hundred dense pages, and dealing mostly with sectarian movements of the 17th century, is so boring that it would be rather inhuman to ask you to wade through it)—at least you had no such reason as long as you were not trying to criticize my views on the subject. Therefore your indignant "By what right . . ." seems to be more appropriate when retorted to you.

Unfortunately, your article teems with such cases when you shift the subject and you try to make yourself believe that I said something you think I should have said on the basis of some general beliefs you attribute to me. I am sure you do this unconsciously, according to a peculiar logic of beliefs which has always been very characteristic of dogmatic communist thinking, where the difference between those reasonings which are truth-functional and those which are not entirely disappeared; however even if it were true that A entails B, it would not follow that if someone believes A, he believes B. (The wilful rejection of this rather unsophisticated distinction has always allowed the communist press to give its readers information constructed approximately in this way: "The American President said that, in defiance of the protest of the whole peace-loving mankind, he would carry on with the genocidal war in Vietnam" or "Chinese leaders declare that their jingoist, anti-leninist policy aims at the destruction of the socialist camp in order to help imperialists".) There is a consistence in this grotesque Wonderland logic and I rather dislike your reasonings echoing it. But there is more than that. Since you think about society in categories of global "systems"—capitalism or socialism—you believe that: 1) socialism, imperfect though it is, is essentially a higher stage of mankind's development and this superiority of the "system" is valid irrespectively of whether or not it can be shown in any particular facts related to human life; 2) all negative facts to be found in the non-socialist world—apartheid in South Africa, torture in Brazil, hunger in Nigeria or inadequate health service in Britain—are to be imputed to the "system", while similar facts occurring within the socialist world have to be accounted for by the "system" as well, yet not socialist, but the same capitalist system (survival of old society; impact of encirclement etc.); 3) whoever does not believe in the superiority of the socialist "system" so conceived is bound to believe that "capitalism" is in principle admirable and to justify or to conceal its monstrosities, i.e. to justify apartheid in South Africa, hunger in Nigeria etc. Hence your desperate attempts to force me to have said something I have not. (True, since you consider my case not entirely lost, you try to wake up my conscience and you explain, e.g., that there are spies and bugging devices in Western countries. Really? Are you not joking?) Needless to say, this peculiar way of reasoning is absolutely irrefutable, because it is able to neglect all empirical facts as irrelevant (whatever bad happens within the "capitalist system" is by definition the product of capitalism; whatever bad happens in "the socialist system" is by the same definition the product of the same capitalism). And socialism is defined within this "system-thinking" as total or nearly total state ownership of the means of production; you obviously cannot define socialism in terms of the abolition of hired labour, since you know that if empirical socialism differs in this respect from capitalism, this is only in restoring direct slave labour for prisoners, half-slave labour for workers (abolition of the freedom to change one's place of work) and the mediaeval *glebae adscriptio* for peasants. So, within this construction it is consistent to believe that with the private title of ownership the roots of evil, if not all actual evil, on earth are eradicated. But these three statements I mentioned are nothing else but the expression of an ideological commitment, incapable of being either validated or disproved empirically. You say that to think in terms of "system" yields excellent results. I am quite sure it does, not only excellent, but miraculous; it simply solves all problems of mankind at one stroke. This is why people who have not reached this level of scientific consciousness (like myself) do not know such a simple device for the salvation of the world, as is known to any sophomore in Berlin or Nebraska, viz. the socialist world revolution.

*   *   *

I have obviously not exhausted the topics of your text, which restores the dignity of the vanishing art of epistolography. But I believe I have touched on the most controversial ones. The gulf dividing us is at the moment unlikely to be bridged. You still seem to consider yourself as a dissident communist or as a sort of revisionist. I do not, and this for a very long time. You seem to define your position in terms of discussions of 1956 and I do not. This was an important year and its illusions were important, too. But they were crushed just after they had appeared. You probably realize that what was labelled "revisionism" in the people's democracies is virtually dead (possibly with the exception of Yugoslavia) which means that both young and old people in these countries stopped thinking about their situation in terms of "genuine socialism", "genuine Marxism" etc. They want (more often than not in a passive way) more national independence, more political and social freedom, better life conditions—but not because there is anything specifically socialist in these claims. The official state ideology is in a paradoxical position. It is absolutely indispensable, for it is the only way in which the ruling apparatus can legitimize its power; and it is believed by nobody—either the rulers or the ruled (both well aware of the unbelief of the others and of their own). And in Western countries, virtually every intellectual who considers himself socialist (and even communist) will admit in private talk that the socialist idea is in a deep crisis; few will admit this in print, here buoyant jauntiness is obligatory and we must not sow doubts and confusion "in the masses" or supply our foes with arguments. I am not sure if you agree that this is a self-defeating policy, I rather think you do not.

In the meantime some traditionally socialist institutions seem to creep in capitalist societies in a rather unexpected way. Even the most short-sighted politicians realize now that not everything can be bought for money, that a moment might come when no money will buy us clean air, clean water, more land or wasted natural resources. And so, "use value" comes back, slowly, into the economy. A paradoxical "socialism" resulting from the fact that mankind does not know what to do with garbage. The result is growing bureaucracy and the growing role of power centres. The only medicine communism has invented— the centralized, beyond social control, state ownership of the national wealth and one-party rule—is worse than the illness it is supposed to cure; it is less efficient economically and it makes the bureaucratic character of social relations an absolute principle. I appreciate your ideal of the decentralized society with a large autonomy for small communities and I share your attachment to this tradition. But it is silly to deny powerful forces resulting from the technological development itself, and not from the fact of private property, and leading toward greater and greater power of the central bureaucracy. If you pretend to know simple means to cope with this situation, if you imagine to have found the solution in saying "we will make a peaceful revolution and socialism will reverse this trend" you delude yourself and you fall victim to verbal magic. The more society depends on the complex technological network it created, the more problems have to be regulated by central powers, the more powerful state bureaucracy is, the more political democracy and more "formal", "bourgeois" freedom is needed to tame the ruling apparatus and to secure individuals their shrinking rights to remain individuals. There will never be and there cannot be any economical or industrial democracy without political ("bourgeois") democracy with everything it entails. We do not know how to harmonize the contradictory tasks contemporary society imposes upon us, we can only try an uncertain balance between these tasks, we have no prescription for a conflictless and secure society. I will repeat what I wrote once elsewhere: "In private life there is the attitude of those who think about how they could gain at one blow the capital that would allow them to spend the rest of their life without worries, in peace and security; and there is the attitude of those who must worry about how to survive until tomorrow. I think that human society as a whole will never be in the happy position of a rentier, living on dividends and having the guarantee of the secure life to the end, thanks to the capital once acquired. Its position will be rather similar to that of a journeyman who must care about how to survive until tomorrow. The utopians are people who dream about ensuring for mankind the position of rentier and who are convinced that this position is so splendid that no sacrifices (in particular no moral sacrifices) are too great to achieve it."

This does not mean that socialism is a dead option. I do not think so. But I do think that this option was emptied not only by the experience of socialist states; it was emptied by the silly self-complacency and self-confidence of its adherents, by their inability to face both the limits of our efforts to change society and the incompatibility of demands and values which made up their creed; briefly, that the meaning of this option has to be revised entirely, from the very roots.

And when I say "socialism" I do not mean a state of perfection but rather a movement trying to satisfy demands for equality, freedom and efficiency, a movement that is worth trouble only as far as it is aware not only of the complexity of problems hidden in each of these values separately but also of the fact that they limit each other and can be implemented only through compromises. We make fools of ourselves and of others if we think (or pretend to think) otherwise. All institutional changes have to be treated entirely as means at the service of these values and not as ends in themselves and be judged correspondingly, taking into account the price we pay in one value when we reinforce another one. Attempts to consider any of these three values as absolute and to implement it at all costs not only are bound to destroy two others but they are self-defeating—a discovery of venerable antiquity. Absolute equality can be set up only within a despotic system of rule which implies privileges, i.e. destroys equality; total freedom means anarchy and anarchy results in the domination of the physically strongest, i.e. total freedom turns into its opposite; efficiency as a supreme value calls again for despotism and despotism is economically inefficient above a certain level of technology. If I repeat these old truisms this is because they still seem to go unnoticed in utopian thinking; and this is why nothing in the world is easier than writing utopias. I wish we could agree on this point. If we do, we can agree on many others, even after exchanging a few caustic remarks which, I hope, we will be generous enough to forgive each other. Such an agreement will be much less likely if you keep believing that communism was in principle an excellent contrivance, somewhat spoilt in less than excellent application. I hope to have explained to you why, for many years, I have not expected anything from attempts to mend, to renovate, to clean or to correct the communist idea. Alas, poor idea. I knew it, Edward. This skull will never smile again.

Yours in friendship,
Leszek Kolakowski

REVOLUTIONARY INTELLECTUALS AND THE SOVIET UNION*

Rossana Rossanda

A RELATIONSHIP with the socialist countries—with revolutions "else-where"—has been part of the history of the European left, which has not had its revolution, for fifty years. A relationship composed of hopes and disappointments, alliances and recantations, inspiring utopias and depressing realisms. Almost always subordinate, it has become one aspect of the defeat of the left in the "developed capitalist countries". And as a love-hate, hope-disillusion relationship is always in some sense ridiculous and always turns into weakness, the European left has tried more than once to free itself of it by rejecting it as a problem: whatever the nature and the destiny of the "other" revolutions, they have nothing to do with me, mine will be "quite different". But this is no more than an exorcism. The "other" revolutions exist. They define the world in which we live. They define us, whether we like it or not. They cannot be avoided.

And for two reasons. The first is the fact that the unity of the world stage has become obvious: capitalism has created a system, a mechanism in which interactions between the centre and the periphery are more and more immediate and constraining. The second is that the con-ceptual apparatus of Marxism—despite (or perhaps because of) all the distortions it has suffered in the "Vulgate" of the Communist Parties, despite its enervation in the reformist version or admixtures from the mongrel but Marxisant culture of "American radicalism" or other "new cultures"—has provided a common political vocabulary, a grid for reading and interpretation which has in its turn speeded up the unification process. Thus, every break in the imperialist bloc or the capitalist front, or in the "socialist camp" is perceived—however remote its epicentre—not just as a problem agitating all the fronts of the movement, but as an interrogation which is immediately recognizable because it is common to us all: always and everywhere *de te fabula narratur*. The history of *revolutions* appears once again as a pure pheno-menology of the history of *the revolution*.

Hence we are surrounded. The left cannot evade either a factual or a

* This text is reprinted from *Temps Modernes* and has also appeared in *Kursbuch* (Berlin). The translation is by Ben Brewster.

21

value judgement of the socialist countries. Think of the history and of the crises of the European workers' movement and you will find inextricably linked to the history of *commitment* questions concerning the socialist countries. Must they be accepted, and to what extent? Or rejected, and with what consequences? These questions have always had direct consequences for the way the revolution has been understood and for immediate political alliances.

In the Marxist left, those who have rejected, or attempted to reject the need to test themselves on this terrain have been rendered impotent thereby. Starting from opposite positions, the Social Democrats and the Trotskyists have put the socialist countries into parentheses. The Second International, while it still contained within it someone to think for it, failed to see the approach of the revolutions. When it could no longer ignore their irksome presence, it registered it as an accident: history had brought forth monsters. Marx had foreseen the arrival of socialism as a break, admittedly, but also as the consummation of capitalism at the summit of its development, when the impetuous productive forces had come into contradiction with the old relations of production. If such is the schema of the socialist revolution, October 1917 did not have its papers in order; about China the less said the better and as for Cuba, that is quite another matter. Neither substance nor accident, these are phenomena to which the Second-International Marxist can grant no legitimacy, and hence which do not disturb him at all. If need be he can make use of the internal difficulties in the socialist countries to justify his gradualist vocation, his integration; and when the latter has been achieved, it is clear that any reflection on the "socialisms" loses its drama. He who does not believe in the revolution does not find the revolutions a problem.

The Trotskyist current—the respect due to certain exceptions notwithstanding—has given up too, but by the opposite method. Not through indifference, but through excessive dramatization. October 1917 is indisputably the revolution; but it has been transformed into a fatal bureaucratic degeneration. This being so, history is seen as a mistake, a non-history (which, from the political standpoint, amounts to the same thing). I have no wish to offend the susceptibilities of the Trotskyists when I note that the quarrel they have sought with the Eastern countries has been the same for forty years. Like all refusals, their attitude fails either to defeat the inimical reality or to analyse it in itself, in its objective relations with its surroundings, in its development. If for them the USSR is the country of Leninism betrayed, the Chinese revolution is quite simply incomprehensible (and the Cultural Revolution an aberration) nor is it on the terrain of pure principles that they base their sympathy for Cuba—a sympathy which is not returned besides. The result is a world vision in which the revolutions, those which have been realized or others, are permanently compromised; what remains is a theoretically imprecise element with confused features (the degenerated, bureaucratic, workers' state).

It is the militants of the Communist Parties and their more or less distant fellow-travellers for whom the relationship with the socialist countries is inscribed in their life-blood. It has a history, stages, wounds. It contained a real problematic, itself not static. And, more clearly than for the other, it eventually became a symbol, a focus in which, on every occasion, the point of their reflection on the revolution converges.

I

I shall not try to outline this history. To write it seriously would require work of quite a different order, for it is neither simple nor linear. It is neither simple nor linear even for the Communist leaders, despite the fact that they all but managed to prevent their tormented relationship, first with the Third International and then with the socialist countries from filtering through to the outside. Moreover I think that even the most minute research would not change the conclusions that it is possible to draw from this history today.

In the relationship with the socialist countries, the weight accorded to their *existence* and their *international role* has predominated absolutely over the judgement to be made about their *internal* nature. Paradoxical as this may seem—given that the Communist Parties did not criticize the Soviet Union before 1956—this fact very rapidly became clear, precisely in the Parties themselves. I only have first-hand knowledge of the Italian Communist Party, and of certain militants in other Parties; but this knowledge is sufficiently eloquent. In Italy, as early as 1923, after the failure of the councils and the factory occupations, Antonio Gramsci wrote very lucidly that in the ebb of the great European experiment, October, the socialist workers' state, was not so much simply the image of a hope realized, but the guarantee, the sole guarantee that the workers' movement had not been defeated. The result was a change of priorities in his political thought. And when, in 1926, he wrote his famous letter to Stalin condemning him for having broken the unity of the leading group in his rupture with Trotsky (for Gramsci, Trotsky was certainly wrong, but remained a vital component of the Soviet revolution), he was thinking of the future of Communists throughout the world. Togliatti replied—with a harshness of tone that has remained characteristic of the entire attitude of the Communist Parties—that the problem was not whether Stalin was agreeable or not, but that Stalin was from now on the Soviet Union, and that the Soviet Union was the sole guarantee that the class had not been defeated.[1]

Whether Togliatti was right or wrong is of little importance here;

of course, there has been no revolution that has not had to define itself with respect to the socialist countries. But that is not the end of the question, as we shall see later. Here let me simply note that the relationship with the USSR very quickly became more a strategic choice than the recognition of an identity. The Communist Parties' unconditional support for the Soviet state, their inability to give at least a problematic, if not a critical image of it in their press, their refusal of all but apologetic analyses of the "homeland of socialism" and later of the people's democracies, correspond less to a certainty about the identity of the aims of the October Revolution and the concrete reality of the Soviet state than to a deliberate decision not to confront this problem. The USSR was the first socialist country, and an encircled one, too: and that was that. For it and for the Communist Parties, the first priority was to safeguard it. Thus the whole history of the International can be read as a subordination of the Communist Parties to the USSR. It can also be read as the anchoring of the revolutions lacking in Europe to the only reality antagonistic to capital existing *as a state*, and hence capable of opening an objectively new potentiality for class struggle on a world scale.

The itineraries of Paul Nizan, or of Ernst Fischer, or of Jean-Paul Sartre—to take three intellectuals differently implicated in the Communist camp, Nizan a militant and journalist of the PCF, Fischer on the staff of the International, Sartre completely independent of any organizational discipline—show that this grid for political interpretation was fundamental, and not only for the bureaucracies of the Communist Parties.

Is not Nizan the symbol of the militant Communist intellectual shattered in a single day—24 August 1939—by his discovery of the gulf dividing the rationale of the world anti-fascist front and the rationale of the Soviet Union? After a long period of militant activity, which for every intellectual, but for him in particular, had also been a surpassing of himself, of his origins, his weaknesses and his cultural inclinations—with the always slightly morbid satisfaction of "serving the people" through obedience to the Party—Nizan resigned on the spot, departed ostensibly as a volunteer for the war that the USSR did not want to wage, and died less than a year later, at Dunkirk. This death has all the appearances of a suicide (even if it was not one), so emblematic is it, occurring when Nizan had ceased to "live" since his life had been entirely identified with political commitment.

After his death, Nizan was to remain a symbol, the symbol of how low the Communist Parties could sink when they wished to destroy one of their own. He was not yet dead when Maurice Thorez wrote: "Paul Nizan, police informer, made himself the champion of a national communism." And, after the War, Henri Lefebvre and Louis Aragon turned him into the very image of treason.[2] Although on numerous occasions the French Communists have been defied to provide proofs of such an accusation, they have never withdrawn it.

However, Nizan's tragedy was not his disappointment at the nature of Soviet society. That it was not a heaven on earth he must have discovered long before. The ambiguous remark that Simone de Beauvoir records shows this too: after his return from the USSR—on the one hand writing panegyrics in the Party press, on the other evading any sincere assessment with his friends—he had let slip: "It was a very corrupting stay." From what point of view corrupting? Did he fear as an intellectual that he had definitively accepted the USSR as a "positive religion"? The trials—about which he did not write—did not really upset him. The toughness of the situation, the difficulties, the isolation of the Russian revolution, its dramatic initial conditions acted as a counterweight and attenuated the errors, tragic as they were: once Trotsky's thesis that everything happening in Moscow was the deliberate betrayal of the ideas of 1917 was set aside, everything happening in Moscow could be set down as part of the heavy but unavoidable price to be paid, compensated by a different order of conquests. Communists quickly become realists—and this cannot be said to be their worst failing. All the more so given that weight was added to their arguments by all the utterly disillusioned "returns from the USSR" which regularly put the disappointed on the other side of the barricades. In the 1930s, confronted with the rise of fascism, this became less and less acceptable to the honest intellectual. From the Dimitrov trial to the red flags of the Popular Front, via the Seventh Congress of the International, the mass movement against the fascist threat, propelled and sustained by the International, sufficed to suppress the memory, or even the awareness—think of Romain Rolland—of Stalin's trials. It was not just the officials, but also the finest figures of European anti-fascism who allowed themselves to be persuaded that everything else must be put into parentheses before the threat of Hitler.

But when the attitude of the USSR to this threat seemed to change, i.e., in August 1939, everything collapsed for Nizan. Although he tried for some months to maintain his hopes in the Soviet Union, which objectively remained the strategic enemy of fascism, and therefore directed his polemic against the French Communists rather than against Stalin, Nizan finally came to the conclusion that this distinction between long-term objective nature and immediate subjective choices not only represented intolerable juggling, but could not be made without something profound, something of prime importance being damaged or irretrievably lost. If "in order to understand what is happening," he wrote to his wife, "we shall have from now on to refer rather to the history of Charles II than to the complete works of Marx,"[3] that meant that the USSR as a traditional "power" had now indisputably prevailed over the USSR as a "socialist state". Which no doubt led to the consequence that the equation "defence of the USSR = defence of Communism" no longer held. Nizan did not, at least explicitly, reach this conclusion. He probably even hesitated on the brink of it, waiting: "In these days," he wrote in one of his last letters, "I recognize only one virtue; neither courage, nor the will to martyrdom, nor abnegation, nor blindness, but solely the will to understand. The only honour remaining to us is that of understanding."[4]

Understanding? Yes, but what to do once one has understood? We do not know how Nizan would have answered this question; probably— were it not for the infamies which his Party was quick to heap on him— like many other militants who moved away in 1939, he would have rejoined after the War. Stalin and Ribbentrop's notorious handshake would have been redeemed, even buried, by Stalingrad, by the millions dead, by the capture of Berlin. All the questions which seemed to be posed by the drama of 1939—the relation between revolution and state power, between socialist states and Communist movements, between strategic defence of the USSR and tactics on the international chess-board—all this confused and barely extricable tangle fell with the War. Nizan's crisis was no more than the outline of a conflict between politics and ethics from which he had neither the time nor the ability to free himself.

*   *   *

Is not Ernst Fischer's itinerary in a certain respect the counter-test for what I have claimed? Intellectually, Fischer was even less inclined towards Stalinism than Nizan: his culture was all subtleties and careful distinguos; he had a profoundly critical mind, a mind totally foreign to the rhetorical temptations to which the French intellectual was prey and which constitute, for Communists, a convenient alibi for intelligence. Before becoming a Communist, Nizan had been attracted towards right-wing revolt; before he joined the Austrian Party, Fischer had always been a democrat and a socialist. He joined the CP and rapidly became its delegate to the International. Rereading the account in his *Erinnerungen* of his experience in Moscow and even more in speaking to him during the last years of his life, I was struck by the fact that he agreed to commit himself so completely to an experience so totally, intrinsically incompatible with his scale of values, with his most constant and personal note: a delicately critical tolerance, a funda-mental refusal of Manicheeism. It had been enough that in an occasional discussion with Togliatti or Dimitrov, in whom he recognized the same refusal of defeat, he had been told: "Here, in Russia, things could not be otherwise; 'our' socialism will be different, but the USSR

and it alone can guarantee it for us" for him to have adapted himself to
the *Realpolitik* for which he was not really suited. Why? Because of the
weight of the defeat of the revolutions in Europe; also because of Hitler.

During these years, the USSR did not just represent the last strong-
hold. Paradoxically, just when its situation was most serious, its policy—
the Seventh Congress of the International, "frontism"—constituted for
the European Communist Parties, in their last extremity, a framework
in which they could rapidly grow. Similarly, the 1945 victory and the
displacements of forces that followed long appeared not at all as the
sanction for a division of the world that left no space for the revolution
in Europe, but rather as the guarantee of a reorganization of the
movement, of its indestructibility. The *Realpolitik* of the difficult period
seemed to have paid off. Thus Ernst Fischer was not to break with the
Party because of the trials of the 1930s, nor because of the Nazi-Soviet
pact, nor in 1948, nor because of the Prague trials, nor in 1956. Fischer
broke in 1968 when the Soviet state sent its tanks into Prague and thus
carried out an action in which it was no longer possible to recognize the
slightest intention to defend socialism or its principles but solely a logic
of power, in no way distinct from that of the conventional powers and
obtaining their tacit consent. He broke as soon as to be on the side of
the USSR no longer meant to have placed oneself in opposition to the
system. In fact, for Fischer, behind the break with the USSR in 1968,
besides Czechoslovakia of course, there was above all ten years in which,
within the socialist camp, itself, there had emerged a critique of the
international role of the Soviet Union, either explicit, as in the Chinese
case, or indirect, as in the case of Cuba and the revolutionary movements. There was also Khrushchev's ambiguous attitude to Vietnam.
Finally there was, in the 1960s, the exhaustion of what, even in Stalin's
policy and despite his nationalism, made the USSR the hope of a
possible alternative.

When this distinction between the Soviet state and the other states
disappears totally in the consciousness of a Communist, then—but only
then—the relationship is broken. So long as this is not the case, the
bond that unites him to the socialist countries holds firm, reduced to a
single thread, but extremely strong: the "otherness" of the camp. This
bond may be accompanied by a thousand distinctions, critiques,
maintenance of distances, even condemnations, but they are issued
from the same side of the barricades. (See for instance—since it is shared by
a large part of the left, even the non-Communist left—the attitude of the
Italian Communist Party to the USSR, the most autonomous in this
sense.) With a consequence: once the relationship is located on this
terrain, a break becomes very difficult. In fact, if it is easy to recognize
that the USSR *cannot* be identified with the revolution (the left's crisis
of conscience before the War), and if it is now accepted that the USSR

can no longer even be identified in any specific way with an antagonistic contradiction with imperialism (the left's crisis of conscience since
the War, especially in the 1960s), it is qualitatively more difficult to
deny its *difference* with respect to capitalism and imperialism. Hence it
is always possible to find a line of demarcation justifying an alignment.
(Only the Chinese try to erase it by reducing it to an "inter-imperialist
contradiction", i.e., one between imperialism and social-imperialism:
but the use of a different term is enough to leave an open breach, all
the more so since their analysis of when, how and why the USSR
changed its nature is far from satisfactory.)

The objective character of this difference is of great importance; the
socialist countries invoke it continually. The Soviet Union, which
made great use of it in the 1930s, still carries on accompanying its
brash affirmations of strength with the still profitable thesis of the
fortress to be defended against the enemy attack. It is enough
to remember the extraordinary confusion which the invasion of
Czechoslovakia managed to sow precisely in the extreme left, more
than one group of whom regarded it as a "left-wing" intervention
against German intrigues. Undoubtedly, it is Cuba that makes most use
of this argument: small and isolated in the face of the American giant
which would gladly liquidate it, it believes this makes it irreproachable.
A large part of the European left gives in to this argument as far as
Cuba is concerned. Only China—despite the toughness of its polemic—
avoids recourse to the theme: "I am surrounded, everything I do is right.
You must therefore approve it."

Thus the European left can become extremely sceptical towards the
socialist countries and yet choose nonetheless to remain on their side,
so long as they remain in contradiction with imperialism. For example:
if the USSR is no longer the rampart of revolution, it is still true that
it represents a barrage against the fascization process in Europe, and
that an agreement with the Social Democracies is preferable to an
extension of fascism. Or else: it is true that the USSR did not prevent
the Americans from attacking Vietnam; but without Soviet aid, could
Vietnam have held out? Moreover, by a ruse of History, it is those on
the left who used to fear a revolutionary USSR who today make the
best of the USSR as a guarantor of the balances in Europe, just when
the latter is able to take advantage of the post-war crisis of American
imperialism. Thus the semi-skilled Italian worker—not the old
Communist, but the young worker, more advanced, more radically
agressive and more radically sceptical about Brezhnev—hardly warms
to the denunciation of the USSR, because he coolly recognizes the
political importance which its existence on the borders of Europe and
the relationship between equals it has established with the USA retains
vis-à-vis the Italian government, vis-à-vis the "bosses".

But is this not the extreme product of the ambiguous seduction of the "factual" for which Merleau-Ponty attacked Sartre? For in Sartre's itinerary—which is the last I shall take as an example—this type of realistic relationship with the USSR is the most exemplary because it is freely assumed, outside all party discipline and the corresponding moral obligations. Sartre, a late-comer to militant politics during the Second World War, was never a member of the PCF and has never tried to become one.[5] He came closest to the Communists in 1952, not when the Party was triumphant, but when it seemed to have reached the nadir of isolation and crisis. 28 May. The Cold War was at its height. The PCF had called on the masses to demonstrate against Ridgway; the government had banned the demonstration. The masses had retreated and not taken to the streets. All the governmental establishment exulted, naturally, but so did a certain left wing which saw in this abstention a liberation of the French working class from the grip of the Communist Party and the Soviet Union. It was then that Sartre spoke out violently, proclaiming not just for himself, but for the whole class, the necessity for a coalition with the whole of the Communist movement—states and Parties—as its special and indestructible interest. He wrote this in *The Communists and Peace*,[6] which Merleau-Ponty was maliciously to describe as the most eloquent justification and defence of the Communist Parties, unfortunately by arguments which they would not accept. Historically, claimed Sartre, the political being of the class—i.e., the idea and hope of socialism—is linked to the October Revolution and the Soviet state (it is no accident that the reference is to the Lenin of "Better Fewer but Better" which provides a basis for the distinction between the inevitability of the victory of socialism since "capitalism carries within itself the seeds of death", even if the Soviet state were destroyed—a proposition of principle—and the defence of socialism from the concrete historical point of view).[7] Thus those fighting against the USSR and the Communist Party today, for whatever reasons, were fighting against the class and against the revolution. Soviet socialism might or might not be agreeable, the Communist Parties might or might not be agreeable, they still represented the only current element of antagonism in a world which, without them, would have been *entirely* bourgeois. This was the only authentic criterion of discrimination; to depart from it in the name of a different idea of the revolution, of the Party, of the class—which did not for the moment exist and thus constituted neither object nor subject of the confrontation with the system—meant abandoning the true terrain of the struggle.

The strength of Sartre's position in the debate which ensued with Merleau-Ponty on the one hand and Lefort on the other lay entirely in this argument. From a scholarly point of view both were more steeled than he in Marxism. Only the theoretical lucidity that led Lefort to re-establish the party-class relationship more correctly on the plane of principles, also led him to put into parentheses what in his own analysis he called the "improper" crystallization of the class represented by the Parties, that "improper" social reality the socialism of the Soviet revolution. By doing so not only did he desert the line of battle but also, said Sartre, objectively played into the hands of the class enemies, of the government. Willy-nilly. Merleau-Ponty, more skilful than Lefort, sought to evade this dilemma, but did not do much better. He tried in fact to dissociate Communism *as it is* from Communism *as it ought to be*, while refusing to attack Communism *as it is* so as to avoid objectively lining himself up with the bosses.[8] His proposed *a-Communism* was supposed to save him from anti-Communism and to situate him on the side of the workers' movement. But this operation could be no more convincing than the one for which Sartre was to attack Camus: "You blame the European proletariat because it has not publicly emphasized its disapproval of the Soviets, but you also blame the governments of Europe because they are going to allow Spain to join UNESCO: in that case, I can only see one solution for your problem: the Galapagos Islands."[9]

Yet it was Merleau-Ponty who was to give the most lucid definition of the *impasse* which eventually every member of a left which claimed to be Marxist confronted in the Soviet Union and the practice of the Communist Parties. It was condemned, he wrote, to oscillate ridiculously between two impossibilities of remaining faithful to Marx: on the one hand the acceptance of *a factual reality* (this revolution, this Party, this type of contradiction which they maintain with the bourgeoisie) which allowed it effective militant activity, but on condition of sacrificing the principled reasons justifying that activity; on the other refuge in a tranquil philosophical sterility, in the maintenance of principles, which also constitutes a betrayal of Marx because a Marxism cut off from all capacity for immediate action is no more than philosophy "in the worst sense of the term".

But the second term of the dilemma—a Marxism which remains no more than "thought", an imaginary proletariat—comes down to a mere critique of its own inadequacy, to its transformation into pure "ideology", whereas the first term is simply a way of reproducing a series of unresolved problems. Can the "fact" of revolutions, Soviet, Cuban or Chinese, be defined simply by negation, by what they *are not*? If it was a matter of a pure negativity, how could they constitute a political contradiction, object and subject of confrontation and history? But then what is this mongrel factual reality, these movements which are neither "the" revolution nor the "non-revolution", these societies which are neither socialism "as such" nor capitalism, these Parties which are neither the political expression of the class nor a political expression of the bourgeoisie? What are they in relation to the mechanisms of capital, the class struggle, the formation of proletarian consciousness? How are they integrated into history? What are the mechanisms which induce them or deflect them, what mechanisms do they themselves induce, to what will they eventually lead?

Sartre did not need to attempt an answer like *The Communists and Peace* to evade the dilemma Merleau-Ponty spoke of. His profoundly existentialist formation (his most authentic vein) was enough to allow him to abstract from it. This formation made him resist the temptation to exorcise reality, the fact, in the name of an idea. He will always admit that for him it is enough that *this should be*. This is what was to push him, he who is yet so remote intellectually from the Communists, so close to their realism. It is this that was to make him a fellow-traveller, not a very comfortable one, but a reliable one. It is this which separated him unhesitatingly both from Social Democracy—whose "factual reality" is immediately clear, insofar as it lies on the other side of the barricades —and from Trotskyism, in which he saw no more than pure Talmudism. This is what made his relationship with the socialist countries the least passionate, the least dramatized in comparison with those of other European intellectuals. He rarely attempted to idealize them, he rarely sought from them a true response, he did not lose himself in the search for either an original purity—the revolution betrayed—or a purity to be rediscovered, more in Cuba than the USSR, or in China rather than in Cuba. He objectified them (for which they were rarely grateful to him) as experiences *which exist*, and as realities antagonistic to imperialism—so long as the contradiction seemed clear to him.

His real separation from the "historicity" of the Communists only occurred in 1968. But not, as with Fischer, because he reached the nadir of an intolerable disillusion in August, at Prague, but on the contrary because he saw in the month of May, in Paris, a new hope, borne by the working class and youth, which could replace that of the Communist Parties, a new front on which he could relink himself to militancy. A minority reality, with uncertain outlines, an inadequate one, but one very different from the purely ideological solution of a Lefort: a *real* class embryo. A different factual reality. From that moment, the relationship with the socialist countries and the Communist Parties became secondary. They remain a datum in the world framework, but their antagonistic nature has become blurred if not, as in Paris in 1968, reduced completely to nothing. They no longer represent the inevitable reef, the militant's "take it or leave it".

However, the problem seems only to have been resolved for a short time. A short time because the May wave was not long lasting—as a mass movement capable of shifting the fundamental equilibria and opening a new historical period. A short time, above all, because once the ebb tide revealed itself, what remained lost its novelty and its innocence. After having apparently swept away all the old conceptions of the relationship between vanguard and class, tactics and strategy, in a total re-invention of politics, what the wave left behind as a strategic consciousness inevitably tends to relocate itself in the conceptual schemata of the past, in a heavily repetitive manner. In May, and in the movement of the students, a work of purification and reappropriation of the history of Communism seemed to be achieved, via certain exemplary options: Lenin, Rosa Luxemburg, Trotsky, Guevara, Ho Chi-minh, Mao Tse-tung. Each represented the symbol of an immediate need: in the first three, revolutionary rigour with three different emphases (organization, spontaneity, intransigence), in Guevara, the exaltation of subjectivity, in Ho, the proof of the possibility of a victory of the poor, in Mao, egalitarianism. In other words, Communist experience, theoretical and practical, seemed recuperable, without traumas, without too much running foul of the concrete impasses of the past, via a positive selection. But with the ebb-tide of the movement of 1968, this reconciliation became more complicated and impoverished. Lenin, Rosa, Trotsky, Mao were once again the object of theoretical disputes and organizational choices within the minority groups characterized by the most notorious vices of the Communist movement—without even the justification of its grandeur— and often fifty years behind in relation to history.

Sartre has tried in vain this time to exorcize this reality. He has sought to discover beneath the advertised ideological categories new categories, ones which in fact suit him perfectly: the rediscovery of violence, the priority given to exemplary praxis, the identification of politics and ethics.[10] But really this is less a question of a convincing portrait of "France's Maoists" than of three aspects of his own personal return to the ethic of the gesture, to morality more than to politics—an unusual sign of discomfort, the need to indicate in something, in some-one, an inarticulate germ and to rally to it. In twenty years, since 1952, this has forced him to reduce, terrifyingly, what remains "non-bourgeois" in a world which is thus totally integrated. The class and its organizations no longer bear the mark of antagonism that he had recognized in The Communists and Peace. The great optimism of 1968 has overturned into a perhaps unprecedented absence of hope.

And, in this void, the "factual", ungraspable and now inimical, is back on top: the revolutions "as they are", the Communist Parties who have recovered their audience. What is left of the revolutionary movement—now that the flags no longer fly from the occupied faculties and factories and the luminous schematisms of the slogans are no longer enough—realizes that it will have to settle accounts not with the image and words of Guevara, but with the Cuba of the 1970s, that economic crisis has tipped into the Soviets' lap; with a Vietnam which, after twenty terrible years, has attained difficult negotiations and which, if it does eventually win, will still have a struggle for survival ahead of it; with the China of the post-cultural-revolution period, which sees the main enemy on the left. The rationale of history has once again swept away the illusions of ideology. Europe is facing the same problems as before, with one experience more: the problems and impasses that were thought to be those of others reveal themselves in the moment of the rising as in that of retreat to be our own. Nothing has been surpassed, but only—for a brief moment—referred to the hope of a revolution in our countries, to our measure.

II

I might have evoked other itineraries, other protagonists here. The result would certainly have been richer and more complex. But I doubt whether the conclusions drawn from this work could have been anything but the confirmation of a double impasse. To return to Merleau-Ponty's dilemma, those who have refused the historicity of the socialist countries and Communist Parties in Marx's name have first found themselves outside history and then been caught out by it. But those who have recognized the reality of the socialist societies (and hence of the Communist Parties, the two things going together) in the name of this same Marxist enlightenment, have been caught up in the wheels of an uncontrollable, coercive and disillusioning logic and in the last analysis found themselves once again facing the problem they thought they had evaded.

In fact, the socialist countries can be liquidated neither by the ideological Trotskyist, nor by the now relativistic and sceptical orthodox Communist. To the former they counter the weight of their existence and what that has given rise to since the beginning of the century; to the latter they periodically present the state not only of their international position but also that of their internal nature. In his last years Togliatti may have tried to save what could be saved by agitating for the "plurality of roads to socialism", according to which each post-revolutionary society would only have to measure itself by its own standards, would represent no model and yet could be recognized in a common front, but this is no more than a "realist" hypostasis which reality is only too ready to explode. For the "nature" of each socialist country determines not only its inner being but also its relations with the other socialist countries, with the revolutionary movement, with other states. Moreover, it is the expression of a totalizing and tendentially global outlook which cannot be made to coexist relatively with the others; hence it may constitute a powerful disintegrating factor in the "camp". It is difficult to be simultaneously with Brezhnev and Mao, with Dubcek and Husak, with Castro and Tito, with the guerrillas and with Allende. The problem of *socialism*—and not just of *socialisms*—has become deeper, with all its contrasts and trials, it has been active in upsetting the balances of the post-war world, and that just as the left succeeded in washing its hands of it with its thesis of the "national roads to socialism".

In other words, the attempt to separate alliance with the socialist countries from analysis of their revolutions has not outlived the cold war. When the two questions have tended to recombine, the left, Communist and non-Communist, has had no choice but to recognize its own political and theoretical disarray—betrayed every time by attempts to escape the historical and political analysis of the revolutions in one way or another. This critical and theoretical inadequacy might be said to be simply a consequence of its lack of revolution: the European left, politically disarmed, lacks adequate investigatory instruments. But the opposite could just as well be true: this kind of intellectual blockage—which is all too easily blamed on the Communist "Vulgate" —is itself a brake or an alibi for the inability to think one's own revolution. It is an "ideology" in its turn, in the sense of a false consciousness.

The extraordinary inability—since Lenin and Rosa Luxemburg—to rethink the mechanisms of imperialism (if we also call inability the heart-breaking attempts of the revolutionary groups to replace all investigation, all analysis by a few sterile schemata) may well be the proof that, for those who are inside the imperialist fortress, it is perhaps not so crucial to know the monster to defeat it. The Western left shakes its head at the inadequacy of the peremptory theses that come from the third world—even if it does periodically look to that world for re-generation. But these theses do at least reflect a need for liberation which does perhaps impel them towards over-rapid definitions, whereas the laziness of the Western left reflects a long familiarity with the advantages of false consciousness. Similarly, no one will dissuade me. that if the revolution is so long delayed in the West it is because in the crisis shaking it the part of integration is equal to that of revolt, the Communist imperative has as a counterpart the passive acceptance of the Western model of consumption, and the two have formed and are in conflict in a framework where subsistence is more than guaranteed. I am thus inclined to believe that the many lacerations and the lack of serious analyses induced by the relationship with the socialist countries also betray an unconscious flight, an unavowed complicity.

What other explanation could there be for the scarcity of interpretative hypotheses about the socialist societies in the last fifty years? Eliminating the anti-Communist arsenal, itself hardly rich in innovations, it is clear that all the reflection of the European left has either been oriented towards Trotskyist theses (in the broad sense) or has not been oriented in any direction at all. All, or almost all of its analysis can be summed up as follows: the Soviet Union is not the direct and indisputable expression of the power of the proletariat. Question: why? Answer: because once capitalism was abolished and the bases of socialism had been laid, the class's power of political expression degenerated. Second question: why did it degenerate? Answer: because of a subjective failing (with many tautological variants which bring it very close to: because it degenerated. Because power was not democratic, because it was centralized, because it was bureaucratized, because it fell into dangerous or incompetent hands, or hands insufficiently armed ideologically. Because power is power, and those who hold it will not let it go). Final corollary: either, on the left (Maoists and Trotskyists), the situation can be redressed if power is restored to the base; or, in the centre (the Communists), the situation can be redressed, and will necessarily be redressed, because the development of the productive forces itself will lead to an extension of power to the masses; on the right (the Social Democrats), the situation is irremediable because the masses can exercise power only through the institutions of the modern bourgeoisie.

There is no way out here. And from this viewpoint, it is surprising that Trotsky's procedure corresponds conceptually to that of the Communist Parties, even of those in power. A re-reading of *My Life* or *The Revolution Betrayed* confirms that not only is the accent laid entirely on the phenomenology of power, at the social-psychological level,[11] but also in the rest of the analysis this vision of history is deliberately brought to the fore, in opposition to the conquests which make the USSR otherwise a guaranteed proletarian state. Only one "social basis" is taken into consideration: the apparatus of power, i.e., the bureaucratic caste, seizes the levers controlling the distribution of goods for its own purposes—and, in doing so, this caste sets itself in contradiction with the socialist nature of the state, thus creating a situation of instability which leads either to the adaptation of distribution to the "socialist norms" already governing property, or to the adaptation of property to the "bourgeois norms" of distribution.

The critique of Stalin made at the Twentieth Congress and the secret speech are not based on a fundamentally different reasoning, even if they are silent about the problem of the enrichment of the bureaucracy and go on much more about the violations of socialist legality. This is not fundamentally different because the appearance of Stalinist deformation is reduced entirely to the subjectivity of the man or of the "anti-Party" group, and hence of the apparatus that the latter constructed. In other words, it is a matter that takes place entirely in the "political" sphere in the narrow sense of the term and which can be remedied by changes in the "political", i.e., formal, mechanisms of power—i.e., the re-establishment of socialist "legality" and of "collective responsibility", the "democratization" of the state. The same pre-occupation is found in Trotsky, in Khrushchev and in the Mao of the essays of 1956, those on "The Historical Experience of the Dictatorship of the Proletariat" (if they are by him as is claimed), and this is all the more interesting given the fact that the three have nothing else in common. All three separate these degenerated political elements from a social body whose base has not been changed since it has become *socialist* with the seizure of political power and the abolition of the private ownership of the means of production.

Only the Chinese have, quite recently, broken with this schema, and not without a basic contradiction, as we shall soon see. All the rest of the Communist movement and the greater part of the European left accepts it. It accepted it before the Twentieth Congress, and this enabled it to believe that the worst epoch of Stalinism could be redeemed not only, as we have seen, by reason of the inter-national function of the Soviet Union against fascism, but also by a correction of the mechanisms of power, which remain foreign to the nature of the system. (Trotsky himself never renounced his defence of the USSR as a proletarian, workers' state, suffering only from a bureaucratic degeneration.) When, at the Twentieth Congress in 1956, this critique was unfolded, based as it is on the affirmation of a dis-crepancy (for which Stalinism alone is responsible) between a socialist economic base and a superstructure which is not yet socialist, the European left favourably welcomed this diagnosis of the evil and the hopeful prognosis, and anxiously awaited the process of "liberalization", of "political democratization". Even those who had no illusions about Khrushchev dreamed for a moment after the Polish October of a more radical democratization, of the re-establishment of workers' "councils", of a new "sovietism" that could be obtained by a mere transfer of power from the summit towards the instances at the base.

There is more. All the left was to accept the Soviet thesis, a thesis that goes back to the 1920s anyway, according to which the difficulties and delays in the democratization had an almost fatal cause: the "scarcity" of resources, the socio-economic backwardness of Russia in 1917, necessarily led to a phase of authoritarianism, centralization, hyper-stratification, in which it was necessary—for the survival of the youthful revolution—to give priority to the objectives of the "material construction" of socialism, to strengthening it economically and, in consequence, to the state apparatus that guaranteed it. Once a certain level was attained, it would be possible to move on to objective no. 2, the socialist transformations. This thesis can also be found in Sartre in

1952. It was even to appear in Guevara much later: a certain dose of Stalinism is the price to be paid for the escape from backwardness. And the Twentieth Congress is all in the same vein: "*Now* that the USSR has reached this level of the productive forces, it is possible, as it was not hitherto, to crown our work by transforming human relations in a socialist direction." It had even become almost obligatory, since excessive centralization of power was no longer a motor but rather a brake on the development of mass initiative. At the Twenty-Second Congress, Khrushchev was to say that things had advanced to such a point that it was now possible to dispense with a centralized power (necessarily similar to that of the bourgeois state) and even with the dictatorship of the proletariat—the state already belonging to "the whole people" and the self-government of the workers being capable of realization between then and 1980.

And yet, since the Twentieth Congress we have seen such an alternation between timid attempts at "liberalization" and sharp backward steps where repression is concerned, that it is easy to declare (almost twenty years having passed) that the hypothesis built on the Twentieth Congress of the CPSU was quite unrealistic. The new course, and the invasion of Hungary which followed are the most dramatic symbol of this. But other, less obvious signs confirm the tendency: Poland, where the class struggles attained a higher level than in the other socialist countries and where the repression took more skilful and complex forms; Yugoslavia which, at the cost of a vertical crisis in the League of Communists, put a brake on the manifestation of an already complete process of disintegration. Even in the—quite specific—case of Cuba, there is a recurrent alternation of centralization and extension of democracy; the most politically significant example being the self-critical speech after the failure of the 1970 *zafra* made by Castro who had seemed at one time to represent the whole history and structure of power in Cuba and who, a few months later, promoted a management in which the Soviet line slowly but surely prevailed.

Hence it is essential to ask what is wrong with this type of interpretation. Why does the superstructure fail to become "socialist" on a basis which is already supposed to be so? Why does it manage this neither when the development of the revolution is hindered by backwardness nor when it has overcome it?

Interesting perspectives may be opened up by the attempt to answer these questions. I shall restrict myself to advancing a few elements as the first guide-lines to a later, more serious investigation. First of all, it is striking that the vast majority of analyses of the degeneration, or the difficulties, or the delays (according to the varying optimism of those who discuss it) of the socialist societies accept totally a separation between the economic sphere, the (socialist) base and the sphere of relations between men, or superstructure (which is not yet socialist). Let us ignore a first contradiction which all the defenders of this thesis quickly leap over: after all, it was a superstructure (the Party, the revolutionary vanguard) which changed that base in a socialist direction; and since it is usually admitted that state and power are now in the hands of this vanguard, it should follow that in the socialist societies the superstructure is simultaneously behind and in advance of the base. Even if the Party, the state, the cultural institutions, the press, the radio, etc. . . . . are "socialist"—as any Communist will claim—the result is that there is only one domain to which this socialist nature does not extend: the relations between citizen and state, what is generally called the relations between the governors and the governed. Following this logic one should really speak of a *divided* superstructure rather than of a backward superstructure. For the Communist Parties it follows nonetheless that this disparity and this partial backwardness of the superstructure is what prevents direct democracy and implies "a reinforcement of the state until the moment of its withering away"; a rather obscure statement at the very least, fashionable since the 1920s, and which Mikoyan repeated again imperturbably at the Twenty-Second Congress of the CPSU, which predicted the transition to communism by 1980.

But even if one accepts this vision of a society divided into socialist bits and bits which are not socialist, why is there resistance to the progression towards a socialist totality, to what correspond the "not yet socialist relations" in the political sphere, what are their social bases? Trotsky, as we have seen, did not think that the bureaucratic, non-socialist degeneration of Soviet power derived from the old classes. It was born within the vanguard itself, as a mortal crisis. Inside the Bolshevik Party this resistance was at first reduced to the persistence of the interests of the former classes. But in 1936, Stalin declared as a position of principle that this type of class struggle had come to an end, given the hegemony of the socialist sector. And when in 1952, he returned to this problem of class conflicts, he tended to reduce it to the survival of residual and marginal elements of resistance from the past. The Chinese Cultural Revolution was to talk for quite a long time rather about a resistance caused by "old ideas", thus referring the superstructure to the superstructure.

The result of this interpretation, which is still found in the discussions of the left, is that socialism is a socio-historical formation characterized by a marked disequilibrium between superstructure and base: the former still lags behind the latter for decades and decades, as a consciousness which is now no longer the expression of a social being but which draws from itself an extraordinary capacity for reproduction. Hence it is supposed to be easier to liquidate capitalism than its projection in the customs and relations between man and man. And this despite the fact that a large part of the superstructure—the state, the legislative power, educational instruments and those of propaganda —are in the hands of a vanguard regarded as a guarantee of the "socialization" of the structure. The unlikelihood of this series of correlations from a Marxist point of view stares one in the face. And in fact, Marx, intensively utilized in the study of the mechanisms of capitalist societies, is most often set aside as soon as discussion turns to the transitional societies: the economy is studied in classical, quantitative or technical terms, and the political sphere through a kind of sociology of power which, in the best of cases, turns into nothing more than the history of the choices and ideology of the leading groups. *The Short Course on the History of the CPSU (b)* is no exception to this rule.

The theoretical eclecticism, the loss of Marxist identity represented by this discussion of the socialist societies—together with the paradoxes that I have briefly mentioned—is a result, in my opinion, of the generally accepted premiss that the base is "socialized" at the moment of the seizure of political power by the abolition of the private ownership of the means of production.[12]

Even those—and this means the leaders of the Communist Parties— who have recognized that the seizure of political power is not the "initial" moment of the revolution implicitly assume that the transformation of property essentially signifies the abolition of capitalism as a mode of production. There is an underlying identification of "structure" and "ownership of the means of production"—in fact a distorted and reductive reading of Marx. Marx may have said that capital is not a thing but a relation between men mediated by things; he may have written—in the famous *Preface* to *A Contribution to the Critique of Political Economy* which is the source of so many errors in the interpretation of structure-superstructure relations—that the structure is formed out of the "definite relations which are independent of their will" that men have with one another and that these "relations of production" are "appropriate to a given stage in the development of their material forces of production"; he may have said that it is "*the totality of these relations of production*" that constitutes the "economic structure of society, the real foundation, on which arises a legal and political superstructure and to which correspond definite forms of social consciousness"; in other words, he may have claimed that structure and superstructure are two distinct levels of relations between men the first of which—those formed in the "social production of their existence"—are pre-eminent, but the ordinary reading has been quite different. The base has been assimilated to the system of ownership of the means of production, capitalism to their *private* ownership and the capitalist mode of production to a mere consequence, destined to fall or lose its meaning with the disappearance of this mode of property. With the result that the post-revolutionary societies have thought that the *socialist* nature of the base was guaranteed by a no longer private management, a management by the working class through its political representation—the Party for Lenin, the "councils" for the Luxemburgists—of the same organizational and technical system of production that capitalism had created and left them as an inheritance (and, it goes without saying, of the same productive forces). The whole discussion in the 1920s in the Soviet Union, despite certain important allusions by Lenin to "state capitalism", seems to move within these theoretical limits.

But capitalism, as a historical formation and as a system of production, cannot be assimilated to the existence of a class of proprietors. It is a whole productive civilization born around a certain type of accumulation and reproduction, which has given birth to the most complex and simultaneously the most distorted web of relations known to history. The fact that the holder of capital is no longer a private individual and that—practically—that part of the profit which does not go to feed the accumulation fund changes its destination, does not change the substance and the mechanisms of the productive system. In Marx this is quite simply implicit, however obvious it is on the logical plane. All Marx's interest is concentrated precisely on this global system of relations, in which the private ownership of the means of production (like all property relations in general, cf. the *Introduction* to *A Contribution to the Critique of Political Economy*) is only one aspect. A particularly profound examination of *Capital* is not indispensable to realize this; the most famous pages of the *Grundrisse*, "Pre-capitalist Economic Formations", are enough. In them Marx traces the history of the loss and reappropriation by man of his labour, of the product of his labour, hence of himself, and in them he suggests the complexity of the relations that designate the "productive civilization" introduced by capital, the capitalist world of production—an extremely close relationship between the material character of the productive fact, the inter-human relation between producer, wage-labourer and the holder or manager of capital, the "objectivity" of the system of accumulation and reproduction of capital, the political and social history which follows from it. The result is that the stake of the "socialist revolution" is very different from a change in the ownership of the means of production pure and simple, with the fairer distribution of profit that follows and without all the other relations of commodities and reification being touched. What is at issue is a total decomposition and recomposition of the relations between men, between men and things, the revolutionization of the "social mode of production of their existence". In other words, it is the tendential end of the present image of the worker, of alienation, of the separation between labour and the product of labour, of the existence of the two as commodities.

Without this, the seizure of power and the abolition of a class of proprietors represent only a preliminary and incomplete condition for the struggle against the capitalist mode of production *which continues to operate under a different management.* This type of argument has long been rejected. Trotsky rejected it when he stated that the bureaucracy is not a class because it does not *own* the means of production and hence cannot hand them down to the next generation. Of more recent and interesting investigations of the socialist societies, many reject it too.[13] And yet, if one re-reads (and reflects on) the debate that followed Lenin's death, it is this illumination that makes the only sense of the development of Soviet society. Here I shall only take up one example: the discussion about *socialist accumulation,* for it showed clearly that the almost ineluctable resistance of the mode of production inherited from the past could only be surmounted if the premises were brought back into question. In Preobrazhensky's most lucid pages—Preobrazhensky, whom Stalin liquidated after assimilating his theses—the theoretical impasse is obvious.[14] An accumulation was necessary, he said; and would have been had not the revolution included an enormous loss of resources. But how was it to be realised? Capitalism does it in three ways: by a levy on workers' labour in industry (surplus-value, surplus product), by the "brutal plunder" of the countryside, described by Marx, and by the even more brutal plunder of all the productive sectors of the colonies by the metropoles. The youthful republic of the Soviets had no colonies. It had therefore—maintained Preobrazhensky —to accumulate from workers' labour and the countryside. "The source of this accumulation," he recognized in relation to the former point, "is the same as under capitalism, that is the labour of the working class, whose wages must be less than the total value of the products they create". With a "number of very important distinctions . . . *in the forms in which labour power is used and is paid for*" (my emphasis), i.e., within the *limit* set on its exploitation from the physical and wage point of view. Now since they had inherited an industrial sector needing total reconstruction and structurally backward, accumulation would have to be realized less on the basis of a levy on workers' labour, which would hardly suffice to reconstitute resources, than on a massive levy on the countryside, which Preobrazhensky rather significantly called "our colonies". What had been called the "brutal plunder" carried out by capitalism was here also called a "transfer of resources from the pre-socialist sector to the socialist sector"; the process was the same. This ideological precaution is purely formal: industry is a "socialist" sector because in it the private ownership of the means of production has been abolished; the countryside is not yet a "socialist" sector because ownership of the land still survives, and this justifies the levy (which, as is well known anyway, is produced and continues to be produced in *all* forms of property in land, even if the phenomenon is less important today because of tenacious peasant resistance). In reality it was a matter of an accumulation corresponding to a model of development of the productive forces forged by the industrial revolution, a historical form of capitalist production and one indissolubly linked to it. There was no escape. With all the consequences that this implied: the aggravation of the division between town and country, social stratification, the low level of social mobility, the accumulation of discrepancies from region to region, selection in culture and in roles, i.e., the reproduction of the *structural* inequality proper to capitalist development.

The theoretical problem posed is obvious. Indeed, how could a political revolution, i.e., the mere seizure of state power and the transformation of private property into state property, modify an already formed organization of the productive forces whose destruction would imply famine (and hence the rapid defeat of the revolution) and whose maintenance included the reproduction of the obligatory mechanisms of capitalist production? In other words, what can and must a socialist revolution destroy, what may it retain, and for how long, what mechanisms must it set in motion if it would not remain prisoner either of the destruction or of the retention of the capitalist mode of production? The question is important, and relates to an ambiguity present throughout Marxist thought, which sees the revolution simultaneously as the *crowning* and as the *overthrow* of capitalist development. It seems to me that the heart of the Maoist thought of the Chinese revolution has been the only one to confront it, the Mao of the 1956 speech on the "Ten Great Relations", of the "Great Leap Forward", of the beginning of the cultural revolution. This Maoism's only concern is to confront and overcome the challenge of the productive forces and of their organization, inherited and made obligatory by capital and the pre-capitalist structure, while at the same time rejecting all its internal consequences, opposing its natural logic, forcing it with the aim of creating the outlines of a different economic "rationality" able even to debouch onto the end of the model of development born with industrial mechanization and able to formulate a new relation between industry and agriculture at the productive level.

But this once said—and in my opinion it is the central theoretical problem of the construction of socialism—it is the political aspect that stares us in the face. If "socialist" accumulation has to be realized as it was in practice realized, through the persistence of working-class exploitation[15] and a "levy" on the countryside as a whole—two measures dictated by the desire to reorganize resources so as to make possible an acceleration of the model of development characteristic of the most advanced capitalism—the consequence must be a state "centralization". These economic priorities prohibit the construction of worker and peasant self-government, they remove the social base for it: in this way one can explain the impossibility of the survival of the soviets in the 1920s. No-one can deliberately preside over his own spoliation. Mao Tse-tung understood this very well when he refused to gamble on an accelerated industrialization at the expense of the countryside; when he chose a balanced development at the level of the whole of economic life, *at the same time as* a struggle against every mechanism of capitalist rationality, a development based on a relationship which granted a large place to agriculture with respect to industry, to light industry with respect to heavy industry. By this Mao avoided setting one part of society against the other (industry against agriculture, whereas the true conflict lies in class against class). And at the same time he allowed these two sectors (and most easily the countryside) to retain a proportion of the power, allowed them to direct themselves towards solutions of self-government (the communes) in which the pre-eminence of state centralization is organized on other bases. All this is possible insofar as it is founded on a different rationality of the *base*. It is no accident that, in this orientation, the cultural revolution revealed in its development the opposite of what is ordinarily stated. In China or in the USSR it was not just a matter of defeating the "old ideas" but also the "capitalist road", the capitalist mode of production which, while persisting and reproducing itself, also reproduces the superstructural forms of the *bourgeois state* and thus constitutes a permanent reproblematization of the dictatorship of the proletariat.

From this point of view, the delays, the difficulties and the *political* degeneration of the socialist states, their inability to realize the ideals of liberty and equality for which they were born, the persistence of the subaltern character of the class, the separate nature of the power apparatuses appear as the *necessary* projection of a structure which is only partly socialized. There is not a discrepancy between base and superstructure but a correspondence. Socialist society is a *transitional* society in the full sense of the term; it is a historical form in which elements of capital continue to exist, mingled with other elements, and to exercise decisive pressure on the political sphere, on the relationship between men, on the relationship between governors and governed. In their turn, these elements of the past (or present) mode of production refer to the productive forces; the *social* revolution appears as an uninterrupted process, only begun by the political revolution, and which the latter does not necessarily guarantee. The history of the USSR shows it, but so does that of Cuba and China—the cultural revolution is an extraordinary indication of it, with the level it attained and the ebb it has experienced.

But if this is the case, the relationship between the European left and the socialist countries must be doubly re-envisaged. It can disengage itself from the alternation of hope and disillusion, utopia and realism which has always bogged it down, and provide a healthy and lucid analysis of the processes of transition. It can thus always distinguish between the moments of advance and the moments of retreat, the order of the contradictions, the class equilibria—in the full sense of the term class—and hence also the degree of antagonism attained, global, partial or zero, by the struggle of the system at the international level. This is the replacement of a relation between religion and apostasy by a "secular" relation. This type of analysis of the socialist countries is then, and in reality, a type of reflection on the *socialist revolution* and immediately becomes a reference point for our militancy in the West. The difficulty of taking up this different relationship surely reveals a curious "ideological" deformation, the difficulty we have in cutting the deepest root of the evolutionism of the Second International. That of conceiving a *different* model of development, of the productive forces, of society, which is not the capitalist model in which we live and which, in a by no means disinterested way, we transfer to the "socialist" societies while asking them for all that to accompany them with a system of political and social relations. Is it not here that lies the extreme ambiguity of Western Marxism and its most authentically revisionist vein, shared by militants and others—the political and theoretical vice which has hitherto blocked the revolution in the West? This tenacious umbilical cord, which links our way of thinking the revolution of the capitalist matrix of our societies, was cut by China at the most fruitful moment of Maoism, during the Cultural Revolution. By Europe, too, in the "refusal" of the students of 1967–8 and certain Italian workers' struggles against the capitalist organization of labour. In the heat of the struggle and in the clarity of a radical antagonism the necessity of a revolution not only in the world but also in ourselves, the total re-foundation discussed by Marx in *The German Ideology*, has been intuitively understood: a revolution in which we shall save nothing if not the ideas of liberty and equality, finally rediscovered in their material roots and guarantees—another way for men to organize their existence.

Summer 1972

NOTES

1. Cf. the exchange of letters published in *Rinascità*, the PCI weekly, in May 1964.
2. In his *L'Existentialisme*, Lefebvre describes him as follows: "Paul Nizan had few friends and we wondered what his secret was, the secret of his obsession and of his torment. Today we know. All his books revolved around the idea of betrayal." As

for Aragon, he depicts Nizan in his novel *Les Communistes* in the figure of Patrice Orfilat, traitor, paid agent, naturally with a certain sympathy for the Trotskyists defined by the positive character (Politzer) as *"flics"*.

3. *Paul Nizan, intellectuel communiste*, selected and presented by J.-J. Brochier, Maspero, Paris, 1970, vol. II, p. 110.

4. Ibid., p. 115. On 30 September, i.e. a few days after his resignation, he wrote to his wife: "Have read the complete text of the Kremlin agreement. I seem to understand Iossif Vissarionovich's game: the least that can be said is that it is double and *cousu de fil rouge* [a play on *cousu de fil blanc*, i.e., blatant]. . . ." And on 22 October: "It is not because I hold its agreement with Berlin against the USSR that I took the decision I did. It is precisely because I thought the French Communists lacked the necessary political cynicism and the political capacity to lie it required to draw the maximum political advantages from a risky political operation." In other words, the PCF should, while approving the USSR's action, have dissociated itself from it so as to avoid the after-effects of what was for Stalin an obligatory choice, whereas "to imitate the Russians to the letter was to mistake them entirely in spirit", it was to be no more than their "faithful imitators". However, the invasion of Poland seemed intolerable to him: "Stalin's policy disgusts me." From October 1939 to May 1940, the contradiction seemed insurmountable to him. The book presented by Brochier is very rich in hitherto unpublished documents on this question.

5. Just as the PCF never courted him. In "Matérialisme et révolution", which appeared in *Les Temps Modernes* from June to July 1946, Sartre tells how Jean Kanapa had proposed to him a meeting with Garaudy and Mougin at René Maublanc's house. Sartre, who was then concerned to maintain good relations with the Communists, went along. But to his astonishment he was greeted with a violent attack from Garaudy and the meeting at no point took the direction that the young Kanapa perhaps desired of a conquest of Sartre for the Party. Nor did this happen subsequently, although Sartre has always been concerned to define himself as a fellow traveller and his attacks on the PCF have been rare.

6. Cf. *Les Temps Modernes*, July and October–November 1952, and the subsequent polemic with Claude Lefort in April 1973, translated into English by Irene Clephane as *The Communists and Peace, with An Answer to Claude Lefort*, Hamish Hamilton, London, 1969.

7. "Russia is not the one way of reaching the final solution. Born in the antagonisms which provoked the war of 1914–18, it could disappear: the antagonisms will survive it, and the capitalist nations will in the end collapse. In this precise sense, the safeguarding of the USSR is not the *necessary* condition for world revolution. But these considerations are not *historical*: historically the opportunity of the proletariat, its 'example' and the source of 'the strength of revolutionary penetration' are in the USSR." "Les communistes et la paix", I, *Les Temps Modernes*, July 1952; *The Communists and Peace*, op. cit., p. 10.

8. Merleau-Ponty briefly characterizes the dilemma as follows: "Sartre's attitude is first a reminder of the facts. It is true that today the most active portion of the working class supports the PCF and the CGT. Hence it is true that every defeat of the PCF decreases the weight of the working class in the political struggle, that those who celebrate the failure of a strike called by the PCF as a victory of the working class are abandoning the working class that exists and is in a majority Communist. The left-wing anti-Communist gets out of this by calling the working class's fatigue lucidity and its disheartenment revolutiohary spirit. He is walking with an imaginary proletariat towards a revolution at last freed from Communist tutelage and graces a politics which triumphs or suffers simultaneously with Pinay's government with the name proletarian politics. . . . If you are prepared to treat the PCF as the enemy number one and to think your politics in consequence,

your enemy number two, capitalism, is relatively speaking your ally; if your first concern is to weaken the Communist Party, you will lack the time and the desire to weaken its adversaries. . . . All this is true and had to be said." (Cf. "Sartre et l'ultrabolchévisme", in *Les Aventures de la dialectique*, Gallimard, Paris, 1953, pp. 140–1, where the whole argument that I have briefly reported here is developed.

9. Cf. "Réponse à Albert Camus", *Les Temps Modernes*, August 1952.

10. Cf. his preface to Michèle Manceaux's book *Les Maos en France*, Gallimard, Paris, 1972.

11. See Chapter XLI in *My Life*, "Lenin's Death and the Shift of Power". "The leading groups of the party that emerged from underground were inspired by the revolutionary tendencies which the leaders of the first period of the revolution were able to formulate clearly and to carry out completely and successfully in practice. It was exactly this that made them the leaders of the party, and, through the party, leaders of the working class, and, through the working class, leaders of the country. It was thus that certain individuals had concentrated power in their hands. But the ideas of the first period of the revolution were imperceptibly losing their influence in the consciousness of the party stratum that held the direct power over the country. In the country itself, processes were shaping themselves that one may sum up under the general name of reaction. These extended, in varying degree, to the working class as well, including even its party. The stratum that made up the apparatus of power developed its own independent aims and tried to subordinate the revolution to them. A division began to reveal itself between the leaders who expressed the historical line of the class and could see beyond the apparatus, and the apparatus itself—a huge, cumbrous, heterogeneous thing that easily sucked in the average communist. . . ." And further on: "I am here limiting myself to the psychological aspect of the matter, and disregarding its social basis, that is, the changes in the anatomy of the revolutionary society. In the final reckoning, it is, of course, these latter changes that decide. But in actual life it is their psychological reflection that one encounters directly." In the rest of the book he never returns to the "social basis". See *My Life*, Grosset and Dunlap, New York, 1960, pp. 502 and 504.

12. See also the debate in *Le Monde*, 3 November 1972, on Roy Medvedev's book *Let History Judge: The Origins and Consequences of Stalinism*, Macmillan, London, 1972. Jean Ellenstein, for the PCF, repeats notably: "This pertains to the fact that the USSR possessed a socialist economy, that society there was socialist and simultaneously, at the level of the superstructures, where the government of men and the management of things are concerned, there was considerable backwardness. . . ." It is clear—and I shall not linger long over the problem—that any judgement of Stalin is reduced to a superstructural phenomenon. As much for those who seek justifications (the Communists insist on the cultural backwardness of Russian society; Isaac Deutscher, who was not a Communist, explains the centralization and hence the excesses by general social backwardness) as for those who do not (like Medvedev or the orthodox Trotskyists, for whom the advance might, without Stalin, have been less bloody and more rapid).

13. In contrast, the question has been globally confronted in the fundamental debate between Paul Sweezy and Charles Bettelheim, with two different analyses, a debate recently published by Monthly Review Press; and in general in the analyses of the *Centre d'Etudes et de Planification socialiste*, directed by Bettelheim also.

14. "The Fundamental Law of Primitive Socialist Accumulation." This text by Preobrazhensky was published in *Vestnik Kommunisticeskoj Akademii*, VIII, 1924. With some alterations, it constitutes a chapter of his *The New Economics*, translated by Brian Pearce, introduced by Alec Nove, The Clarendon Press, Oxford, 1965.

15. Preobrazhensky attempts to soften this harsh reality by maintaining that, during the revolution, the working class is *no longer the object, but rather the subject of the exploitation* since it is in a position to decide, on the basis of its being and political practice, to exploit itself.

SOLZHENITSYN: A POLITICAL ANALYSIS

Jean-Marie Chauvier

Introduction

IT would be a relief if Solzhenitsyn were really a writer left over from the 19th century, a purely anachronistic spirit, a Great-Russian chauvinist with nothing ultimately very new or very credible to contribute to our understanding of Stalinism or of Soviet history and Soviet society. It would at any rate relieve the Left in the West of a daunting task— that of deciphering a message which, like many others that are now reaching it from the East, fails to offer an echo to the Western Left's hopes or illusions. However, in order to quell a fever it is not enough to smash the thermometer.

Even if the diagnosis of "fever" is a plausible one, it still remains necessary not merely to justify this but also to explain how a body of writing inspired by such backward-looking ideas can have succeeded in fascinating, even stirring, by its "authenticity", its "skill in saying what is hardest to say", even those who belatedly discover, with astonishment, what the writer's political conclusions are. One still has to account for the pre-eminence of this body of writing in the Soviet literature of the last ten or fifteen years: the audience, the esteem, even the influence that it enjoys among the most outstanding representatives of Soviet prose and poetry, among the Soviet intelligentsia, and, in general, among Russian readers. And, finally, one has to account for the strange dread which it seems increasingly to have cast upon official circles in the USSR. How is it that the rulers of such a great power, claiming to be the ideological leaders of the Communist movement, can be afraid of the books and speeches of an Old-Believer, an apostle of early-mediaeval Orthodoxy?

There is certainly something disconcerting about this *starets*, this venerable sage from the world of legend, who has wandered into the second half of the 20th century. Those who have subjected Solzhenitsyn to censorship, fond though they are of "ideological struggle", have not managed to join battle with him on any point whatsoever, but have felt able to deal with him only by means of sordid measures of persecution, culminating in a barbarous banishment—an admission, if ever there was one, of their impotence, but also a proof of the validity of that accusation of tyranny, of "survivals of serfdom", that the writer has always levelled against the rulers of his country.

Solzhenitsyn has been a no less baffling surprise for the Left of the West, who would have liked to see in the author of *One Day in the Life of Ivan Denisovich*—seemingly so unlikely to produce *The Gulag Archipelago*, which was nevertheless already in preparation—the reassuring critic of a Stalinism that belonged to the past, the harbinger of a regenerated socialism.

Many of his bourgeois admirers, dazzled at first by this unexpected gift, have also been taken aback: although the indictment of the Soviet order was most pleasing to them, its religious, Russophil and even anti-capitalist tones made "the conscience of mankind" less easy to exploit than had been hoped.

All these aspects of the Solzhenitsyn phenomenon—the coincidence of a literary achievement and a struggle, the power his writings have shown to upset people, the idolatry that they have been accorded in the West—most certainly call for a *political study*.

I appreciate the danger of *reduction* that such a study involves. Some commentators will exclaim, outraged, that Art with a big A cannot be examined and interpreted in this way "at the level of the conjuncture". Has not Solzhenitsyn himself rejected plainly enough all ideology, "the ephemeral requirements of politics and of petty social ideals"?

It remains none the less true that a particular "conjuncture" and the "ephemeral requirements" of a certain kind of politics are what have conferred upon Solzhenitsyn his status as "the conscience of mankind", and that both his *ideas* and his *social ideals* (which are far from petty) thrust him into the midst of the vital disputes of our time, which are essentially political: about the balance-sheet of Stalinism and of the Soviet revolution, about the past, present and future of socialism.

The spirit of Solzhenitsyn, that of those who scorn him, and also that, however elegantly draped in aestheticism it may be, of his pious proselytes, all quite clearly belong to the realm of approaches and contexts which are eminently *ideological* and *political*.

I

The published work of Alexander Isayevich Solzhenitsyn extends from 1962, when his first story appeared, to the present time. (He actually began writing in 1936–9.) His writings fall into four sections, which are not "stages" but the differing manifestations of one and the same approach. The first section consists of "long short stories" (novellas), most notably *One Day in the Life of Ivan Denisovich* and *Matryona's House*, in which the writer was revealed to us. Their sobriety, their language, their narrative method make them akin to the *skaz*, originating from the depths of the people and transcribing an orally-told tale.

The *skaz* enjoyed its period of glory in the 1920s, when this genre was practised by such virtuosi as Isaac Babel and Boris Pilnyak. This is doubtless why Lukács sees grounds for finding in Solzhenitsyn a revival of "socialist realism" in its original form.

The author of the great novels, with their numerous characters, descriptive realism and moral tendencies, is naturally linked with the great realistic tradition of 19th century Russian literature, outstandingly represented by Tolstoy. We do not find in Solzhenitsyn, however, either the slow pace, or the ponderous descriptions, or the fatalism that are characteristic of *War and Peace*. The way in which he tackles situations, the "polyphonic" construction of his work (as he himself has described this),[1] the richness of his language (country expressions, religious archaisms, Soviet neologisms, words of the author's own devising), and the topical nature of his ethical preoccupations (even when he projects these upon the world of *August 1914*) show us a writer who is deeply original and in touch with present-day realities.

The trials that have set their mark upon Solzhenitsyn—the war, the camp, cancer—have led him to reinstate the theme of death: confronted with imminent death, the writer questions the meaning of life and of the values of this world.

His testimony-cum-indictment on *The Gulag Archipelago*[2] has enabled Solzhenitsyn to define his view of the history of the Soviet Union, from which he deduces, among other things, his political philosophy. The latter has been outlined for us in a fourth section of his work—his public statements, the most significant of which to date is his *Letter to Soviet Leaders*.[3]

*   *   *

The first reports from Moscow which in 1962 announced the appearance in *Novy Mir* of *One Day in the Life of Ivan Denisovich* hailed a sort of event in political journalism: the first account to be published in the USSR of one of Stalin's concentration camps. Pierre Daix tells how he heard, from Elsa Triolet, that what it signified was something much more than that: "great Russian prose . . . a real classic". And Claude Roy declared that *One Day* "has emerged as a masterpiece of literature, a book to be set beside Dostoyevsky's *Memoirs from the House of the Dead*". From that moment when criticism of Stalinism was joined with great literary talent, Solzhenitsyn became, for numberless readers in the West who were trying to grasp what had happened in Russia, the writer whom they accepted as their guide. The Left was especially anxious to take him over, to recognize themselves in this "Soviet" author who seemed to have the backing of his country's leaders. A critic "from within" who was also an emphatically modern writer—did not the hope embodied in this phenomenon make up for the shock they had suffered through the revelation of the world of the camps? The fact that Ivan Denisovich's mental horizon lacked any hope for the future, that there was no reference made to socialist ideology, to the "baby" which it was said one ought not to throw out with the "bathwater", certainly gave reason for feeling some perplexity. But Solzhenitsyn, it was supposed, was not shutting any door. When *Matryona's House* appeared, these readers were not too willing to see in it the black picture of rural life in the Soviet Union, or the sort of religion of Russia's continuity, which broke through the socialist frame of reference: the beauty of his art, the genius of his language were sufficient to maintain their belief in Solzhenitsyn's greatness. In *Cancer Ward*, and even in *The First Circle*, people strove to discover the consolation of a socialist promise in full conformity with the anti-Stalinist criticism made by "liberal" or Khrushchevite Communism, or even compatible with the denunciation of "bureaucratic degeneration" as conceived, since Trotsky, by the various "Left" adversaries of Stalinism. Georg Lukács did not differ greatly from this way of seeing Solzhenitsyn, in whom he found a "plebeian critique" of Stalinism, together with a kinship with the socialist-realist tradition of the 1920s—a first step in the critique of Stalinism, inevitably limited in character, but a marker for future progress.[4]

As Solzhenitsyn's ideas became plainly displayed, however, in *The First Circle* and then in his (undelivered) *Nobel Prize Lecture* of 1972, this endeavour to "absorb" the writer was found impossible to maintain. Pierre Daix said: "Solzhenitsyn does not echo our dreams"; for him, revolution was a lost cause. "The system does not contain potentialities for its own transformation. This transformation will take place from outside it."[5] But Daix still believed Solzhenitsyn's attitude to be compatible with Marxism, with the hope of a "21st-century socialism". *The Gulag Archipelago* and the *Letter to Soviet Leaders* were to perform the task of ruling out this last hoped-for compromise: Solzhenitsyn is profoundly hostile to Marxism, and for him socialism is neither a problem nor a hope.

It may be thought that this break in Solzhenitsyn's thinking took place gradually, being perhaps hastened by the disillusionment and the manifold harassments that the writer was obliged to endure after the euphoric interval of de-Stalinization. However, a re-reading of Solzhenitsyn in the light of his most recent writings suggests that there has been a fundamental continuity. *One Day* already contains the ideas that were to come to flower in *The Gulag Archipelago*. The latter book was begun at the end of the 1950s, and the author did not share the political hopes that were current at that time. "Re-Stalinization" was to be, in his eyes, merely the confirmation that what is called Stalinism has never ceased to exist—that it is inherent in the basic characteristics of the system.

From the first novellas to *The Gulag Archipelago* and the *Letter to Soviet Leaders*, by way of the great novels, a sort of theory of moral values, an axiology, develops, which organizes through successive inductions what can indeed be called "Solzhenitsyn's thought". It is thought which is radically alien to Communism.

One Day exposed what most Communists had refused to admit until then—the existence of concentration camps in the land of socialism. Daix, who experienced Mauthausen, does not hesitate to compare these camps to the Nazi ones. The documentary aspect of the story is nevertheless very secondary. Shalanov and Ginzburg have given much more detailed descriptions of the world of the exiles.[6] *One Day in the Life of Ivan Denisovich* is an ordinary day, when nothing much happened, "almost a happy day", similar to the other "three thousand six hundred and fifty-three days in his sentence. . . . The three extra days were because of the leap-years."[7] In contrast to accounts which lay stress on atrocities and tortures, the horror of concentration camp life is here epitomized in this stripping-bare, this perfectly ordinary, routine, *political* task of dehumanization, of disintegration of the human personality for which the camp serves as instrument. *One Day* is, in fact, only an allegory, with the camp as a microcosm of Stalinist society, a concentration of the essence of the system, of the "socialist community", which here takes the form of a building-site where slaves are set to work: "a barren field covered with snow-drifts, and before anything could be done there, they would have to dig holes, erect posts and put up barbed wire between the posts—to prevent themselves from escaping. And only then could they begin to build."[8] Because it is a concentration of the essence of the system it cannot be a "cancer", surgical elimination of which would be accomplished by the system itself—in other words, a malign excrescence that a body which had remained healthy could get rid of. There is no salvation within this system. Captain Buinovsky, who shouts at the guards: "You're not true Soviets! You're not Communists", is awarded ten days in the cells, a frightful punishment.[9] Readers have perceived how unbearable it must be for the guards to be confronted with the values they are supposed to be representing. But Buinovsky's cry reveals also the uselessness of this sort of nostalgia for "true Communism". Salvation is not to be found in the Idea, which still allows a bond of complicity to continue to link the victims with their executioners. It lies in that deep quality of humanity which unites the victims alone, whoever they may be. It lies above all, and more precisely, in the love of work, of creation, the qualities of endurance and the stoicism of the Russian people, embodied in the *muzhik* Shukhov. He alone gets by, managing, by refusal to make any compromise, but also without engaging in any futile rebellion, to save his humanity, at the bottom of a well into which no light penetrates any more—in a world wherein one must abandon all hope except what comes "from within". . . .

*   *   *

Returning from exile, Solzhenitsyn draws us into the midst of Russia, where the forests roar in the wind, into villages whose evocatively sonorous names tell us that we are in "the heart of Russia". Here he finds and tells us about Matryona (the Motherland), humble matron and "righteous person" of her village, embodying the ancient peasant wisdom that survives all upheavals and patiently resists the craziness of the collective-farm bureaucracy. Not often does an "immersion in Russia" bring such ecstatic enjoyment as this story does, with its air of authenticity which is still further underlined in the Russian text by language drawn from the speech of countryfolk, sensuous and full of sounds that powerfully evoke the meanings of words—language of which Solzhenitsyn is a past master, and which, it must be said, baffles the reader who knows only the Russian of the newspapers.

It would be pointless here to charge the author with lack of objectivity in depicting the collective-farm countryside in such dark colours. Villages like Matryona's do exist. Whoever travels, as I have some-times travelled, across central Russia, the countryside that begins at the gates of Moscow, can testify to this rural scene, apparently un-changing, where only the coming of electricity and radio, following the Second World War, seems to have introduced something new and of importance since the time of Tolstoy, despite the cataclysms of the collectivization campaign and the War, and despite the "collective-farm revolution". Down to the middle 1950s agricultural Russia had remained outside the technical progress being realized in the developing cities, and in a state close to destitution. One might contrast with this picture the richer aspect offered by the black-earth lands of the Ukraine, the success achieved by the cotton-producing collective farms in Uzbekistan, or the relatively prosperous standard of living of the peasants of Estonia, as so many proofs of the régime's ability to bring about progress in agriculture. No doubt, indeed, one might—but the writer's purpose is not sociological or statistical in character, it is aesthetic. The essential lesson of the story about Matryona is surely the moral defeat of the ruling ideology, which has done no more than touch the surface of reality, without penetrating into people's consciousness: while on the other hand, the spirit of Matryona, a sister to Ivan Denisovich, bears witness once again to the purifying ascesis of con-scientious labour, to the immanent and anonymous justice that waits in the depths of the people. "None of us who lived close to her perceived that she was that one righteous person without whom, as the saying goes, no city can stand. Nor the world."[10]

* * *

Critics have not failed to reproach Solzhenitsyn with his fixation on the "dark side" alone of Soviet life. The view taken is that, as with Stalin, there is a "positive" element and a "negative" one, clearly separable and capable of arithmetical evaluation: the repressions and the camps in one scale of the balance, and the great technical and social achievements in the other, with what decisive superiority! It must be appreciated that in the mental journey that has brought him to the point of repudiating the revolution, Solzhenitsyn has not in the least overlooked the factors of enthusiasm and devotion to the socialist cause that enter into the life of the Soviet people. The novella entitled *For the Good of the Cause* grapples with just this "edifying" theme, and the author even employs in it the contemporary Soviet jargon used by technicians, young people and officials.

Here, we are a long way from Matryona. In a provincial town the Principal, the teaching staff and the students of a technical college resolve to build with their own hands the new building and installations which they urgently need. They devote to this task—without receiving the least encouragement (quite the contrary) from the ruling authorities —an entire year of work, sacrificing their free time and their holidays, in the spirit of the *subbotniki*, the "Communist Saturdays" that were dear to Lenin. Without exaggerating, it is a socialist epic, and, to employ the current jargon, a fine example of "self-management". When the work is completed, and the reward so greatly desired at last within reach, a commission composed of high officials arrives and decides to assign the new building to a research institute engaged in "work vital to the State"—not without "observing" that the cramped old premises are perfectly adequate for the needs of the technical college. A struggle is waged against this bureaucratic decision, but it proves hopeless. The point is that certain prospects of promotion are involved: promotion for Khabalygin, who will become head of the new institute, and for Knorozov, the regional party leader, who finds the decision splendid, because "we'll move at once into a different class of town—towns on the scale of Gorky and Sverdlovsk".[11] The point is, above all, that there is no appeal from the fatality of omnipotent arbitrariness.

And what about the people concerned, those who had given so much in order to rebuild their college? What explanation are they to be offered? "The institute is vital to the state and it's not up to us to question its suitability", says a Party secretary to those who cannot accept the *fait accompli.* "Call meetings? Have a special discussion of the issue? No, that would be a political error. In fact, we must do the opposite: if the students of the Komsomol committee insist on a meeting, we must dissuade them from holding it."[12] There is no way round it: all that can be done is to clench one's fists and blink back one's tears.

To be sure, the Principal of the college does find someone ready to listen to him—Grachikov, the secretary of the town's Party Committee. There is always, somewhere or other, an honest official, a true Communist. This one goes to see his superior, Knorozov. Replying to the frank but too unjust declarations of this petty chieftain, Grachikov crosses the Rubicon, finding words for a righteous and stinging rejoinder: "We're not medieval barons trying to outdo each other by adding more quarterings to our coats of arms. The honour of our town lies in the fact that these children put up that building themselves, and did it for the love of it, and it's our duty to back them up. But if you take the building away they'll never forget we've cheated them. If you cheat people once, then they realize that you may cheat them again." And later, abandoning all restraint, he bursts out: "Why are we arguing over a heap of stones? . . . Communism will not be built with stones but people. . . . It's a harder and longer task, but if we were to finish the whole structure tomorrow and it was built of nothing but stones, we would never have Communism."

All that Knorozov can say in answer to that is: "You're not mature enough for the post of secretary of the town Party committee. . . . We overlooked that."

Never mind: in that moment Grachikov has chosen his fate—he is "sick to the teeth" with this style of command.[13] Soon he will be thinking that profiteers and parasites of every sort "should be immediately expelled from the Party"—not reprimanded, but expelled, for their conduct "implied a completely alien mentality, that of an inherent capitalist".[14]

While the author's sympathy is with the volunteer builders and with the Communist Grachikov, he allows them no chance of success. The evil that destroyed the inmates of the camp is the same evil that dooms enthusiasm to sterility. The fight for a just cause breaks helplessly against the rock of arbitrary power and bureaucracy. In contrast to most Soviet works that deal with this type of subject, there is here no appeal, no gleam of hope inside the system. And the question arises: what will become of the young people who are being shaped by trials such as this?

* * *

In proceeding from the novellas to the great polyphonic novels the writer merely widens his field of investigation and deepens his subject-matter. There is not only continuity but also simultaneity between the modernistic author of the novellas and the novelist who is said to have revived the great tradition of Russian literature. Thus, *The First Circle*, the scene of which is the prison-cum-research-institute where the author spent four years of detention in the company of privileged slaves (scientists and scholars) precedes (1955–8) *One Day*, which takes place in the lowest circle of Hell (1959). *The Gulag Archipelago* began to be written in the same period. *Cancer Ward* was intended at first (1963) to be a novella, to be followed by other tales.

Masterpieces of a literature of denunciation, *The First Circle* and *Cancer Ward*, attack the Stalinist system in its entirety by way of two distinct sub-entities which, in their characteristic features, nevertheless reveal both the oneness of what is being denounced and that of the accuser's approach to it.

In *The First Circle*, the *sharashka*, that "monkey-house" where the first-class prisoners work, inspires the author to make his first major indictment, violent and sometimes caricatural, of the police system quartering Stalinist Russia.

In *Cancer Ward* the country has, like the author, emerged from the nightmare of terror, and is convalescing. This only means that it is seeking even more deeply for "the reasons why".

Here, three key characters, all faced with death, are made to serve the argument. There is Rusanov, the one-time Communist worker who has become an official and privileged beneficiary of the régime, an informer, a "representative of the proletariat" who has landed up, to his great embarrassment, in the public ward of a hospital. There is Kostoglotov, the survivor of the camps, the incorruptible one who has returned to life, to a life that he wishes to be full and worthy. And there is Shulubin, the one who has experienced Stalinism "in freedom", in fear and abjuration, but finds the strength to rise above it. In face of death the values by which these men have lived are brought to the test, and unavoidable choices loom before them.

The values of the "Marxist" Rusanov seem the most vulnerable, and also the least deserving of respect, for they lack sincerity. They are made up of dusty dogmas, terribly brittle assumptions, and, ultimately, of a totalitarian system of thought which is now confronted with ideas and facts that elude its tyrannical rationality. The denunciation of "Rusanovism", moreover, is a denunciation of bureaucratic parasitism, of the privileged set at the head of the Stalinist power-system, un-scrupulous opportunists with stunted minds, loaded with privileges and exemptions of all kinds. Solzhenitsyn does not conceal his profound contempt for them, which is nourished by egalitarian ideals that are typically populist and revolutionary—Shulubin quotes Lenin—and are expressed in cutting words uttered by Kostoglotov: "You think that while we're working towards communism the privileges some have over others ought to be increased, do you? You mean that to become equal we must first become unequal, is that right? You call that dialectics, do you?"[15]

Rusanov had just been explaining the importance, under socialism, of differences in wages, and stressing the difference between the contributions made to the national income by the person at the head of the public health service and by the person who washes the floor in the clinic.

Rusanov is not unlike Drozdov in *Not By Bread Alone*. Dudintsev and Solzhenitsyn have written some of the most vigorous pages in Russian literature on the subject of those whom Konstantin Paustovsky called "the new race of carnivores and property-owners which has nothing in common with the revolution". But whereas, for Dudintsev and Paustovsky, salvation is sought in a socialism restored to its original revolutionary purity, Solzhenitsyn's characters are bringing to ripeness meditations of a different sort. Kostoglotov no longer wants to distinguish between the camps and the régime, and displays a radical scepticism. Shulubin advocates a kind of ethical socialism: " 'But is socialism to blame? We made a very quick turn-around, we thought it was enough to change the mode of production and people would immediately change with it. But did they? The hell they did! They didn't change a bit. Man is a biological type. It takes thousands of years to change him.'

" 'Can there be socialism, then?'

" 'Can there indeed? It's an enigma, isn't it? They talk about "democratic" socialism, but that's just superficial, it doesn't get to the essence of socialism, it only refers to the form in which socialism is introduced, the structure of the state that applies it. It's merely a declaration that heads will not roll, but it doesn't say a word about what this socialism will be built on. You can't build socialism on an abundance of material goods, because people sometimes behave like buffaloes, they stampede and trample the goods into the ground. Nor can you have socialism that's always banging on about hatred, because social life cannot be built on hatred. After a man has burned with hatred year in, year out, he can't simply announce one fine day, "That's enough! As from today I'm finished with hatred, from now on I'm only going to love!" ' "

Shulubin eventually defines the socialism he wants to see: a moral socialism, "a society in which all relationships, fundamental principles and laws flow directly from ethics", and from them alone. Ethical considerations must determine all considerations: how to bring up children, what to train them for, to what end the work of grown-ups should be directed, and how their leisure should be occupied. As for scientific research, it should only be conducted where it doesn't damage morality, in the first instance where it doesn't damage the researchers themselves. The same should apply to foreign policy. But what is this morality? Shulubin does not clarify his idea any further. What we do know is that there will no longer be any question of the pursuit of a chimerical happiness for future generations that have not been consulted. It will be a morality of "mutual affection". Shulubin's references are to Vladimir Soloviev, Kropotkin and Mikhaylovsky. These are perhaps, to some extent, Solzhenitsyn's own "authorities": I shall come back to this point.[16]

*   *   *

But Solzhenitsyn's grand design is situated on the plane of history. He wants to join up again the broken thread of Russian continuity, to examine the events through which Russia was suddenly swept into the turmoil of revolution.

A monumental work on the war of 1914–18 is to serve to accomplish this design. The author looks upon it as his most important task: he had conceived the idea of it already when he was leaving adolescence, all his other writings being merely products of circumstances and of the "peculiarities" of his life-story. This opinion may evoke surprise. More than one reader will, like myself, have felt when reading *August 1914*, the first instalment of this huge undertaking, that the "first" Solzhenitsyn, concerned with what he had personally experienced, and moving us because of the authenticity of his tone, had gone away from us.

Half-way between a testimony and a reconstitution of events, *The Gulag Archipelago* already marks a certain stage reached along the road to this recovery of the collective memory. The realm of fiction is abandoned here in favour of that of documentary *montage*: autobiography, collected testimonies, investigation on the basis of official documents, personal reflections—these are the materials used for this enormous fresco of the world of the concentration camps, the two first parts of which (out of the seven planned) were published almost by accident.[17]

We are here standing, without any doubt, at the foot of a tremendous monument of the literature of denunciation. It is above all a work resulting from a powerful emotional discharge, the ejaculation of a long-restrained cry. We recall the author's words in his *Nobel Prize Lecture*: "During our exhausting forced marches in the camps, as we were taken to work and back again to our huts, with those little chains of lanterns just shining through the mist of the evening frost—many was the time that there arose in our throat those words which we would have liked to shout out to the whole of the world, if only the world could have heard just one of us."[18]

The historian's approach is governed by passion that is ethical in nature. Passion to perform the service due to the memory of the martyrs: "I dedicate this book to all those who did not live long enough to tell what is told here. May they forgive me for not having been able to see everything, retain the memory of everything and fathom everything." Passion of a kind of purificatory catharsis. If he points his finger at the murderers who have gone unpunished (they are still around, either torturers making new careers in various departments, or major operators of the terror, like Molotov, living in comfortable retirement), he does so not in order to demand vengeance on the scale of the crimes he committed, but to oblige the nation to sit in moral judgement: to speak the truth, to condemn the criminals, but above all to condemn their crime, this seems to him to be the key to the deliverance from evil, the method of collective psychotherapy whereby the Russian people can recover their moral balance. "What message will Russia be able to leave to the world if she does not root out this rottenness?" This descent into Hell is not weighed down with the crude imagery of vulgar propaganda: the anger does not need emphasis, the sorrow is conveyed without ostentation. The pamphleteer has not betrayed, in his haste and eagerness to denounce, the artist, the master of words and of feeling.

The author's intention, as he announces in his subtitle, does not go beyond an "attempt at a literary investigation". This modesty is praiseworthy and proper. Let us not then try to find here, as some Western zealots in apologetics have tried, the history, "revealed at last", of the Soviet Union, the "scientific rigour" from which the "myth of Lenin the Good", it is said, will never recover. Although his method is indeed literary, however, the author's ambition is that of an historian, and furthermore one who does not content himself with describing the facts but also propounds a sovereign judgement upon the history he records. This does not happen without some ambiguity. The author's central thesis is, indeed, that what is called the "Stalin" terror resulted from the very quintessence of the régime that was born in October 1917 and continues to exist today. His proof that this is so is far from being demonstrated by scientific method and argument—a point to which I shall come back. In particular, the "terroristic" quotations from Lenin, isolated from their context, are not adequate to support a critique of Leninism which, in fact, does not enter into the writer's preoccupations. Social-Democratic and Anarchist critics have done much better in this line. Roy Medvedev himself, even though he stops short of breaking the "taboo" on a critical re-evaluation of the Lenin period, provides a body of systematic information and analysis on the subject of Stalinism to which *The Gulag Archipelago* cannot be compared. When it is said that Solzhenitsyn "establishes the truth" it must be made clear that, behind and beyond the partial truths assembled in *The Gulag Archipelago*, the great "Truth" towards which the writer strives is not historical or social in nature, but *moral*.

The Gulag Archipelago begins at the point of time when Solzhenitsyn's series of books on the war of 1914–18 is to conclude, assuming that he succeeds in completing this task, which, by his own account, may take him twenty years, and for which "most probably" his life "will not be long enough".

The form of this work is that of a trilogy of novels. *August 1914* is the first panel of the triptych, or, more precisely, the "first node". By "node" the author means a decisive event in the unfolding of history— here, Russia's defeat at Tannenberg. Description of military operations is mingled with description of Russia as it was then, the Russia which, as later became apparent, was in its death-throes.

The author is working in virgin territory. He did not himself live through the situations he describes, although one feels that he has projected upon them his own experience of war. Witnesses are few, Government archives not accessible. The writer therefore draws upon oral tradition and the memories of former generals, published abroad. The reconstitution accomplished is all the more remarkable: not only the events, but the atmosphere, the language, which is quite archaic ("Church Russian", a reader notes),[19] make of it a kind of literary "museum of Russia" which has not failed to dumbfound Soviet visitors to it. Nothing here recalls the ideas that are generally accepted in the USSR, where the entire process of the ending of old Russia is "arranged" so as to lead up to the outcome: the Revolution. It is clear that Solzhenitsyn's purpose is to show that the latter, contrary to what Soviet historiography implies, was not an inevitable occurrence— a point of view which, in itself, is not in the least sacrilegious for Marxists! The writer therefore sets himself to reconstruct all the potentialities of Russian society on the eve of the great turning-point. To be sure, stormladen clouds are not lacking: military defeat, negligence on the part of high authorities in the Army and the State, intrigues in the Tsar's entourage, the unworthy role being played by the Church, that of the liberal intelligentsia. . . . But the Russia of 1914 is also a society filled with dynamism. Released at last from serfdom and its sequelae, agriculture is recording successes that are not to be matched again for a long time.[20] Industry is in full "take-off". The towns are expanding: in Moscow an underground railway is being built (the War was to interrupt this work). Cultural life has been showing, since the turn of the century, a no less remarkable degree of vitality: is not Moscow on the way to becoming one of the centres of the international artistic movement, particularly in the plastic arts?

In all respects, the picture that the writer paints of the Russia of 1914 is the opposite of the picture of a backward poverty-stricken country, a picture to justify the Revolution, which was to be subsequently retained in the USSR. Solzhenitsyn's picture is certainly the true one where many points are concerned: but it overlooks the dark areas that are no less deserving of attention. The Russia of the *muzhiks* and the "lower depths", the country with more than a hundred million illiterates, of proletarian misery, of epidemics and still frequent famines (despite the high production of wheat, a large part of which was exported), of economic colonialism—none of *that* figures in Solzhenitsyn's landscape. The working class and the poor peasantry are, moreover, entirely absent from *August 1914*, except as they appear wearing the greatcoat of the Russian soldier, whose courage and endurance are extolled. The officers, the well-to-do peasantry, the intelligentsia, the engineers, the teachers: these are the protagonists of history as Solzhenitsyn relates it. It has been said that, in restoring "all the options" that were then open to Russia, Solzhenitsyn has favoured none above the rest, and that, furthermore, neither the structure nor the development of his novel is "pre-determined". My own impression is very different. While rejecting the retroactive "determinism" of October 1917, Solzhenitsyn is concerned to suggest, *a contrario*, not only that the Revolution was not inevitable but *that it would have been desirable that it should not have occurred.* True, one cannot pre-judge the way the story is to develop in the remaining instalments. But *August 1914* already provides us with enough "pre-determinations" and value-judgements (none of which should surprise us) to show that history is being re-written in accordance with a "higher" moral truth. This truth comes through in the sympathies revealed by the author and the views, obviously representing his own, that he puts into the mouths of certain characters.

Thus, Solzhenitsyn's sympathy clearly lies with the new bourgeoisie of engineers and entrepreneurs, whereas the revolutionary intelligentsia inspires him only with apprehension or contempt. "Even in those days [the late 90s] the students were split between the revolutionaries and the engineers—the destroyers and the builders. In those days I, too, thought that to build was impossible. But one only had to spend some time in the West to be amazed at how peacefully the anarchists lived there and how hard they worked. As for industry, anyone who has created something with his own hands knows that production is neither capitalist nor socialist, but *one* thing only: it is what creates national wealth, the common material basis without which no country can exist." The character who in this way crosses swords with young "contesta-tionists" gives an example of how he sees the class struggle:

"Along comes a bunch of arts students and they explain to the workers that they are earning too little, and that that little engineer in spectacles over there is earning God knows how much, and that it's sheer bribery!

And these simple, uneducated people believe it and get indignant: they can understand the value of their own work, but they're incapable of understanding or putting a price on somebody else's."[21]

In another passage, a wise old man questions the worthwhile-ness of the line taken by youngsters who have chosen as their path of salvation that of service to the people: "But what if that sacrifice proves to have been misconceived? Don't the people have any *obligations?* Or do they only have *rights?* Are they simply meant to sit and wait while we first supply them with happiness, then provide for their 'eternal interests'? And what if the people themselves aren't ready?"[22] The coming of the Revolution is heralded in apocalyptic terms. An engineer exclaims angrily: "I have built two hundred mills, steam and electric, in southern Russia, and if those starvelings really do arise and start lashing out, how many of those mills will be left to grind the corn? And what will we have to eat—even at this table?"[23]

Two minorities, at opposite extremes, will suffice, it seems, to render the clash inevitable: " 'On one side—the Black Hundreds, on the other—the Red Hundreds! And in the middle'—he formed his hands into the shape of a ship's keel—'a dozen people who want to pass through to get on with a job of work! Impossible!' He opened his hands and clapped them together. 'They are crushed! Flattened!' "[24]

The destructive force of the Revolution, the "lie" of the class struggle, the arrogance of youngsters who "contest" without knowledge, the continuity of history which it is costly to try and break, the irresponsibility of the revolutionary intellectuals, the suffering of the Russian people, so rich in men and women of powerful spirit: so many images of Russia, of the anxious or vindictive ideas which did, perhaps, occupy the minds of a *certain* section of Russian society in the year 1914.

What is very much less open to doubt is that these ideas occupy Solzhenitsyn's mind today.

II

The Solzhenitsyn of the mythology which has arisen with him as its object of veneration appears as "the seeker after truth", the creator, the Good Man who is resolutely independent of ideology, of any ideology at all. But what is more *ideological* than Solzhenitsyn's presentation of Truth, of Creation, of Good? While the author of *One Day*, of *Cancer Ward* or of *The Gulag Archipelago* certainly does not set forth any doctrine, any coherent system of thought, he does develop in those works some *ideas* which, in his important public statements, like the *Nobel Prize Lecture* and the *Letter to Soviet Leaders*, express a political philosophy with fairly definite features.

Alexander Solzhenitsyn's thought is organized around a few essential axes. The first of these is rejection of an ideology and an ideocratic system which he identifies with lies and violence. The second is affirmation of a universal system of values based on the primacy of the spiritual, an anthropological conception of history, and an ethic, with a mystical basis, of individual responsibility and social action. The third is a reaching back to embrace Russia's national and religious traditions. The whole proceeds from a veritable axiology, a theory of values in which the forefront is occupied by that which gives organization to all the rest—the key concept of *pravda*, which is both Truth and the moral ideal of Justice, the central concept of Russian Christianity.

The *Nobel Prize Lecture*, which extols the virtues of art as the language that unites mankind, appears, on a superficial or indulgent reading, to be a profession of humanist faith which transcends all frontiers and spares no oppressive régime. Actually, it is clear that the only ideology attacked—and to be attacked much more systematically in the *Letter to Soviet Leaders*—is the Soviet ideology. And this applies to all the miseries, faults and tragedies that are denounced.

What does this rejected ideology amount to? A totalitarian ideocracy which has turned Marxism-Leninism into the "science of sciences", the Word without which are only heresy or treason—a determinism that reduces history to the working of "economic laws" and the human being to the status of a cog in a "collective", a class, a party, or the Soviet Fatherland.

This ideology is false in that it conceals the real relationships, like a piece of "stage scenery" (this comes close to Marx's "false consciousness"). Between falsehood and violence there is an inevitable association: "Violence can only be concealed by the lie, and the lie can only be maintained by violence. Any man who has once proclaimed violence as his *method* is inevitably forced to take the lie as his *principle*."[25]

The "necessity of the lie" is, according to the *Letter to Soviet Leaders*, no longer so obvious, since "nobody believes in it any more", and it is now only the ridiculous mask worn by a reality that everyone has learnt to recognize. But long before it became this insipid "piece of stage scenery", the lie was the tribute that had to be paid by political voluntarism; in other words, the Revolution. In order to build a new society it is indispensable that men should learn not to see depressing realities, should learn to despise "petty truths" so as to devote themselves to the "great truth": the former are bound up with things as they *are*, the latter expresses the tendency towards things as they *will be*, or (and to an ever greater degree) as they *ought to be*. This is a dispute that is as old as Soviet literature itself, and which has broken out again in connection with Solzhenitsyn. In the 1920s, Boris Pilnyak gave a notable formulation of this logic of the lie: "I have thought a great deal about the will to see, and I have set it in relation to the will to want.

What emerges is that there is another will, too: the will *not to see*, when the will to want comes into conflict with the will to see. Russia is living by the will to want and not to see."[26]

The services rendered to the cause by lies both big and small are not negligible. But Soviet literature and Soviet life have in recent times shown the baneful consequences of falsehood: deception no longer spares anyone, the gulf between words and facts grows wider, and a type of split (schizoid) personality is being formed as a result of this situation.

But Solzhenitsyn does not linger on the subject, or perhaps does not see in this ideology what it may contain that is special, distorted, perverted, in relation to Marxism and Leninism: indeed, he does not study the origins and historical functions of these bodies of thought. On the contrary, it is "Marxism" in general that he rejects. For him it is an imported ideology, alien to the Russian spirit, "primitive, super-ficial", which has been wrong about everything, has predicted nothing, and is, in the last analysis, the source of all the misfortunes that have afflicted Russia. "Cast off this cracked ideology! Relinquish it to your [Chinese] rivals. . . ." This is the appeal he addresses to the leaders of the Soviet Union; an appeal which the author is not, apparently, convinced is doomed to remain entirely without echo. According to him, all that is needed is to bring what is said into line with what actually happens: "For a long time now, everything has rested solely on material calculation and the subjection of the people, and not on any upsurge of ideological enthusiasm, as you perfectly well know. This ideology does nothing now but sap our strength and bind us."[27] This is the same ideology, moreover, that the writer denounces as being present in the movements of "world revolution" instigated by the USSR, the youth movements which "are blissfully repeating the discredited platitudes of our Russian 19th century". These naïve young people do not realize that justice cannot result from their revolts, and the older people who know this to be so take good care not to teach it to them: "There are those who have lived a little, who understand, who could argue with these young men and women, but many of them *do not dare* to argue. Instead they try to worm their way in among them —anything rather than be labelled 'conservative'. Once again, we had this in Russia in the 19th century. Dostoyevsky called it 'becoming a slave to silly little progressive ideas.' "[28]

Similarly, through and behind the facts denounced in *The Gulag Archipelago*, all revolutionary violence is condemned. "Intensive study has convinced me that bloody mass revolutions are always disastrous for the people in whose midst they occur."[29] Thus the "warning" given in *August 1914* is confirmed: "Above all, no revolution ever strengthens a country: it tears it apart, and for a long, long time. What's more, the bloodier and longer-drawn-out it is, and the dearer the country pays for it—the more likely the revolution is to be given the title of 'great'."[30] (Here the writer is evidently alluding to the quasi-ritual adjective used in the Soviet Union when referring to the October Revolution.)

Nothing that Solzhenitsyn is now saying about violence ought to surprise those who read his *Nobel Prize Lecture* of 1972. The picture he then drew of the struggles taking place in the world arena was indeed most eloquent: "The same old cave-man impulses—greed, envy, lack of restraint, mutual ill-will—still tear and rip our world apart, though now they have adopted such 'decent' labels as class conflict, race war, the struggle of the masses or the trade unions (*klassovoy, rasovoy, massovoy, profsoyuznoy borbui*). A primitive refusal to compromise has been turned into a theoretical principle and is seen as the great virtue of orthodoxy. It demands victims by the million in still unfinished civil wars, and still dins into our brains the fact that there are no firm, generally-approved concepts of goodness and justice, that all such concepts are fluid and liable to change, which means that one should always act in the way that is most profitable to one's own party. Groups of workers or professional men wait for every suitable moment to grab a bit extra, whether they have earned it or not, whether they need it or not, and then they seize it, and to hell with the whole of society."[31]

The "devils" who are creeping across the world appear, in Solzhenitsyn's eyes, to wear the quite distinctive faces of the Palestinian terrorists who at the time he was writing (summer 1972) were the objects of much publicity: "And now they hijack aeroplanes, seize hostages, cause fires and explosions. All their work of recent years is evidence of their determination to shake out and destroy civilization. And they may well succeed."[32]

In Vietnam, to be sure, "civilization" was putting up a good defence. . . .

* * *

The system of values from which Solzhenitsyn seeks to draw his answer to the crisis of civilization is supposed, of course, to be unconnected with any ideology, and in particular with any sort of rationalism. (The crisis of civilization affects, indeed, "the entire culture and world outlook which were conceived at the time of the Renaissance and attained the acme of their expression with the 18th-century Enlightenment."[33]) The keystone of this system seems to be the idea of "truth" which is so deeply rooted in Russian Christian tradition. *Pravda*, a concept that is untranslatable and is not to be reduced to concrete truth (*istina*) is in this tradition not identified with objectivity, or with the correlation of reason with itself, or with the Kantian sense of co-ordination of ideas. Nor is it, either, as with Kierkegaard, inherent in subjectivity. It is "trans-subjective" (Berdyaev) in the sense that it belongs to man's spiritual dimension, which is distinct from his consciousness in the strict meaning of that word. Its revelation, in every spiritual manifestation, in every creative act by which man rises above his enslavement to objects, is therefore not at all a matter of rational cognition. It is above all "an evaluation" (Berdyaev), a value judgement, and thereby, through the creative act, the divine presence is made known.[34]

To Russia's youth, tired of a utilitarian morality (with varying and contradictory uses) Solzhenitsyn offers a "truth" that ignores secular contingencies and opportunisms. He explains to some student readers that "there is nothing relative about justice, as there is nothing relative about conscience. . . . You will never err if you act in any social situation in accordance with justice (the old way of saying it in Russian is: to live by truth)."[35]

Inward order, moral order—ensuring the primacy of the spiritual factor in human activities—undoubtedly has Tolstoyan resonances. But Solzhenitsyn professes a much more voluntarist and individualist conception of history and of man's responsibility in history than we find in Tolstoy.

True, history is free from the social determinisms proclaimed by Marxism. "Our intelligence is usually not sufficient to grasp, to understand, and to foresee the course of history. . . ."[36] "History is irrational. . . . It has its own, and to us perhaps incomprehensible, organic structure."[37] At the same time, however, one is aware, in August 1914, for instance, of the extent to which men's responsibility, the choices they make, their mistakes, are what determine the way events develop. The theme of responsibility, of shared guilt, of self-accusation, is also present in the works that deal with the Stalin period. Individuals are for Solzhenitsyn the protagonists of history—not the masses, nor the classes, and still less the accidental, chance things that happen. This outlook separates Solzhenitsyn both from historical materialism and from a fatalistic idealism.

Man, the maker of history, makes himself as well, in the creative act. It was at the bottom of the concentration-camp abyss that Solzhenitsyn appears to have discovered in work (a value already sublimated in Soviet tradition) the last redoubt of the human personality, that un-conquerable area where it is possible for a transcendence, or, to employ another concept typical of Russian Christianity, a "transfiguration" of life to take place. Creative labour, like a genuine work of art, like every transcending of biological and social limitations that man achieves, tends towards the spiritual "feat" (*podvig*)—another familiar concept in religious writing, and closely related to that of resurrection. Solzhenitsyn's ethic could be defined as a personalism with a mystical basis.

The reflections upon socialism in *Cancer Ward*, the appeal for solidarity among writers in the *Nobel Prize Lecture*, and above all the programme of moral rearmament set forth in the *Letter to Soviet Leaders* show, moreover, that his aim is to lay the foundations for a kind of social action: he wants to see the coming of a "moral society".

Is Solzhenitsyn, like his character Shulubin, an advocate of "moral socialism"? It seems likely that that was a residual expression which the writer does not adopt on his own account. He has never, certainly, expressed opposition to the collective taking-over of the factories in 1917–18. His work contains sufficient harsh passages about capitalism or the "consumer society" for us not to suspect him of "bourgeois" sympathies. On the other hand, he calls upon the Soviet leaders to "give up the forced collective farms and leave just the voluntary ones", abandoning "ideological agriculture".[38] But, in fact, questions of the organization of society occupy a very small place in Solzhenitsyn's concerns: socialism is not his problem. What does concern him, however, is the moral grounds for the choices to be made regarding national development. To the discredited Marxist ideology he counterposes the moral foundations of "ancient Orthodoxy". He has no belief in the virtues of democracy in a country (such as the Russia of 1917, and *a fortiori*, the Russia of today) which has not been prepared for it. An authoritarian régime would suit Russia perfectly. "It is not authoritarianism itself that is intolerable, but the ideological lies that are daily foisted upon us. Not so much authoritarianism as arbitrariness and illegality. . . ." Russia lived for a thousand years under an authoritarian order—"and at the beginning of the 20th century both the physical and spiritual health of her people were still intact". This order rested, *inter alia*, upon "the Land Assemblies of Muscovite Russia, Novgorod, the early Cossacks, the village commune". The author also recalls "the real power of the Soviets", which existed until 6 July 1918, and which he suggests might be restored. He demands "a free art and literature, the free publication not just of political books—God preserve us!"[39]

Socialism? It would be safer to say that the political system favoured by Solzhenitsyn contains both elements from Russia's traditions of patriarchal rule and community organization and from a legalism of more recent origin. Popular and depoliticized Soviets, freedom under supervision, unrestricted development of religions and of philosophical discussions: this is, at least, the "minimum programme" which Solzhenitsyn summons the leaders of the USSR to implement.

*   *   *

Solzhenitsyn's adhesion to the Orthodox Church bears a special (critical) significance. The Church's enslavement to the State, its administration by a state council for religious affairs ("a church directed dictatorially by atheists"[40]), is intolerable to him. Desire for separation of the Church from the State does not relate for Solzhenitsyn merely to the present period, in which the State is identified with atheist rule. It forms part of the old Orthodox conception by which the Church, charged with a messianic task (the Third Rome) was to guide the State while remaining independent of it. In his letter to the Soviet leaders Solzhenitsyn is quite clear on this point. He invokes "the ancient, seven-centuries-old Orthodoxy of Sergei Radonezhsky and Nil Sorsky, before it was battered by Patriarch Nikon and bureaucratized by Peter the Great".[41] Indeed, the Church's claims to independence and to the primacy of the spiritual power proved unable to withstand the strengthening of monarchical absolutism. The necessary subjection of the Church to the State began, with the help of Patriarch Nikon, in the 1650s, through a reform of the liturgy (uniformization of the rites of the Churches of Russia and the Ukraine, correction of the Scriptures in accordance with the Greek texts). This reform was to give rise to the schism (*raskol*) of the Old-Believers. To this day the old faith has been able to find underground channels of survival and influence. Some religious philosophers of the late 19th century and of the present century, including Nikolai Berdyaev, have sought to revive it.[42] This appears to be the spiritual line of descent to which Solzhenitsyn belongs: a primitive, spiritual, ascetic Christianity which is yet impregnated with pagan feelings, as we see from the cult of the Earth and of the Forest (in *Matryona's House*, *August 1914*, the "roots of life" in *Cancer Ward*, etc.)[43]

Nothing provides better justification for this attitude than the present situation of the Orthodox Church. The liquidation of the old structures of rural life in the 1930s, urban growth, atheist propaganda and the whole arsenal of repressive measures (closing of churches, exiling of believers, etc.) put into effect under Stalin deprived Orthodoxy of its mass basis and the chance to influence the rising generations. The régime's anti-religious policy underwent an eclipse during the War, when the Church became one of the chief props of the spirit of national resistance. Strangely enough, it was during the Khrushchev period, between 1958 and 1964, that the anti-religious campaign was resumed more vigorously even than before: some 12,000 churches were closed, not without acts of violence and plundering. Solzhenitsyn denounces "backward and frenzied atheism".[44] That was the period when the official in charge of the ideological department of the Party's Central Committee, Ilyichev, declared that extirpation of religious sentiments was one of the "pre-requisites" for the achievement of Communism—

the latter being, of course, a matter of the immediate future. (On this question he was publicly contradicted by Palmiro Togliatti and Roger Garaudy.) During that testing time Russian Christianity perhaps gained in fervour and in spirit of abnegation, which would explain the influence it has won over a narrow fringe of the rising generations. But the official Church, set in its immutable liturgy, resistant to all the currents of ideas that have revived Christianity in the West, and even the Polish Church, obsessed with preserving the slender possibilities of survival allowed to it by the State in exchange for good and loyal service, presents the picture of a petrified institution.

Following the example given by the Dissenting communities, sectarian but amazingly alive, such as the Baptists (Alyosha in *One Day*), the neo-Orthodox like Solzhenitsyn want to rescue their Church from its torpor and give it back a sense of militant evangelism, even at the price of a further martyrdom. This ambition is closely linked with that of reviving the national traditions. Solzhenitsyn recalls "that radiant Christian ethical atmosphere in which over a period of a thousand years were established our mores, way of life, view of the world and folklore, even the very name in Russian for the Russian peasants—*krestyane*".[45]

*   *   *

Solzhenitsyn's patriotism has been variously characterized as "Russophilism", "Slavophilism", "isolationism" and even "Great-Russian chauvinism".[46] The confusion in the terms used reflects the confusion of the thinking: neither Solzhenitsyn's ideas nor the Slavophil tradition seem to have been understood correctly.

Great-Power ideology has, in the Russia of today, nothing oppositional about it and does not need to be smuggled in. On the contrary, it finds expression both in the policies and in the language of official circles. It was especially overt at the time of the invasion of Czechoslovakia and of the clashes with Chinese forces on the River Ussuri. A whole literature has flourished for several years now, with full official approval, which exhales the scent of the Russian soil, singing the beauty of Russia's countryside and of Russian architecture, recalling with emotion the greatness and the wars of the past, of the conquest of Siberia by the Cossack chieftain Yermak, and so on. . . . This tendency is not a new one: we can date its resurgence exactly—along with the restoration of officers' epaulettes and the dropping of the *Internationale* as the state anthem—to the time when, in the early 1940s, Stalin rallied to the Great-Russian national tradition. What is new is the intensity, the aggressiveness with which chauvinism is thrusting itself into the cracks, which are certainly considerable, in the allegedly internationalist official ideology. The poet Yevgeny Yevtushenko alluded to this at the

Fifth Writers' Congress in 1971, when he mentioned the historico-literary "reconstitutions" which have been popular in the Soviet cinema in recent years. In these films, he noted, the "nests of gentlefolk" are idealized: "the camera glides so tenderly over the curves of a piece of old oak furniture, brought from some antique-shop, and over the family jewels. No oppressors, no oppressed, but splendid landowners, an idealized picture of Russia with peasant-girls crowned with wild flowers who have come straight out of the pre-Revolution magazine *Niva*."

Great-Russian chauvinism seems to have found very active adepts in the leadership of the Komsomol, of its publishing house ("Molodaya Gvardiya"), of the newspaper *Sovietskaya Rossiya* (the Party's daily organ for the Russian Republic) and the illustrated weekly *Ogonyok*. The Rodina club, officially devoted to restoring historical monuments (which means, mainly, churches) has become the rallying centre of this trend, which is naturally inclined towards xenophobia and antisemitism. Alongside these official *Russity*, or *pochvenniki* ("men of the soil") are active dissident groups enjoying a greater or lesser degree of toleration, such as the group that has been formed around the *samizdat* review called *Veche*, edited by Osipov. These circles, unlike Solzhenitsyn, proclaim their loyal attitude towards the ruling authorities, just as they integrate the "Russian Revolution" of 1917 into the patrimony of Russia's national greatness. It is therefore not accidental that this same review *Veche* accused the author of *August 1914* of being a "germanophil" and a "slanderer of Russia".[47]

One of the main ideas developed by Solzhenitsyn in his *Letter to Soviet Leaders* is precisely that "ideological" Great-Power objectives should be renounced, whether in relation to China or to the Mediterranean. Nothing gives us reason to assume that Solzhenitsyn's patriotism includes any leanings whatsoever towards chauvinism or national exclusivism.

"Slavophilism" itself needs to be understood with attention to its different shades. In the first place, the idealization of the past and the belief in Russia's "spiritual mission" on the part of the Slavophil thinkers of last century, such as Khomyakov, did not necessarily imply the imperialistic use of these attitudes that was made by the Tsars. The idea of domination, of a "chosen people" is, in any case, not to be found in Solzhenitsyn's work. On the contrary, he reveals himself as being, in his own way, intensely universalist, in his *Nobel Prize Lecture*. Solzhenitsyn's Russophilism is consequently not without a certain originality. It is linked both with his conception of history as "organic", of the role of nations, and with a utopian vision of Russia's "restoration". Solzhenitsyn believes in the continuity of Russia. This forms part of the "organic tissue" of history, which reason cannot grasp. History, therefore, in contrast to the Marxist conception of it, which sees history as being accomplished through the dialectic of social contradictions, with the class struggle as its "guiding thread", tends rather towards a slow, harmonious, "organic" development. This, at any rate, is its tendential "truth", the moral idea that a nation can set up for itself: an accidental tragedy like the October Revolution may divert it from this path, but this is only a diversion, and, sooner or later, continuity will be re-established.

Solzhenitsyn has recourse to the classical symbolism of the tree: "History grows like a living tree. And as far as that tree is concerned, reason is an axe: you'll never make it grow better by applying reason to it. Or, if you prefer, history is a river; it has its own laws which govern its flow, its bends, the way it meanders. Then along come some clever people who say that it's a stagnant pond and must be diverted into another and better channel: all that's needed is to choose a better place and dig a new river-bed. But the course of a river can't be interrupted—block it at all and it won't flow any longer. And we're being told that the bed must be forcibly diverted by several thousand yards. The bonds between generations, bonds of institutions, traditions, custom, are what hold the banks of the river-bed together and keep the stream flowing."[48]

For Solzhenitsyn the national idea implies no sort of superiority or self-sufficiency. It merely signifies a cult of *difference*. The "growing unity of mankind" appears as a unity in diversity, a striving for a symphony of differences. "In recent times it has been fashionable to speak of a levelling of nations and of a disappearance of peoples in the melting pot of modern civilization. I do not agree with this, but any discussion of it would be a separate issue. Here it is right that I should say just this: were nations to disappear, we would be impoverished in exactly the same way as if all people suddenly became alike, with the same character and the same face. Nations are part of the wealth of the human race. Although generalized, they are its individuals. The smallest of them has its own special colours and hides in itself some facet of God's design."[49] At the same time, the nations must seek a common language, exchange their experiences, fight against mutual indifference: "The fact is that in our cramped, little world there are no longer any 'internal affairs'. Man's salvation depends upon everyone making it his business to know everything. It depends on the people of the East not being entirely indifferent to the opinions of people of the West, on people in the West not being entirely indifferent to what is happening in the East."[50] The international solidarity for which Solzhenitsyn calls here is certainly very restricted in its scope: it is the solidarity that he thinks the international community of writers ought to show towards oppressed colleagues in the East and towards the Czechoslovak people.

Nevertheless, Solzhenitsyn's universalism is incompatible with the "isolationism" of which he has been accused. Between someone like Sakharov who is for a convergence between East and West, a Roy Medvedev whose inclination is rather towards a coming-together of the progressive forces, specifically, of East and West, and the Russophilism of Solzhenitsyn, the dispute is no mere repetition of the old dispute among the Russian intelligentsia of the 19th century, in which "Slavophils" opposed "Westernizers". Even at the time the dispute was not so clear-cut as all that. A "Slavophil" attitude might, in the case of Alexander Herzen, form part of a progressive social outlook. The "Westernizers" were split between Liberalism and Marxism. The socialist idea drew strength from both trends. Today the dispute has arisen again in a very different setting—that of a world unified by capitalism, and a Russia profoundly transformed and linked with the outside world (capitalism, the socialist countries, the revolutionary movements) by a complete network of relations.

Stalinism nevertheless prepared the ground for a come-back by Russophilism. Solzhenitsyn is certainly mistaken when he rages against the *avant-garde* outlook and contempt for tradition which he thinks he can perceive in the official ideology—the "Progressive World-View", as he scornfully refers to it. The *avant-garde* stance, futurism, progressivism with a world-wide mission all belong to the mental world of the Revolution and the 1920s. Stalinism merely perpetuated a fleshless caricature of all that: itself, it enforced a cultural autarky to which Solzhenitsyn's political ignorance bears witness. What the appearance of the new Russophils, or *Russity*, strikingly proves is that this autarkic ideology, more and more completely withdrawing into chauvinistic values, has not succeeded in filling the gap left by the ebbing of internationalist Marxism. It is true that Stalinism was, in the last analysis, not so much a "return to Russia" as a *retreat into Russia*, with all that that could imply in perversions, by a policy that was highly Westernizing, European or, if there must be an analogy, "Petrine". In notable contrast with a certain type of Western anti-Stalinism, disposed to denounce "Oriental despotism", Solzhenitsyn blames the "blind imitation" of Western civilization. And—the height of seeming paradox—his critique is not lacking in environmentalist overtones which seem almost familiar to us in the West. "We had to be dragged along the whole of the Western bourgeois-industrial and Marxist path in order to discover, at the end of the 20th century, and again from progressive Western scholars [Solzhenitsyn refers to 'the Teilhard de Chardin Society and the Club of Rome'], what any village greybeard in the Ukraine or Russia had understood from time immemorial and could have explained to the progressive commentators ages ago, had the commentators ever found the time in that dizzy fever of theirs to consult him: that a dozen maggots can't go on gnawing the same apple *forever;* that if the earth is a *finite* object, then its expanses and resources are finite also, and that the *endless, infinite* progress dinned into our heads by the dreamers of the Enlightenment cannot be accomplished on it."[51] According to Solzhenitsyn, we must turn our backs on economic progress. (He uses the word *progress* and not *rost*, i.e. "growth", as some translations of his writings might suggest.) But this is possible only at the price of saying goodbye to Marxism: "If we renounce industrial development, what about the working class, socialism, communism, unlimited increase in productivity, and all the rest?" Solzhenitsyn asks why socialism has shown itself "so dolefully unoriginal in technology, and why have we so unthinkingly, so blindly copied Western civilization?" And yet "one might have thought that, with the central planning of which we are so proud, we of all people had the chance *not* to spoil Russia's natural beauty, *not* to create anti-human, multi-million concentrations of people. But we've done everything the other way round: we've dirtied and defiled the wide Russian spaces and disfigured the heart of Russia, our beloved Moscow. . . . We have squandered our resources foolishly without so much as a backward glance, sapped our soil, mutilated our vast expanses. . . ."[52] The ecologist critique corresponds to a concern that is widespread, both in official circles and among the "dissident" elements of the population: more than once in recent years the alarm has been sounded in connection with the wasting of natural resources, the pollution of certain lakes, the disfigurement of Moscow by the building of such architectural monstrosities as the giant Hotel Rossiya, next door to the Kremlin.[53] Never till now, though, has this critique been directed so radically at the pattern of industrialization, the giantism of production and cities, or the uselessness of the "conquest of space". Soviet industrialization, although less anarchical than ours, and undoubtedly more careful, for several years now, to preserve resources and the environment of human life, continues to secrete the phenomena of gigantomania, urban concentration and differences between town and country which were supposed to fade away as the march to Communism progressed.

The way out, or at least the way of atonement for the mistakes committed, lies, according to Solzhenitsyn in opening up in an original manner the vast undeveloped territories of Russia's North-East. As a pole of attraction, a hope, a "source of stability", the North-East would be, in a sense, the place where the wounded nation might *convalesce.* Solzhenitsyn sees this region as a land of "clean air and clean water", of health-giving silence, where towns will once more belong to those who live in them, and where a new youth will arise, freed from the obligations of military service. "Utopia or death" seems to be his message, delivered in his own fashion—which is not however, that of a René Dumont or an Ivan Ilitch. In his case, the Utopia is wholly and profoundly *backward-looking*, as he says himself: "let us go back". "Back" means, for him, to the golden age of old Russia, to "our old towns . . . towns which were humane, friendly, cosy places, where the air was always clean, which were snow-clad in winter and in spring redolent with garden aromas streaming through the fences into the streets". "Back" means, for him, schools where the pupils "respect their teachers", and families in which the wife can devote herself solely to her household "toils and troubles" without being forced to go out and earn "a separate pay-packet".[54]

Now, there is nothing here, as regards fundamentals, that should surprise us. The rejection of Marxism and of the class struggle, the personalist ethic, the return to the sources of Russian Christianity, the "organic" conception of history, all go together: Solzhenitsyn's moral society is a society based on religious values, the only values that can ensure national "continuity", which for him means re-establishing the link with medieval Russia.

In this regard Solzhenitsyn's ideas remind us of the "Christian policy" conceived in the last century by Vladimir Soloviev, to whom the writer several times refers. He has also been influenced by the ethical and personalistic conceptions of Mikhaylovsky, one of the theoreticians of Narodnism, and of the Anarchist Kropotkin (quoted in *Cancer Ward*). But it is above all Soloviev, the advocate of an economy with moral purposes, Dostoyevsky, with his theocratic Utopia, and perhaps also Berdyaev, the theoretician of a religious socialism of communities and "councils", who seem to have been closest to Solzhenitsyn at a time when (being in the USSR) his knowledge of Russian religious philosophy was still, inevitably, limited. Solzhenitsyn's thought has doubtless not yet attained its final form.

III

Solzhenitsyn's moral condemnation of violence is directed at a clearly defined *type* of violence—that which frankly comes forward into the open, justifying itself by some ideology. Solzhenitsyn's point of view sees neither causes nor cures for violence other than those of a moral order, whether ideological or anti-ideological. It is the same where the class struggle is concerned. The Marxists have made an ideology of it—but are those who "refute" it any less devoted to constructing an ideology? There lies the whole problem.

What is Solzhenitsyn's thesis regarding the Stalin terror? Leninism contained the germ of it, and October 1917 made it inevitable. This terror was therefore not "Stalin's", but was, quite logically and without any breach in continuity, *revolutionary*.

There is no shortage of arguments to sustain this thesis. In the weeks following the October Revolution the Bolsheviks dispersed the Constituent Assembly, banned the Cadet Party and arrested the office-workers' strike committee. Counter-revolution was brought under fire, but so also, very soon and at the same time, were "anarchy", "drunkards and hooligans", the printing workers of Petrograd, landowners, priests and monks, members of the religious sects, the Tolstoyan pacifists, the Christians engaged in the first agrarian communes where complete communism was practised—everything and everybody that hindered the dictatorship of the Party. Lenin called for the land of Russia to be "cleansed of all vermin". And Solzhenitsyn lists the many passages in which the head of the young Soviet State incited to intolerance, hardness, mass application of the death penalty.

The "cleansing" assumed an unprecedented form: the Cheka, the Extraordinary Commission for Combating Sabotage and Counter-Revolution, was the first instance in history of a state police force that concentrated in its own hands all powers of investigation, arrest, examination, trial and execution. Founded in December 1917 it possessed at first only limited powers of preliminary investigation. In practice, however, it took to itself additional powers with every passing day. On 21 February 1918 it superseded the judiciary. In the course of eighteen months (1918 and the first half of 1919) it shot 8,389 persons and arrested 87,000. Thenceforth arbitrary power was absolute in Russia.[55]

Among the instruments of Red Terror were the concentration camps. The first in Russia to use the term was Leon Trotsky, on 4 June 1918. Sent there, one after the other, were Czechoslovak mutineers, Russian officers who refused to serve the Soviet state, persons suspected of anti-Soviet agitation, saboteurs, parasites, speculators, etc. . . .[56] Under War Communism, compulsory labour service tended to make more widespread the institution of forced labour. "Deserters from labour" were sent to the camps.[57] Dzerzhinsky recommended that separate camps be established for the bourgeoisie and for the workers and peasants—so that the former should not contaminate the latter. The camps continued in being during the 1920s, under the New Economic Policy, especially for "re-education through labour". Political and common-law prisoners arrived in droves from 1923 onward in the Solovki, the special camps on the Solovetsky Islands. There it was that was to be tried out in the mid-1920s (and glorified in Soviet literature) the new type of slavery which, during the reign of Stalin and of Gulag became a mass phenomenon that was not merely political and repressive in nature but also economic, supplying a reserve force of labour for the great works of the industrialization programme.[58] In his desire to justify the measures of War Communism Trotsky had already provided a certain theoretical foundation for this resort to forced labour: "We are now heading towards the type of labour that is socially regulated on the basis of an economic plan, obligatory for the whole country, compulsory for every worker. This is the basis of socialism. . . . The militarization of labour, in this fundamental sense of which I have spoken, is the indispensable basic method for the organization of our labour forces. . . . Is it true that compulsory labour is always unproductive? . . . This is the most wretched and miserable liberal prejudice: chattel slavery, too, was productive. . . . Compulsory serf labour did not grow out of the feudal lords' ill-will. It was (in its time) a progressive phenomenon."[59]

As we have seen, the terror is for Solzhenitsyn not something exclusively connected with Stalinism or with some "bureaucratic degeneration" or other. It is integral to the régime and ideology that prevailed under Lenin and Trotsky. But its inevitability goes back even before that time, being inherent in the Revolution itself. "Well before any sort of civil war began, it was clear that Russia, given the nature of her population, could not, of course, be led towards any sort of socialism, that she had spoiled everything." Why had this spoiling come about? The writer intends, in the successive instalments of his great novel about the war of 1914–18, to try to throw some light on this question.

In his book, which parallels *The Gulag Archipelago*, Michel Heller offers his answer to the question: the Revolution lacked a social basis, and in particular lacked the proletariat in whose name it was made. Accordingly, "from the earliest days of Soviet power coercion emerged as an absolute necessity. This was not just coercion in general, or that coercion directed against the hostile classes which is inevitable in any revolution: it was coercion imposed upon the working people, peasants as well as workers."[60] Even while it was being glorified, labour became a punishment. The experiment with workers' control, the taking over of the enterprises by those who worked in them, which was attempted at the end of 1917 and the beginning of 1918, ended in catastrophe, with production completely disorganized. After having upheld the view that every cook must be able to rule the state, Lenin turned back to the thoroughly traditional notion that only compulsion can overcome disorder and idleness. The move in the direction of the militarizing of labour coincided with Lenin's recognition of the merits of the Taylor system, which was increasingly adopted in Russian industry from the NEP period onward.

Was the coming of the terror a matter of will, of inevitability, or of continuity with what had gone before? While there is room for an investigation aimed at bringing out the significance of deliberate choices made, of the compelling pressure of circumstances, and of a concatenation of terrorist measures obeying their own logic, the deductions drawn from all this by Solzhenitsyn, as by Heller, are neither so obvious nor so irrefutably well-supported as may seem at first sight to be the case.

Although the October Revolution was indeed carried through by "violence", "the midwife of history", the majority of those who witnessed it or have written about it acknowledge that this violence was not excessive, and that the Bolsheviks showed "relative but very genuine moderation" in their use of it against the Revolution's adversaries. "It was a moderation that was sometimes reminiscent of the generosity that had occasionally accompanied the euphoria of earlier revolutionary victories." For example, the Red Guards released the officer-cadets who had fought against them, requiring only that they give their word not to take up arms against the Revolution any more— an undertaking which the cadets hastened to violate only a few days later. Some ministers in the Provisional Government who had been arrested were set free. General Krasnov, who had tried to reconquer Petrograd, was allowed his freedom in return for a promise not to resume battle against the Soviets—and almost immediately joined the anti-Bolshevik forces gathering in the South. Moreover, "during the first months of their rule, the Bolsheviks, far from inflaming the anger and vindictiveness of the masses, sought to set bounds to the manifestation of such feelings". No death-sentences were passed during the first three months of the new régime, and, indeed, one of the Soviet Government's first decrees abolished the death-penalty. This moderation contrasted with the multiplying acts of violence by counter-revolutionaries and the first outbursts of White Terror, such as the massacre of their "Red" prisoners by the officer-cadets in Moscow, and the slaughter of between ten and twenty thousand "Reds" in Finland.[61] Roy Medvedev records that during 1918, even at the height of the civil war, the Cheka's activities were "moderate" as compared with those of the Whites, and kept in check by the political authority. He recalls that a demand for torture to be used, since the Revolution's foes were using it, met with "widespread indignation in Party circles".[62]

If reprisals became ever more frequent and arbitrary methods were introduced, if the death-penalty was restored, if concentration camps were established—undeniably, and with "chronological" proofs at hand—the fact is that these developments took place in response to the increasing onslaught of the counter-revolutionary White armies and the intervention by foreign expeditionary forces sent to help them.

But it is precisely the counter-revolution and the foreign intervention, the attempted murder of the young Soviet Republic by all the exploiting classes and reactionary groups, expropriated or seized by panic, in Russia and the entire bourgeois world, that Solzhenitsyn either ignores or plays down.

It is true that, as Solzhenitsyn observes, the "wide range of targets" (Liebman's phrase) proposed by Lenin for attention by the organs of Red Terror —Tsarist military men, kulaks, prostitutes, bureaucrats, speculators, "unstable elements" were all marked down for extermination—soon makes an apocalyptic impression on the reader. Some of Lenin's orders seem to echo the command of one of the White generals, as reported by Victor Serge: "The orders are to hang all arrested workers in the street. The bodies are to be exhibited for three days."

Lenin's psychology and his tendency to verbal excesses are probably only of secondary importance in explaining how the Red Terror mounted in intensity. There is a logic in this matter, which is well described by Isaac Deutscher: "The terror has its own momentum. Every revolutionary party at first imagines that its task is simple: it has to suppress a 'handful' of tyrants or exploiters. It is true that usually the tyrants and exploiters form an insignificant minority. But the old ruling class has not lived in isolation from the rest of society. In the course of its long domination it has surrounded itself by a network of institutions embracing groups and individuals of many classes; and it has brought to life many attachments and loyalties which even a revolution does not destroy altogether. The anatomy of society is never so simple that it is possible surgically to separate one of the limbs from the rest of the body. Every social class is connected with its immediate neighbour by many almost imperceptible gradations. The aristocracy shades off into the upper middle class; the latter into the lower layers of the bourgeoisie; the lower middle class branches off into the working class; and the proletariat, especially in Russia, is bound by innumerable filiations to the peasantry. The political parties are similarly interconnected. The revolution cannot deal a blow at the party most hostile and dangerous to it without forcing not only that party but its immediate neighbour to answer with a counter-blow."[63]

This complexity of the social and political fabric shows how dangerous are the hasty schemas and the cult of violence characteristic of various "ultra-left" elements. Civil war rarely splits society into "exploiters" and "exploited": it almost always raises up against the progressive forces not merely the reactionary classes but also broad strata of the people who still side with the latter owing to ideology, cultural backwardness and the weight of certain clerical influences, not to mention fear of "upheaval", an apolitical outlook, and all the manoeuvres and provocations to which poverty and forced idleness can give rise among the most deprived sections of the population.

It cannot be denied that the policy and style of repression that were inaugurated by the civil war survived that conflict, even if only, during the 1920s, in a mitigated form. On the initiative of Lenin, who recommended re-abolition of the death penalty already in 1920, the Cheka's prerogatives were sharply restricted. The GPU, its successor, was made subject to the political authorities, and had to accept that "the power of judgement belonged exclusively to the Courts". But this was only a precarious interval.[64] The GPU retained the Cheka's power of administrative repression and internment in camps.[65] At a time when Lenin was waging a desperate struggle against bureaucracy and Great-Russian chauvinism, and when he acknowledged the right of the trade unions to defend the workers against their own "workers' state with bureaucratic distortions",[66] he does not seem to have paid overmuch attention to the problem of the rule of law, which was constantly being undermined by police (and even political) tyranny. In a letter dated 10 February 1922, unpublished, and circulated by *samizdat* methods some years ago, after its inclusion in Lenin's "Complete Works" in 55 volumes had been turned down by the censors, Lenin shows himself especially ruthless in his attitude to the clergy, who were resisting confiscation of the Church's valuables. (The immediate purpose of this confiscation, it should be mentioned, was to obtain means for famine relief.) "The bigger the number of representatives of the bourgeoisie and the reactionary clergy that we manage to shoot, the better that will be. What we have to do, in fact, is to educate those people in such a way that for decades to come they will not be able even to think of putting up any sort of resistance." The letter was addressed (as a communication classified "secret") "to Comrade Molotov and the members of the Politburo".[67] In other documents of the same year Lenin insists on continuation of the terror, and even defines a new category of offenders, namely, whoever "gave help objectively" to the external foes of the Soviet régime.[68]

Liebman asks: "Is not the origin of the often gratuitous terror of Stalinism to be found in the largely uncontrolled and uncontrollable violence of the years 1917 to 1920?"[69] The origin of Stalinism is seemingly to be found not only in the stigmata of this period but also in the political consequences of the civil war: the elimination of all political forces other than the Bolsheviks themselves which might have co-operated with the new régime, and some of which showed readiness to do this (e.g. the Left-wing Mensheviks and some sections of the Anarchists); the replacement of the dictatorship of a proletariat which had been decimated or scattered by the war by a "dictatorship of the proletariat" that was exercised by the Communist Party in its name; the devitalizing of the Soviets, which might, in particular, have ensured wide participation by the poor and middle peasantry in the government of the country; and the prohibition of tendencies and factions in the Party in 1921 (a measure described as "temporary" but which is still in force. In other words it was this one-party and bureaucratic regime, born of circumstances rather than of any deliberate choice, more or less accepted and at the same time feared by the Bolshevik leaders, but which quickly changed from a necessity into a virtue in the eyes of Lenin and Trotsky, and soon, under Stalin, became identified as the political system appropriate to socialism—it was this régime, together with the exigencies of industrialization, speeded up from 1928 onwards, that was to manifest a sort of "structural" need to resort to tyranny and repression.

What Stalinism did, however, was to free this "need" from all the safeguards provided by the political intentions, the democratism and the international outlook which, in spite of everything, continued to be characteristic of Lenin's struggle. The discontinuity between Leninism and Stalinism is therefore not without importance.[70] Police methods became the norm, the axis, and not something exceptional or auxiliary, in the way the country was governed.

It was no longer only or even mainly "class enemies" that the Stalin terror crushed, but real or potential *allies* (poor and middle peasants), and soon the workers themselves and the most faithful cadres of the Revolution (Oppositionists first, then loyal Stalinists as well). The bulk of this terror's victims were *imaginary* enemies of the Revolution, if not of Stalin himself.

Along with Solzhenitsyn we can doubtless accept that there is a fatality of violence in every revolutionary process. Not that this must necessarily—as it did, almost inevitably in Russia—take the extreme form of a civil and even an international war, but because profound changes in social structures, overthrowing propertied classes and sweeping away modes of production that have outlived themselves, cannot take place *without* violence. It is in this sense that the latter has been, throughout the centuries, "the midwife of history", as Engels put it.

But Solzhenitsyn fails to see the roots of this violence, and its scope, perceiving only, and then in a distorting light, the *revolutionary* element in it. This abstract preaching of non-violence, which almost always has for corollary a condemnation of the violence of the oppressed, goes back a very long way.

The pattern of the revolutionary "break" does not depend wholly upon the methods chosen by those who promote it: Lenin and Trotsky in Russia, Mao in China, or Castro in Cuba. It also mirrors the social relations that it confronts. In Russia the survivals of patriarchal and feudal relations and ways of thought, and the centralized and authoritarian political system prevailing in Russia since Peter the Great's transformations, did not go for nothing in determining the pattern of the revolutionary struggle and, subsequently, the building of the Soviet state.

The ignorance, isolation and brutality that marked the life of the peasants did not prepare them, either, for a revolution "in the spirit of the Enlightenment". A people reared under the knout and in fear of the gendarme will not produce a revolution such as might be dreamed up by a study-commission of the Parti Socialiste Unifié. Nor was the Revolution like the one that the Russian revolutionary intellectuals had expected. When the common people forced their way into the boulevards of St Petersburg or into the old palaces of the Romanovs, littering the former with spat-out sunflower-seeds, and in the latter using precious vases from Sèvres, Saxony or the Orient as chamber-pots, they seemed not so much the bringers of an uplifting future as creatures moved by zeal to destroy, in the eyes of those very persons who, in books, had prayed that they would rise up. Furthermore, that which gave strength to the Russian Revolution, the fact that it "broke the chain of imperialism at its weakest link", became a source of weakness as soon as isolated, deprived of the prospect of world revolution that had nourished it, suffering from the "sanitary" blockade imposed by the industrialized countries of the West, and betrayed by the Right-wing Social-Democrats, Soviet Russia found itself alone with the burdensome heritage of the past, the devastations of the war and the ruin of the productive forces that had been accumulated between 1900 and 1913, and faced with the task of building a socialism that appeared increasingly both hypothetical and hypothecated.

The "break" deplored by Solzhenitsyn certainly occurred, a "break" that was indeed deplorable and which went much further than the mere "smashing of the State" aimed at in October—but not necessarily in the sense that Solzhenitsyn means, for the Soviet régime took upon itself, even if unwillingly, a certain "Russian continuity" of bureaucracy and chauvinism, against which real internationalist socialists like Lenin and Trotsky were to wage a last desperate struggle. What did occur was a "break" in economic life and professional traditions, and a break, to the greatest misfortune, with the West—its technology, its universalist culture, its working-class movement.

The violence of the propertied classes, moreover, is neither governed nor disciplined by a project for social liberation. It is merely a matter of defending property and privilege, and nothing more than that. It is not encumbered by any humanitarian scruples. And this is why a cold and determined savagery can so easily sweep away all the baggage of refinement and humanism of which these classes seem to be the heirs. In this connection the conduct of the former Tsarist officers fully lived up to a tradition that runs from the "Versaillais" of 1871 to the generals who made the putsch in Chile, and includes the Ruhr tycoons and Prussian aristocrats who served Hitler.

In any case, as Liebman writes, "there is often an element of hypocrisy in the reproach brought against the nascent Communist movement and the Bolshevik leaders that they employed methods of terror, as though the violence that broke out in Russia somehow defiled an epoch of peace and progress". Solzhenitsyn's condemnation of terrorism belongs, it must be said, to this same category of hypocrisy. "People have been refusing to accept as terrorism a treacherous assault under peaceful conditions against peaceful people by military forces that have been surreptitiously armed and are frequently dressed up in civilian clothes. They demand that we study the aims of the terrorist groups, the base that supports them and their ideology, and then perhaps accept them as sacred 'guerrillas' (in South America they have even gone so far as to give them the comic description 'urban guerrillas')." Further on, he writes: "The bestial mass murders in Hué,[71] which had been reliably proven to have taken place, were only noted in passing and almost immediately forgiven—because society's sympathy leaned *to that side* and nobody wished to oppose the consensus." Again: " 'Hijacking' and all other types of terrorism have increased tenfold simply because people have capitulated to them too quickly. But when one shows firmness, one wins over terrorism—mark my words."[72]

As we see, Solzhenitsyn, who has more than once shown his lack of tenderness for the terrorism of movements by oppressed people, none the less calls for "firmness". Firmness by whom and against whom? It is clear that the preaching of non-violence, where Solzhenitsyn is concerned, has nothing in common with Gandhism or with the attitude of the War Resisters' International. It is quite frankly a stand in favour of "order" and "civil peace", as this is understood by the defenders of the "free world". Solzhenitsyn's voice has never been raised against the massacres carried out by the imperialists in Vietnam, Chile and so many other places where "firmness" reigns.

Finally, the *class character* of the acts of violence perpetrated during the civil war is ignored completely in Solzhenitsyn's analysis, and not without reason. The impression is given that an incomprehensible cataclysm engulfed the good people of Russia, destroying their way of life and their precious values.

That cataclysm, for such it was, began with the Great War, and that war resulted from the striving to conquer markets and *Lebensraum*, from the repartition of the world: it was a consequence of capitalism, and millions of workers and peasants, all over Europe, were its victims. This is a rudimentary but nevertheless enlightening Marxism fact which enables one to grasp. In this cruel conflict the clash between fatherlands, between nations, took precedence over the conflict between classes, and the International of the proletariat did not survive it. With flowers in the muzzles of their rifles, workers and peasants went forth to fight other workers and peasants. For what interests? Here was an opportunity for the author of *August 1914*, so sensitive to ideological falsehood, to detect what the stance and talk of "the Fatherland in danger" concealed by way of ideology—and what sort of ideology?—with the purpose of breaking up some solidarities in favour of others—to whose advantage? The revolution, a class war, proceeding from other interests and a different ideology, sought, in the shaken edifice of the world imperialist system, to find a crack through which it could enter, and this it found in Russia. One logic spurned the other. Among the most symbolic scenes of the Revolution was that in which, at the front, Russian, German and Austrian soldiers embraced each other—men who had, until that moment, been occupied in killing each other. What attitude will Solzhenitsyn take towards that scene?

Was not the violence that, in their turn, the White generals, the fallen barons, the politicians cast by October "into the dustbin of history", unleashed against the Revolution—was this not class violence?

The fact that this broad picture included, in inextricable confusion, such tortured personal destinies as that of Doctor Zhivago, experiences, ideas and feelings that have only a distant, often invisible, relation to this socio-historical truth, justifies us, perhaps, in "qualifying" it with a whole range of partial truths, but not in rejecting it, *in the last analysis*.

Revolutionary violence is, moreover, identified by Solzhenitsyn with terror and destruction. This is an approach that both *misrepresents* and *reduces* the revolutionary phenomenon, ultimately rendering it incomprehensible. The Red Army fought at the front—but also strove to overcome popular illiteracy. The Cheka and the GPU carried out repression—but their creation of the first colonies for re-education through labour, replacing the old prisons, their organization of labour communes governed on their own behalf by young criminals, also form part of that great effort to establish a new way of life of which, among others, Wilhelm Reich and Anton Makarenko wrote.[73] Lenin showed no pity for the enemies of the revolution, but his uncompromising attitude went along with a continual appeal for initiative and cultural improvement on the part of the masses. It is interesting, in this connection, to restore to its context a little phrase that is frequently quoted in *The Gulag Archipelago*. The passage in which Lenin demands, in incredibly harsh tones, that the land of Russia be "cleansed of vermin", and sets forth a whole catalogue of terroristic measures to this effect, comes from an essay entitled *How To Organise Competition?* written in December 1917 (old style). What Solzhenitsyn does not mention is that this essay is above all a stirring plea in favour of the dignity of the working class. The "vermin" of whom he writes are "yesterday's slaveowners", the "rogues", "idlers" and "rowdies", and the intellectual "lackeys" who refuse to put their knowledge at the service of the people. Against all these, Lenin calls above all for a spirit of initiative and emulation to find expression: "Every factory from which the capitalist has been ejected, or in which he has at least been curbed by workers' control, every village from which the landowning exploiter has been smoked out and his land confiscated has only now become a field in which the working man can reveal his talents, unbend his back a little, rise to his full height, and feel he is a human being. For the first time after centuries of working for others, of forced labour for the exploiter, it has become possible to *work for oneself* and moreover to employ all the achievements of modern technology and culture in one's work. . . . At all costs we must break the old, *absurd*, savage, despicable and disgusting prejudice that only the rich, and those who have gone through the school of the rich, are capable of administering the State and directing the organizational development of Socialist society." And this essay, an improperly isolated phrase from which Solzhenitsyn seeks to use to overwhelm Lenin, ends with these words: "In what commune, in what district of a large town, in what factory and in what village are there *no* starving people, *no* unemployed, *no* idle rich, *no* despicable lackeys of the bourgeoisie, saboteurs who call themselves intellectuals? Where has most been done to raise the productivity of labour, to build good new houses for the poor, to put the poor in the houses of the rich, to regularly provide a bottle of milk for every child of every poor family? It is on these points that *competition* should develop between the communes, communities, producer-consumers' societies and associations, and Soviets of Workers', Soldiers' and Peasants' Deputies. This is the work in which *talented organizers* should come to the fore *in practice* and be promoted to work in State administration. There is a great deal of talent among the people. It is merely suppressed. It must be given an opportunity to display itself. It *and it alone*, with the support of the people, can save Russia and save the cause of socialism."[74] Milk for poor children and the workers as masters of their fate—this is the inspiration of Lenin's hunting-down of "vermin". . . .

This restatement brings us to consider one of the most intense moments of revolutionary violence, what has been called "the period of the Red Guard attack on capital", and which was marked by the spread of workers' control, at the same time as, in the countryside, the peasants were taking possession of the estates confiscated from the big landowners and the Church, and the State was leaving them to enjoy it. "The land to the peasants, the factories to the workers"—revolutionary violence, in its initial phase, also meant that. Michel Heller is caricaturally unfair when he ascribes to the revolutionaries this idea: "Everything seemed very simple. Once the workers had established their control over production, all economic problems would immediately be solved."[75] In the thinking of the revolutionaries, on the contrary, nothing was more complicated than this apprenticeship to management.

"Workers' control" was a spontaneous creation of the proletariat, from February 1917 onward, which was encouraged by Lenin (unlike other Bolsheviks, who preferred state control) and was gradually brought under regulation by the new Soviet power. Now this "control" implicitly demonstrates that the immediate objective of the revolutionary authority was not to take over production: it was merely a matter of the workers' exercising a right of supervision and veto which was eminently political in character. The libertarian urge of the masses, but also, and most important, the employers' and engineers' refusal to co-operate, and their actual sabotage, caused this plan to be thwarted: gradually, workers' control became transformed into collectivization, and even "wildcat" self-management, and it was doubtless prematurely that the Soviet Republic found itself, at the beginning of the summer of 1918, confronted with the obligation to manage a large part of Russia's industry. It is no less caricatural to attribute to workers' control, as Heller suggests, responsibility for the economic catastrophe that then descended upon Russia. Not that anarchy and the absence of an effective co-ordinating authority did not make their contribution—but the war, the lack of raw materials and fuel, and sabotage by the bourgeoisie, were infinitely more decisive factors.[76] The disappointing experience of workers' control, which was succeeded rather quickly by the system of authoritarian management of enterprises, nevertheless served as a school from which emerged a number of future worker-administrators, and in which, above all, as in the Soviets which covered Russia for a few months, a huge mass of people had undergone an apprenticeship to an intoxicating and genuine freedom.

This cannot be left out of account when the problem of the "non-existent" social basis of the Revolution is considered. On the one hand, this basis certainly shrank during the civil war: the proletariat emerged from its battles greatly weakened, the frightful economic situation fostered discontent among the peasants and workers to which the Red Army and the Cheka replied bluntly (as at Kronstadt); the phenomena of "de-classing" of the working class occurred of which Lenin speaks; the Soviets were rendered insubstantial; and at the end of the civil war, the Bolsheviks' military victory was lumbered with a political defeat—the Party had largely lost the confidence of the masses and was ruling Russia in spite of them and even against them.

On the other hand, however, how are we to understand this victory over the Whites, achieved in face of the hostile coalition of the bourgeois world, and after coming to the brink of disaster? How could a revolution "without a social basis" have succeeded in meeting so deadly a challenge? Even an historian so openly hostile to the Bolshevik Revolution as Adam B. Ulam is not satisfied, in answering this question, to refer to the inadequacy of the outside aid given to the Whites, their lack of unity and their military mistakes, their extortions from the civil population, the anti-Jewish pogroms and the execution of prisoners, which certainly contributed greatly to discredit them. Although he sees the division in the ranks of the Whites as a major cause of their defeat, this writer nevertheless does not remain silent about a series of other causes, which most historians of the Revolution have emphasized. Movements of hostility against the commissars and the Cheka in the Russian provinces only rarely took precedence over hatred of the old régime, and did not affect the people's attachment to the Soviets, so that there took shape in the popular mind "the legend of the golden period of Bolshevik rule, the period of the Soviets". On the other hand, "without a massive foreign intervention, the Civil War in Russia could have ended in a Bolshevik defeat only if the opposite side had produced a leader of unusual appeal and organizing ability, or if the Whites . . . could have produced a political organization possessing the cohesion and sense of mission of the Communist Party". Finally, to Denikin, who expressed contempt for "formulas", Ulam replies: "But what, if not declarations and formulas, were 'All power to the Soviets', 'All land to the peasants', 'The right of every nationality to choose its own form of government', which certainly helped sway the course of the Russian revolution and the civil war?"[77] Formulas? But by what accident was it that these particular "formulas" were those *of the Bolsheviks?*

An astonishing contradiction is contained in the attempt to reduce the Revolution and the Soviet régime to a system of "terror and lies". On the one hand we are shown a revolution that is the work of a tiny minority, a coup d'état, in fact, imposed upon a people 150 millions strong. On the other, we are told that this people, especially in the 1930s, is a victim of the régime's ideological lying.

That the Revolution made use of force and the Stalin régime of lies is absolutely true. But by what miracle tens of millions of men who had been "forced" to accept the new régime bestowed upon it thereafter such blind devotion—that is something that, after all, calls for some further explanation! Some polemicists in a hurry will quote other notable instances of mass spell-binding in history—the Nazi period in Germany, say, don't forget that. Without going into the detail of possible comparisons, the brittleness of this analogy seems obvious, so far as the "spell-binding" aspect is concerned, at any rate. From the technical standpoint alone, Soviet rule, including its Stalin phase, possessed neither the means of persuasion nor the network of communications needed for such a conditioning of the masses as could be effected in highly-industrialized Germany. Till the end of the 1920s illiterates were still numerous in Russia, and radio sets rather few. Consequently the impact of strictly ideological means of manipulation was considerably less than in Germany. But this is not the main thing. The Nazis appealed to values that *united* the people—the nation, the race, antisemitism, the spirit of superiority and conquest. The Soviet régime—including the Stalin régime, at least until the early 1940s— was driven by ideals of *differentiation*: class struggle, socialist revolution, cultural revolution, destruction of the religious heritage (the spiritual cement of Russian tradition), international proletarian solidarity ("aid for Spain"), antifascist solidarity. It is unnecessary to point out, in addition, how fundamentally different were the respective values of the two régimes, and therefore their ideological motivations. In order to explain why the masses rallied round the Soviet régime we need to find more convincing arguments: terror and "conditioning" do not account for everything, or even for what is most important.

This is not the place to go at length into what would constitute part of a history of Soviet society, and more especially a social history of Stalinism, which no-one has so far attempted.[78] In the 1920s the regime was able to draw the majority of the youth and of the proletariat behind it in pursuit of aims of civilizing (and Europeanizing) Russia and, to some degree reorganizing life on socialist lines. This meant, on the one hand, opportunities for social advancement through education and the "proletarianization" of the country's leadership at all levels. But it also meant mass participation in political life, an explosion of cultural and artistic activity, the search for a new way of life through art, the theatre, modern architecture, sexual reform, new ways in teaching, in psychiatry. . . . Without spreading oneself on this theme and without idealizing phenomena which remained, after all, very much the concern of minorities only, and largely premature at that, is it not the case that any attempt to assess the past and foretell the future in the Soviet Union must include a re-discovery of this "heritage of the 1920s", which is still largely unexploited, and which the kind of concern with the past that is characteristic of Solzhenitsyn necessarily ignores?

After the phase of social experimentation, coinciding with the ambiguous period of the New Economic Policy, the social transformations accompanying Stalin's industrialization campaign formed the basic background to the régime of terror which historians, including Medvedev—and, of course, Solzhenitsyn—tend to detach from its context: final disappearance of the old exploiting classes, formation of a new working class and a peasantry that was either proletarianized (in the State farms) or collectivized, and on this basis, new stratifications of society that provided Stalinism with its social foundation (to a much greater extent than the Bolshevik Party apparatus and the vestiges of the old ruling classes); the determining role played by education, liquidation of illiteracy, ending of infectious diseases, and so on. . . . How is it possible to close one's eyes to this gigantic "stirring up" of the former *muzhik* masses, this revolution that was both social and cultural and meant turning upside down the society of the former Russian Empire, bringing it greater homogeneity and in particular the capacity to resist attack from without (as was shown in 1941–5)? It is beyond doubt that the history of Soviet society is not to be reduced to that of a "world of concentration camps", and its present characteristics are not definable either, by Andrei Sakharov's polemical formula: "one huge concentration camp".

*   *   *

The problem of morality holds a central position in Solzhenitsyn's work. Its importance in Soviet literature since the time of the 20th Party Congress corresponds to the crisis of ideals engendered by the revelation then made of the crimes, and, more generally, the deceptions of the Stalin period. But it certainly has deeper roots than that.

It was by way of revisionism and moralistic criticism that after 1956 a revival began in social thought in the USSR, including interest in Marxism and the Communist ideal. And this was no accident. The "dictatorship of the proletariat", the "higher (historical) interests of the proletariat", the "class struggle", with the Stalinist variant whereby "the class struggle grows more intense as the building of socialism proceeds", "class" morality—all this had served as ideological camouflage for tyranny, the concentration-camp system, the massacre of millions of citizens, including many Communists. It would be futile to expect that these same concepts should, as though by magic, become operative once more in exposing the trick that had been played. There is certainly nothing surprising in the fact that they were deeply discredited, and that the socialist ideal, when it again sought to find its identity, endeavoured to assume "a human face". But it was not merely a few formulas that were discredited. The "return to Lenin" was not adequate to close the account of the deception that had been experienced, and the moral defeat suffered by the régime, with its incapacity to create, transcending the class struggle and its harsh exigencies, an ethic for the new way of life corresponding to a society on the road to communism, in which the class struggle would have ceased to be the driving force of history and man would become the *subject* of history. Consequently, the revelation of the gap between "official truth" and reality effected by Solzhenitsyn and other moralistic critics, even when this has been done in a disguised form, has proved more important than all the tons of learned "Marxist" works that have been devoted, in the East as in the West, to dodging the real problems. From this it does not follow that Solzhenitsyn is acceptable either in the way that he presents these problems or in the solutions that he advocates. It does follow, however, that Marxism will not succeed in working out its own solutions unless it recognizes its own limitations, and overcomes them.

One of the adepts of the new moral socialism, Georgii Pomerantz, formulates the question in these terms: "Crude civilizations are incapable of filling the ideological vacuum. They collapse like a house of cards. One of the principal causes of the vacuum arises from the collision between two conceptions of the world: the religious one and the scientific. Mankind's centuries-old heritage has been codified in the world religions. The scientific revolution has shaken the world religions, but without proving capable of creating, at the same time, symbols of a beauty that can stand comparison with those of Buddha or Christ." Pomerantz sees the way out through reviving the dialogue between Marxism and the old philosophies: this seems to him to provide the key to a new culture. This position is certainly different from that of Solzhenitsyn, who is less concerned with such a dialogue than with a new theocratism. It also differs from the ideas of Krasnov-Levitin, who seems to see in Christian spirituality a kind of addition of a soul as leaven to socialist democracy. (This trend is truly representative of a "Christian socialism".) What reply can Marxism give to the needs that find expression through the new moral doctrines?

Official ideology confines itself to the "moral code of the builders of Communism", an improved version of Stalinist moral doctrine. The "testament" of Eugen Varga noted the "petty-bourgeois view of the world" that lurked beneath the bark of this official morality. Roy Medvedev acknowledges the undeveloped character of the "ethical conception" in Marxism-Leninism, and considers it impossible to "construct a solid system of morality" on such a "simplistic" foundation as: "whatever helps the Revolution is moral".

This criticism hits indirectly at Lenin, for whom proletarian morality had to be "wholly subordinated to the interests of the class struggle of the proletariat"—a conception which, with all that follows from it on the practical plane, was defended with talent by Leon Trotsky. "Whoever accepts the end . . . must accept the means. . . . Nevertheless, do not lying and violence 'in themselves' warrant condemnation? Of course, even as does the class society which generates them. A society without social contradictions will naturally be a society without lies and violence. However, there is no way of building a bridge to that society save by revolutionary, that is, violent, means."[79] The author of _Their Morals and Ours_ bursts out angrily against the indictment brought against Bolshevism by "moralists" of every variety, at the time of the Spanish civil war and the Moscow trials: "A slaveowner who through cunning and violence shackles a slave in chains, and a slave who through cunning or violence breaks the chains—let not the contemptible eunuchs tell us that they are equals before a court of morality".[80] And yet Stalinism is far from being justified by this conception. Trotsky gives a definition of Bolshevik morality that is perhaps wider than Lenin's, when he writes that not everything is permissible. "That is permissible . . . which *really* leads to the liberation of mankind . . . when we say that the end justifies the means, then for us the conclusion follows that the great revolutionary end spurns those base means and ways which set one part of the working class against other parts, or attempt to make the masses happy without their participation: or lower the faith of the masses in themselves and their organizations, replacing it by worship of the 'leaders'."[81] But, above all, Trotsky emphasizes the interdependence of means and ends: "Seeds of wheat must be sown in order to yield an ear of wheat."[82]

The Soviet experience offers a good illustration of the truth of this proposition of Trotsky's. Putting it the other way round, the crop that comes up shows what was sown. The moral consequences of Stalinism cause us to look back at the means employed, and from these means we look back at the nature of the "socialism" which inspired them: the dictatorship of the proletariat through an interposed bureaucracy, and perhaps the entire conception of building socialism on the basis of first of all accumulating the productive forces, at a rapid rate. We need to investigate how these two major conditions not only determined the resort to violence and lying on the grand scale but, more generally, how they postponed, hindered and in the end seriously compromised the régime's socialist aim, namely, the creation of new social relations of a liberating kind.

*   *   *

But although Solzhenitsyn does give expression to the alienated relation, which he has experienced, of millions of men to the mega-industrial reality, the way he expresses it is clearly warped by an ideology turned towards the past and in no way concerned with recasting social relations in a liberating form.

Ignorance of the discontinuities of history (the mutations of the growing tree!) has, in fact, several consequences for Solzhenitsyn. The first and most obvious is his nostalgia for an idealized version of a Russia without internal antagonisms, without class struggles, that never existed outside the writer's dreams: here he is, recalling, after many other nostalgic sighs, that, "for centuries Russia *exported* grain,"[83] whereas nowadays she has to import it—forgetting to mention that the existence of this exportable "surplus" did not prevent many peasants from dying of hunger in certain periods.[84]

The second consequence is his failure to grasp what is irreversible in the "discontinuity" of October 1917 and Stalin's achievement, even if, contrary to what is implied by official apologetics, they constitute neither the beginning nor the end of Russian and Soviet history, which is said to be open henceforth only to "improvements" to a path that has in essentials been finally laid down for the future. History is neither "closed" nor is it reversible.

In the third place, Solzhenitsyn seems to be unaware of the *Soviet* constituent in the Russian patriotism of today. This patriotism cannot be understood—nor the chauvinism that arises from it, either—without taking into account the revolution, the industrial achievements, the scientific and cultural successes, the victorious war with Hitlerite Germany, the new building-sites in Siberia—in short, everything that in the last half century has enriched the heritage of the Russian people and those associated with it in the Soviet Union. It must be added that "patriarchal" values have little chance of making much appeal to the young people and the women of present-day Russia. Even in the depths of the countryside, where attachment to the land is strong enough to make the authorities attempt experiments in "personalizing" its cultivation, the dream of the boys and girls of today is not so much to perpetuate or enlarge the petty domestic economy, with all that this means in advantages, but also in burdens, as to study, acquire a well-esteemed trade or profession, and enjoy those comforts and "leisure" opportunities that are appropriate to an urban way of life.

Finally, and above all, the Soviet Union exists. It is made up of an economic, historical, social, and to an increasing extent cultural reality, in which a tremendous mingling of population has taken place, through mixed marriages, and a type of human being has emerged having a composite personality in which the "Soviet" characteristics jostle with distinctive national peculiarities that are more or less pronounced. It would be as absurd to deny this reality as to claim that the Russian, Georgian, Uzbek, Estonian, etc., cultures are no longer "national" except in form, and "socialist", Soviet in their content. Solzhenitsyn does not deny this reality. He simply shuts his eyes to it.

Is this because it is only, after all, an "ideological" reality? In any case, Russia forms an integral part of this reality, and Solzhenitsyn's Russocentrism, unless it takes account of *this* dimension of present-day Russia, can offer no prospects in which the non-Russian peoples of the Union can recognize themselves. To "civilisation in an impasse" Solzhenitsyn's answer is the impasse of a retrograde turning towards the past, incapable of integrating and thereby transcending the substrata that history has left in men's way of life and thought. The return to Holy Russia may serve as a theme for a new poetry of "compensation", but it cannot help to bring about new social relations in the Soviet society of this last quarter of the 20th century.

IV

The *"affaire* Solzhenitsyn"—the persecution and banishment of the writer and the use of him as a political tool—has been revealing in several interesting ways.

It has revealed, in the first place, the vulnerability of the Soviet leaders to a critique the anachronistic character of which, and complete lack of influence among the Soviet people, they were pleased to emphasize without troubling about the contradiction implied, although, logically, what they said about it should mean that it had no prospect of being "subversive". It has also revealed the unscrupulousness and shamelessness of certain circles in political life and the mass media in the West, which have transformed the writer (with his consent) into a consumer-product for anti-Communism of a particularly vulgar sort. Finally, it has revealed the embarrassment into which this kind of event continues to plunge the Left in the West—especially, of course, the Communist Parties linked with the Soviet Union.

Undoubtedly Solzhenitsyn owes to the officials of the Writers' Union, the KGB and the CPSU a considerable proportion of his international audience and his reputation as "the conscience of mankind". His talent and his personal courage, however great they may be, would not have sufficed for this. The banishment of Solzhenitsyn, though it may have seemed the shrewdest possible action to take, among several evils, having regard to the political repercussions of the affair, has nevertheless done severe damage to the Soviet Union's prestige, especially in intellectual circles and among sympathetic progressives. It is true that the leaders of the USSR are a great deal more concerned today to win economic and trading partners from among the most representative and stable forces of world capitalism than they are to develop a serious, and inevitably critical, dialogue with sympathizers or potential allies in the international Left. No one any longer doubts that a stable Gaullist or post-Gaullist France is more welcome in Moscow than would be a France which set out along the hazardous path of an uncontrollable socialism. But what is it that obliges the Soviet leaders to take risks with their own recalcitrant intellectuals which entail such serious harm to their socialist "brand-image"?

The answer most commonly given to this question is that the writers who criticize the set-up, and Solzhenitsyn in particular, would become widely influential in a situation in which the rulers were discharging some ballast. In the restricted circles in which they have circulated for some years now, Solzhenitsyn's works have indeed had considerable impact. "One will no longer be able to write or to think, from now on, as if he had not existed", say young Soviet intellectuals who are nevertheless not greatly disposed to agree with the theses of the *Letter to Soviet Leaders*. The brilliance of the writing, even if it counts for much, is not enough to account for this audience. A significant complicity has been entered into between the world of Solzhenitsyn's writings and the intimate spiritual life of his readers.

"The dumb have, thanks to you, recovered their power of speech", the writer Lydia Chukovskaya wrote to Solzhenitsyn. "I don't know of any writer more eagerly awaited or more indispensable than you. Where the word is still living, the future is safe. Your bitter books at once wound and heal our soul. You have given back to Russian literature its formidable strength." Even readers who are remote from Solzhenitsyn's ideas will subscribe to those words. There is no shortage of writers of talent in the Soviet Union. Most of them write something "for the drawer" or for circulation in *samizdat* form. Some very valuable books are also published, in the most normal manner, and without any whiff of scandal attracting to them the too selective sense of smell of the world's newspapers. All this is true. But no-one, perhaps, has so completely freed himself from "Aesopian language" and found such authentic and profound accents in which to express the tragedy which, since the return from the camps, has gnawed at the consciences of very many Soviet people. Only a minority? That is undeniable. The anti-Stalinist intellectuals, the "dissidents", acknowledge their isolation. "A sound-proof wall", writes Chukovskaya, "methodically and hatefully erected by the leaders between the creators of spiritual values and those very people for whom these values have been created, has been made thicker. . . ."

But does not the very fact that this wall is kept in good repair show that the leaders fear the contagion of subversive ideas?

The problem here is not whether or not Solzhenitsyn's political attitudes might or might not find a wide public to support them if they were allowed free circulation. This is doubtfully the case. Not that a favourable soil does not exist for backward-looking and Slavophil ideas—with or without Solzhenitsyn, moreover. But the attraction of technocratic-liberal ideologies is felt more strongly among the intellectual youth. And, besides, the attachment of the broad masses to the conquests of October, the social and cultural achievements of the régime, the familiarity of the system of collective ownership of the means of production, are firmly rooted enough to make unlikely the success of any "anti-Sovietism" in the strict sense of the word. Anti-Stalinism itself does not appear to be the current of opinion that the leaders have most to fear so far as the mass of the population and the young generations are concerned.

The problem is that any breach, however narrow and debatable it may be, in the monopoly of ideas and information, involves the risk of bringing about fatal consequences for the stability of the established order. An open discussion about Stalinism and about all the problems of current politics—which might start, say, from the beginnings made by Sakharov and Solzhenitsyn, but would quickly advance beyond them, in all probability—would cause to manifest itself in the country an unsuspected potential of criticism and aspiration. In this respect, the agitation of the "dissident" minorities is not the only factor that has to be taken into consideration. Recent discussions in the Party on the subject of methods of management, among collective farmers on the subject of the experiment of "collective-farmers' councils", in the trade-union organizations about the rights of works committees, all reflect the presence of social movements, favourable to a democratization of the machinery of society. To be sure, these still barely perceptible "movements" may seem very remote from the preoccupations, and very far short of the demands, formulated by the dissident groups. The latter are, moreover, inclined towards a paralysing pessimism as to the possibilities of change in the immediate or fairly near future. This pessimism and political despair is reflected, among other things, in the urge to emigrate. The "atmosphere of departure" has become dominant in certain intellectual circles. The example set by the Jews has had a lot to do with this. Some Russian writers or scientists who have no "new homeland" to kiss are also tempted by the prospect of emigration, and the authorities are not in every case resistant to their wishes. . . .

On the other hand, Roy Medvedev continues to hold the view that a movement for the democratization of Soviet society can develop only given an initiative from the top.

The extraordinary "power of words" in the USSR is related, obviously, to realities that are not familiar to Westerners. In this connection one remembers the moral and messianic traditions of Russian literature. And also the "ersatz" for a political debate that can be constituted by a novel or a poem (and the collective celebration of such works, such as poetry meetings, encounters between writers and their public, etc.) in a country in which public opinion is without adequate means of expression in the form of newspapers and institutions. But this "power of words", or at least of ideas, results also from the nature of the cultural advance and certain changes that are in progress in Soviet society. In the context of "ideocracy", producers of ideas, and therefore writers, are traditionally charged with a high civic mission. A very large public has been formed, and continues to be formed, for the consumption of the régime's cultural values, which vary a great deal in quality. The thirst for knowledge is tremendous. Quite recently Marc Chagall, returning from his first visit to the USSR since 1922, bore witness to this: "Nowhere else in the world have we seen such a love of reading and of art. In spite of omnipresent television, everyone carries books and reads, in the parks, the public gardens and the Metro. You should see and feel how they can listen to music. . . . Such attraction towards and respect for culture is quite simply amazing and overwhelming." Furthermore, the advance in education, the changes in the ways in which the working class is reinforced and trained, the establishment of a new way of life in the towns, the modernization of the country districts during the last decade have all caused new forms of behaviour and new needs to appear, which cannot be neglected in any serious analysis of Soviet society today.

Among the intelligentsia circles that are most sensitive to moral and political questions it is necessary also to reckon with the profound disillusionment that followed the stopping of "de-Stalinization", which culminated in the April Plenum of 1968 (the signal for a vast internal campaign of ideological prophylaxis) and intervention in Czechoslovakia in August of that year. Political *samizdat* did not really "take off" until after 1964. At the time, "anti-Stalinist" criticism still, as a general rule, developed within the setting of the ideas of the 20th and 22nd (1961) Congresses of the CPSU. Thereafter, and especially after 1968, the most radical, frankly anti-Communist documents circulated in great numbers. It was inevitable that Lenin and Bolshevism should be called in question as this intellectual maturation proceeded. This criticism took the form, with some, almost inevitably, of systematic iconoclasm. Solzhenitsyn's thought thus matched a movement of ideas that was not confined to himself.

Is this to be seen as a "reactionary" movement? Undoubtedly this question, as Pierre Daix says, has "come out of our world, our society". The old Bolsheviks, Anarchists and Christians who have shared a common fate in Stalin's camps are less concerned with their differences among themselves than with what marks them off from those who formerly held them in captivity and torment. The Communist writer Alexander Tvardovsky, the historian Roy Medvedev (a member until recently of the CPSU) and even General Grigorenko, well-known for his radical neo-Bolshevism, are closer to the "reactionary" Solzhenitsyn, in the political spectrum of the USSR, than they are to the "progressives" in the leadership of the Party or the KGB. It is hard to construct a "Right-Left" typology of the oppositionist currents in accordance with our Western criteria. The first priority, struggle for freedom of thought and expression, cuts across philosophical differences. But nevertheless these exist, and are becoming clearer. Around two or three ideological axes—Liberal Westernism, Russophil Christianity, socialism—a spiritual life is reawakening which had been numbed but not entirely extinguished by more than forty years of monolithism.

The "Marxism" that Solzhenitsyn attacks so crudely, calling it

"economico-mechanistic", is obviously a Marxism-Leninism impoverished by the officially-approved form in which it is presented, and
which has, moreover, been cut off from all living Marxist tradition for
half a century: in a country where even the writings of Rosa Luxemburg
are still "censored" there can clearly be no question of publishing
Lukács, Gramsci, Lefebvre, Mandel, Marcuse, Gorz, etc. Marxism in
the Soviet Union is impoverished to such an extent that it is no longer
being developed, nor can it come to grips with the other systems and
trends of thought that have constituted the heritage of Western culture
for the last fifty years: sociology, economics, psychology, psycho-
analysis, etc.

This poverty of social thought and of official Marxism (or simply of
what is known of Marxism) does not fail to affect the quality of
oppositionist thinking. In comparison with the intellectual richness
that preceded and marked the movement of socialist rebirth in
Czechoslovakia, the moralistic type of protest that has appeared in the
USSR cannot but disappoint. Yet it arises from a unique experience,
and constitutes a probably necessary element in the "reawakening of
consciousnesses".

In any case, it is not Solzhenitsyn's political thinking that will
dissuade us from letting Marxism have a chance, and recognizing its
necessary part in the critical analysis of Soviet society that Soviet
Marxists will develop. It was probably as a joke that, in an important
Brussels newspaper, Nikita Struve, publisher of *The Gulag Archipelago*,
assured us that Solzhenitsyn's work deals a "quasi-mortal blow" to
Marxism-Leninism.[85]

While, however, this statement, if it was not made as a joke, must
cause us to doubt the perspicacity of the man who uttered it, tells us
a great deal about one of the aspects of the political campaign of which
Solzhenitsyn has become the unfortunate plaything. Undoubtedly,
anti-Sovietism, in the Western world which is now involved in the
dialectic of the rapprochement between East and West, has reasons for
existence that derive not merely from the nostalgias of people for whom
the Cold War has never ended, but also from the very dialectic of this
rapprochement, in which factors of co-operation do not eliminate the
antagonistic realities of the two systems. But it is above all anti-
socialism, anti-Marxism, in a context of multiple crises, that explains
why certain testimonies are exploited in what is often a quite frenzied
fashion.

The attitude of part of the Left in the West, especially the Communist
Parties, continues to lay itself open to such exploitation. I have in mind
here not merely the obtuse reactions of a Georges Marchais, or the
active participation of several Communist Party papers (particularly in
Austria and in France) in the campaign of slander against Solzhenitsyn

in connection with the Vlasov affair. In the most liberal reactions—which are, of course, to be welcomed—a persistent short-sightedness is apparent. Thus, people become indignant when they find that Solzhenitsyn is not a "socialist", at the same time as they urge that the "Soviet comrades" ought to have published him, in order the better to criticize him.

This short-sightedness is clearly possible only in so far as the "case of Solzhenitsyn" is treated independently of the historical and political realities that gave rise to it. A study of these realities does not fail to inform us that anti-socialism is a perfectly conceivable attitude among the Soviet intelligentsia of 1974, and that "free discussion" of Solzhenitsyn in the USSR is not among the "options" that are open to the leaders within the framework of the present political régime in that country. At the very least, Solzhenitsyn's testimony, and the sad *"affaire"* that has taken possession of it, remind the Left in the West of tasks which other events will not omit to render urgent: critical, Marxist analysis of the Soviet experience; critical reflection upon the ties (in the case of the CPs, ties of subordination) between the working-class movement and the leadership of the USSR, and the need to establish "bridges" between the progressive movements in East and West, to resume a dialogue that has been suspended for too long and is certainly burdened with serious misunderstandings.

NOTES

1. A novel in which several voices speak, with the author intervening discreetly in the argument between his characters.
2. *Gulag* is the acronym formed from the Russian title of the "central administration of labour camps" which existed under Stalin.
3. Addressed to the leaders of the USSR under date 5 September 1973, having been written six months previously. Published by the YMCA Press in February 1974: English translation, by Hilary Sternberg, published in April 1974 by Index on Censorship, London. Quotations are from this translation.
4. Georg Lukács, *Solzhenitsyn* (English translation), London, 1970.
5. Pierre Daix, *Ce que je sais de Soljénitsyne*, Paris, 1973.
6. Cf. V. Chalanov (Shalanov), *Article 58*, Paris, 1969, and E. S. Ginzburg, *Into the Whirlwind*, London, 1967.
7. *One Day in the Life of Ivan Denisovich*, translated by Gillon Aitken, London (The Bodley Head), 1971, p. 174. Quotations are all from this translation.
8. Ibid., p. 7.
9. Ibid., p. 35.
10. "Matryona's House," in Solzhenitsyn, *Stories and Prose Poems*, translated by Michael Glenny, London, 1971, p. 54.
11. "For the Good of the Cause," in ibid., p. 112.
12. Ibid., 105.
13. Ibid., pp. 113–14.

14. Ibid., p. 117.
15. *Cancer Ward, Part Two*, translated by Nicholas Bethell and David Burg, London (The Bodley Head), 1969, p. 135.
16. Quotations from ibid., pp. 173–6.
17. It was the seizure of a copy of the manuscript in the possession of a woman friend in Leningrad, who killed herself after interrogation by the KGB, at the beginning of September 1973, that caused the writer to decide to publish a work that he had originally intended should not appear until after his death.
18. *Nobel Prize Lecture*, translated by Nicholas Bethell, London (Stenvalley Press), 1973, p. 17.
19. "*Avgust Chetyrnadtsatogo*" *chitayut na rodine* (a survey of reactions to *August 1914* by readers inside the USSR, published in Paris by the YMCA Press).
20. Not until the 1950s did the USSR surpass the quantities of grain harvested and the numbers of cattle that Russia could boast of in 1913.
21. *August 1914*, translated by Michael Glenny, London (Bodley Head), 1972, pp. 601–2.
22. Ibid., p. 425.
23. Ibid., p. 606.
24. Ibid., p. 608. The Black Hundreds were a terrorist organization of the extreme Right, especially notorious for pogroms against the Jews. The implications suggested by the expression "Red Hundreds" will be appreciated.
25. *Nobel Prize Lecture*, op. cit., p. 53.
26. Quoted by Michel Heller, *La Monde concentrationnaire et la littérature soviétique*, Paris, 1974 p. 103.
27. *Letter to Soviet Leaders*, op. cit., pp. 46–7.
28. *Nobel Prize Lecture*, op. cit., p. 39.
29. *Letter to Soviet Leaders*, op. cit., p. 50.
30. *August 1914*, op. cit., p. 605.
31. *Nobel Prize Lecture*, op. cit., p. 37.
32. Ibid., p. 39.
33. *Letter to Soviet Leaders*, op. cit., p. 12.
34. N. Berdyaev, *The Realm of Spirit and the Realm of Caesar*, London, 1952, pp. 18, 19.
35. *Letter to Three Students*, October 1967, in *Solzhenitsyn: A Documentary Record*, ed. L. Labedz, London (Penguin), 1972, p. 151.
36. Ibid., p. 151.
37. *August 1914*, op. cit., p. 429.
38. *Letter to Soviet Leaders*, op. cit., pp. 33–4.
39. Ibid., pp. 52–4, 56.
40. *A Lenten Letter to Pimen, Patriarch of All Russia*, English translation, Minneapolis, 1972.
41. *Letter to Soviet Leaders*, op. cit., p. 52. [Solzhenitsyn is referring to St Sergius of Radonezh, who died in 1391—he founded the famous Troitsk Monastery, and played an important part in uniting the Russians in resistance to the Mongol yoke, as Solzhenitsyn recalls in his story *Zakhar-the-Pouch*: and to St Nilus of the Sora, who died in 1508—an ascetic, he fought strongly against corruption and worldliness in the Church—*Translator.*]
42. Berdyaev, op. cit., and also *The Origin of Russian Communism*, London, 1937.
43. This same filiation and this same sensibility are expressed in Tarkovsky's film *Andrei Rublyov* [about a great Russian painter of the 15th century who was a monk in St Sergius's monastery—*Translator.*]
44. It is true that this atheist propaganda sometimes has to wrestle with a religiosity that is no less "backward" and "frenzied": an anthropomorphic notion of God, and obscurantist sectarian practices such as refusal to conform to standards of hygiene or to compulsory education.
45. *A Lenten Letter . . .*, op. cit.

46. *Cahiers marxistes*, Brussels, May 1974.
47. *"Avgust chetyrnadtsatogo" chitayut na rodine*, op. cit.
48. *August 1914*, op. cit., pp. 429–30.
49. *Nobel Prize Lecture*, op. cit., p. 33.
50. Ibid., pp. 49, 51.
51. *Letter to Soviet Leaders*, op. cit., p. 21.
52. Ibid., pp. 24–6.
53. A. S. Sakharov, *Thoughts on Progress, Peaceful Coexistence and Intellectual Freedom* (London, 1968); R. Medvedev, *De la Démocratie socialiste;* M. Sholokhov, speech at the 23rd Party Congress.
54. *Letter to Soviet Leaders*, pp. 37, 39, 40.
55. *The Gulag Archipelago*, Chapters 2 and 7.
56. Michel Heller, op. cit.
57. Isaac Deutscher, *The Prophet Armed*, London, 1954, p. 499.
58. Heller, op. cit.
59. Trotsky, speech at 3rd All-Russia Trades Union Congress, quoted in Deutscher, op. cit., p. 501.
60. Heller, op. cit., p. 23.
61. Marcel Liebman, *The Russian Revolution*, London, 1970, and *Le Léninisme sous Lénine*, Vol. 2, Paris, 1973 (an English translation is shortly to be published by Jonathan Cape), quoting Victor Serge, J. L. H. Keep, F. Kaplan, Boris Souvarine, etc.; also E. H. Carr, *A History of Soviet Russia: The Bolshevik Revolution, 1917–23*, Vol. 1, London, 1950.
62. Roy Medvedev, *Let History Judge*, London, 1972, pp. 261–2.
63. Deutscher, op. cit., pp. 338–9.
64. Medvedev, *Let History Judge*, op. cit., p. 391.
65. Heller, op. cit.
66. See on this subject Moshe Lewin, *Lenin's Last Struggle*, London, 1969, and *Le Testament de Varga* (preface by Roger Garaudy), Paris, 1970.
67. Published in *Vestnik russkogo studencheskogo khristianskogo dvizheniya* (Paris and New York: organ of Russian Students' Christian Action), No. 98, April 1970.
68. Lenin, *Polnoye sobranie sochineniya* (Complete Collected Works), Vol. 45 (published 1964), p. 191. [The phrase occurs in a letter to Kursky dated 17 May 1922. The document is omitted from the *Collected Works*, 4th edition, English version, Vol. 42: see p. 419 and note 477—*Translator*.]
69. Liebman, *Le Léninisme sous Lénine*, Vol. 2, op. cit., p. 163.
70. In his last writings, Lenin declared himself plainly against any hastiness in carrying forward the socialist process, and in favour of a *gradual* collectivization of agriculture.
71. A city in Vietnam bombarded in February 1968 by the National Liberation Front, during the Têt offensive. [Hué was briefly *occupied* by the Communist forces during this offensive, and after its recapture by the South Vietnamese forces about a thousand bodies of executed persons were reported to have been found buried in mass graves—*Translator*.]
72. Letter to the Oslo newspaper *Aftenposten*, 5 September 1973, nominating Academician Sakharov for the Nobel Peace Prize. English translation in *Index*, Winter 1973, pp. 47, 48, 50.
73. See Wilhelm Reich, *The Sexual Revolution*, London, 1969, and A. S. Makarenko, *The Road to Life: An Epic of Education*, Moscow, 1951.
74. First published in *Pravda*, 20 January 1929 [*sic*]: *Collected Works*, 4th edition, English version, Vol. 26 (1964), pp. 404–15.
75. Heller, op. cit., p. 14.
76. J.-M. Chauvier, "Contrôle ouvrier et 'autogestion sauvage' en Russie (1917–1921)", in *Revue des Pays de l'Est* (Brussels), No. 1 of 1973.

77. Adam B. Ulam, *Lenin and the Bolsheviks*, London, 1966, pp. 433, 437, 440.
78. An outline of such a history will be found in Roy Medvedev's *Let History Judge*.
79. Trotsky, *Their Morals and Ours* (1938), London (New Park Publications), 1968, p. 30.
80. Ibid., p. 32.
81. Ibid., pp. 43–4.
82. Ibid., p. 45.
83. *Letter to Soviet Leaders*, op. cit., p. 34.
84. The Russia of Pugachev, of Stenka Razin and the great peasant revolts is no less "traditional" than that of the Old-Believers!
85. Interview in *Le Soir*, 22 March 1974.

MARX ON DEMOCRATIC FORMS OF GOVERNMENT

Hal Draper

THIS is one chapter in a work on *Karl Marx's Theory of Revolution* which will be published in the near future. Many questions connected with the subject of this chapter and which are only briefly mentioned here are of course discussed in detail in other parts of the work.

In a general way, Marx's socialism (communism) as a political programme may be most quickly defined, from the Marxist standpoint, as *the complete democratization of society*, not merely of political forms.* But the democratic movement of the 19th century began by putting the struggle for advanced political forms in the forefront; and so did Marx, in a different programmatic context. For Marx, the fight for democratic forms of government—democratization in the state—was a leading edge of the socialist effort; not its be-all and end-all but an integral part of it all.

Throughout the history of the socialist/communist movements, one of the persistent problems has been to establish the relation, in theory and practice, between the struggle for socialism and for democracy (or democratic rights), between socialist issues and democratic issues. Every distinctive socialist current or school has had its own characteristic answer to this problem. On one extreme end of the spectrum is the view (held consciously in theory or expressed in practice) which puts the advocacy of democratic forms in the forefront, for their own sake, and subjoins the advocacy of socialistic ideas as an appurtenance. (From the Marxist standpoint, this is merely the leftmost wing of bourgeois-democratic liberalism extruding into the socialist spectrum.) On the other extreme is the type of radical ideology which *counterposes* socialistic ideas—in the sense of anti-capitalist views—against concern with democratic struggles, considering the latter as unimportant or harmful. Every conceivable mixture of the two approaches has cropped

---

* As a liberal Marx-critic, A. D. Lindsay, put it from his own viewpoint: "the Liberal, if to be a Liberal is to believe in democracy, must explain why he will not extend democracy to the government of the collective labourer and become a socialist. Socialism is for Marx essentially the democratization of the collective labourer. Because it was that, he regarded it as inevitable; for a society in which 'the notion of human equality has already acquired the fixity of a popular prejudice', and in which the prevailing form of production is social and involves government, is already in principle committed to it."[1]

101

up too, but they all form a single family insofar as they are *mixtures*. (For example: in the tension between socialist aims and democratic means, is your concern 50–50, 60–40, 30–70, etc.?)

Marx's approach is qualitatively different from this sort of eclecticism, and does not attempt to establish a sliding scale of *concern* with the two sides of the duality. For him, the task of theory is to integrate the two objectively. The characteristic answer to the problem emerging from Marx's theory was already heralded in his notebook critique of Hegel's philosophy of right,[2] where he sought to show that "true democracy" requires a new social content—socialism; and it will be rounded off with his analysis of the Paris Commune, which showed that a state with a new social content entailed truly democratic forms. Marx's theory moves in the direction of *defining consistent democracy in socialist terms, and consistent socialism in democratic terms.* The task of theory, then, is not to adjudicate a clash between the two considerations (a hopeless job once the problem is seen in that light), but rather to grasp the social dynamics of the situation under which the apparent contradiction between the two is resolved.

Marx did not work this out simply within his skull; progress toward a solution came only in the course of the first historical experience which he went through in which this problem was concretely posed. This was the period of the 1848–9 revolution, when democratic demands and socialist aims seemed to be at swords' point. One of the results was his so-called theory of permanent revolution: we will follow this process in some detail in a later part, and the problem will remain with us throughout.

Against "The Old Thesis"

From the start there was the problem of self-styled radicals who held the same attitude of hostility and contempt for democratic forms that emanated from the old régime, though presumably from an opposite direction. This is an aspect of the almost unanimous anti-democracy of pre-Marxist socialism.[3] When Marx referred to it in *The German Ideology*, he already called it contemptuously "the old thesis": "The old thesis, which has often been put forward both by revolutionaries and reactionaries, that in a democracy individuals only exercise their sovereignty for a moment, and then at once retreat from their rule. . . ."[4] (The polemic here is against the anarchoid Stirner.) This was only one favourite anti-democratic argument among many, one which flourishes today as lustily as two centuries ago. Marx gave them all short shrift, in the apparent belief (wrong, as it turned out) that they were simply vestiges of the past and had no future.*

---

* An example: Among the backward-looking anti-democrats that Marx ran into was the maverick David Urquhart, against whom Marx warned in an article: "there is

This rejection of anything connected with bourgeois democracy would later become associated mainly with ultra-left radicalism, but its beginnings were another matter. Engels described a case in a letter to Marx from Paris, where he was trying to work with one K. L. Bernays, an editor of the Paris *Vorwärts*, the German émigré paper. Bernays insists on writing anti-bourgeois articles for a Berlin paper which is anti-bourgeois from a reactionary (absolutist) standpoint.

> "He writes in the *Berliner Zeitungs-Halle* and rejoices like a child to see his *soi-disant* communist expectorations against the bourgeoisie printed there. Naturally the editors and the censorship let stand whatever is simply against the bourgeois and strike out the few allusions that could be offensive to themselves too. He rails against the jury system, 'bourgeois freedom of the press', the representative system, etc. I explain to him that this means working literally *pour le roi de Prusse* and indirectly against our party. . . . I make clear that the *Zeitungs-Halle* is in the pay of the government. . . ."[6]

"Working *pour le roi de Prusse* [for the king of Prussia]" meant, in French idiom, *working for nothing;* but Engels argued that Bernays was unwittingly working for the Prussian régime *literally*, since publishing attacks on democratic institutions in absolutist Prussia only helped the régime discredit the democratic movement. But, continued Engels, Bernays, a-gush with sentimentality, could understand none of this; he could not comprehend, he said, an approach which went easy on people he had always hated, *viz.* the bourgeoisie. Engels added:

> "I have read umpteen of these Paris-datelined articles [by Bernays]; they are *on ne peut plus* [to the fullest extent possible] in the interest of the government and in the style of True-Socialism."

Marx and Engels' approach to the question of democratic forms (rights, liberties, institutions, etc.) was completely different. The reason a type like Bernays could not comprehend their approach was that his socialism, such as it was, was merely anti-capitalist and not pro-proletarian; it was not a theory about a class movement but simply a predilection for a certain social reorganization. It had nothing to do with putting power in the hands of the masses of people, but rather

another clique of 'wise men' emerging in England, who are discontented with the Government and the ruling classes as much as with the Chartists. What do the Chartists want? they exclaim. They want to increase and extend the omnipotence of Parliament by elevating it to people's power. They are not breaking up parliamentarism but are raising it to a higher power. The right thing to do is to break up the representative system! A wise man from the East, *David Urquhart*, heads that clique."[5] Marx goes on to explain that Urquhart wants to turn the clock back on civilization, to return to the old Anglo-Saxon conditions, "or, better still, to the Oriental state", to localism, to economic conditions prior to the modern division of labour and concentrated capital. The subject of social tendencies hostile to both capitalism and the proletariat is reserved for separate consideration.

looked to any men of good will who wanted to make the changes envisaged. For such a man, popular control over government could be a danger, since the Stupid Masses might well be more hostile to his schemes than enlightened souls.

Popular control over government: in the middle of the 19th century it was much clearer than it is today that the problem of democracy was the effective establishment of full popular control over government, for the simple reason that no government (except perhaps the American) pretended that this happy state of affairs already existed. It had not yet become necessary or fashionable to redefine democracy out of existence; it was therefore quite common, in those benighted days, for enemies of popular sovereignty to attack the democratic idea openly and forthrightly, instead of embracing it in a crushing vice. For the "democratic extremist," popular control meant *unlimited* popular control, the elimination of all juridical, structural and socio-economic restraints on or distortions of popular control from below. For Marx, this is why popular control pointed to socialism.

But in a country which had not yet had its 1789, like Germany, the extension of popular control still had to pass through its bourgeois phase; under semi-feudal absolutism, the bourgeoisie was a part of the "popular masses" too, even if a limited and privileged part. For Marx, the problem resolved itself into this: how to pass through this phase—through and *out*—in such a way as to shift power to the underlying working strata of the population as expeditiously as possible. This is what will define the problem of the "permanent revolution".

At any rate, from the standpoint of this theoretical approach Bernays' inability to see more than his "hatred" of the bourgeois system did not mean that he hated the bourgeoisie more than Marx; it was a reflection of his non-class point of view. Marx did not have to weigh "hatred of the bourgeoisie" against the advantages of bourgeois democracy—an impossible calculus. It was rather a matter of making a class analysis of the elements of bourgeois democracy: sorting out what was specifically bourgeois (e.g. property qualifications for voting) from what furthered the widest extension of popular control.*

For Revolution and Democracy

The revolutions of 1848–9 temporarily established bourgeois-democratic governments in both France and Germany, the two countries with which Marx was mainly concerned. These governments

---

* In this explanation we have used "democracy" and "democratic" in their modern sense; but in mid-19th century, especially on the Continent before 1848, the democratic forms involved were more commonly labelled "liberties", specific "freedoms" (e.g. freedom of press, expression, etc.), specific "rights" (right of organization or association, etc.), "popular" institutions, including "popular sovereignty", and so on.

were thoroughly bourgeois and more or less democratic as compared with the previous régimes; they therefore raised innumerable concrete problems of what political forms should clothe democratization. In the case of Germany, Marx and Engels' articles in their *Neue Rheinische Zeitung* had to deal with many problems day by day, not merely in historical hindsight; hence they took up smaller-scale questions than are usually found in their synoptic analyses of the events in France.

The over-all criterion is: what will maximize the influence exercised from below by the masses-in-movement, on the political forces above? These political forces were two above all: the monarchist régime and its government, which was still the executive, though now on the defensive; and the representatives of the people in the assemblies established by the revolutionary upsurge. The latter represented the potentiality of "popular sovereignty", i.e. democratic control by the people. But when the National Assembly, elected from the various German states, met in Frankfurt on 18 May, it showed that the bourgeois-democratic delegates shrank from a clash with the monarchy. In the first issue of the *Neue Rheinische Zeitung*, on 1 June, Engels summarized the situation:

> "Since two weeks ago, Germany has a national constituent assembly which is the product of a vote by the whole German people.
>
> "The German people had won its sovereignty in the streets of almost all the big and little cities of the country, especially on the barricades of Vienna and Berlin. It had exercised this sovereignty in the elections for the National Assembly.
>
> "The first act of the National Assembly had to be to proclaim this sovereignty of the German people loudly and publicly.
>
> "Its second act had to be to work out a German constitution on the basis of the sovereignty of the people, and to get rid of everything in the actually existing state of affairs in Germany which contradicts the principle of the sovereignty of the people.
>
> "All during its session it had to take the necessary measures to thwart all efforts by the reaction, to maintain the revolutionary grounds on which it stands, to secure the revolution's conquest, the sovereignty of the people, against all attacks.
>
> "The German National Assembly has now already held a dozen sessions and has done nothing of all this."[7]

Instead, continued Engels, the authorities still violate the rights of citizens with impunity, while the Assembly pays more attention to its dinner hours than to its democratic tasks.[8]

As the year wore on, even the Frankfurt "Left", the consciously liberal wing, showed what little stomach it had for a fight with the real state power headed by the Crown. In a later article on the assembly's deliberations, Engels quotes the liberal deputy Ruge* as an example of

---

* This is the same Arnold Ruge who, five years before, had been Marx's co-editor of the *Deutsch-Französische Jahrbücher*, complaining that the German people were hopelessly apathetic and could never make a revolution. He was prominent among those who helped to fulfil his prophecy. By the 1870s he wound up on the pension rolls of the far-from-apathetic Bismarck.[9]

empty rhetoric: "We do not want to quarrel, gentlemen," Ruge told
the Assembly, "over whether we aim at a democratic monarchy, a
democratized monarchy[!] or a pure democracy; *on the whole we want
the same thing*, liberty, popular liberty, the rule of the people!" (The
emphasis and interpolated exclamation are by Engels.) With much
disgust Engels comments that this speaks volumes about a so-called
Left which says it wants the same thing as the Right, and "Which
forgets everything as soon as it hears a couple of hollow catchwords like
'popular liberty' and 'rule of the people'. "[10]

The difference between hollow rhetoric about "liberty" and a real
revolutionary-democratic struggle could only be spelled out in terms of
concrete issues. One of the most elementary and basic was the issue
that had been the first subject of Marx's political pen, freedom of the
the press. From the first number of the *NRZ*, Marx and Engels made
this a major battle-cry.[11]

The government, wrote Marx, is trying to apply the Penal Code
provisions against so-called "slander" in order to prevent any criticism
of the régime. Indeed, if a paper protests that the government is curbing
freedom of the press, *that* is punishable as a "slander" even if it is true.*
This application of the Penal Code means

> "the real, definitive finish-blow to the 19th of March [the revolution], to the clubs,
> and to freedom of the press! What is a club without freedom of speech? And what is
> freedom of speech with §§367, 368, 370 of the Penal Code? And what is the 19th of
> March without clubs and freedom of speech?"[13]

As this already indicates, freedom of the press could hardly be
separated from freedom of expression in all its forms. The whole
existence of the *Neue Rheinische Zeitung* was a battle for survival against
government suppression. Haled into court, Marx, Engels and others of
the group were acquitted by a Cologne jury, after defence speeches that
were mainly political expositions; but when the counterrevolution
gained confidence, the paper was suppressed by simple decree. In the
court case—as Engels wrote much later—they attacked "the monstrous
notion that anyone can place himself outside the common law by
maintaining an opinion. This is the pure police-state. . . ."[14]

As the *NRZ* began its third week, Engels asked what the revolution
had won, besides bringing the big bourgeoisie to governmental power:

* Marx was also acquainted with the government device of allegedly suppressing
only "false" statements by the press. This became prominent under the Bonaparte
dictatorship in France, which claimed to be for freedom of the press to tell the "truth"
but not its freedom to tell "lies". In an 1858 article Marx derisively quoted the Bonapartist press: "The duty of the press is to enlighten the public, and not deceive it," and
demonstrated that this was only a façade for the principle that the duty of the press is
to obey the government's orders on how to deceive the public.[12]

"It gave the people the weapon of freedom of the press without security-bonds, the right of organization,* and partly at least also the material weapon, the musket," he answered.[15] Marx and Engels saw freedom of the press as a barometer of governmental arbitrariness, among other things. When the Hansemann ministry submitted an "interim law" to regulate the press, i.e. to muzzle criticism, Marx wrote that "in short, we again meet the most classic monuments to the Napoleonic despotism over the press", and—

> "From the day this law goes into effect, government officials can with impunity commit any arbitrary act, any tyranny, any illegality; they can calmly administer or permit floggings, or make arrests, or hold without trial; the only effective control, the press, is rendered ineffectual. On the day this law goes into effect, the bureaucracy can hold a celebration: it becomes more powerful and unrestrained, stronger than it was before March."[16]

As the government tried "to cheat the revolution of its democratic fruits",[17] the *NRZ* was the loudest voice raised in Germany. In July the government suppressed the club movement in two cities; Engels warned:

> "You believe you have finished with the police-state? Delusion!—You believe you possess the right of free assembly, freedom of the press, arming of the people, and other fine slogans that were shouted from the March barricades? Delusion, nothing but delusion!"[18]

As the government was in process of chopping off the "democratic fruits" of the revolution, a militia bill was proposed which would restrict the rights of its citizen members to nearly nothing. Marx asked: What does this mean for the citizen militiaman?

> "The worthy man has gotten arms and uniform on the condition of renouncing above all his prime political rights, the right to organize, etc. His task of protecting 'constitutional liberty' will be fulfilled in accordance with the 'spirit of his destiny' when he blindly executes the orders of the authorities, when he exchanges the customary civil liberty that was tolerated even under the absolute monarchy for the passive, will-less and self-less obedience of the soldier. A fine school in which to bring up the republicans of the future! . . . What has our *citizen* been made into? A thing somewhere between a Prussian gendarme and an English constable. . . . Instead of disbanding the army into the people, wasn't it an original idea to disband the people into the army?
>
> "It is truly a bizarre spectacle, this *transformation of constitutional phrases into Prussian realities*."[19]

The *NRZ* carried on other campaigns for democratic rights against government pressure, including the Frankfurt Left's programme for "immediate establishment, proclamation and guarantee of the fundamental rights of the German people against all possible attacks by the

* Lit., the "right of association"; so throughout.

individual governments [of the German states]". It criticized the Assembly liberals for being too vague on the issue of direct suffrage versus indirect suffrage, and denounced all anti-democratic forms of elections.[20]

For Marx and Engels, the right of assembly also meant the right of the people to exercise pressure against their "own" representatives. This came into question when the right-wing press denounced the pressure put on the Prussian Assembly in Berlin by the presence of thousands at its deliberations. Marx wrote:

> "The right of the democratic mass of the people to exert a moral influence on the attitude of the constituent assembly is an old revolutionary right of the people which, since the English and French revolutions, could not be dispensed with in any period of stormy action. It is to this right that history owes almost all energetic steps taken by such assemblies. If . . . the fainthearted and philistine friends of 'freedom of deliberations' wail against it, the only basis they have is that they don't want any energetic decisions taken anyway."

This alleged "freedom of deliberations" is infringed, argued Marx, on the one side by the pressures from the existing state and its army, courts, etc. And likewise "the 'freedom of deliberations' is infringed by freedom of the press, by freedom of assembly and speech, by the right of the people to bear arms" on the other side, since these too exercise unwanted pressure on the representatives. Between the two species of "intimidation", the representatives have only this choice: "Intimidation by the unarmed people or intimidation by the armed soldiery: let the Assembly choose."[21]

The Maximization of Democratic Control

But should a government permit activities, even such as are sanctified by democratic rights, which may result in its own overthrow? Marx and Engels' answer was: If the exercise of the people's rights endangers the government, then so much the worse for the government. Governments have a habit of believing that activities dangerous to them are infringements on "liberty"—namely, their own "liberty" to exist. Marx did not believe that the people were called on to sacrifice their own rights in order to relieve the government's problem:

> "The 'Ministry of Action' [Hansemann ministry] seems to espouse peculiar oriental-mystical notions, a kind of Moloch cult. In order to protect the 'constitutional liberty' of presidents, burgomasters, police chiefs [a long list of government officials follows here] . . . in order to protect the 'constitutional liberty' of this elite of the nation, all the rest of the nation must let its constitutional liberties, up to and including personal liberty, die a bloody death as a sacrifice on the altar of the fatherland. Pends-toi, Figaro! Tu n'aurais pas inventé cela!"*[22]

* This catch-line, adapted from Beaumarchais, amounts to a sarcastic "What a brilliant idea!"

The next day's *NRZ* had a similar comment by Engels on another issue. A motion by the left liberal deputy Jacoby had proposed that the Assembly's decisions have the force of law without anyone else's consent: a crucial issue of the revolution. Deputy Berg had denounced this as the attempt by a parliamentary minority to win outside support, an attempt whose consequences "must lead to civil war". But, replied Engels, the "outsiders" who must not be appealed to—who were they? "The voters, i.e. the people who *make* the legislative body."

> "In a word: Herr Berg's principle would lead to the abolition of all political agitation. Agitation is nothing more than the application of representatives' immunity, freedom of the press, right to organize—i.e. the liberties now juridically in existence in Prussia. Whether these liberties do or do not lead to civil war is not our concern; it is enough that they exist, and we shall see where it 'leads' if the attack on them continues."[23]

A week later, the question came up again, on an even more fateful issue. Local Democratic Associations were being suppressed by the governments, first in Stuttgart and Heidelberg, now in Baden; this made a mockery of the Assembly's phrases about the right to organize.

> "The basic condition [wrote Engels] of the free right of organization is that no association or society can be dissolved or prohibited by the police, that this can take place only as a result of a judicial verdict establishing the illegality of the association or of its acts and aims and punishing the authors of these acts."[24]

What was the government's ground?

> "The motivations given for this new act of police violence are extremely edifying. The Associations wanted to affiliate to the organization of Democratic Associations for all Germany, set up by the Democratic Congress at Frankfurt. This congress 'set a democratic republic as its goal' (as if that is forbidden!) 'and the means envisaged to attain this goal flow, among other things, from the sympathy expressed in those resolutions in favour of the agitators' (since when is 'sympathy' an illegal 'means'?)....
> "According to Herr Mathy [liberal Baden politician], the Associations in Baden are therefore responsible for the resolutions of the Central Committee [of the Democratic Associations] *even if they have not put them into practice.*"

Mathy had argued further that it "seems inadmissible and pernicious for the foundation of the constitution to be undermined and thus the whole state structure shaken by the Associations' power". Engels commented:

> "The right to organize, Herr Mathy, exists precisely so that one can 'undermine' the constitution with impunity—in legal form, of course. And if the Associations' power is greater than that of the state, so much the worse for the state!"[25]

Another vital issue on which the *NRZ* hit hard was a corollary of the "sovereignty of the people", viz. the sovereignty of the Assembly elected by the people, as against the power of the government set up by the Crown. The revolution had given rise to two lines of power which were diverging, wrote Engels:

> "The results of the revolution were, on one hand, the arming of the people, the right of organization, the *de facto* achievement of popular sovereignty; on the other, the maintenance of the monarchy and the Camphausen-Hansemann ministry, i.e. the government of the representatives of the big bourgeoisie.
> "The revolution thus had two series of results which necessarily had to diverge. The people had been victorious, they had won freedoms of a decisively democratic nature; but the immediate ruling power passed not into their hands but into the big bourgeoisie's.
> "In short, the revolution was not completed."[26]

Marx and Engels' line was strongly for all power to the Assembly as the representation of popular sovereignty, as against the Assembly majority's goal of a deal with the Crown. The Jacoby motion, previously mentioned, that the Assembly's decisions should have the force of law without further ado, was a *sine qua non*. It would be incredible to other peoples, wrote Engels, that the German assembly had to debate a motion asserting that it is sovereign with respect to the government. "But we are in the land of the oak and linden, and so we should not be easily astonished by anything." The Assembly was "irresolute, flabby and lackadaisical".[27]

Marx presented the revolutionary-democratic proposal in terms of the concentration of both legislative and governmental (executive) power in the hands of the people's elected representatives. The Radical wing of the Assembly, he wrote, was calling for a governmental executive "elected for a period determined *by* the National Assembly and responsible to it". But that was not enough. This executive power must be selected out of the ranks of the Assembly itself, as was demanded by the left-wingers among the Radicals. Since the National Assembly was a constituent body—i.e. no constitution as yet existed—there could be no government except the Assembly itself: "it is the National Assembly itself that must govern".[28] Above all, it must take the initiative away from the governments of the German states:

> "A national constituent assembly must above all be an *activist*, revolutionary-activist assembly. The assembly in Frankfurt does parliamentary school-exercises and lets the governments act. Supposing that this learned council succeeds after the maturest deliberations in figuring out the best agenda and the best constitution, what were the good of the best agenda and the constitution if in the meantime the governments put the bayonet on the agenda?"[29]

This course was driven home as the *NRZ* analysed the Assembly debates.[30] If the Assembly declined to take over all the powers of the state, if in particular it was even deprived of the right to exercise control over the executive through its commissions of inquiry, then this amounted to "a renunciation of the sovereignty of the people."[31] The issue of the deputies' immunity from arrest by the government was one very concrete aspect of the question of sovereignty: the *NRZ* campaigned for full and unabridged immunity with no loopholes[32].

But in fact, instead of the Assembly's taking over executive power, it was the governmental power that used every means to strengthen itself. Marx used the Militia Bill as an example: the idea of a popular militia was converted into a plan for a bureaucratic force.

"Prussian perspicacity has nosed out that every new constitutional institution offers a most interesting occasion for new penal laws, new regulations, new disciplinary measures, new surveillance, new chicanery, and a new bureaucracy."[33]

This reflects a leitmotiv of Marx's attitude toward the problems of democratization: minimization of the executive power, the state bureaucracy—maximization of the weight in the governmental structure of the representative system. And not only in the period of revolution.

Analysis of a Constitution

It was in the decade following the defeat of the 1848–9 revolutions that Marx wrote most extensively on specific problems of constitutional democratic forms. What emerged particularly was this principle: one of the chief marks of a truly democratic constitution was the degree to which it *limited and restrained the independent scope of the executive power*.

This follows naturally from the view that democracy is genuine insofar as it means popular control from below. Let us see how the point is made in a number of rather detailed criticisms which Marx made of particular constitutions.

The first such constitutional analysis by Marx, written in 1851, dealt with "The Constitution of the French Republic Adopted November 4, 1848".* The main fraud in this constitution, repeatedly pointed out by Marx, is that it leaves room for its alleged democratic guarantees to be nullified by subsequent laws put through by the governmental power.

Here is his first example of the type of provision which pretends to

* This article was written by Marx for Ernest Jones' paper as part of a series on "The Constitutions of Europe". It is therefore very specifically concerned with the exact provisions of the document, thus providing a supplement to the broader political analysis of this constitution which Marx had written the year before, in his *Class Struggles in France*.[34] A year later, Marx, reviewing the same history in *The Eighteenth Brumaire*, included the constitutional points too, as discussed below.

establish a democratic right but vitiates itself by allowing for "exceptions made by law".

" '§3. The residence of every one on French territory is inviolable—and it is not allowed to enter it otherwise than in the forms prescribed by law.'
"Observe here and throughout that the French constitution guarantees liberty, but always with the proviso *of exceptions made by law*, or which may STILL BE MADE!"[35]

Another provision ensures freedom of association, opinion, press, etc. but it adds, "The enjoyment of these rights has no other limit, than the equal rights of others, and the public safety". Marx points to the last phrase as the joker:

"That the limitation made by the 'public safety', takes away the enjoyment of the right altogether, is clearly shewn by the following facts. . . . [Marx then cites what actually happened in France.]"

Again, the constitution says "The right of tuition is free."

"Here the old joke is repeated. 'Tuition is free', but 'under the conditions fixed by law', and these are precisely the conditions that take away the freedom altogether."[36]

And so on. Marx sums up the character of this constitution:

". . . from beginning to end it is a mass of fine words, hiding a most treacherous design. From its very wording, it is rendered *impossible* to violate it, for every one of its provisions contains its own antithesis—utterly nullifies itself. For instance: 'the vote is direct and universal',—'*excepting* those cases which the *law* shall determine'."

The repeated formula is that this or that freedom shall be determined by an "organic law" to be adopted—"and these 'organic laws' 'determine' the promised freedom by destroying it".[37]

The following year Marx incorporated the substance of this review of the French constitutional device in his *Eighteenth Brumaire*. After making the point and giving some examples, Marx writes that the "organic laws" regulated all the liberties granted "in such manner that the bourgeoisie in its enjoyment of them finds itself unhindered by the equal rights of the other classes". For anything that contravenes its own safety is obviously not "in the interest of public safety".

"In the sequel, both sides accordingly appeal with complete justice to the Constitution: the friends of order, who abrogated all these liberties, as well as the democrats, who demanded all of them. For each paragraph of the Constitution contains its own antithesis, its own Upper and Lower House, namely, liberty in the general phrase, abrogation of liberty in the marginal note. Thus, so long as the *name* of freedom was respected and only its actual realization prevented, of course in a legal way, the constitutional existence of liberty remained intact, inviolate, however mortal the blows dealt to its existence *in actual life*."[38]

In the 1851 article, Marx also included a powerful denunciation of another device by which the government bureaucracy exercised *de facto* control over the liberties of the individual regardless of constitutional or other façades. This device is the internal passport and "labour book".

> "The excess of despotism reached in France will be apparent by the following regulations as to working men.
> "Every working man is supplied with a book by the police—the first page of which contains his name, age, birthplace, trade or calling, and a description of his person. He is therein obliged to enter the name of the master for whom he works, and the reasons why he leaves him. But this is not all: the book is placed in the master's hands, and deposited by him in the bureau of the police with the character of the man by the master. When a workman leaves his employment, he must go and fetch this book from the police office; and is not allowed to obtain another situation without producing it. Thus the workman's bread is utterly dependent on the police. But this again, is not all: this book serves the purpose of a passport. If he is obnoxious, the police write 'bon pour retourner chez lui' in it, and the workman is obliged to return to his parish! No comment is needed on this terrific revelation! Let the reader picture to himself its full working, and trace it to its actual consequences. No serfdom of the feudal ages—no pariahdom of India has its parallel. What wonder if the French people pant for the hour of insurrection. What wonder if their indignation take the aspect of a storm."[39]

Twenty years later Marx denounced the use of the same system by the Versaillese government; one of his counts against the police-state methods of the Thiers régime was "the reintroduction of passports for travelling from one place to another."[40] In both cases the French government used the internal-passport system for population control in the wake of a revolutionary upsurge.

Minimization of the Executive Power

In 1853 Marx analyzed the provisions in the new draft constitutions for Schleswig and Holstein, noting their undemocratic character. In addition, he notes that one of the "most remarkable paragraphs . . . deprives the courts of law of their ancient right of cancelling administrative decrees. . . ."[41]

Such provisions are bad because it is the "power of the bureaucracy" which has to be kept down: this is also spelled out in Marx's analysis, written in 1858, of the Prussian constitution of 1850. Once again he sees constitutional rights nullified by the freedom of action accorded to the executive power:

> "The question of ministerial responsibility possesses in Prussia, as it did in the France of Louis Philippe, an exceptional importance, because it means, in fact, the responsibility of bureaucracy. The ministers are the chiefs of that omnipotent, all-intermeddling parasitic body, and to them alone, according to article 106 of the Constitution, have the subaltern members of the administration to look, without taking

upon themselves to inquire into the legality of their ordinances, or incurring any
responsibility by executing them. Thus, the power of the bureaucracy, and by the
bureaucracy, of the executive, has been maintained intact, while the constitutional
'Rights of the Prussians' have been reduced to a dead letter."[42]

The Prussian reality, writes Marx, shows the gulf between constitutional theory and actual practice:

"Every step of yours, simple locomotion even, is tampered with by the omnipotent
action of bureaucracy, this second providence of genuine Prussian growth. You can
neither live nor die, nor marry, nor write letters, nor think, nor print, nor take to
business, nor teach, nor be taught, nor get up a meeting, nor build a manufactory,
nor emigrate, nor do any thing without '*obrigkeitliche Erlaubnis*'—permission on the
part of the authorities. As to the liberty of science or religion, or abolition of patri-
monial jurisdiction, or suppression of caste privileges, or the doing away with entails
and primogeniture, it is all mere bosh."

Marx explains why this is so in the same way as he explained the self-
vitiation of the French constitution of 1848: all the liberties are granted
only within "the limits of the law", which in this case means the
absolutist law predating the Constitution.

"Thus there exists a deadly antagonism between the law of the Constitution and the
constitution of the law, the latter reducing, in fact, the former to mere moonshine.
On the other hand, the Charter in the most decisive points refers to organic laws. . . .
They [the organic laws now adopted] have done away with guarantees even existing
at the worst times of the absolute Monarchy, with the independence, for instance, of
the Judges of the executive Government. Not content with these combined dis-
solvents, the old and the new-fangled laws, the Charter preserves to the King the
right of suspending it in all its political bearings, whenever he may think proper."[43]

This is the second time that we have seen Marx upholding the
independence of the courts against the executive power. It is clear,
however, that this is only one aspect of his advocacy of every possible
means of minimizing the autonomous power of the executive. In 1859
Marx wrote an analysis of the Hessian constitution of 1831 which
praised it as "the most liberal fundamental law ever proclaimed in
Europe", except for its undemocratic method of electing representatives.
Naturally, this praise was relative to the times; but what stirred this
enthusiastic description?

"There is no other Constitution which restrains the powers of the executive within
limits so narrow, makes the Administration more dependent on the Legislature, and
confides such a supreme control to the judicial benches."[44]

The article spells out the detailed reasons for this tribute, including
the fact that "the Courts of law, empowered to decide definitively upon
all the acts of the Executive, were rendered omnipotent". The courts

also have the final say "in all questions of bureaucratic discipline". The representatives can remove any minister declared guilty of misinterpreting its resolutions; the Prince's "right of grace" is shorn, and also his control over members of the Administration. "The Representative Chamber selects out of its members a permanent committee, forming a sort of Areopagus, watching and controlling the Government, and impeaching the officials for violation of the Constitution, no exception being granted on behalf of orders received by subalterns from their superiors in rank. In this way, the members of the bureaucracy were emancipated from the Crown." Military officers are similarly bound to the Constitution, not to the Crown. "The representation, consisting of one single Chamber, possesses the right of stopping all taxes, imposts and duties, on every conflict with the executive." Later, mentions Marx, the revolution of 1848–9 democratized the election forms and made two other improvements. Both of the latter were likewise directed against the power of the executive: "by putting the nomination of the members of the Supreme Court into the hands of the legislature, and, lastly, by taking out of the hands of the Prince the supreme control of the army, and making it over to the Minister of War, a personage responsible to the representatives of the people".

In the same article Marx points to another democratic feature of this constitution: "Communal councillors, nominated by popular election, had to administer not only the local, but also the general police." Over a decade later, Marx pointed to the Paris Commune's system of community control of the police as a democratic achievement.[45] In general, Marx's views on the minimization, or thorough subordination, of the executive power reached fullest expression in his analysis of the Paris Commune.

Safety-valves for the Bourgeoisie

Comments on various aspects of democratic rights are, of course, scattered through the later writings of Marx and Engels, though not the subject of any systematic work. Examples of aspects not yet mentioned may have some interest:

(1) *Freedom of opinion.* Discussing the Bonapartization of France in 1851, even before the coup d'état, Marx commented that the very last straw was the 1850 law which restored censorship of the drama. "Thus freedom of opinion was banished from its last literary refuge."[46]

(2) *Restrictions on voter eligibility.* In the same connection—the antidemocratic swing in France after the 1848 defeat—Marx noted two infringements dealing with voting limitations. The law of 31 May 1850 not only excluded political offenders "but it actually established domiciliary restrictions, by which TWO-THIRDS of the French people are incapable of voting"! A little further there is a related point: "By

the law of August 7, 1848, all those who cannot read and write are
erased from the jury list, thus disqualifying two-thirds of the adult
population!"[47]

In his article on the Schleswig and Holstein constitutions, Marx also
noted a related question: among the undemocratic restrictions is the
provision "making the right of election dependent on the holding of
landed property, and limiting its exercise by the condition of 'domicile'
in the respective electoral districts".[48] In his already mentioned article
on the Prussian constitution of 1850, he remarked that although it
allows payment of deputies and voting rights from the age of 25, "The
electoral rights, however, and the machinery of election, have been
managed in such a way as to exclude not only the bulk of the people,
but to subject the privileged remnant to the most unbridled bureaucratic interference. There are two degrees of election."[49]

(3) *Gerrymandering.* The "unbridled bureaucratic interference" in the
Prussian electoral system included more than the complicated system
of grouping voters by the amount of tax paid, etc.

"As if this complicated process of filtering was not sufficient, the bureaucracy has,
moreover, the right to divide, combine, change, separate and recompose the
electoral districts at pleasure. Thus, for instance, if there exists a town suspected of
liberal sympathies, it may be swamped by reactionary country votes, the Minister,
by simple ordinance, blending the liberal town with the reactionary country into the
same electoral district."

Marx concludes: "Such are the fetters which shackle the electoral
movement, and which, only in the great cities, can exceptionally be
broken through."[50]

(4) *Unicameralism.* In general, Marx was for a single representative
assembly, not the bicameral system devised to check the exuberance of
popular sovereignty. In his article on the Hessian constitution, he
noted approvingly that "The representation, consisting of one single
Chamber, possesses the right of stopping all taxes, imposts and duties,
on every conflict with the executive."[51]

(5) *Right to demonstrate.* The following case in point has a special
interest. In 1872 a Hyde Park demonstration was organized by Irish
members of the International, to demand a general amnesty. But at the
last session of Parliament the government had put through a law
regulating public meetings in parks: it required two days' prior
notification to the police, including the speakers' names. Engels wrote:

"This regulation carefully kept hidden from the London press destroyed with one
stroke of the pen one of the most precious rights of London's working people—the
right to hold meetings in parks when and how they please. To submit to this regulation would be to sacrifice one of the people's rights.

"The Irish, who represent the most revolutionary element of the population, were not men to display such weakness. The committee unanimously decided to act as if it did not know of the existence of this regulation and to hold their meeting in defiance of the Government's decree."[52]

The police decided not to intervene after all.

(6) *The informer system.* The use of informers, spies and stool-pigeons (*mouchards* in French and also in Marx and Engels most of the time) was, of course, the common instrument of the governments and a constant plague in the radical and labour movements. Here, however, is an important variant.

The Austrian commander in Milan, after suppressing an insurrection, decreed that anyone who failed to denounce another's illegal act was himself guilty. Marx reported this bitterly:

> "Whoever will not become a spy and informer for the Hapsburg shall be liable to become the lawful prey of the Croat [Austrian troops]. In a word, Radetsky proclaims a new system of wholesale plunder."[53]

(7) *Freedom in wartime.* After the outbreak of the Franco-Prussian war, Bebel and Liebknecht were arrested by the Bismarck government on charges of high treason—

> "simply because they dared to fulfil their duties as German national representatives, viz. to protest in the Reichstag against the annexation of Alsace and Lorraine, vote against new war subsidies, express their sympathy with the French Republic, and denounce the attempt at the conversion of Germany into one Prussian barrack."

So Marx, in a protest published in the London press. His letters also described the governmental repression of other anti-war socialists, and added:

> "The few independent German journals existing outside Prussia are forbidden admission into the Hohenzollern estates. German workmen's meetings in favour of a peace honourable for France are daily dispersed by the police. According to the official Prussian doctrine . . . every German 'trying to counteract the prospective aims of the Prussian warfare in France', is guilty of high treason."[54]

He compares the liberty existing in France (where the Empire had just been overthrown—it is the interlude between Sedan and the Paris Commune):

> "The French soil is infested by about a million of German invaders. Yet the French Government can safely dispense with that Prussian method of 'rendering possible the free expression of opinion'. Look at this picture and at that!"[55]

In truth, the French republican government could hardly do otherwise; it had come into being through a mass upsurge in the streets after

Sedan, and a revolution loomed before it. Revolutionary pressures ensured its democratic distinction from Prussianism.

In England, pressure against freedom in wartime was political. During the Crimean war, John Bright accused the government of undermining "the Parliamentary system of this country" by its intolerance of criticism. Marx commented:

> "It may be asked of what use this system is? Domestic questions must not be agitated because the country is at war. Because the country is at war, war must not be discussed. Then why remains Parliament? Old [William] Cobbett has revealed the secret. As a safety-valve for the effervescing passions of the country."[56]

It could be put more generally: for bourgeois democracy, not only a parliament but the whole structure of democratic rights and institutions was, in good part, "a safety-valve for the effervescing passions of the country". Or, as we put it in another connection in another part of the work, it was used as a means of containing popular pressures, not expressing them.

The "Democratic Swindle"

As in the case of most political problems, it is not possible to extract from Marx and Engels' writings a systematic account of what Marx called the "democratic swindle"—the methods whereby the bourgeoisie utilized (used and abused) democratic forms for the purpose of stabilizing its socio-economic rule; besides the present and preceding chapters, aspects of the subject will emerge subsequently. But a couple of basic points may be made here.

The "democratic swindle" was a swindle not insofar as it was democratic but, on the contrary, insofar as it utilized democratic forms to frustrate genuine democratic control from below. The phrase itself comes from a reference by Marx to the country which, he well understood, was the *most* democratic in constitutional form at this time: the United States. It was, indeed, "the model country of the democratic swindle"[57] not because it was less democratic than others but for precisely the opposite reason. The fact that the US had developed the formal structure of the constitutional republic in the most democratic forms meant that its bourgeoisie likewise had to develop to its highest point the art of keeping the expression of popular opinion within channels satisfactory to its class interests.

In Marx's time there was no problem about putting the finger on the main method of this enterprise: the system of rank political corruption mentioned in the preceding chapter. As long as it was possible to work it, within the cadre of a country that was expanding economically and geographically, social explosions could be avoided. The expense was worth while to gain "a safety-valve for the effervescing passions of the country".

The expense of buying up public opinion, however, should not be confused with the expensiveness on a social scale of a democratic structure as against an authoritarian one. Other things being equal, a democratic state form is cheaper to operate than a despotism; as long as it is possible, it is a bargain for a ruling class interested in keeping down overhead costs. This is true not only in terms of hard cash outlay (necessary for any swollen state apparatus) but also in terms of intangibles, such as the willing interest of the mass of the population in cooperating in their own exploitation. Marx pointed to the difference in his polemic against the liberal Heinzen:

> "The monarchy involves great expenses. No doubt. Just take a look at governmental finances in North America and compare them with what our 38 duodecimo fatherlands [the German states] have to pay for being administered and kept under discipline!"[58]

In England the main representatives of the bourgeoisie in politics aim ideally at bargain-rate government, and therefore—

> "to these champions of the British Bourgeoisie, to the men of the Manchester School, every institution of Old England appears in the light of a piece of machinery as costly as it is useless, and which fulfills no other purpose but to prevent the nation from producing the greatest possible quantity at the least possible expense, and to exchange its products in freedom. Necessarily their last word is the Bourgeois Republic, in which free competition rules supreme in all spheres of life; in which there remains altogether that *minimum* only of government which is indispensable for the administration, internally and externally, of the common class interest and business of the Bourgeoisie; and where this minimum of government is as soberly, as economically organized as possible. Such a party, in other countries, would be called *democratic*."[59]

Time and again Marx or Engels analysed bourgeois-democratic politics as an exercise in convincing a maximum of the people that they were participating in state power, by means of a minimum of concessions to democratic forms. On the eve of the 1848 revolution—the preceding November, to be exact—Engels took up the programmatic manifesto issued by Lamartine, the poet-politician who headed the moderate republican party.

> "What, then, is the meaning of the political measures proposed by M. de Lamartine? To give the government into the hands of the inferior *bourgeoisie*, but under the semblance of giving it to the whole people (this, and nothing else, is the meaning of his universal suffrage, with his double system of elections)."[60]

The century saw a plethora of clever electoral systems devised to insert a manipulative factor into the forms of a more or less universal suffrage, beginning with the American Constitution. As Engels indicated in the case of Lamartine, the mechanisms were calibrated to achieve a single type of effect: *How far down in the social scale, in the hands of what class or class stratum, was political power expected to reside?* This was the link between the class struggle and often technical-sounding questions of constitutional forms; that is, between a political programme in the narrow sense and a social programme. A movement that aimed to place political power in the hands of the working-class masses could afford to press for complete democratization with no twists.

Toward the Socialization of Democracy

Lamartine, wrote Engels, might be able to inspire poets and philosophers with enthusiasm for "his system of graduated election, poor rate, and philanthrophic charity", but not the people.

> "The principles, indeed, of social and political regeneration have been found fifty years ago. Universal suffrage, direct election, paid representation—these are the essential conditions of political sovereignty. . . . What we want, is not English middle-class expediency, but quite a new system of social economy, to realize the rights and satisfy the wants of all."[61]

This was published in a Chartist paper and written for the eyes of Chartist workers, who were indeed already battling for what was then the political programme of the democratic extremists. But Engels' friends in the left wing of Chartism, Harney and Jones above all, were fighting for "the Charter and Something Else", i.e. for the extension of the democratic idea to a social programme. This, of course, had been what Engels had also urged since his arrival in England. As we have seen,[62] he began by counterposing "communism" *against* democracy, in the wake of Proudhon and Weitling. By 1844 he had corrected this to advocating going over from mere political democracy to a more basic social transformation.

In an 1844 article which Engels wrote for a German paper in Paris, he analysed the constitutional forms of British democracy in this spirit.* Conceding that "England is undoubtedly the freest, that is, the least unfree country in the world, North America not excepted", he undertook an examination of the methods and forms of the political system "on purely empirical lines", to show how the structure is designed toward "making concessions merely in order to preserve this derelict structure as long as possible", and maintaining the rule of the middle class in partnership with the progressive-minded aristocracy.[63] Since

---

* This was *before* Engels teamed up with Marx, and while he was still denouncing "all state forms" in principle, in anarchoid language which can be found in the same article. The contradiction is striking.

the representative chamber, the House of Commons, wielded all power (he thought), it followed that "England should be a pure democracy, if only the democratic element itself were really democratic". It is the latter condition that he subjects to detailed analysis, measuring constitutional and formal pretensions against the "empirical" facts of class power. His conclusion is that "The Englishman is not free because of the law, but despite the law, if he can be considered free at all",[64] for it is the constant threat from below that ensures the recognition of democratic rights in practice.

It is, he argues, likewise the struggle of classes which will move matters still further:

> "The struggle is already on. The constitution has been shaken in its foundations. How things will turn out in the near future can be seen from what has been said. The new alien elements in the constitution are of a democratic nature; public opinion too, as time will show, develops in accordance with the democratic side; England's near future is democracy.
>
> "But what a democracy! Not that the French Revolution, whose antithesis was the monarchy and feudalism, but that democracy whose antithesis is the middle class and property. This is evident from the entire preceding development. The middle class and property are in power; the poor man is bereft of rights, oppressed and sweated; the constitution disowns him, the law maltreats him; the struggle of democracy against the aristocracy in England is the struggle of the poor against the rich. The democracy which England is heading for is a *social* democracy.
>
> "But mere democracy is unable to remedy social evils. Democratic equality is a chimera, the struggle of the poor against the rich cannot be fought out on the ground of democracy or politics in general. Hence this stage too is only a transition, the last purely political measure that still is to be tried and from which a new element must immediately develop, a principle transcending everything political.
>
> "This principle is the principle of socialism."[65]

"Mere democracy" is merely *political* democracy, democracy which stops with governmental forms and does not extend to the "social question", to the democratization of socio-economic life.

In sum: Marx and Engels always saw the two sides of the complex of democratic institutions and rights which arose under bourgeois democracy. The two sides corresponded to the two classes which fought it out within this framework. One side was the utilization of democratic forms as a cheap and versatile means of keeping the exploited masses from shaking the system, of providing the illusion of participation in the state while the economic sway of the ruling class ensured the real centres of power. This was the side of the "democratic swindle". The other side was the struggle to give the democratic forms a new *social* (class) content, above all by pushing them to the democratic extreme of popular control from below, which in turn entailed extending the application of democratic forms out of the merely political sphere into the organization of the whole society.

In any case, the key was popular control from below. This phrase was best translated by Marx in a comment on a slippery slogan, the Lassallean catchword of a "free state". Taking it literally, Marx replied that we do not want a *state* that is free, but rather a state that is completely subordinate to society.

> "Free state—what is this?
> "It is by no means the aim of the workers, who have got rid of the narrow mentality of humble subjects, to set the state free. In the [Bismarckian] German Empire the 'state' is almost as 'free' as in Russia. Freedom consists in converting the state from an organ superimposed upon society into one completely subordinate to it, and today, too, the forms of state are more or less free to the extent that they restrict the 'freedom of the state'."[66]

This proposes a basic test for, and measure of, freedom in the sense of popular control from below, and it applies equally before and after the social revolution.

NOTES

MEW	= Marx-Engels *Werke*, Berlin, Dietz, 1961–8. (Vol. and page no. abbreviated in colon form; e.g. 2:363 = Vol. 2, p. 363.)
ME:SW	= Marx-Engels, *Selected Works in three volumes*, Moscow, Progress Pub., 1969–70.
ME: *Art. Brit.*	= Marx-Engels, *Articles on Britain*. Moscow, Progress Pub., 1971.
NRZ	= *Neue Rheinische Zeitung*.
NYT	= *New York (Daily) Tribune*.
ME	= Marx and Engels.
M/E	= Marx or Engels.

1. A. D. Lindsay, *Karl Marx's Capital* (London, 1937,), 105.
2. This refers to Marx's 1843 manuscript; in the O'Malley translation (the only complete one available, Cambridge University Press, 1970), pp. 30–1 are especially relevant.
3. See my *The Two Souls of Socialism* (Berkeley, 1966; or in *New Politics*, Winter 1966, 57–84).
4. ME: *The German Ideology* (Moscow, P.P., 1964), 362.
5. M: "The Association for Administrative Reform", in ME: *Art. Brit.*, 236–7.
6. E. to M., 9 March 1847, MEW 27:78.
7. E. in NRZ, 1 June 1848, MEW 5:14.
8. Ibid., 15–17.
9. For Ruge's political evolution, see W. J. Brazill, *The Young Hegelians* (Yale U.P., 1970), 256–9.
10. E. in NRZ, 3 September 1848, MEW 5:358.
11. For the first number, see M/E in NRZ, 1 June 1848, MEW 5:18; besides the passages quoted further along, there was constant emphasis on the issue, e.g. E. in NRZ, 20 July 1848, MEW 5:238.
12. M: "France", in NYT, 30 April 1858.
13. M. in NRZ, 11 July 1848, MEW 5:200.

14. E: Preface to *Karl Marx vor den Kölner Geschwornen* (1885), in MEW 21:201.
15. E. in NRZ, 15 June 1848, MEW 5:68–9.
16. M. in NRZ, 20 July 1848, MEW 5:241.
17. M/E in NRZ, 23 June 1848, MEW 5:97.
18. E. in NRZ, 20 July 1848, MEW 5:238.
19. M. in NRZ, 21 July 1848, MEW 5:244–5.
20. M/E in NRZ, 7 June 1848, MEW 5:39; M. in NRZ, 2 June 1848, MEW 5:23; M/E in NRZ, 4 June 1848, MEW 5:30.
21. M/E in NRZ, 17 September 1848, MEW 5:406–7.
22. M. in NRZ, 21 July 1848, MEW 5:251.
23. E. in NRZ, 22 July 1848, MEW 5:229.
24. E. in NRZ, 28 July 1848, MEW 5:276.
25. Ibid., 276–7.
26. E. in NRZ, 14 June 1848, MEW 5:64–5.
27. E. in NRZ, 18 June 1848, MEW 5:222–3.
28. M/E in NRZ, 7 June 1848, MEW 5:39–40.
29. Ibid., 40.
30. E.g. in E. in NRZ, 8 June 1848, MEW 5:49, 52.
31. M/E in NRZ, 8 June 1848, MEW 5:53.
32. M/E in NRZ, 19 June 1848, MEW 5:83; ditto 21 June 1848, MEW 5:90–3.
33. M. in NRZ, 21 July 1848, MEW 5:245.
34. M: *Class Struggles in France*, in ME:SW 1:233–6.
35. M: "The Constitution of the French Republic [etc.]", in *Notes to the People*, No. 7, June 1851, Vol. 1, p. 125.
36. Ibid., p. 126.
37. Ibid., p. 129.
38. M: *Eighteenth Brumaire of L. B.*, in ME:SW 1:409.
39. M: "The Constitution of the French Republic . . .", 129.
40. M: *Civil War in France*, First Draft, in ME: *Writings on the Paris Commune*, ed. Draper (N.Y., 1971), 134.
41. M. in NYT, 5 November 1853 (untitled article).
42. M: "Affairs in Prussia", NYT, 8 November 1858.
43. M: "Affairs in Prussia", NYT, 3 November 1858.
44. M: "Trouble in Germany", NYT, 2 December 1859.
45. M: *Civil War in France*, First Draft, in ME: *Writings on the Paris Commune*, 152; and Second Draft, ibid., 200. For the final version, see ME:SW 2:220.
46. M: "The Constitution of the French Republic . . ." 126.
47. Ibid., 127, 128. See also M: *Eighteenth Brumaire*, in ME:SW 1:408.
48. M. in NYT, 5 November 1853 (untitled article).
49. M: "Affairs in Prussia", NYT, 8 November 1858.
50. Ibid.
51. M: "Trouble in Germany", NYT, 2 December 1859.
52. E: "Letters from London, 3", in ME: *Art. Brit.*, 364.
53. M: "The Attack on Francis Joseph [etc.]," NYT, 8 March 1853.
54. M: Letter to *Daily News*, 19 January 1871, in ME: *Selected Corr.*, 2nd ed. (Moscow, P.P., 1965), 254–55.
55. Ibid., 255.
56. M. in NYT, 12 June 1854 (untitled).
57. Letter, M. to E., 7 September 1864, in ME: *The Civil War in the US*. 3rd ed. (N.Y., Citadel Press, 1961), 271.
58. M: "Die moralisierende Kritik [etc.]", 1847, in MEW 4:348.
59. M: "The Chartists", NYT, 25 August 1852, in ME: *Art. Brit.*, 117–18.
60. E: "The Manifesto of M. de Lamartine", in MEGA I, 6:339.
61. Ibid., 340.

62. [In a previous chapter.]
63. E: "The Condition of England: 2. The English Constitution", in ME: *Art. Brit.*, 32, 33, 34, 41.
64. Ibid., 38, 57.
65. Ibid., 57–8, revised after MEW 1:592.
66. M: "Critique of the Gotha Programme", in ME:SW 3:25.

GRAMSCI AND LENIN 1917–1922

Alastair Davidson

I

ANTONIO GRAMSCI was twenty-six at the beginning of 1917.[1] The "sewer of his past" on whose seething resentments he had built a "sardist" view of the world ("Into the sea with the Italians") only showed in too many coffees and cigarettes and an enormous capacity for work. He had given up his "sardist" world-view for what he and a great many other educated Italians regarded as a satisfactory view of the world: "crocianism". Throughout 1917 Gramsci was still "crocian in his views",[2] although he had been a Socialist for over three years and was working full-time for the Socialist newspapers *Avanti* and *Grido del Popolo*, although his "crocian" friends of university days had gone to war, and although he had considerable contact with workers, who were always dropping in from the nearby Casa del Popolo to see him because he "had the great gift of knowing how to talk to everybody".[3]

Theoretically, he agreed with the views in Benedetto Croce's recent *Teoria delle storia della storiografia*. In particular these were: 1) a rejection of positivism as inverted idealism; 2) a consequent rejection of any history which claimed to relate what truly happened once and for all; and therefore 3) a belief that all immanent world-views had been "thought up" in terms of the contemporary level of knowledge.[4] It followed that Gramsci believed that men were never the prisoners of their past in the sense that they could not free themselves through their own wilful actions, but only be freed by some structural conjunction of events. They could, of course, well be the prisoners of their understanding of that past, and therefore fail to comprehend the realities of their present situation. Gramsci's theoretical and emotional beliefs are summed up in words he wrote in early 1917: "For natural laws, the fatal progress of things of pseudo-scientists, has been substituted the tenacious will of men", and in rather more moralizing tones: "Some people whimper pitifully, others curse obscenely, but none, or few, ask themselves: if I had done my duty, if I had attempted to impose my will, my opinion, would what has happened have happened?—I hate the apathetic."[5]

This theoretical rejection of determinism was, however, only a "starting point" for Gramsci, who proceeded through the crocian view that contemporary levels of knowledge were based on contemporary needs, and through the theory of Giovanni Gentile of the "act", to that variety of marxism which best accorded with the notion that the revolution would not come automatically but would have to be made in a conscious wilful act by men who understood that the cause of their misery was capitalism. By 1917 he had found this in the interpretation of Antonio Labriola, who denied that marxism described the "apocalyptic" workings of history and claimed that it was a theory based on the historical need for socialism and marked a stage in men's understanding of their situation. Labriola typified this view overall as a "philosophy of praxis", thus stressing the affinity between his concerns and those of the early Croce, who had also written a *Philosophy of Practice*.[6] Influenced by Labriola's work, Gramsci, who had read by 1917 Marx's: *Holy Family*; *The Poverty of Philosophy*; *The Communist Manifesto*; *Revolution and Counter-Revolution in Germany* and a *Contribution to the Critique of Political Economy*, was even able to dub Engels' *Anti-Duhring* a humanist work, and within a year to endorse firmly Labriola's belief that *Capital* was "not the first great book of critical theory but the last great book of political economy".[7] From the Labriolan position that the revolution would take place only when men "understood and overcame"[8] (taken directly from Hegel), Gramsci had reached the ideological concerns which really interested him in 1917: how to make men "understand and overcome".

Ideologically, Gramsci was influenced by Charles Péguy and Romain Rolland, both of whom agreed with the proposition that "Fate is the excuse of men without wills" and who preached on a more practical level the same sort of views and morality as Croce. This amounted above all to the belief that it was the task of the intellectuals (and Gramsci defined himself as an intellectual) to tear the veil of misunderstanding from men's eyes and help build the "City of God".[9] Gramsci endorsed this notion, and consequently, that the main socialist task was education. After he got his first job on *Avanti* in 1916 he argued in a series of important articles that: "The problem of education is the most important class-problem" and that ". . . the first step in emancipating oneself from political and social slavery is that of freeing the mind". This education was necessary because it was clear from history that such freedom did not come according to a "fatal law" or spontaneous evolution. Man was "above all mind, historical creation and not nature" and all his knowledge of himself had been obtained as the result of "intelligent reflection" on the nature of social oppression, first by "a few men" and only later, after "an immense labour of criticism and cultural penetration", by the many, who initially resisted the new ideas. Gramsci pointed to the enlightenment for proof of his proposition that revolutions only took place after this "immense labour"—in Italy, Napoleon had found his way paved for him "by an invisible army of books, which had prepared men". The initial labour of education which Gramsci proposed was directed not to having men acquire masses of facts but to attaining that self-knowledge which would enable them to realize their "own historical value", their "own function in life", their "rights and duties".[10]

In 1917 he was still preaching these views forcefully through *Grido del Popolo* and in the single issue of *Citta Futura*, the journal of the Youth Federation of the Italian Socialist Party, but his attention was beginning to shift to the practical application of his educational programme as well.[11] This brought him to the crucial question of the *method* or *mode* of this educative process. His answer was the completely traditional, and idealist, method of indoctrination through the press, lectures and seminars.

Practically, he engaged in "cultural messianism" among the young members of the party. He lectured frequently to the Youth Federation and the workers of Turin, urging them to read Croce or even reflect on Marcus Aurelius's character (!). He ran study circles on Marx, and in December 1917 formed the Club di Vita Morale, whose activities he described in these terms: "At Turin we believe that preaching about the principles and moral maxims which should necessarily become established with the coming of a socialist civilization is not enough. We have tried to give this preaching an organized form; to give new examples (for Italy) of how to work together. So the Club de Vita Morale has recently emerged. Through it we propose to accustom young people in the socialist movement to dispassionate discussion about social and ethical problems. We want them to become used to research, to read in a methodical and disciplined fashion, to expound their convictions simply and with equanimity. It works out like this: I, who have had to accept the role of *excubitor*, because I began the association, assign a paper to some young person: a chapter of Croce's 'Cultura e Vita morale'; Salvemini's 'Problemi educativi e sociali' or his *French Revolution* or 'Cultura e laicita', the *Communist Manifesto* or the Commentary of Croce in *Critica* or something else, which, however, reflects the existing idealist movement: then I or someone else replies."[12]

This "cultural messianism"—the practical outcome of Gramsci's "crocian" "starting point"—was completely against the current at the time. The Club lasted three meetings. The bulk of young socialists still preferred Mussolini's and Bordiga's view that "class-consciousness" came through struggle and not from any cultural policy. In 1912 Bordiga had proclaimed scornfully that: "The need for study should be proclaimed in a congress of school-teachers, not socialists. You don't become a socialist through instruction but through experiencing the real needs of the class to which you belong", and Mussolini proclaimed even more bluntly that it would be good riddance if all the "brains" in the Socialist Party left.[13] Faced with continuous failure, Gramsci had started by 1918 tentatively to question "cultural messianism", in principle, if not in practice.[14] But in 1917 his views on the levels of theory, ideology and practice were still comparatively homogeneous. He was already a man with formed opinions when he first faced the implicit and explicit teachings of the Russian revolutions. He believed that men made revolutions in acts of collective will; that the main problem was to make them see that they could change the world, and he had therefore engaged in an activity of "moral re-education" which had, however, not gone much beyond a series of "didactic homilies" which workers found difficult to stomach and which they rejected.

II

The news of the February revolution only gradually crept through the wartime censorship and not until April 1917 did Gramsci publish his first known commentary on its significance. He denied outright that it was a bourgeois revolution. "We are persuaded that the Russian revolution is proletarian in character, as it has been so far in its deeds, and that it will naturally result in a socialist régime."[15] We need not dwell on whether this was a correct assessment or not—perhaps Gramsci already perceived that the bourgeois February revolution would develop into the proletarian October revolution. However, it is clear that in one sense he quite misunderstood what was going on. Although he had heard of Lenin before 1917, he saw Chernov as the leading practical revolutionary of the Russian "maximalists". Lenin was the ". . . master of life, the stirrer of consciences, the awakener of sleeping souls. Chernov is the realizer, the man with the concrete programme to put into practice, an entirely socialist programme which permits no collaboration, which cannot be accepted by the bourgeoisie because it destroys the system of private property, because it finally begins the socialist revolution, the entry into world history of collectivist socialism".[16]

This misunderstanding was not his fault entirely, or that of the censorship. His major source of information at this time about the revolutions and Russia generally was *Avanti*, which had started to rely on the reports of an emigré Russian, Vassily Suchomlin, for its explanation of what was occurring in Russia. Suchomlin's loyalties were to the Social-Revolutionaries of that country and not only strongly biased in their favour, but also biased against Lenin.[17] Gramsci's fundamental misunderstanding indicates, however, how little he knew about the history or contemporary developments of Russian socialism. Not only was a "crocian" facing the implications of the February revolution, but a "crocian" who knew very little about the men who were making the revolution. As if to make up for these errors of fact, Gramsci showed an enthusiastic preference for Lenin from July onwards, dubbing him the "tomorrow of the revolution" and ascribing to him the task of preventing any compromise between the "Idea" and the incubus of the past.[18]

It is important to note at this juncture that before he had any real idea about what was going on in Russia, he had already begun an interpretation of Lenin, identifying him in "crocian" terms as the bearer of the "Idea". He continued to find a Lenin who shared his views even in 1918 when the more reliable Balabanoff had replaced Suchomlin as *Avanti*'s Russian correspondent. This Lenin was the "practical expression" of "our Marx", whom Gramsci described in May 1918 as "not a Messiah who left a string of parables laden with categorical imperatives and absolutely incontrovertible norms outside the categories of time and space. The only categorical imperative, the single norm, is 'workers of the world unite'."[19] The Bolsheviks, whom he had by now identified correctly as the practitioners of revolution, "live marxist thought, the part of it which cannot die, that part which is the continuation of German and Italian idealism, and which in Marx himself became contaminated by positivistic and naturalistic encrustations. And this thought considers not economic facts the main force in history, but man, the society of men, of men who are close to each other, who understand each other, and develop through these contacts [civilization] a social and collective will and understand, judge and order to their wishes these economic facts, so that their wishes become the motor of the economy." He summed up the theoretical conclusions he was drawing from the Bolshevik revolution in the title he gave to the article in which these words appeared: "The Revolt against *Capital*."[20] This view was again made clear in these lines of July 1918: "If you find Lenin a utopian, if you say that the attempt to set up the dictatorship of the proletariat in Russia is a utopian effort, you cannot be a socialist, who is aware, and who builds up his culture by studying the doctrine of historical materialism: you are a Catholic, bogged down in the *Syllabus*: you are the only utopian really.

"Utopia consists precisely in not being able to see history as free development."

In sum, the main lesson he drew from the Bolshevik revolution, even in 1918, was that it showed that history was free development, and this lesson endorsed the educative policies he had been following in the Italian proletariat. He denied that much could be learnt from the particular facts of the Bolshevik revolution, at least until some years had gone by and it could be the object of mature reflection.[21]

Yet at about the same time he decided that "what is happening in Russia shows us the way" and started to "seek for" the works of Lenin to discover how the Russian had educated the masses to a level where a socialist revolution could be conducted when "cultural messianism" alone obviously did not work. Why? Gramsci had apparently given up his belief that the revolution could be conducted only *after* a long, slow, cultural work of freeing minds and had decided that the revolution was actual given the conditions of Italy. By the beginning of 1918 he was supporting Bordiga's demand that the Socialist Party "act now" in terms which were earning him the undeserved reputation of "bergsonian voluntarist" among the more cautious maximalist leaders of the party.[22]

But, as Togliatti recalled, "matters were neither simple nor clear" in those early days[23] and Gramsci reputedly only saw a collection of Lenin's works for the first time in the middle of 1919, when they were shown to him by the ex-syndicalist Alfredo Polledro.[24] Moreover, there was practically nothing of Lenin translated into Italian in May 1920, when Gramsci bitterly criticized the Socialist Party for being so remiss and arranged for the publication of the first edition of Lenin's work in Italian. This was published in July 1920. So Gramsci had to turn to the newspapers in the only language which he read without difficulty: French. Leonetti recalls that "the source was always in French". And so it was that Gramsci obtained his view of the Revolution and its implicit theory and practice through the following newspapers and journals: *Communist International, La Vie Ouvrière* (1919–); *Le Phare* (1919–); *Demain* (1919–); *Nouvelle Internationale* (1919–); *Bulletin Communiste* (1920–); *Revue Communiste* (1920–); and *Clarté* (1920–).[25] Readers will note that because of the censorship none of these sources were available to him until 1919. The only writings of Lenin to appear in these newspapers in 1919 were his letter to "Our American Comrades"; a short article declaring that the Second International was finished, and a portion of the *Proletarian Revolution and the Renegade Kautsky*, which appeared in *Nouvelle Internationale* on 30 April 1919.[26] However, a very definite picture of Lenin and Lenin's views was given in the reports of Arthur Ransome. Some indicative lines in "Conversations with Lenin" appeared in Gramsci's most important source, *La Vie Ouvrière*, on 20 August 1919. "He [Lenin] told me that he had read a comparison of his own theories with those of the American Daniel de Leon in an English socialist newspaper. He had immediately borrowed some of de Leon's pamphlets from Reinstein (who belongs to the party which de Leon founded in the United States) and had been struck by how much and how early the thought of de Leon had started following the same course as that of the Russians."[27] Small wonder that the paper should claim that "our Russian comrades have carried out in practice the main theoretical objects of syndicalism", and that their main achievement had been the rejection of parliament in favour of direct action through the workers councils.[28]

If Gramsci knew no Lenin he certainly knew something about the theories of de Leon, whom his French sources suggested presented much the same theory as Lenin, since he and Togliatti had started to study IWW theory in 1916, and had, indeed, first learnt of Lenin through the *Liberator*, the IWW paper of Deleonite tendency. By mid-1919 he showed quite clearly that he had decided that the leninist theory of revolution was a theory of the primary role played by the soviets in raising revolutionary consciousness, or, in his terms, educating the masses. Given what he felt to be the great similarity between Russia and Italy—in both he isolated the war as the single most important catalyst for revolution because the bourgeoisie "had not been able to avoid giving a terrible practical lesson in revolutionary socialism" to the predominantly peasant population—he called on the Turinese workers to "create (their) own soviets within the limits allowed".[30] He and his friends set up the newspaper *Ordine Nuovo* a month later, after discussions with interested workers, mainly from the "rigid" minority of the Metalworkers' Federation (FIOM). At first this paper was no more than a renewed venture in "cultural messianism", because Angelo Tasca (another "crocian") had found the money for it and he was unable to envisage it as anything but "a ragbag anthology—a collection of abstract cultural items and a strong leaning towards nasty stories and well-intentioned wood-cuts".[31] But in July 1919, Gramsci, Togliatti and Umberto Terracini conducted the editorial *coup d'état* which led to the paper's conversion into a promoter of the transformation of the *commissioni interne*, or shop-stewards' committees, into "workers' councils" which would eventually become an alternative state power: "This state does not pop up by magic: the Bolsheviks worked for eight months to spread and make their slogans concrete: all power to the Soviets, and the Soviets were already known to the Russian workers in 1905. Italian communists must treasure the Russian experience and save on time and labour: the work of reconstruction alone will demand so much time and work that every act, every day must be directed towards it."[32] Gramsci made clear that the function of this self-organization was educatory in the sense in which he had understood education in 1916–17. It would "cause a radical transformation in working-class psychology, making the working-class better prepared to exercise power, and, through spontaneously generated common historical experience, spread an awareness of the rights and duties of comrades and workers".[33]

The first documents of the Communist International to be published in Italy, and especially the manifesto drafted by Trotsky, must have encouraged Gramsci's belief that the way to power was through councils which educated men through a constant class-struggle at their place of work and allowed them both to understand and have the will to change the world. In the second half of 1919 and early 1920 he and his followers began an endless round of talks and agitation in the factories in favour of the establishment of workers' councils. They found the working-class contacts he had built up among the FIOM "rigids", like Giovanni Parodi, invaluable in obtaining *entrée* for them.[34] Together they and their audiences elaborated a complicated analysis of Italy's post-war problems and their solution which formed the basis of the articles in *Ordine Nuovo*. We may sum up this analysis as: 1) the problem of capitalist society was that it alienated men from one another, and thus destroyed the possibility of their uniting to overthrow it; 2) therefore, "associating men together can and must be assumed to be the essential fact of the proletarian revolution" and, 3) as the Russian, Hungarian, and German experience showed, the one effective way to do this was to form councils to unite men together and prepare them for a successful socialist revolution.[35] Gramsci wrote years later in a catalogue of the lessons of the factory council movement that "our actions always had an almost immediate and wide success, and seemed like the interpretation of a diffuse, deeply-felt need, never as the cold application of an intellectual schema . . ." because they "never took action without sounding out the opinion of the worker in various ways. . . ."[36]

In September 1919 the workers of Fiat Brevetti met to set up the first of the factory councils, starting a movement which had spread through the Turin factories by the end of 1919. It was not, at first, a movement dominated by the socialists of *Ordine Nuovo* although they worked hard to develop its revolutionary qualities and thus win it to their point of view through their School of Cultural and Social Propaganda.[37] It is worthwhile emphasizing the enormous effort Gramsci put into these endeavours. Tasca wrote: "We must note the intense activity of Gramsci. . . . *Avanti*, the Central Executive of the Party, *Ordine Nuovo*, *Sotto la Mole*, lectures for the factory councils . . . prodigious activity, a sickly body and a steely will . . . he is a leader."[38] These words remind us that revolutions do not make themselves, and that at the beginning of 1920 Gramsci was actively committed in a practical and organizational sense to a particular course of action. He could not therefore avoid the implications of this activity for his understanding of leninism when he began to become more acquainted with leninism in 1920.

By May 1920 his French sources had made available to him Lenin's work on the *Problems of Soviet Power; The Heroes of the Berne International;*

The Third International and its Place in History and some work on the economic and social problems of the transition to socialism. In June further articles by Lenin on the proposal to reconstruct the Berne International appeared, and in July *Bulletin Communiste* published Lenin's letter to Sylvia Pankhurst condemning her refusal to participate in parliamentary activity. In December the same journal carried the first two chapters of *Left-Wing Communism an Infantile Disorder*.[39] Nearly all of these writings stressed the bankruptcy of the Second International and its mechanical marxism and the importance of the Soviets, but, with the exception of *Left-Wing Communism an Infantile Disorder*, none are really important works of Lenin.

However, there was one account of Lenin and his theory which stood out among the rather lyrical accounts of Ransome, Goode, Sadoul and others, for whom Lenin's major discovery was still the soviets. This was Zinoviev's speech of 6 September 1918, made after the attempt on Lenin's life, which appeared in *Vie Ouvrière* on 16 April 1920. We do not know if Gramsci read it, but it was interesting because it contained the only account of *What is to be Done?* in these sources. The article stated that the first article in the *Spark* contained the "quintessence of bolshevism" and then gave a simple account of the contents of *What is to be Done?* making clear its stress not only on "conscious" activity being necessary on a political level if a revolution was to be made, but that it was all-important to organize a revolutionary party. Yet Zinoviev also negated this emphasis by suggesting that concern with the party was only an early development in Lenin's thought (he also skated over *Materialism and Empirio-Criticism*) which proceeded to the crucial theoretical contribution of Lenin, the theory of the role of the soviets which he had supposedly developed since 1905, and his corresponding teaching on the State: "In Lenin the government of the soviets found not only its greatest political leader, a practitioner, an organizer, a fiery propagandist, a poet, but also its greatest theoretician, a Karl Marx." So even when the fundamental text for Lenin's teaching on the party was discussed, its importance was lost in the stress that Lenin's greatest contribution to marxism was his theory of the State.

It is clear that at this juncture Gramsci, too, still regarded the main teaching of Lenin to be that in the *State and Revolution*,[40] since he recommended it warmly as "useful to everybody".[41] Interestingly, his knowledge of this book ante-dated that of his French sources, which only translated it over a year later, when they were very enthusiastic about it.[42]

How important the role of the party was in leninist revolutionary theory only became more clear when the reports of the Second Congress of the Communist International began to be published in August and September 1920, in France and Italy. It is important to recall that the emphasis on party politics at this congress, the first at which western revolutionary socialists were present in any numbers, was accompanied by a call for moderation in their anti-parliamentarism. *Left-Wing Communism* became available in French at about the same time as the Second Comintern Congress. There was a noticeable change in the attitudes of Gramsci's French sources towards Lenin. They gave *Left-Wing Communism* a mixed reception and tended to start lending more support to Trotsky than to Lenin, whose opinions had already been dubbed "rightist", or moderate, in tendency much earlier.[43]

It is not clear whether Gramsci shared their resistance to a party leninism rather than a "sovietist" or "syndicalist" leninism, but he certainly continued to regard Lenin as a "conciliar" theorist throughout 1920, equating the views of Lenin, Luxemburg and Pannekoek and writing in October 1920: "The syndicalist tendencies of *Ordine Nuovo* are also a myth: we simply make the mistake of believing that only the masses can make the revolution, that a party secretary or president cannot make it through decrees: it seems that this was the opinion of Karl Marx and Rosa Luxemburg, and the opinion of Lenin."[44] He also published a whole series of eyewitness accounts of the revolution which stressed the same view of Lenin. Moreover, in the only reference to *What is to be Done?* which appeared in *Ordine Nuovo* (in an account by Charles Rapaport), Gramsci's accompanying caption dismissed it as an "old thesis".[45]

If Lenin's theory of the party had not begun to affect Gramsci by the end of 1920, he had certainly begun to use the concept of imperialism more frequently. However, the fact that he did not realize that Lenin did not agree entirely with Hilferding, or Adler and Kautsky, suggests that he had not grasped the nuances of Lenin's theory, and was, as earlier writings indicate, developing the theory autonomously.[46] Moreover, he absolutely refused to regard such world-wide developments of capitalism as shifting the main locus of the class-struggle outside the factory.

At the end of 1920 accounts of Lenin's theory of the party had obviously not become sufficiently clear or predominant to make Gramsci reconsider his belief that the Russian's main contribution was a "conciliar" theory. It was still possible to have this view of leninism and the role accorded to a party in such a theory even late in 1920 because of ambivalences in the formulations of Lenin himself. For example, in his letter published in Italy in September 1920 condemning the Italian Socialist Party and supporting a Turinese demand that the party "renew" itself, Lenin suggested that the revolution started from below and that the task of the party was to "generalize, and give watchwords".[47] But Gramsci's own activity during that year pushed him ever more strongly in the direction of favouring a renewal of the

PSI and then, *faute de mieux*, a split from the PSI and the formation of a Communist Party. He was forced to consider the problem of a revolutionary party because his factory councils threatened the hegemony of the traditional union and PSI leaders in Turin. When they attacked him, and not before, he was compelled to embark on a critique, first of the unions, and then of the party. Both, he argued, were organized not to take power, but to come to agreements within the bourgeois State, and their policies and structures were therefore determined by capitalism. In the course of their dispute each side sought their allies where they could and Gramsci turned particularly to the anti-party workers, both anarchist and "abstentionist", whose leaders now controlled the FIOM. The rupture with the PSI took place after its leaders refused to lend national assistance to the Turinese workers, who were locked out in April 1920 by their employers, who had a much greater understanding of the revolutionary implications of the councils than the PSI's leaders.[48] In May Gramsci's bitter denunciation of the PSI was read at its Milan conference. He called upon the PSI to prepare for revolution through organization and education, since the contemporary period would mark either the success of a proletarian revolution or usher in "the most terrible of reactions". He claimed that the PSI leaders had failed to help the strikers because they did not live "immersed in the reality of the class-struggle", because the party was too bureaucratic. "The existence of a strongly disciplined and cohesive Communist Party, which through its nuclei in the factory, unions and co-operatives, coordinates and takes central control in its executive committee of all revolutionary actions of the proletariat is the fundamental and indispensable condition for attempting any Soviet experiment. . . ."[49]

The PSI rejected this critique, denying the possibility of any immediate revolution although they had committed themselves to its actuality when they joined the Comintern in December 1919. Lenin learnt of the exchange through intermediaries who favoured the Turinese and at the Second Congress of the Comintern in July–August 1920 made clear that "the II Congress of the Third International regards the criticism of the party, and the practical proposals put before the national congress of the Italian Socialist Party by the Turinese section of the party in *Ordine Nuovo* of 8 May 1920 as substantially correct. They correspond fully to the fundamental principles of the Third International."[50] The PSI delegation was flabbergasted, and it was made quite clear to Lenin that the Turinese were considered "syndicalist", and at least implicitly anti-party.[51] Lenin then withdrew his blanket approval of Gramsci's policies and limited his endorsement to the text of the document, not the intentions of its authors.[52]

What this amounts to is an endorsement by Lenin of Gramsci's

views on the PSI before he knew what they really meant and before
Gramsci had read any of Lenin's views on the party. From the time of
this refusal by Lenin to endorse any "syndicalist" interpretation of the
role of the party we can observe a growing tension between Gramsci's
and Lenin's views. For although Gramsci denied that he was a
syndicalist he did continue to equate the Russian revolution with
councils, and these with what was common in the writings of Marx,
Lenin and de Leon.[53] Not without some justification.[54] On the other
hand, the Russian was making clear that the party would have
primacy over the soviet both in theory and practice. By March 1921
Clarté had published *Right-wing Socialism and Counter-Revolution* which
made clear the leading role of the party in Lenin's thought: "When
people talk about the unity of the proletariat it is difficult to listen to
them without smiling . . . we know through experience that the unity
of the proletariat can only be ensured by a revolutionary marxist
party, and only by a struggle without mercy by this party against the
others."[55] Throughout early 1921 in the preparations for the Third
Comintern Congress it was made clear that when the leninist theory of
imperialism was put together with the democratic centralism of the
twenty-one conditions of admission to the Communist International
the result was a hierarchy of command in which the whole of the
"world communist party" was obliged to obey the Comintern's
Executive Committee in Moscow, no matter what the line laid down.

Although also pushed to consider the role of the party by the
continuous failure of the PSI to lead, Gramsci was drawing very
different conclusions in the second half of 1920. In July he wrote in a
consideration of how the party should renew itself, that it should be:
"a party of the masses who wish to free themselves through their own
efforts, by themselves, from political and industrial slavery, through the
organization of the social economy, and not a party which uses the
masses to attempt heroic imitations of the French Jacobins."[56] He set
to work not to replace the existing leaders of the PSI or to split away
from it, as his co-editors wished and as the "abstentionists" in the
factory councils also wished, but to organize education groups which
"can offer the proletariat for its emancipation, neither communal
councils nor union leaders, but work in the field of mass action; for
communist groups in the factory and union, for the Workers' Council,
for proletarian unity in the face of menace to its cohesion. . . ."[57] This
activity he typified as one which escaped from the "magic circle" of
concern with political leadership and, implicitly, saw the problem of
the failure of the revolution to eventuate in the nature of the existing
relationship between the party and the real organic life of the masses.
But the correct relationship he proposed was one which did away with
the leading role of the party, which was to become no more than the

"agent" of a process of revolution taking place on the factory floor. "The Party and the union ought not to consider themselves the tutors or ready-made superstructures of the [council]. . . . They must consider themselves the conscious agents of its liberation from the forces of oppression centred in the bourgeois state. They must organize the general (political) external conditions in which the process of revolution will develop its greatest speed and in which the liberated productive forces will find their greatest expansion."[58]

Gramsci's analysis of the role of the party did not stop at such "anti-Jacobin" formulations. New events caused him to elaborate further after July 1920. The great industrialists were determined by the second half of 1920 to smash the revolutionary pretensions of the workers once and for all. They adopted a completely uncompromising position in negotiations for better conditions. So the Metalworkers' trade union federation called on the workers to occupy their factories as a defensive move aimed at making the government intervene in favour of the workers. Gramsci considered the move ill-timed and likely to foster illusions. In September 1920 the workers started to occupy their factories throughout Italy, though especially in the North. Gramsci then warned that merely occupying a factory did not bring about a revolution. He penned an important article which revealed clearly that in denying a leading role to a party he was not denying that it played an important part in making a revolution. A revolution was only made (and here the influence of *State and Revolution* on him seems obvious) when the State power of the bourgeoisie was smashed, and to do this the proletariat needed an armed force to take power and coerce the reaction. He obviously did not feel that the PSI was able to take these initiatives, but he also obviously believed that nation-wide initiatives, and therefore a national party, was needed as it would have to lead the assault on the State.[59]

In this state of mind, knowing that a party was necessary for a revolution, and that councils alone could not make the revolution, he sat in factories with the workers and watched the PSI ("Barnum's circus") shilly-shally and fritter away its chances. The occupations, which had started as a defensive move, were obviously becoming more and more offensive in their nature. The trade union leaders who had sown the wind began nervously to watch the approaching whirlwind. Unity of purpose was rapidly lost among the leaders of the unions and the Socialist Party. While encouraging the belief that there could be a revolution through aggressive and demagogic sloganeering and manifestoes, they simultaneously engaged in negotiations with the industrialists and the government to prevent such an outcome. Gramsci commented wryly that the Socialist Party was "no different from the English Labour Party and revolutionary . . . only in its programme".

It was really a conglomerate of parties and had become as a result an organization to be exploited by adventurists and careerists, and incapable of showing any initiative and responsibility.[60] Small wonder that mutual distrust was obvious when Togliatti visited Milan to discuss policy with the trade union leaders, just as the crisis reached its peak. The trade union leaders asked whether the Turin workers would initiate the assault on the State by coming out into the streets. Togliatti saw in this proposal a plot to destroy the factory council movement once and for all and refused flatly: ". . . to do it a simultaneous action throughout the country is necessary, and above all a nation-wide action".[61]

The responsibility was too much for the leaders of both the unions and the Socialist party. Some offered to resign to avoid having to make the decision, others declared that since it was a "political matter" it did not really involve them, as they were union leaders. Finally, the problem was resolved, to the relief of the majority, by putting the issue of whether to extend the movement to a vote, that ultimate fetish of the irresolute. By a majority the "revolution was lost".

It was only after the revolution was lost that Gramsci started organizing to establish a new communist party, though he recognized that it was really too late to be useful since he himself had stated in May that either the revolution would triumph or there would begin the most "terrible of reactions". It was only in a situation which he characterized as the "chaos and collapse" of Italian socialism, when he felt himself "overwhelmed by events", that he agreed to split the PSI.[62] In the desperate scramble to retrieve something from the wreckage, Gramsci helped to create the sort of party he did not want, and the sort of party which neither Lenin, Trotsky nor the Comintern wanted.

III

In 1958, at the first conference of Gramscian studies, Palmiro Togliatti, the secretary of the Italian Communist Party, stated the official orthodoxy about the relationship between Gramsci and Lenin. He affirmed that between 1919–22 Gramsci read: *What is to be Done?*; *One Step Forward, Two Steps Back*; *Two Tactics of Social-Democracy*; *Imperialism, the Highest Stage of Capitalism*; *The State and Revolution*; *The Proletarian Revolution and the Renegade Kautsky*; *The Development of Capitalism in Russia* and *Materialism and Empirio-Criticism*; that he accepted the theory in them and rejected his "crocianism"; and, in particular, that he accepted the leninist theory of the party.[63] We have shown that up to mid-1921 Gramsci could only have read some of the works on Togliatti's list; could, necessarily, only have accepted some of the theory in the *ensemble* of those works, and did not subscribe to the leninist theory of a leading role party before the formation of the PCI in 1921. This is not to argue that Gramsci did not wish to become a leninist in 1917–21, or that he did not devour avidly what Lenin was available to him and spread Lenin's theory among his comrades, but merely that when we follow Cicerchia's suggestion and discover how Lenin's thought permeated through Eastern Europe to the West and how it was taken up, we are left, in Terracini's words, with the fact that Lenin ". . . was known more as a revolutionary than as a marxist theoretician".[64] Again, this is not to argue that he did not read those works of Lenin listed by Togliatti, after 1921, and espouse them, in part, or in their entirety.

It seems from a historical reconstruction that the leninism which Gramsci knew before 1921, and *accepted*, was a "sovietist" leninism (or, as critics would have it, a "syndicalist" deviation) which stressed that a revolution is made from below by masses of men learning in the practice of organizing themselves for united action. His Lenin was a man who never lost sight of "the mainspring of all political and economic activity: the class-struggle".[65] This class struggle—because it never lost sight of the "sole categorical imperative in Marx 'Workers of the World Unite' "—took place in a special form—through workers' councils organized at the place of work.

Is this "sovietist" leninism—the "translation" of leninism into the West in 1919–21—*really* leninism? Many commentators say no. Spriano is blunt: "We cannot identify leninism with a conception of *revolution from below*, with a *molecular process* of the formation of the workers' State, which Gramsci places at the base of his theory of power. . . ."[66] Caracciolo, Soave and Berti more or less agree. They thus come into agreement with the extreme left students of Gramsci who maintain that Gramsci was not a leninist because he neglected or underestimated the role of the party.[67] Both groups of commentators, despite other abiding disagreements, share the view that Gramsci was not really a Leninist because they agree that the unifying problematic in Lenin's theory is the leading role a party must play in making a revolution. The nub of such a view of the relationship between the theory of Gramsci and that of Lenin must rest, *not* on the claim that he ignored the role a party can play—we have shown that after April 1920 Gramsci clearly realized that a party is essential, not so much for raising consciousness as *What is to be Done?* argues, but for the co-ordination of national initiatives which begin at council level, and for the assault on the bourgeois State machine. In a whole series of articles Gramsci and his followers called for renewal of the PSI; that it be changed by "the communist groups in the factory" from an assembly expressing the "psychology of the crow" into an "association" based on the factory and composed of "delegates [from the factory] with imperative mandates".—Rather, such a view must rest on the claim that the problematic in Gramsci's theory denies *a leading role* to the party—that Gramsci takes an "anti-Jacobin" view of the revolution. It is difficult to disagree with the claim that Gramsci was an "anti-Jacobin" up to 1921. He not only wrote in 1918 that "Jacobinism was the substitution of one authoritarian régime for another", but he claimed that the Russian revolution could not be Jacobin because it was proletarian.[68] In other words, a proletarian revolution and Jacobin positions were mutually exclusive. Gramsci understood Jacobinism in a variety of senses, but the key sense was that in 1918 Jacobinism could be equated with "cultural messianism". "Cultural messianism" had the following qualities and logic, making it the opposite of revolutionary. It believed that "the majority of men were fundamentally honest and upright, but prey to and the victims of ignorance of their own real interests and the goals that they could more usefully aim for" and therefore, "cultural messianism" proposed a work of "discussion and propaganda" in which it had "infinite faith", particularly through a newspaper which would unite and clarify the diverse aims of men; but when its reason failed to unite men, it "saw the maleficent influence of perverse wills", which are finally identified with "the leaders", who it condemns to universal execration.[69]

Two points need to be made here. First, that it is easy to show that Lenin frequently asserted the identity of Jacobinism and the proletarian revolutionary. In *One Step Forward, Two Steps Back* he wrote: "A Jacobin who wholly identifies himself with the *organization* of the proletariat—a proletariat *conscious* of its class interests—is a *revolutionary Social-Democrat*."[70] At the same time as Gramsci condemned Jacobinism and described him as an anti-Jacobin, Lenin wrote: "Bourgeois historians see Jacobinism as a decline. Proletarian historians see Jacobinism as one of the highest points reached by an oppressed class in the struggle for its emancipation. . . . It is a characteristic of the bourgeois class to execrate Jacobinism. It is a characteristic of the petty-bourgeoisie to fear it. Conscious workers and proletarians believe that power should pass to the revolutionary class, the oppressed, and that is where the essence of Jacobinism lies."[71] Second, it is easy to show that in 1902–4 Lenin meant by Jacobinism the "cultural messianism" Gramsci condemned. The dissimilarities between the contents of *What is to be Done?* and Gramsci's "cultural messianism" are too striking to be ignored. When we add *One Step Forward* we see that Lenin justified the purging of the party of "opportunists" by reference to the experience of Jacobinism. In sum, it is clear that in 1904 Lenin called himself a "present-day" Jacobin because he thought that the role of party leadership was all-important in making a revolution, and Gramsci was an "anti-Jacobin" because he did not.

A *prima facie* case exists for the claim that Gramsci was not a leninist because of this fundamental difference of emphasis. It is a useful base on which to distinguish their theory as it directs attention to what is novel in Gramsci's views. Unlike Lenin, Gramsci never organized to split the party even when it needed to be renewed, because he did not consider the fundamental problem of the "conscious" revolution to be one of leadership, but one of the relationship between the leaders and the masses. For him, the real weakness of the PSI as a revolutionary force was that its leaders did not live "immersed" in proletarian life, in the class struggle, and therefore "could not express the communist solution to contemporary problems: proletarian control of production and distribution, disarmament of mercenary armed forces, and control of the municipalities by the workers' organizations":[72] *and* that the workers were not united and disciplined enough to overcome their inability to see their problems on a national level, to overcome their tendency to "see everything rosily and to like songs and fanfares more than sacrifices"[73] and to seize power on a national level after organizing their own armed forces. Both sides need to step out of the "magic circle" where each blamed the other for their failures and saw the problem as either that of political leadership *or* mass consciousness, and instead to engage in the process of "mass work" in the factory and the union "for Workers' Council, for proletarian unity in the face of menace to its cohesion".

This displacement of the problem of revolution in the West from the party (theory) and the masses (practice) to the relations and links between them is what constitutes Gramsci's novelty and explains how and why he was already by 1922 advising a revolutionary strategy of replacing "a bourgeois personnel . . . by a communist personnel in all vital and dynamic functions organized in the State". Such suggestions preluded the concerns developed later in his *Prison Notebooks*, in particular the concern with the intellectuals as the real expression of the link between practice and theory.

Yet, while it is obviously useful to draw the distinction between Gramsci and Lenin—"anti-Jacobin" versus "Jacobin"—as it indicates the precise *locus* of Gramscian theory, it is useful to make a reservation about the blunt assertion that Gramsci was not a "leninist" before 1921. This essay has been devoted to enquiring about the degree to which the ideas of Gramsci were dependent upon those of Lenin. Most other work on the relationship between the Russian and the Italian has been devoted, in one sense, to such inquiry. We have reached common conclusions that Gramsci's ideas were not dependent on those of Lenin and that in fundamental respects their views were different up to 1921. There is, however, another way of examining the relationship which has not been attempted here, because our object has been to demystify the relationship by breaking away from the presupposition that all revolutionaries must be "leninists" (in the sense that their thought paraphrases that of the Russian) through using a *historical* method. The alternative way of examining their relationship should placate proponents of the view that Gramsci was a "leninist". It examines both theories from the point of view of the history of marxist theory as a whole, and takes as its starting point the marxist position that the meaning of marxist writings is determined by the *present* stage in the understanding of revolutionary marxist theory: it looks at them from the end-point in a historical development of which they form a part. In this enquiry the meaning of both theories is theoretically, but perhaps not practically, *outside them* and what is significant in their work is established not by *what they thought was significant*, nor by *what they directed most of their attention to*, but *by what our present revolutionary/practical understanding renders significant* in their work. This reading is an *implicit* reading in which our perspective renders *visible* what was *latent*.

To explicate to our own satisfaction what is involved in such *revolutionary* reading would involve writing a history of marxism *qua* theory of practice, which we cannot hope to do here. But some interesting implications for Lenin's rather than Gramsci's theory emerge from such a reading, which *practically* means reading the former in the light of the latter. We make this last assertion because we agree with A. M. Macciocchi in *Pour Gramsci* (Seuil, Paris, 1974) that Gramsci and Mao hold similar views and constitute the height of contemporary revolutionary theory, though each in their own environment, and with their own real objects. As an aside, we note that contemporary theory of a "structuralist" sort does not help us make a *social* revolution, whatever its contribution to philosophy. We also concede that it is theoretically inevitable that Gramsci himself will eventually have to be subjected to the same reduction in terms of future revolutionary theory, and thus our perspective on Lenin will change.

Reading Lenin from the point of view of contemporary revolutionary marxist thought, that is, from the point of view of Gramsci, shows that the significant development in his thought is a movement away from the positivist, fatalist views of the Second International towards a philosophy of praxis: towards the point where, if we may be permitted the image, he hands the baton on to Gramsci. In this sense his theory is a "revolt against *Capital*". This handing on of the baton is not understood simply as a filiation of ideas—we have already shown the limitations of such a *hegelian* view in practice—rather it is to be understood as the meeting of two separate revolutionary practices, in which the practice determines the validity of the theory. Moreover, the overall reading does not deny the established facts of Lenin's life: it re-orders them to render them comprehensible.

Briefly, Lenin's starting point should be seen as that of a man trying to make a revolution—where there was no real alternative—with the tools of understanding and action provided by the Second International. His theoretical paraphernalia, readers will recall, started with *Capital* and Plekhanov's *Our Differences*, which, when read in isolation, suggested that Marx's writings had already established how this world worked. Lenin, like most marxists of the Second International, not only read Marx backwards, but also did not read crucial sections of Marx until later, if he read them at all (*The Parisian Manuscripts*, the *Grundrisse*). Together these theoretical tools provided by the Second International contained an implicit logic, which was explicated by theoreticians like Bernstein and, later, Kautsky. This logic was that marxism was a fatalism which described the automatic development of capitalism into its own contradictory death, and led *politically* towards an *evolutionary* practice in its conclusions.

Lenin could not accept these political *conclusions* and rejected them in *Where to Begin?* and *What is to be Done?* in 1901–2. It is important to stress that it was the *conclusions* rather than their premises which he rejected, as in retaining the premises he retained a contradiction which would vitiate the practical action he took to make a revolution. As most readers of *Socialist Register* know, he proposed to create a revolutionary consciousness among the Russian workers through "combining all the activities of the local groups" of revolutionaries who had preceded him, and had been unsuccessful in their propaganda efforts because of their lack of *organization*. Since Lenin is often misunderstood as primarily an organizer, it is important to stress that the object of this organization of fragmented groups into a *party* was to facilitate the raising of a revolutionary consciousness among the Russian workers. This political intervention to make a revolution marks a step forward from the do-nothing politics of the Second International, but it failed in its object, which was to raise a revolutionary consciousness. There is not the space in this article to go into the history of this failure. What concerns us is why there was such a failure.

The crucial problem was not merely a matter of organization for revolution in the abstract, but how and where to organize. Lenin proposed to organize, and organized, on the *political* level first, to raise what seemed a perennial social revolt to the level of a *political* revolution. More lies behind this choice than the apparent realities of Russia—which were undoubtedly compellingly present. To explain the choice we must realize that Lenin was still working on the basis of the premises of the Second International's marxism on at least two levels: first, he still believed that conditions created *class-consciousness*, as distinct from a *revolutionary consciousness* and confined his critique of "spontaneity" to the Socialist notion that *class-consciousness* automatically developed into *revolutionary consciousness*; second, and this partly explained his first limitation, he still thought that Marx's works contained a final description of how the world worked, and therefore, that the problem of raising a *class-consciousness* to a *revolutionary consciousness* was primarily a matter of transmission of Marx by those who knew the contents of those works to those who did not. His concept was naturally one of a revolution from *above* where "twelve wise men" were worth a "hundred fools" and where the immediate and crucial problem was one of *leadership*. Hence the over-all theme in Lenin's work up to 1905 was that theory preceded practice.

However, his political practice, and especially his observation of the 1905 revolution in Russia, called into question the belief that theory preceded practice, and hence led back to rejection of the notion that the crucial problem was that of *leadership*. The lesson he drew from 1905 was clear: "The proletariat sensed sooner than its leaders the change in the objective conditions of the struggle and the need for a transition from a strike to an uprising. As is always the case, practice marched ahead of theory." [74] This was a discovery of immense theoretical as well as practical importance, but Lenin only realized it practically at first. He refused to draw the conclusions implicit in it for marxist theory and therefore reaffirmed categorically a residual fatalism ". . . the idea of seeking the salvation of the working class in anything but the further development of capitalism is reactionary". [75] After 1905 Lenin still believed that objective conditions created *class-consciousness*, that is, that the process of the *class-in-itself* into the *class-for-itself* is automatic. So while he affirmed the limited historical relevance of the notions in *What is to be Done?* after 1905 and tended to devote more attention to the problem of galvanizing struggle by direct organizational activity in the working class than to the party, he simultaneously made clear his theoretical limitations to the positions of the Second International in *Materialism and Empirio-Criticism*. What is important for his further development, which, of course, had its ups and downs, is that over-all his views were informed by the following sort of notion: "The real education of the masses can never be separated from their independent political and especially revolutionary struggle. Only struggle educates the exploited class." [76] There is an enormous wealth of nuance in such a notion, which combined started battering down the still-present vestiges of the elitist view that education (the creation of a *revolutionary consciousness*) comes from *above*, and the corresponding view that *class-consciousness* arises automatically. The whole problematic of automatic marxism is called into question.

Since the "educative struggle" took place in specific form, that of Soviets, Lenin became more and more a theoretician of the role of the Soviets, though first he only theorized their role practically. While the Russian revolutionary movement remained revolutionary (up to *circa* 1921), this change in Lenin's concerns from the party to the Soviet was clearly recognized by the leaders of that movement (e.g. in Zinoviev's speech of 1918 cited on p. 133 of this article), but it was later clouded by a return to concern with the leading role of the party after 1921, and particularly under Stalin. Moreover, the more rapid realization by Trotsky of what role the Soviets played, obscured the fact that in a slower fashion Lenin, too, was revising his views of how a revolution was made.

Implicitly, after 1905, the problem of organization is seen in two ways by Lenin: organization must take place on 1) a political or party level, and 2) on a pre-political, or social and class level. The stress in *What is to be Done?* shifts as well. Instead of party organization being primarily important, and organization at the level of production being secondary, the emphasis changes. The real organization for revolution takes place at the level of the class *qua* producers and the role of the party shifts implicitly from that of *the* educator ("who knows") to that of agent of the working class, especially in its assault on the State. Indeed, when the issue of insurrection became paramount in 1917 it became clear that its role was primarily that of overthrowing the bourgeois State power. The important theoretical works of that year include not only the *State and Revolution*, but apparently more practical works like *Marxism and Insurrection*. When insurrection became the order of the day, it also became clear that the development of *class consciousness* through the Soviets did not mean a corresponding readiness to overthrow the State in any concrete fashion: ". . . the majority of the soldiers sympathized with the Bolsheviks, voted for them, elected them, but also expected them to decide things". This real reaffirmation of the essentiality of the party, did not, however, prevent Lenin stating that the main lesson of 1917 was: "The history of the Russian revolution has shown precisely that no argument can convince the great masses of the working class, the peasants, the small employees, if they are not convinced by their own experience."[77] Did the implicit affirmation that men must change the world in order to know it—this "philosophy of practice"—mean an implicit or explicit realization by Lenin that theoretical marxism was yet to be written? Had he himself realized the theoretical implications of such statements? The answer probably depends on what status we are to accord to the criticism he made of all previous marxist theory, including his own, when he read Hegel's work. An affirmative answer, which we do not feel capable of supporting or denying, would have important implications for the relations between Lenin and Gramsci since it would situate a rupture in the understanding of marxism in Lenin's life as well as in Gramsci's.

We prefer to rest with the proposition that from the point of view of the history of marxism, leninism at its end-point and gramscianism at its beginning are closely linked, and that Gramsci certainly developed many of the implications of a "philosophy of practice" from 1919 onwards. By this we mean that just as we have described leninism as a proving in practice of the limitations of the Second International's marxism, so we can understand gramscianism as the proving in practice and the exposition in theory of the relevance of the end-point of leninism. This very method, which allows us to see a strong convergence in 1917–21, as Lenin moves from a theory of the party to a theory of councils and Gramsci follows the reverse process, both for practical reasons rather than through the influence of the ideas of the first upon the second, also compels us to see Gramsci's thought as a development *away* from that point of convergence—once again the image of men in a relay race comes to mind. This movement *away* and *beyond* leninism is what allows Gramsci to give a much clearer theoretical formulation of his own practice than Lenin did, especially with regard to the creation of *class consciousness* through the reorganization of social life. Later it allowed him to write the invaluable *Prison Notes*, which clothe with concrete meaning, and political advice for Western revolutionaries, Marx's words: "The materialist doctrine that men are the products of circumstances and upbringing, and that, therefore, changed men are the products of other circumstances and changed upbringing, forgets that it is men who change circumstances and that it is essential to educate the educator himself. Hence, this doctrine necessarily arrives at dividing society into two parts, one of which is superior to society (in Robert Owen, for example).

"The coincidence of the changing of circumstances and of human activity can be conceived and rationally understood only as revolutionizing practice."

NOTES

1. This section of this essay is covered at much greater length in my *The Young Gramsci: Towards an Intellectual Biography* (forthcoming). Gramsci was born at Ales, Sardinia, on 23 January 1891. His father, Francesco, was a civil servant employed in the Land Registry. His mother, Giuseppina, was a member of a local land-owning family, the Corrias. Gramsci had a privileged life by Sardinian standards until he was injured in a fall at the age of four and started to develop a hunch-back. Then his life became a cycle of misery: first his father was jailed in the course of a political feud; then, because he was a fallen member of the middle class in a society where the middle class had usually brutally oppressed the peasantry, he was mercilessly persecuted by his peasant school companions. He lived a life of physical and emotional deprivation—like a "bear" looking out of his lair, "convinced that no-one could love him". For compensation he turned to reading, and by the time he had finished high-school in Cagliari he had moved to the top of his class. In 1910 he won a scholarship to Turin University, where once again

he lived the life of a withdrawn scholar, whose brilliant potential was thwarted by starvation and a body racked by illness. His social outlook was affected by this life. As Garuglieri puts it "... being mocked at because of his deformity developed in him a great love for all those who suffer unjustly, and the need to give them succour, drove him to sacrifice himself generously in their cause". As a child he blamed the miseries of life on the Italian imperialism which exploited Sardinia, a view shared by many Sardinians, and he associated himself emotionally with the Sardinian nationalist movement known as sardism. But under the influence of his university teachers he was attracted to socialism, joined the Italian Socialist Party in 1913, and became a full-time journalist on the socialist newspapers *Avanti* and *Grido del Popolo*. This began a long career of revolutionary militancy, first as a Socialist, and then as a leader of the Communist Party of Italy formed in 1921. In his political practice he evolved the ideas which found their culmination in the now famous *Prison Notebooks*.

2. In 1916 Gramsci stated that the views in Croce's, *Teoria e storia della storiografia* constituted his "starting point", and in 1918 that they were still "undoubtedly right". *Sotto la Mole* (Einaudi, Turin, 1960, pp. 145, 365).

3. G. Amoretti, "Con Gramsci sotto la Mole" in *Gramsci, Scritti di Palmiro Togliatti ed altri* (Unita, Rome, 1945), p. 44.

4. For Gramsci's expression of these principles see *Sotto la Mole*, p. 365 where he wrote: "To be history, and not merely graphic marks, or source material, or aids to memory, past events must be thought up again, and this rethinking brings them up to date, since the evaluation or ordering of those facts necessarily depends on the 'contemporary' knowledge of the person rethinking the past event, about who makes history, and who made it in the past." It followed that Gramsci maintained that men were never the prisoners of their past in the sense that they could not fire themselves through their own wilful action. Indeed, he denied that men could only be freed by some structural conjunction of events.

5. *La Citta futura*, 11 February 1917. See reprint in G. Ferrata and N. Gallo, eds., *Due mila pagine di Gramsci* (Il Saggiatore, Milan, 1964), I, pp. 233–5.

6. A. Labriola, *La concezione materialistica della storia* (Laterza, Bari, 1953), pp. 31, 151.

7. Ibid., p. 73; *Sotto la Mole* (3 April 1916), pp. 101–2.

8. Ibid., p. 76.

9. See Al Leonetti, "Romain Rolland e Gramsci" in *Note su Gramsci* (Argalia, Urbino, 1971 (?)), pp. 209–21; Romain Rolland, *Jean-Christopher* (Michel, Paris, 1956), p. 22; *Au-dessus de la melée* (Michel, Paris, 1953), pp. 64, 80, 88, 124.

10. "Socialismo e cultura", *Il Grido del Popolo* (29 January 1916) in G. Ferrata and N. Gallo, I, pp. 189–93; *Avanti* (Turin) (9 December 1916) in S. Caprioglio, *Scritti 1915–1921* (Il Corpo, 1968), pp. 23–5.

11. P. Gobetti, "Storia dei comunisti torinesi scritto da un liberale", *Rivoluzione liberale*, IV, 2, 1922.

12. For the lectures and the strongly pro-crocian tone of the suggested reading see Amoretti, p. 45; for the club see the letter from Gramsci to Giuseppe Lombardo-Radice (March (?) 1918) in *Rinascita*, 7 March 1964; Leonetti, op. cit., pp. 105–8.

13. See *Avanguardia*, 20 October 1912 for Bordiga's statement and L. Cortesi ed., *Il Socialismo italiano tra riforme e rivoluzione 1892–1921 Atti congressuali del PSI* (Laterza, Bari, 1969) for the full report of Mussolini's opinions at the 1914 Ancona conference of the PSI; for the attitude of young workers at that time see M. Montagnana, *Ricordi di un operaio torinese* (Rinascita, Rome, 1949), p. 28; A. Tasca in *Il Mondo*, 18 August 1953.

14. In 1918, in an article rejecting the positivism of his former hero, Gaetano Salvemini, which is also interesting for other reasons, Gramsci wrote: "Jacobinism is a messianic view of history: it always speaks in abstractions: evil/good; oppression/liberty; light/shade; which exist absolutely, generically, and not in

historical forms. Jacobin messianism is completed by cultural messianism, which is represented in Italy by Gaetano Salvemini and has given birth to idealist movements like that of *La Voce* in the past and *l'Unita* at the present time. . . . Even cultural messianism abstracts from the concrete forms of economic and political life, and proposes an absolute outside time and space . . . and ends up being utopian." See *Scritti giovanili* (Einaudi, Turin, 1958), pp. 271–3.

15. *Il Grido del Popolo* (29 April 1917) in Ferrata and Gallo, I, pp. 251–2.

16. Ibid., (29 September 1917) in Caprioglio, *Scritti*, pp. 31–6. Victor Mikhailovitch Chernov (1876–1952)—one of the leaders and theoreticians of the Socialist-Revolutionary Party. After the February 1917 revolution, he was Minister for Agriculture in the Provisional Government; organizer of severe repressive measures against peasants who seized landed estates. After the October Revolution, Chernov was one of the organizers of anti-Soviet revolts. In 1920, he emigrated and continued his anti-Soviet activities from abroad.

17. S. Caprioglio, "Un articolo di Gramsci alla vigilia di Ottobre", *Rinascita*, 13 October 1967; P. Spriano, *Torino operaia nella grande guerra 1914–1918* (Einaudi, Turin, 1960), p. 210.

18. *Il Grido del Popolo* (29 July 1917) in *Scritti giovanili*, pp. 122–4.

19. "Il Nostro Marx" in *Il Grido del popolo* (4 May 1918) in *Scritti giovanili*, pp. 217–21.

20. "La rivoluzione contro il *Capitale*", *Avanti* (Milan) (24 November 1917) in ibid., pp. 149–53.

21. "L'utopia russa", *Il Grido del Popolo* (27 July 1918) in Ferrata and Gallo, I, p. 317.

22. G. Germanetto, *Memoirs of a Barber* (Co-operative Publishing Society of Foreign Workers in the USSR, Moscow-Leningrad, 1934), p. 138; P. Spriano, *Torino operaia*, pp. 286–7.

23. *Trent'anni di vita e lotte del PCI* (Quaderni di Rinascita, II), p. 37; M. and M. Ferrara, *Conversando con Togliatti* (Edizioni di Cultura culturali, Rome, 1952), p. 43.

24. S. Caprioglio in *Rinascita*, 13 October 1967. Alfonso Leonetti casts doubt on this account in a letter to me dated 14 March 1974. He writes: "All relations between Gramsci and Polledro were broken off after the latter became a 'social-patriot', that is to say, in 1914. Perhaps you mean Gobetti, who took Russian lessons from Polledro's wife. That is possible."

25. A. Leonetti, Letter to *Rinascita*, 22 February 1964; *Note su Gramsci*, p. 109. The sources were also apparently sometimes in English and German, which Togliatti translated, but this was rarely so after 1919. The contents of Leonetti's anthology, which he claims in his letter to me of 14 March 1974 ". . . contains everything essentially important among Lenin's writings then known in Italy . . ." are: *The Third International; Bourgeois Democracy or Proletarian Democracy; The Victory of the Soviets; The Proletarian Revolution and the Renegade Kautsky; The Heroes of the Berne International; Can exploiters and exploited be equal?; Democracy and Dictatorship in Germany; To the Workers in the Field; The National and Colonial Question; The Young International; Voluntary and Obligatory Work; The Emancipation of Women; The Struggle for Bread; The Political and Economic Situation in the World and the Task of the Third International.* See Nicola Lenin, *Pagine scelte* a cura di A. Leonetti (Facchi, Milan, 1920), pp. 190.

26. I have been able to check the complete files of all these newspapers and journals for 1919, 1920 and 1921 mainly at the magnificent Bibliothèque de documentation internationale contemporaine at the University of Paris -X (Nanterre).

27. *La Vie Ouvrière*, 20 August 1919.

28. Ibid., 2 July 1919.

29. Ibid., also ibid., 21 November 1919; *Clarté*, 2 November 1919.

30. The quotation is from an article by one of his close associates. See the "Dawn of Ordine Nuovo", *Avanguardia*, 9 March 1919.

31. "Il programma dell Ordine Nuovo", *Ordine Nuovo* (Einaudi, Turin, 1955), p. 148.
32. See "Democrazia operaia" (21 June 1919), in ibid., pp. 10–15.
33. Ibid. He also wrote that through the factory councils "began that education and that change in psychology, which, according to Karl Marx, must be considered the most promising symptom of the incipient realization of communism". Resoconto in *Avanti*, 25 June 1919, republished in A. Caracciolo, "Il movimento torinese dei consigli di fabbrica', *Mondo operaio*, 2 February 1958, pp. 16–27.
34. G. Parodi, "Gramsci con gli operai", in *Gramsci*, op. cit., p. 67; U. Terracini, "I consigli di fabbrica: vicende e problemi dall'Inghilterra alla Russia, dalla Germania a Torino", *Almanacco socialista 1920*.
35. For a fuller account see my forthcoming essay in *Australian Left Review*.
36. Gramsci to Togliatti, 27 March 1924 in P. Togliatti ed., *La formazione del gruppo dirigente del PCI* (Riuniti, Rome, 1962), p. 255.
37. P. Spriano, *l'Ordine Nuovo* (Einaudi, Turin, 1963), p. 37, fn. 1.
38. Quoted in G. Berti, *I primi dieci anni vita del PCI. Documenti inediti dall' Archivio Tasca* (Feltrinelli, Milan, 1969), p. 67.
39. *Bulletin Communiste*, 23 December 1920.
40. "Per un rinnovamento del Partito Socialista italiano" (8 May 1920), *Ordine Nuovo*, pp. 117–21; Leonetti, p. 24.
41. "Per un rinnovamento . . .", op. cit.
42. *La Vie Ouvrière*, 25 November 1921.
43. See e.g. *Clarté*, 29 November 1919: the association with Trotsky dated back many years in the case of *La Vie Ouvrière*. See Dolléans, *Histoire du Mouvement Ouvrier 1871–1920* (Colin, Paris, 1957), II, p. 234.
44. *Ordine Nuovo* (5 June 1920); (9 October 1920) in *Ordine Nuovo*, pp. 130, 489.
45. See *Ordine Nuovo*, 10 January 1920; L. Paggi, *Gramsci e il Moderno Principe* (Riuniti, Rome, 1970), I, p. 303, suggests that this indicates that Gramsci did not understand its significance in Lenin's thought at this time.
46. See *Ordine Nuovo*, pp. 130, 153, 490.
47. Ibid.; *Korrispondenz Internationale*, No. 13, 1920, col. 260.
48. See my article in *Australian Left Review*.
49. "Per un rinnovamento . . .", op. cit.
50. V. I. Lenin, *Sul Movimento Operaio Italiano* (Rinascita, Rome, 1952), p. 140; see *Communist International*, II, No. 15, August 1920, cols. 2487–2492 for the republication of the Turinese criticism.
51. *Il Soviet*, III, No. 24, October 1920, cited by P. Spriano, *Storia del Partito Comunista italiano* (Einaudi, Turin, 1967), I, p. 73.
52. Ibid.
53. "Il programma dell'Ordine Nuovo", *Ordine Nuovo*, pp. 146ff.; "La relazione Tasca e il congresso camerale di Torino," *Ordine Nuovo* (5 June 1920) in *Ordine Nuovo*, pp. 27ff.
54. *Korrispondenz internationale*, No. 13, 1920, col. 260.
55. *Clarté*, 11 March 1921.
56. "Due Rivoluzioni" (3 July 1920) in *Ordine Nuovo*, p. 140.
57. *Avanti*, 12 August 1920 reprinted in F. Ferri, "La situazione interna della sezione socialista torinese nell'estate del 1920", *Rinascita*, April 1958.
58. "Il Consiglio di Fabbrica" (5 June 1920) in *Ordine Nuovo*, p. 127.
59. "L'Occupazione" (2 September 1920) in Caprioglio, *Scritti*, pp. 130–2.
60. "Il Partito comunista" (4–9 September 1920) in *Ordine Nuovo*, p. 161.
61. Cited in Paolo Spriano, *L'Occupazione delle fabbriche* (Einaudi, Turin, 1964), p. 103.
62. "Contro il pessimismo" (15 March 1924) in Spriano, *Gramsci Scritti politici* (Einaudi, Turin, 1967), p. 546.

63. P. Togliatti, "Il leninismo nel pensiero e nell'azione di A. Gramsci" in *Studi gramsciani, Atti del convegno tenuto a Roma nei giorni 11–13 gennaio 1958* (Riuniti, Rome, 1969), pp. 16–19.
64. U. Terracini, "Three Meetings with Lenin" in S. F. Bezveselny and D. Y. Grunberg, *They Knew Lenin* (Foreign Languages Publishing House, Moscow, 1968), p. 211.
65. "L'Opera di Lenin" (14 September 1918) in *Scritti giovanili 1918–1919* (Einaudi, Turin, 1958), p. 308.
66. Spriano, *Storia del Partito Comunista Italiano*, I, p. 62.
67. See A. Caracciolo, "A proposito di Gramsci, la Russia, e il movimento bolscevico", in *Studi gramsciani*, pp. 95–105; E. Soave, "Appunti sulle origini teoriche e pratiche dei consigli di fabbrica a Torino", *Rivista storica del socialismo*, VII, No. 21, January–April 1964; Berti, op. cit. The best representative "left" article is A. de Clementi, "La politica del partito comunista d'Italia nel 1921–1922 e il rapporto Bordiga-Gramsci", *Rivista storica del socialismo*, No. 28, 1966.
68. "Note sulla rivoluzione russa" (29 April 1917) in *Scritti giovanili*, p. 106.
69. "La Politica del 'se' " (29 June 1918) in ibid., pp. 272–3.
70. V. I. Lenin, *Selected Works* (Progress Publishers, Moscow, 1967), I, p. 412.
71. Lenin, *Oeuvres complètes*, XXV, pp. 124–5.
72. "I Gruppi comunisti" (17 July 1920) in *Ordine Nuovo*, pp. 140–3; "Due rivoluzioni" (3 July 1920) in ibid., pp. 135–40.
73. Letter to Zino Zini in *Rinascita*, XXI, p. 17, 25 April 1964; *Avanti*, 2 September 1920 in Caprioglio, pp. 130–2, 134.
74. Lenin, *Selected Works*, I, p. 579.
75. Ibid., p. 486.
76. Ibid., p. 792.
77. Lenin, *Sulmovimento operaio*, p. 146.

RECONSTRUCTING AUSTRALIAN COMMUNISM

Winton Higgins

IN December, 1971, the Communist Party of Australia suffered its second split in eight years. In 1963, a relatively small grouping had left the party to form the Peking-oriented Communist Party of Australia (Marxist–Leninist). By comparison, the later split was far more traumatic: it took three years—during part of which period the party was virtually paralysed—to come to a head; it compromised the CPA internationally; and the new party, the Socialist Party of Australia, took with it much of the CPA's trade union support and many of its most experienced cadres. In this article I shall attempt to show that this trauma represented an important stage in the party's coming to terms with its own history, and was inevitable if the party was to develop as an effective revolutionary force. Further, I shall argue that, despite its critical weakness immediately following the 1971 split, the CPA is now demonstrating the potential to lead a viable communist movement in Australia.

The Origins of Australian Labourism and Communism

Contemporary Australian society presents a fairly orthodox, advanced capitalist appearance. It is highly industrialized and urbanized, and its monopolistic economic structure is thoroughly penetrated by foreign capital. The final touch to this normality is a new social democratic régime armed with working class electoral support on the one hand, and the latest OECD capitalist development plans on the other. But a closer examination of this social formation reveals unique— and politically significant—characteristics, the product of the peculiar development of capitalism in Australia.[1]

When this development began in the early nineteenth century, the capitalist mode of production was already dominant in England, along with large-scale industry. In contrast to the process of capitalist development in Europe, Australian capitalism did not emerge from the upheavals of any transition from feudalism: its components, human and material, were at first simply imported. While capital formation presented few difficulties, the absence of a class dependent for its livelihood on the sale of its labour-power was a constant obstacle. The

151

convicts and free settlers, who made up the earliest workforce, found plenty of scope for their entrepreneurial talents in the large tracts of cheap and arable land, and on the goldfields from 1851. The availability of land, and the fact that fortunes—or at least sufficient personal wealth to ensure financial independence—could be literally picked up off the ground without any capital outlay, played havoc with the class structure upon which capitalist production depends. (In the concluding pages of Volume One of *Capital*, Marx draws attention to this problem in the case of a Mr Peel who prudently imported his own supply of labour-power into Western Australia, only to see it lured away on arrival by better prospects than those offered by Mr Peel's subsistence wages.) Labour-power thus became an expensive commodity indeed: even convicts, who were forced to work for wages, received more than their "free" proletarian brethren in England, and real wages doubled in Australia between 1840 and 1890.

This early experience had a profound influence on the formation of working class organizations and ideology. What were probably the best wages and conditions in the world, together with the excellent prospects of social "betterment", obscured the basic antagonism between capital and labour. Social inequalities were neither as extreme nor as inescapable as in Europe, and this comparison fostered the myth of Australia as a "classless society" and "the workingman's paradise". The small craft unions that emerged in the latter half of the nineteenth century, far from being expressions of class antagonisms, were associations of solid, respectable citizens, only too willing to unite with other sections of the community to "keep the water on and the foreigners off". In many cases, their charters expressed their main function to be upholding of law and order, and even the Word of God. The early capitalists, for their part, had little need for labour-repressive policies. Primary accumulation was facilitated by the importation of capital, the discovery of gold and high prices for agricultural exports. Scarcity of labour militated against the establishment of labour-intensive industries, but profit-rates were high in mining, grazing and other enterprises in which labour was a relatively minor factor.

The colonial administrations played a typically interventionist role in capitalist development, in the provision of investment funds, transport and subsidies. Moreover, all classes united and easily thwarted the squatters' attempt to limit access to representative institutions by establishing a hereditary assembly of "the bunyip aristocracy". The first trade union representative was elected to the New South Wales Legislative Assembly as early as 1859; ease of access to such bodies bolstered the illusion that the state was a neutral umpire in any clash of interests and any legitimate interest could only benefit from its intervention.

In these circumstances, the emergence of labour parties in the Australian colonies in the 1890s hardly represented a working class assault on the representative institutions of the state. They were pragmatic organizations formed to co-ordinate the activities of the existing parliamentary representatives of the small craft unions. These representatives, who were in many cases propertied notables, pursued policies in which genuine working class interests were dissolved in class collaborationist practices and which were wrapped up in an ideology that combined petty bourgeois radicalism, populism, racism, chauvinism and idolatry of state power. That is not to say that they were unfaithful to their constituents, still less to their own class origins. Capitalist and worker perceived common enemies: Russian and Japanese military invasion, an influx of Asian immigrant workers or cheap foreign commodities, and the "squatocracy's" predilection for free trade.

From the 1890s on, when the first "long boom" ended, industrial strife did break out, and workers were violently suppressed by troops and police. In spite of these obvious manifestations of class violence and partisanship on the part of the state, the fact remained, as Humphrey McQueen put it, "Unionists wanted nothing better than to talk to their employers; and when the employers refused to talk, the unionists wanted the government to make them."[2]

The stage was thus set in 1907 for a deal between the trade unions and capital that was to set the pattern for Australia's economic and political development for decades. Compulsory arbitration of industrial disputes by state appointees, a White Australia policy and protectionism were the elements of that deal, and the Australian Labour Party, above all, remained unshakeably loyal to these three great national institutions for the next sixty-six years. It is a grim irony that the trade union movement itself initiated the arbitration system which has allowed the state to bind the unions to it in a way that Edward Heath could only envy. In 1911 a Labour Attorney-General proposed the notorious "penal powers" which, in their developed form, armed the state with power to fine and de-register unions, and to imprison union officials who refused to pay fines, disobeyed injunctions or otherwise found themselves "in contempt of court".

It is true that, from its formation up to the late 1960s, the ALP proclaimed the intention to introduce greater social equality and ultimately even "socialism". But its "socialist" vision was as innocent of any marxist influence as it was of class combativity, proletarian internationalism or criticism of capitalist social relations. Its egalitarianism was as much an aggressive nationalist celebration of existing Australian society as it was a—passively enunciated—prophecy of its eventual evolution to socialism. While the occasional threats to "cut off the heads of the tall poppies" have not been welcomed in ruling circles, the ALP's actual record in office could only inspire their confidence. A Labour government in 1910 made Australia the first English-speaking country to introduce military training in peacetime, and Labour governments have been entrusted with the nation's affairs in both world wars. While in office, the ALP has demonstrated its sensitivity to the interests of capital in energetic strike-breaking, featherbedding inefficient industries by raising tariffs whenever called upon, and financing the expansion of local and foreign-owned enterprises. Even the establishment of General Motors, the largest car manufacturer in Australia, was originally financed by a Labour Government.

In the 1890s, when the long boom ended, a series of bitter and protracted strikes occurred among miners, shearers and some other industries where greater concentrations of workers were to be found. These strikes, and the working class movement that slowly emerged in the aftermath, were the first stirrings of proletarian organization and ideology in the country. In the early years of the twentieth century, the IWW was the backbone of this movement, but small, socialist groupings grew up at the same time.

By the time the Bolshevik Revolution occurred, the ALP had already extended its influence over the trade union movement as a whole, although this influence remained weakest in the few unions based on relatively large-scale industries. The development of these industries, and the rise of larger concentrations of workers, were the still unfulfilled preconditions of a revolutionary proletarian movement. When the first reports of the events in Russia reached Australia, the few expressions of unmixed enthusiasm came mainly from small syndicalist, anarchist and socialist groups. It was an enthusiasm uninformed by any knowledge of Bolshevism as such. In the wake of the Russian Revolution, some of these groups came together to form the Communist Party of Australia[3] in October, 1920, but the new party was a highly unstable amalgam, none of whose elements could be described as marxist in any real sense.

From its first attendance at Comintern congresses in 1921, the CPA began to receive the former's literature and ideas, but these had little impact in stimulating an interest in marxist theory. By the time Australian communists were becoming aware of the advantages of prefiguring their activity in theoretical terms, the Comintern had fallen under Stalin's influence and had ceased to be an inspiration for the development of marxist theory. While its theoretical analyses and tactical pronouncements were never denied the lip-serivce of the CPA, they were often shelved in practice. Some commentators have interpreted the shifts in CPA theory and practice in terms of a constant struggle between two influences: a native radical tradition that supposedly inspired its constituent elements on the one hand, and a rag-bag of foreign doctrines imported from the Comintern on the other. But it was an instinctive sensitivity to local conditions that prompted deviations from Comintern policy, rather than an alternative strategic perspective.

The Depression dealt a heavy blow to the Australian working class: half a million were unemployed, and those who retained their jobs were forced to accept large cuts in wages and increases in working hours. The CPA threw its weight behind two important movements—the Unemployed Workers' Movement and the Militant Minority Movement. Through the latter, it established rank-and-file organizations within trade unions to mobilize support for militants opposing conservative and opportunist leaderships. The party first captured official trade union positions in this way in the Miners Federation in 1933, and similar success followed, especially on the waterfront, which became a traditional preserve of communist influence. The party itself grew from 500 members in 1929 to 2,500 by the end of 1931, and its lack of political coherence at this time was matched by its militancy and "mass style of work". In the same period, the party established a mass anti-fascist movement which attracted many liberal intellectuals and other non-proletarian elements who had no other affinity with marxism than a recoil from fascism. The main focus of party work, however, remained in the unions.

This emphasis was crucial for the external and internal development of the party. Within the trade unions, the prospects of dislodging more and more rightwing leaderships, and even of achieving dominance over the Australian Council of Trade Unions, were good. On the other hand, the obstacles to even modest electoral success—single member constituencies, the established two-party system, weighting of rural votes and gerrymandering—were insuperable. Communist participation in elections could then be no more than an opportunity to inveigh against the farce of bourgeois democracy, and the CPA ran a much smaller risk of falling into "parliamentary cretinism" than many of its fraternal parties.

But trade union politics proved to have its own dangers for a revolutionary party. Once elected to office, communists were forced to operate within bureaucratic frameworks and to fight the employers and the state with the weapons available within those frameworks. In consolidating their positions, elected officials often resorted to the same manipulative tactics as their opponents. The party's preoccupation with gaining and holding official positions, together with its lack of political development, left it incapable of resisting its militants' degeneration into economism and bureaucratism. Moreover, as the number of communist trade union officials grew, so did their influence within the party, which increasingly reflected their economist outlook and bureaucratic style. The gradual penetration of stalinist dogmatism and authoritarianism merely reinforced these tendencies, hindering the development of revolutionary politics and marxist theory.

The Second World War brought another massive influx of members into the CPA: at the end of the war its membership was estimated at 23,000. This membership was an insubstantial pageant, swelled by "Red Army communists" who quickly melted away on the unglamorous battlefield of the cold war. Nonetheless the CPA, enjoying greater prestige and the reflected glory of triumphant Soviet armies, felt emboldened to confront the ALP (then in office) with a good deal more animus than it had shown in the Third Period (1928–35) when the Comintern had called on Communists to direct "the main blow" against social democratic parties. Its political line against social democracy in general brought it into open conflict with the CPGB. In view of the present restraint on mutual criticism within the international communist movement, not to speak of the liquidationist strategies many communist parties promote in collaborating with social democratic parties, it is refreshing to reread the polemics between the CPGB and the CPA, however wooden their style may seem to us now. The debate began with a letter from the CPA Political Committee criticizing the CPGB's support of the Attlee government:

> "The false estimation of the role of social democracy and of the economic and political condition of Britain reached its climax in the [CPGB] Central Committee's pronouncement that Britain was 'in transition to socialism'. The non-marxist character of this estimation is quite clear when it is remembered that we are here dealing with the second strongest imperialist power in the world, where monopoly capitalism is in complete control and the bourgeois state has not been undermined and the government is led by social democrats whose role is so well-known to all students of marxism-leninism as that of the saviours of capitalism, more particularly in the moments of gravest crisis.
>
> "The 'transition to socialism' theory is plainly without any foundation in fact but reinforces the assertions of the Labour Government leaders that they are marching to socialism along the 'middle path', thus again strengthening the social democratic illusions among the masses. This false estimation of social democracy is still continued, in our opinion, by the new slogan of the so-called 'Left Labour Government'. The whole line . . . is a tailing behind social-democratic leaders and it led to the illusion, oft repeated, that the Labour Government 'could be forced to operate a socialist policy at home and abroad'. It is true that mass pressure could force a policy of peace and co-operation with the Soviet Union, but this does not yet constitute a Socialist policy. Consequently, the idle chatter about forcing the enemies of Socialism to adopt a socialist policy at home and abroad merely helped in the deception of the masses."[4]

The party's new confidence was bolstered by the rapid development of heavy industry in Australia during the war and in the boom that followed it. The party had never made significant inroads into rural and small craft unions, but its efforts in the larger unions during the thirties and forties had been crowned with success. Immediately after the war, communists added to their prestige by leading a number of well-timed strikes, and were clearly threatening the ALP's hegemony in the trade union movement as a whole. Within the ALP, however, attitudes towards the communists were hardening, and certain catholic elements, actively supported by the church hierarchy, began a virulent anti-communist campaign within the trade unions. In 1949 communists, overestimating their own support, led a coalminers' strike which disrupted many other industries. The Labour Government sensed the growing isolation of the communist strike-leaders, enacted draconian legislation to counter their agitation, and finally sent troops in to work the mines. The breaking of this strike was a major turning point in the party's fortunes, the beginning of a decline that only ended in the early seventies. The party simplistically interpreted this defeat as due to "sectarianism" towards the ALP, and during the fifties, it constantly vacillated between united front policies and renewed bouts of "sectarianism". The extent of the ALP's hostility can be judged by that party's decision in 1950 not to oppose the new Liberal Government's legislation outlawing the CPA. When the High Court declared the new law unconstitutional, it was submitted to a referendum. It was largely due to the influence of the new ALP leader, H. V. Evatt, that Labour now opposed the anti-communist legislation, and the referendum was defeated by a narrow margin.

In the fifties, the party was diminished, isolated, and very much on the defensive. Its only comfort was the consolidation of Soviet power in Eastern Europe and the victory of the Chinese Revolution. But the more it identified with international communism and reproduced the latter's line, the more it contributed to its cold war image as a foreign incubus in the Australian body politic. It was in this decade, however, that a large number of CPA cadres went to China for extensive training, in which they gained a solid grounding in marxist theory and imbibed the "central lesson" of the Chinese experience as their mentors saw it: a successful revolutionary strategy is based upon an analysis of the national situation rather than upon the mechanical application of universal prescriptions. Given the prominent part later played by Chinese-trained leaders in initiating the present trends in the CPA and in engendering within it a theoretical debate, the CPC must be seen as a decisive influence in the development of a self-generating marxist tradition in Australia.

The habit of independent analysis, however, had little time to develop before the Sino-Soviet dispute presented the party with one of its most serious dilemmas. The leadership wavered between support for the one side then the other, and a clear division emerged within the ranks of prominent cadres. The issues themselves were complex enough: the validity of the Soviet-proclaimed peaceful co-existence strategy (based upon the assumption that world imperialism would be outstripped, and thereby destroyed, by the economic development of the Soviet bloc), the peaceful—not to mention parliamentary—road to socialism in advanced capitalist countries, and the independent role of wars of national liberation in the anti-imperialist struggle. The CPA's experience with labourism and state intervention in defence of capital at home, and its contacts with Chinese, Vietnamese and Indonesian communism abroad, gave it good grounds to doubt the entire Soviet strategy.[5]

But in the party's internal struggle, these issues were skewed and overlaid by the pro-Chinese faction's loyalty to Stalin, and the stalinist manoeuvring, demagoguery and vulgarization of theory indulged in by both sides. In fact, the split that eventually occurred in 1963 was a classic illustration of the self-destructive tendencies inherent in stalinist parties, particularly in their unresponsiveness to any influence but the inscrutable pronouncements of their leaders, and *raison d'état* glossed over with dogmatic phrases. The opacity of the salient terms of the debate ("creative marxism", "the struggle for peace", "neo-trotskyism" etc.) was the measure of the distance that the party would have to traverse if it was ever to achieve a clear perception of its political tasks and what the tasks demanded of it.

For the Communist Party of Australia (Marxist–Leninist), which the pro-Chinese faction founded in 1964, this journey never began. Though dependent on Chinese patronage, it has remained untouched by the theoretical contributions of Chinese communism.[6] It fairly quickly degenerated into a sect with secret membership and a prolific press which does little but repetitively celebrate Chinese development, heap personal abuse on CPA leaders and advocate armed struggle. About 200 ex-CPA members, almost all from Melbourne, joined it, including some prominent trade union officials.

Immediately after the 1963 split, the CPA could hardly have presented a more orthodox appearance. Those who had been disquieted by the revelations of the CPSU Twentieth Congress had failed to force a timely reappraisal of the past, and the leadership had failed to so much as circulate the text of Khrushchev's speech, let alone unleash a debate on its implications for the CPA. The crushing of the Hungarian uprising shortly after had been met with the same complacency, even though the combined effect of the two events was a mass exodus from the party, especially by intellectuals. The party organization was of a classic bureaucratic centralist type in which internal debate was almost totally absent. Indeed, a talent for infiltrating and controlling bureaucratic structures was encouraged by the internal workings of the party and it was an indispensable skill for the party's style of intervention into trade union affairs. This skill was regarded as sufficient qualification for a revolutionary cadre.

The orthodox appearance of the party, however, was not able to mask for long trends that were eventually to lead the party out of the mainstream of the international communist movement. The CPSU Twentieth Congress had left a permanent question mark over party infallibility, however inadequate its "revelations" were from a marxist viewpoint and however the CPA continued to avoid its real implications. Similarly, the Sino-Soviet dispute had irreversibly shattered the monolith of "the socialist world" and had created two competing systems of revealed truth, neither of which was exactly illuminating the CPA's way forward. By 1964 the old "internationalist" leadership was being replaced by new leaders such as Laurie and Eric Aarons, John Sendy and Bernie Taft. Even though this group was at first indistinguishable from its predecessors on the issue of orientation towards the Soviet Union, they had all undergone training in China in the preceding decade, and shared an—as yet unexpressed—impatience with the banal prescriptions which the Kremlin dispensed to the faithful in the international communist movement. Their accession marked the beginning of the CPA's slow and groping development of an independent stance.

The Developing Crisis

The growth of a critical attitude towards the Soviet régime in the mid-sixties provoked little articulate opposition within the CPA. In line with a decision of the Political Committee, an Australian delegation to the USSR in 1964 criticized the manner of Khrushchev's removal and the subsequent expunging of his name from official history. It called for discussion of anti-semitism and political censorship in the USSR. Soon after, the CPA Central Committee voiced criticisms of the trial of Daniel and Sinyavsky. On his return from Moscow in 1964, Laurie Aarons declared, "We do not follow a Moscow line, a Peking line or an Italian line. Ours is an Australian line." The following year, a CPA delegation visiting Moscow was asked to sign a long anti-Chinese article which had actually been written by CPSU publicists. The delegation's refusal (later unanimously endorsed by the CPA Political Committee) strained relations between the two parties.[7] The fact that these and other demonstrations of independence went virtually unchallenged in the party up to the invasion of Czechoslovakia, far from signifying unanimity, was due to the conception of party discipline held by the more orthodox cadres—a conception which proscribed the public airing of differences, even in defence of the Socialist Motherland.

The growing critical attitude to the Soviet Union was only an outward sign of a more important process of theoretical development within the CPA from 1964 to 1968. Notwithstanding the above disclaimer of an "Italian line", the PCI was a natural focus of Australian attention at the time. Its legitimation of a national analysis and its mass work were readily appreciated by Chinese-trained cadres. Moreover, the Italians had criticized Soviet "democracy" and had advanced a concept of socialist pluralism which the CPA leadership saw as a far more appropriate model for western socialism than its monolithic Soviet counterpart. PCI policies, however, have never been accepted *in toto:* its predilection for gradualism and parliamentarism were foreign to the traditions of the CPA.

The new task assumed by the leadership now revealed the extent of the party's theoretical impoverishment and isolation from the debate in the intellectual community. For the resurgence of marxist thought was beginning to have an impact in Australian universities, and it was clearly in the party's interests to participate in the revivified radical intellectual movement. In 1965 it was decided to discontinue the party's theoretical journal, *Communist Review*, and start another to be called *Australian Left Review*. The aim of the new publication was to sensitize the party to the most recent developments in western marxism, and provide a forum for exploratory theoretical contributions from the party itself. Above all, it was intended to attract contributions from non-party intellectuals, and for this purpose the new journal was placed under an independent editorial collective whose members were not necessarily in the party. It has always suffered from the tension between its purpose of breaking new theoretical ground and its need to appeal to a broad readership, but it nevertheless played a central role in introducing new concepts and issues into the party, and stimulating debate on fundamental questions which had formerly been answered by "authoritative pronouncements".

The re-orientation of the party was given enormous impetus by the social and political radicalization from 1965. In the twenty years since the end of the Second World War, the "long boom" had done much to deaden political life in Australia. The myth of "the lucky country" had a good deal of factual basis, in a world economic conjuncture which favoured Australian agricultural exports and which attracted a large capital inflow to stimulate its new secondary and mining industries. The "unlucky" ones were also the silent or readily silenced—the 20% of the population who lived below the poverty line, the Aborigines who were totally isolated (if not actually interned) on "reserves", cattle stations and in shanty towns, and the migrants who, because of their ethnic divisions and inexperience of local conditions, were easy prey to super-exploitation. Thanks to these conditions and to the cold war, the Menzies Liberal government had been able to maintain its sixteen year dominance in spite of its mediocrity, ineptitude and conservatism. But from 1965, when Menzies introduced a harsh conscription scheme and committed troops in Vietnam, the consensus collapsed. As in the United States, the peace and anti-draft movement was centred in the universities, where there was already widespread dissatisfaction with the parlous state to which Liberal policy and mismanagement had reduced the education system.

The CPA leadership correctly predicted the explosive potential in this political situation, and pushed for the party's active participation in new radical struggles. Far from being prompted by a shrewd opportunism, this orientation went hand in hand with the growth of a new conception of the revolutionary process in advanced capitalist society, and the relation between the revolutionary party and the wider movement. The inapplicability of the Soviet model of revolution was tacitly admitted, but this admission was only the beginning of a painstaking process of coming to grips with the strategic implications of a more complex society, defended (in Gramsci's phrase) by so many superstructural "forward trenches". The work of analysing contemporary capitalism was closely related to the ideological struggle which the leadership now initiated.

The CPA Twenty-first Congress in mid-1967 approved sweeping changes in party organization and orientation. The old "democratic centralist" apparatus was replaced by a new constitution designed to facilitate internal democracy and greater rank-and-file intervention in the workings of the party's decision-making bodies. It also adopted a document entitled *Communists and the Battle of Ideas* which called for greater intervention in ideological debate. But the break with the past was most evident in the searching, 44-page Report of the Central Committee, delivered by Laurie Aarons. The tone of the Report was far from that of an "authoritative pronouncement": it was tentative in its conclusions and self-critical of the anti-intellectualism, sectarianism and lack of theoretical vitality that plagued the party in the past. It raised the problem of the complexity of class structure and the specificity of Australian monopoly capitalism. It presented socialist revolution, no longer as the project of a monolithic working class, but rather that of a bloc of diverse social forces and mass movements: it could only be made by "a coalition of left forces" and would result in a multi-party state. Within the trade unions, unity should not be sought through alliances between factions "at the top", a strategy which holds the labour movement back to conservative programmes based on the lowest common denominator: unity should be forged at the base, within the rank-and-file. Bureaucratic control could only be confronted by rigorous, grass-roots activism which would democratize and unify the trade union movement and lead in turn to the latter's intervention in political and social issues. The CPA's change in trade union policy at this congress took concrete form in its raising the demand for workers' control in industrial enterprises.

At this point, opposition to the changes was scattered and inarticulate. The main opposition came from party trade union officials disquieted by what they saw as a shift away from a working class orientation towards a preoccupation with student and intellectual issues. Many no doubt felt that the new industrial policies denigrated their own expertise and hard-won positions in existing union apparatuses, and that the political demands they were being asked to raise were "in advance" of the workers. Some of these fears may have been well-founded, but the resistance met was much more a product of the party's earlier neglect of political issues and failure to politicize its industrial cadres. The leadership could not but have been aware that they were making a "revolution from above" and that the process could not be rushed without risk. On the other hand, if the party was to play a leading part in the ongoing mobilization around the new radical demands, it could not afford the time to set its own house in order. The innovations therefore continued apace.

In 1968, two further influences were evident. The first of these was the interest in Gramsci's work. At this stage, his *Prison Notebooks* were untranslated, and no reliable account of his marxism was available. It is not surprising that a distorted conception of "gramscianism" was imported into the CPA[8]—a conception that inflated the role of intellectuals and confined the problem of hegemony to the sphere of ethics and ideology in a way that obscured the problem of the state. Even industrial agitation tended to be posed in "counter-hegemonic" terms that devalued economic struggles rather than locating them in a comprehensive strategy.

The second influence in this period was the new régime in Czechoslovakia, immediately relevant since the critique of Soviet institutions implicit in the "Prague Spring" echoed that already expressed by the CPA. But more importantly, the Action Programme of the Czechoslovakian party concretized the socialist democracy and "humanist values" which the CPA leadership was at pains to build into its own model of socialist society. The liberalization of Czech society received wide and enthusiastic coverage in the CPA weekly, *Tribune*, and in June, 1968, Eric Aarons wrote a lengthy appreciation of the Action Programme itself[9] and its relevance to the development of theory in the CPA.

Given the CPA leadership's pro-Dubcek stand, events in Czechoslovakia could not have avoided precipitating a confrontation with the still silent opposition within the party. In mid-July, 1968, the

National Committee met to discuss the Czech situation and its attitude in the event of a Soviet invasion. It issued a statement[10] declaring support for the CCP programme "for socialist regeneration and democratization" and disapproval of the slow withdrawal of Warsaw Pact forces after military manoeuvres in Czechoslovakia. It stated its belief that the CCP not only had the right to decide its own programme without interference, but that the success of this programme was of crucial importance to the struggle for socialism in the west. Cadres' meetings were called throughout the country to mobilize support for the CCP and the stand taken by the CPA National Committee.

Within six hours of the news of the 20th August invasion reaching Australia, the CPA National Executive issued an unqualified condemnation of the Soviet action. Whatever remaining loyalty the leadership may have felt towards the Soviet Union died then and there, and far from being content with a ritualistic denunciation, it organized a series of actions and large public meetings to rally support for its position. At the time, almost all of the pro-Soviet faction joined in this clamour, and the leadership's past and proposed actions were approved by 37 votes to 2 in the National Committee. Had the CPA let the invasion slip into history, it might well have remained in the mainstream of the international communist movement and might also have contained its pro-Soviet minority within some rough consensus. Such a course of action, however, would have amounted to a complete reversal of policies adopted at the previous congress. The invasion was not, then, to be passed off as an isolated and unfortunate mistake.

Two weeks after the invasion, *Tribune* carried an article by Eric Aarons on the significance of the Soviet action. "Clearly, this was no sudden aberration", he asserted, and the origins of this "monumental blunder" were to be found in the deformations of Soviet society itself. Aarons argued that the Soviet leaders identified the interests of international socialism with their own national interests, power was dangerously concentrated in the bureaucracy, the régime regarded democratization as inconsistent with socialism and it had dogmatized and debased marxism into a justification for its own rule.[11] Circulation of *Tribune* was thereupon banned in the Soviet Union.

The following issue of *Australian Left Review* carried another contribution on the Czech question by a member of the National Executive, Ted Bacon. Turning the Soviet justification for the invasion—the internal affairs of a socialist country are the legitimate concern of the whole socialist world—on its head, he stated that the mistakes of the USSR were not the internal affair of that country, but are the concern of the entire international movement:

"The occupation of Czechoslovakia has not only cast a shadow on the sincerity of all [the Soviet leaders'] declarations of principle—it has also demonstrated the necessity for re-examining the past. Denigration of Stalin, Beria, Molotov or Khrushchev were never satisfactory 'explanations' for marxists, but most believed or hoped that the mistakes of the past would never recur, that their causes had been or were being eliminated. Now a continuity of error is revealed and its basic sources must be investigated and properly analysed."[12]

From the Czech crisis on, a dissident minority within the CPA began to materialize. A veteran party functionary, Alf Watt, and the editor of the Miners Federation journal, Edgar Ross, cast the two dissenting votes on the National Committee against the leadership's policy on Czechoslovakia. Two members of the National Executive, Pat Clancy and W. J. Brown, later reversed their stand against the invasion in the light of "new evidence" produced by the Soviet and Czech governments to the effect that a counter-revolutionary coup was imminent immediately prior to the invasion. But it was not the time to organize a right-wing faction, and for another eighteen months the opposition restricted itself to uncoordinated protests against the further implementation of the new policies.

Relations with the CPSU continued to deteriorate throughout 1969, as the Czech issue showed no sign of dying down, and the CPA expressed opposition to the Soviet line before and during the International Meeting of Communist and Workers' Parties held in Moscow in June, 1969. At the preparatory meeting held there three months before, the National President, Richard Dixon, expressed the CPA's disapproval of the draft resolutions intended to be adopted at the main meeting. He declared that it compromised the autonomy of individual parties, camouflaged serious differences over Czechoslovakia and other questions, ignored the growing demands for democratic participation in western societies and its importance for communist movements in those societies. The same criticisms were put more forcefully by Bernie Taft and Laurie Aarons at the Meeting itself, and in the upshot, the CPA refused to endorse those resolutions it had objected to.

In Australia, 1969 saw an intensification of political and social radicalization on many fronts. The most obvious of these was the anti-war and anti-draft movement, but Women's Liberation and the Aboriginal movement were now mobilizing as well. Communists were heavily committed in all these movements, where many cadres were influenced by the New Left. From the right of the party came accusations of adventurism and opportunism, although the party's involvement was clearly in line with its emphasis on self-activating mass movements the thrust of which was "counter-hegemonic" and contributed to a global critique of contemporary capitalism. One challenge that could not be lightly dismissed was directed against the often uncritical acceptance of New Left stances, particularly its branding of all organization as "Stalinist" and its contempt for working class politics.

But it was the party's industrial policies which drew most fire. Agitation around the slogan "Stop work to stop the war!" was seen as "left-adventurist" even though it evoked a positive response: strikes in support of moratoriums, instances of effective black bans on war material bound for Vietnam as well as increasing involvement of workers in the anti-war movement itself.[13] The National Committee's encouragement of grass-roots activism and workers' control initiatives were seen as "left-sectarian", since they were offensive to right-wing union officials whom some communist officials saw as useful allies.[14]

The question of confronting the penal powers—the powers of industrial tribunals to impose criminal sanctions on trade unions and their officials—was a particular bone of contention. As was noted earlier, the compulsory arbitration system has, since its introduction, played the major role in the containment of working class struggle in Australia, acting as a legalistic umbrella for the direct use of state power in industrial disputes. Its long term benefits have been more-or-less effective wage-pegging in non-political guise, and the reduction of trade unions to what one commentator has described as "part of the apparatus of the state".[15] The penal powers were resorted to frequently by employers and the court, and constituted an effective brake on industrial actions. In January, 1969, the CPA National Committee called for mass action directed against the penal powers, which the minority saw as a "political" question which was "too advanced" for the workers at that stage. Four months later, the Secretary of the Victorian Tramways Union, Clarrie O'Shea, was imprisoned indefinitely for contempt of court for refusing to pay fines imposed on his union. The following day, half a million workers went on strike in what was the beginning of a wave of massive strikes and demonstrations throughout the country. The employers were forced to agree to a permanent moratorium on the use of the penal powers.

Theoretical debate within the party intensified sharply from the latter part of 1969 to the Twenty-second Congress in March 1970. The debate focussed on documents[16] circulated by the leadership and intended to be put to the congress for adoption. The debate was carried on in the journal *Discussion* which came out at short intervals and was exclusively concerned with internal discussion of issues arising out of these documents. The importance of raising democratic demands—including workers' control and the imposition of popular control on the economy—in sharpening the struggle for socialism was given particular emphasis, and extra-parliamentary mass struggle conducted by "the coalition of the left" was envisaged as the decisive process in the socialist transformation of society. This transformation is prefigured within the problematic of Gramsci's "war of position" and creation of a socialist hegemony: since the decisive confrontation with the state can only occur when that hegemony has been won, the repressive aspects of "the dictatorship of the proletariat" are not as salient as the orthodoxy suggests and tend to deform post-revolutionary society. Participatory democracy and mass activism were seen as the hallmark of the CPA's strategy for social change and its vision of socialist society. These echoes of Mao's "mass line" once again point to the significance of former links with China. In this context, too, far-reaching criticisms are made of the Soviet bloc, now no longer referred to as "socialist", but as "the socialist-based countries".

The trade unions remained the crucial area of struggle. There was a lengthy analysis of "pressures for integration into the system": economist orientation, reformist ideology, the legalist fetish of seeing the arbitration system as delimiting the perspectives of industrial action, the artificial separation of industrial from political issues, and politically undirected militancy ("too much agitation and too little propaganda"). A special section was devoted to a discussion of "conservatism within the Left". The documents called for a confrontation with the fundamental organizing principles of the system—the "sacred rights" of the capitalist class over enterprises, compulsory arbitration and bourgeois legality—and a conscious intervention by trade unions in all spheres of social life. An immediate task was to replace the existing craft union structure with one which would unify the workers in each industry (thus ending the paralysis produced by "demarcation disputes" between unions) and break down the existing separation between professional and manual workers' organizations.

> "The new unionism based on wider aims, would recognize that the workers' movement faces a more powerful adversary than the individual capitalist—a closely-knit monopoly- arbitration-government structure which works on a general strategy. The essential aim must be to meet this with an overall strategy for social change, which involves a total challenge in all domains to the influence, domination, power and authority of the owner, controller and manipulator of our society."[17]

The minority's attack on the congress documents proceeded from a Soviet-oriented orthodoxy and formalism. The failure to name "marxism-leninism" as the party's source of inspiration was seen as important as the party's lapses from internationalism in failing to recognize the Soviet Union's "leading role" and to endorse the resolutions of the International Meeting and in its recalcitrance over Czechoslovakia. Involvement in the non-proletarian movements was seen as an abandonment of the working class in favour of a left-opportunist practice. The de-emphasis of a repressive proletarian dictatorship constituted a departure from fundamental marxist-leninist principles.

The new practice of open internal debate, and the circulation of written polemics placed the minority at a disadvantage. It was not simply that the habit of internal debate was unfamiliar (or perhaps even unsavoury,) to them: they were also opposed by extremely competent publicists. However, the minority now achieved a measure of coherence in campaigning against the acceptance of the leadership's documents by the Twenty-second Congress. Perhaps the clearest statement of the former's position was Alf Watt's pamphlet "Official CPA Congress Documents Analysed", a vigorous attack on the new policies which, in its positive pronouncements, applied the orthodox strategic and tactical precepts of the international communist movement to Australian conditions. More accurately, it reproduced the conventional collapse of strategy into tactics, and of existing class forces into a naively projected social polarization between "the monopolies" and "the people".

The united front is named as the "key tactic" and is intended "to win economic and political reforms". The united front itself was to mean nothing less than "ALP-Communist Unity" and the primary expression of this unity was to be a parliamentary coalition, since parliament "can be filled with genuine representatives of a people's mass movement against monopoly . . . passing laws around which the mass movement can be further rallied, and becoming an organizing centre against monopoly". This tactic was the unavoidable first stage of a two-stage socialist transformation, and the CPA leadership's attempt to promote radical demands represented a "fatal short cut", an "adventurist dream".

What was missing from Watt's pamphlet was any notion of the positive content of the socialist project, and inevitably there was not even an attempted answer to the strategic question of how that content was to be achieved. This strategic renunciation was expressed in the attitude adopted to the programme of the ACTU and "the progressive aspects" of ALP policy, which, "arising from the struggles of the workers, express their vital interests, though perhaps incompletely, and are the best available programme for united front activity and working class advance". This, and rigid insistence on the Soviet model ("Propaganda for anti-Soviet socialism is not propaganda for socialism at all") as the only possible one, exhausted the available "socialist" perspectives.

Watt equated the CPA's criticism of the Soviet Union and failure to endorse the decisions of the 1969 International Conference with anti-communism and capitulation to imperialism. In this context, he applauded—at some length—the PCI's firm stand against "anti-Sovieteers" when it expelled the *Il Manifesto* group.

The minority coalesced in the support mobilized for an alternative

programme written by Edgar Ross,[18] in consultation with other
prominent members of the minority, for submission to the Twenty-
second Congress. It lacked the clarity and pointedness of Watt's
polemic, but it expressed the same line and echoed the same silences.
It spoke of building "unity on immediate demands" in the unions
without coming to grips with the questions of the level at which this
unity was to be achieved or the nature of the demands. The defence of
"the right to strike" was not informed by a strategy for confrontation
with the system which severely curtails that right. Ross affirmed "the
decisive role" of the USSR internationally and of the marxist-leninist
party nationally, and made the following implicit reference to the CPA
leadership:

> "To be able to play its distinctive role the Communist Party wages an incessant
> struggle against the infiltration of capitalist ideas into its ranks, and the labour move-
> ment as a whole, particularly those which, under the guise of 'bringing marxism-
> leninism up to date' denigrate the role of the working class, suggest that it does not
> need to set up its own political power, its own state organizations to consolidate
> socialism, that not the class struggle but propaganda for general 'truths' and moral
> maxims will bring about socialism and that therefore, not the working class but
> intellectuals are the leaders of the socialist cause."[19]

The worst evils that had to be suppressed in the movement at the
present time, according to Ross, were "anarchists and followers of the
Fourth (Trotskyite) International". In its positive pronouncements, the
Alternative Statement was distinctly reformist:

> "We see as the most important thing the development of a united mass movement
> around immediate issues posed by the capitalist class and in furtherance of a pro-
> gramme of positive demands reflecting itself in parliament and other spheres, laying
> the basis for unity to bring about a revolutionary change in society along the lines of
> the stated objective of the Labour Party and our own—'the socialization of the
> industry, distribution and exchange'."[20]

The references to trotskyism in the CPA were to become more
common as the polemics intensified, although the only "evidence" of
its presence was that a journalist on *Tribune*, Denis Freney, had once
been a member of a Pabloite group. A tactic frequently resorted to by
the minority was the creation of straw men: the leadership's policies
had as little to do with trotskyism as with the abandonment of the
theses that the proletariat is the leading revolutionary force and that it
must replace the bourgeois state with its own state apparatus.

Thus the exchange of polemics made quite explicit two irreconcilable
strategic conceptions, encapsulated in the contradiction between
traditional frontism and the new "coalition of the left", between the
deliberate restriction of the Communist movement to the lowest
common denominator of a broad front and the immediate pursuit of
advanced demands, and between insistence on Soviet dominance in

the international Communist movement and its rejection. These antagonistic strategic conceptions were inseparable from the minority's insistence on the adequacy of Soviet model of socialism and the leadership's conviction that a whole new vision of socialism had to be constructed. The party's involvement in the new industrial militancy and radical mobilization at home, and its partisanship in the controversies raging in the international movement, meant that these antagonisms could not fail to produce diametrically opposed views on day-to-day practice and decisions.

Indeed, the very urgency of these issues was a contributing factor to the theoretical default on both sides. Despite the minority's insistence on a "class approach" in social analysis, any intelligible account of class interests and differentiations was suppressed in the opportunist formula of "the anti-monopoly alliance". The leadership's formulations for their part relied on social categorizations that were in parts vague, ambiguous and lacking any reference to basic capitalist social relations. The minority's programme relied heavily on the assumption of the neutrality of the state, but the fact that this assumption flatly contradicts classical marxist theory did not stimulate any debate about the nature of the capitalist state. Related to this was the lack of analysis on both sides of the political role of the ALP.

The Twenty-second Congress dashed the minority's hopes that the new trends within the CPA could be reversed: the *Statement of Aims* recommended by the National Committee was adopted by 118 votes to 12, and similar majorities were gained on other important issues. Soon afterwards the minority began, in effect, to organize as a faction within the CPA and lay the ground for a future split. Ross and Watt started an enterprise known as Socialist Publications, the main task of which was the publication of a newspaper, *Australian Socialist*, and at the same time they began to form "socialist unity committees" from handpicked dissidents in the CPA. Apart from continuing the polemics, which now included the claim that the decisions of the Twenty-second Congress were vitiated by the leadership's manipulations, they set out to obstruct the circulation of *Tribune* and boycott party meetings. Disciplinary action was finally taken against Ross and Watt, and after they confirmed that they intended to continue these activities, they were expelled. About the same time, Socialist Publications brought out a *Declaration*, signed by over 300 CPA members. It consisted of a restatement of Ross' *Alternative Statement* and a list of the leadership's errors, including "impatient, ultra-left activities", "adventurist policies and tactics", abandonment of united front policies for alliances with "ultra-radical fringe forces", "trotskyism", a "vacillating, opportunist position" and so forth. At this stage, the activities of the minority were seriously damaging the CPA's position in those trade unions in which members of the minority held official positions. While these activities showed no sign of eroding the leadership's majority support in the party, the number of veteran industrial cadres who identified with the minority was sufficiently large to disrupt the functioning of the party. The prolongation of the internal crisis led to a paralysis far more damaging than the eventual split.

When the dispute broke out into the open, the CCP and CPSU joined in. Both *Rude Pravo* and *New Times* published articles[21] on the dispute and referred to the minority as "the genuine marxist-leninists". The *Rude Pravo* article, "Trotskyism or Leninism" (attributed to W. J. Brown) was even reprinted separately by Peace and Socialism Publishers. In accordance with CPA practice, these articles were published in *Tribune* with a reply and a request that the relevant eastern European journals return the favour. This—it goes without saying— was not done. At the same time, the Soviet Embassy lent its financial and moral support to the minority.[22]

In spite of its influence and powerful friends, the minority did not yet feel in a position to form a breakaway grouping outside the party, and it made one more spectacular attempt to discredit the party leadership. Brown laid formal charges against the National Secretary, Laurie Aarons, alleging that he breached party rules by conspiring to change party policy as a result of "discussions with acknowledged trotskyites", notably Freney, and that he thereby brought the party into disrepute nationally and internationally.[23] A committee of five was selected to hear the charges, and for three months it solemnly heard evidence and arguments from the contending parties. The stalinist assumptions underlying these charges, no less than the absence of any evidence to support them, rebounded against the minority: the hearings provided a valuable platform for the majority view, and the inevitable result was a report from the Committee dismissing the charges as grotesque and severely criticizing Brown for having brought them.

During the latter part of 1971, the proposal to split the CPA was gaining support among the minority, although a sizeable section still opposed it. The minority held a meeting of its sympathizers in September, but most of those present opposed a split at that stage. On 5th December a second meeting was held, and a small majority voted for a split. About 400 CPA members thereupon left the party, and the Socialist Party of Australia was formed. The split severely depleted the CPA membership and trade union influence in Adelaide and Sydney, where the party had maintained a constant presence in the maritime unions. Other unionists, as a reaction to hectoring from both sides, left the party and consciously distanced themselves from both groupings.

The 1971 split was no more a clean division on ideological lines than the 1963 split. Many orthodox communists with no enthusiasm for the new policies were repelled by the machinations of the splitting faction, and the heavy-handed interference by the CPSU and the Soviet Embassy in the internal affairs of the CPA. Moreover, communist orthodoxy proscribed splitting a "legitimate" communist party, irrespective of substantive principles involved. The Soviet Union did not promise to withdraw recognition of the CPA (and in fact has not done so to date). Hence the new party, founded on rigid adherence to the CPSU and the official international communist movement, paradoxically was condemned, within the latter, to a somewhat dubious legitimacy. In certain areas, particularly Victoria where the earlier split had hit the party hardest, active steps were taken to prevent the defection of elements which had most in common with the splitters. Thus many who were still steeped in the old stalinist traditions remained in the party. On the other hand, where the splitters were strong, as they were in South Australia, many industrial cadres and trade union officials joined the new party simply in order to remain effective in their existing spheres of activity.

Since the formation of the new party, the Soviet Union has continued to give it all possible encouragement short of exclusive recognition as the Australian section of the international movement. At the end of 1972, both the CPA and the SPA were invited to the celebrations of the fiftieth anniversary of the USSR, and it is clear that the Soviet authorities have no intention of breaking off relations altogether with the CPA while the possibility remains that that party can be coaxed, persuaded or blackmailed into a new conformity.

In terms of industrial strength, SPA's position was at first more promising. It had strongholds in the Waterside Workers' Federation, Seamen's Union and certain unions in the building and motor industries. Inroads have subsequently been made into some of these, especially by the CPA on the Sydney waterfront. In 1973 the SPA lost its representation on the Executive of the ACTU.

The Whitlam Labour Government has received almost unreserved support from SPA since it was elected in December, 1972. Given the small size of the latter, its identification with Labour policy is not so much a united front, as a liquidation, which goes some way to explain its dwindling support and its inability to recruit new members. Another factor in this failure is its mindless celebration of the Soviet bloc, to the point where it has on at least one occasion given pride of place in its newspaper to reprints of *Rude Pravo* features defending treason trials of dissidents. This is hardly the stuff to foment proletarian revolution in Australia.

The CPA after the Split

The CPA held its Twenty-third Congress in April, 1972, in a despondent mood. According to all the immediate indicators, the party was at the nadir of its fortunes: its active membership could not have been more than about 1,500, its sources of funds and channels for working class agitation were severely reduced, many of its branches had been disrupted by the split, and it now had to contend with a possibly powerful rival which had the backing of the Soviet Union as well as the sympathy of many trade union officials. However, the party reaffirmed the new policies, retaining the 1970 documents and adding one more—*The Left Challenge for the Seventies*, which placed even heavier emphasis on the ideological offensive. It anticipated the election of a Labour government in December that year and the new situation that this would pose for the left. It acknowledged the autonomy of the liberation and anti-war movements and called for a non-manipulative but critical involvement in them. In its analysis of the labour movement, it stressed the importance of building on recent experiences of work-ins and intervention in political and social issues—experiences which have developed the self-confidence and class consciousness of the workers involved, and which have done most to erode "the hegemony of capitalist ideas".

In the political and industrial ferment of the six years prior to the split, communists had participated in all radical social movements, often advocating "advanced" policies, but in general participating on the latter's terms. This represented a break with former manipulative practices that had not gone unappreciated by other militants. In spite of this, the party had failed to attract significant numbers of those militants into its own ranks. One reason for this failure was the dominance of New Left ideology which denied the need for party organization altogether. But the more basic reason was the feeling that the CPA's destalinization had not gone far enough, and that the old habits of thought and action were a long time a-dying, the new "line" notwithstanding. The process had been, after all, a "revolution from above" which had avoided as far as possible alienating the more backward elements in the party. The split, however, seemed to have accomplished the catharsis that had been necessary all along, and for the left in general, the CPA took on a new complexion.

New Left groupings were virtually a spent force in 1972, and while many of their former activists disappeared from active politics altogether, others were analysing the reasons for their failure. In Australia as elsewhere, the New Left was crippled by its lack of theoretical rigour, the fragmentation of the movement into loose formations which fell under the domination of cliques, and the restriction of its social base to intellectuals and students. A need was felt once more for a party based on the working class, capable of developing a viable strategy for socialist revolution and of uniting at least some of the scattered elements of the Australian left. For many radicals the CPA, tangibly representing the continuity of the revolutionary socialist tradition in Australia, was now the most likely place to start the party-building process. Hence while young workers are the main group represented in the influx of new members since the split, many students and intellectuals have joined as well. The places of the older members who joined the SPA have been taken by much younger cadres—an essential process for a party which had not seen a substantial inflow of new members since the Second World War.

The CPA's present intervention into trade union affairs and industrial struggles is informed by the complementary themes of workers' control in industry and rank-and-file control of existing trade unions. Its propaganda on these issues sometimes lapses into abstract moralizing and sloganizing which, apart from its ineffectiveness, can alienate militants who are involved in difficult struggles against entrenched bureaucracies and depoliticized memberships. On the other hand, the successful application of the new policies has on occasions achieved dramatic results and invariably has met with the unreserved hostility of government, management and right-wing union officialdom alike.

The workers' control demand has appeared in many different guises. The work-in tactic has become almost a conventional weapon in the defensive armoury of more advanced unionists: it is employed not only to prevent lay-offs, but also to win positive demands.[24] In two large-scale industries—the power and motor industries—workers have successfully regulated production and controlled the speed of the line in the course of protracted disputes. The workers' control concept is also promoted in opposition to the ALP plan to undercut industrial militancy by the introduction of schemes for "workers' participation" in management, "job enrichment" and productivity bargaining. Finally, while not attempting to withdraw from or replace existing trade unions, the CPA has emphasized the need for rank-and-file organizations and shop committees in implementing the demand for workers' control. The latter are seen as important vehicles for industrial militancy in general.

The Builders' Labourers' Federation in New South Wales[25] illustrates the new industrial policies in practice. This union was previously controlled by gangster elements which maintained their grasp on official positions by intimidation. The wages and working conditions in the industry were among the worst in Australia, while the workforce itself was highly unstable and largely made up of migrants. A rank-and-file committee eventually managed to organize sufficient support to take control. A leading communist, Jack Mundey, became secretary of the union and initiated a number of measures to prevent the re-crudescence of bureaucratic power and privilege. A six-year limit was placed on tenure of office, wages paid to full-time union functionaries were to be suspended during general stoppages, and the rank-and-file committee was kept going. At the same time, sweeping demands for better pay and conditions were backed up by strikes, a few cases of industrial sabotage and vigilante teams who prevented the use of scab labour. The success of these campaigns, the consequent growth of the union and popularity of its leadership, and the experience gained by the rank-and-file were the pre-conditions for the builders' labourers' later intervention in issues that went far beyond the economic.

The building industry in New South Wales is the Achilles' heel of Australian capitalism. It has the highest profit rates (swollen by rampant speculation in real estate), and the highest rate of bankruptcies and scandals, which frequently involve prominent members of the State Government. "Development" in Sydney parlance is synonymous with massive social disruption, misallocation of resources, environ-mental destruction and total lack of planning. Entire communities are evicted to make way for office buildings while the housing shortage worsens and two million square feet of office space is unoccupied. The authorities have remained unresponsive to all objections and protests.

In the early seventies, the BLF began to impose "green bans" on demolitions and construction projects in response to requests from resident action committees, conservation groups and the National Trust. Where the bans were not directly enforceable, they were backed up by threats to stop work on all the offending "developer's" current projects. The union repeatedly insisted that these bans were an assertion of its members' right to make and enforce their own decisions on the operation of the industry and on the questions of social policy involved. The building industry, the New South Wales government and the con-servative press mounted a virulent campaign against communism, the workers' control movement, "industrial anarchy" and particularly "illegality". An attempt was made to undermine the solidarity of the workers by arguing that green bans threatened their jobs. But by this time, the builders' labourers had achieved a high degree of unity and politicization and the active support of other unions in the industry, and they were being hailed as the saviours of civilization by Nobel Prize winners, Princes of the Church and other pillars of the com-munity. By 1973, forty green bans were holding up approximately £2,000,000,000 worth of "development" contracts in Sydney. In the same year, the union placed bans simultaneously on work at two Sydney universities. The first was to force the authorities at Macquarie University to reinstate a student who had been expelled from a residential college for homosexuality, and the second was in support of a staff and student strike protesting against the Sydney University Professorial Board's refusal to allow a course in women's studies in the Philosophy Department.

Communist influence in union affairs has also increased in industries that do not provide such scope for spectacular interventions. In these unions, the "new unionism" is gradually being established, tied to a class combativity which is eroding the conservatism, legalistic fetishes and class collaborationist proclivities of union bureaucrats. This is true, for instance, of the Amalgamated Metal Workers Union which, with over 160,000 members (many of whom are in key industries) is by far the largest union in the country. The communist President of the Queensland Building Workers' Industrial Union, summed up the "new unionism" as follows:—

> "Within the union structure, the real decision making must be in the hands of the rank-and-file. This means that more energy, more time, more reliance must be put into building job organization; more stopwork meetings, with pay, to discuss union policy; the development of a job delegate organization much superior to that at present.
>
> "Job organization linked with progressive policies and leadership such as ours, can in a short period develop self-acting democratic structures controlled by the rank-and-file which would more effectively challenge the building industry bosses and challenge the system that bases itself on maximum profit as against the needs of the people.
>
> "This is what I think unionism is all about in the 1970s."[26]

The strength of the CPA's "counter-hegemonic" strategy has been its insistence on the themes of democracy, self-determination, self-generating activity and the use of these themes in a global critique of capitalism, from economic organization and political institutions to culture. An essential part of this strategy is the linking of general social issues to working class struggle: industrial action has been taken by communist influenced unions in the last two years in support of blacks', women's and homosexuals' rights; an embargo was placed on American goods by maritime unions during the concentrated bombing of Hanoi and Haiphong in December, 1972; funds have been collected by unions and other action taken in support of the Vietnamese, and the Chilean left since the 1973 coup.

Lack of development and clarity in key areas of the CPA's strategic thinking will be dealt with in the next section. But it is important to note at this stage the distance the "new policies" have taken the CPA from the theory and practice of the major communist parties in advanced capitalist countries.[27] It has broken with the concept of a two-stage revolution and the timid frontism which constricts strategic demands and perspectives to those acceptable to the lowest common denominator within a front which includes reformist elements. Eric Aarons recently articulated this difference:

"The two-stage idea is that first there will (must) be an anti-monopoly, democratic revolution which will later be followed by a socialist revolution. I am not arguing against possible stages in any revolution, for one must be open-minded to concrete circumstances. What is at stake here, however, is a strategy *based* on two stages. Without going into details, this concept is related to watering down demands and perspectives (which always leads in the direction of economism and an emphasis on 'unity' which buries principles), whereas in my view the conception of socialist revolution to-day must be deepened, and perspectives made more, not less, radical."[28]

This line has left the CPA free to project a socialist perspective in theory, and to adopt advanced positions in practice, to lead rather than tail behind working class and social movements.

The CPA's divergence from the practice of the major western communist parties can be clearly seen in the organizations through which it seeks to work. Hopes are not placed on the ascendency of a Labour Party left or on a possible parliamentary coalition implementing a "common programme". Apart from specific issues, the idea of party ententes within trade union councils has been specifically rejected. Instead, there is a perceived need for independent class organizations which in the short term have to be built up at the point of production; and in the long term, contrary to the implications of the "parliamentary road to socialism", the need for organs of dual power is recognized.

While rejecting conventional frontism, the CPA also rejects the concept of a monolithic party in favour of that of a coalition of revolutionary forces. The adoption of this schema was the first step in its still ambiguous rejection of a "revolutionary legitimacy" inherent in official communist parties. The acknowledgement of trotskyism as a contributor to the revolutionary movement was a break with stalinist demonology which, as we have seen, was seized upon by the right wing in the events leading up to the 1971 split as irrefutable evidence of the party's fall from grace.

The express break with both monolithism and the prefiguring of a one-to-one relation between the revolutionary party and the post-revolutionary state is no doubt an important departure from stalinism, but the very unevenness and underdevelopment of the political organizations of the Australian left effectively limits the application of the "coalition of the left" idea to co-operation with loosely-organized social movements. The SPA's gradualist line and the fact that its practice is limited to that of an electoral machine within the trade union movement and a ginger group to the ALP on the political level, makes it doubtful whether this formation can be realistically included in the left at all. Certainly, the bitterness and rivalry between this party and the CPA, the legacy of the split, makes co-operation between them difficult. The CPA (M-L), for its part, combines an hysterical sectarianism with a flair for unprincipled intrigue and manoeuvring within the unions. While its members hold positions in some unions and actively promote militant activity, the party itself is a declining force. Its dependence on Chinese patronage, its secrecy, deviousness and inept propaganda have effectively isolated it.

In numbers[29] and influence, the CPA, SPA and CPA (M-L) account for almost the entire left. The two aspirants for recognition as the Australian section of the Fourth International are no more than small propaganda groups which concentrate on the publication and sale of their respective newspapers. The relative political sophistication of these groups provides the only possibility of a "left debate" in Australia, and an external critique of the CPA in particular. But the critique as well as potential co-operation are hampered by the trotskyists' insistence that stalinism is the CPA's fixed, metaphysical essence, and thus sufficient reason to count it among the enemies of the working class.

Problems

Trotskyist metaphysics notwithstanding, the recent history of the CPA shows that official communist parties are not necessarily permanently compromised by the traditions of the Third International. The negative lesson in this history consists in the high price of regeneration—loss of influence in the trade unions, loss of membership and long periods of partial paralysis. The major causes of the CPA's decline are not, of course, to be sought in its internal history but in the second long boom from 1949 to the present, and in the success of the anti-communist offensive of the cold war. The internal disputes within the party were for the most part different responses to a social reality that flatly contradicted the nostrums of vulgar marxism and the prognostications of the international communist movement alike. Kelvin Rowley expressed the dilemma as follows:

"In the post-war period, many of those for whom the role of the working class in the struggle for socialism was an article of blind faith, rather than the outcome of rational analysis, have either retained the faith and retreated into dogmatic obscurantism, or have abandoned it and attempted to discover some alternative social base for a socialist movement. Common to both these approaches was an avoidance of the task of actually examining what has happened to Australian workers in the past twenty years. . . . The conclusion is that both the dogmatic and revisionist stances must be rejected: the former because it substitutes a mythical working class which it manufactures out of its own head for the reality; the latter because its assessment of the 'integration' of the working class is superficial and unhistorical. . . . This 'integration' is not due to long-term, structural changes in the nature of capitalism (as such theories require) but rather is due to more transient factors specific to the period which is now drawing to a close. Thus a 'classical' marxist approach is not 'obsolete'; on the contrary, such an approach is indispensable if we are to understand what is happening in the world today. What is obsolete is a tradition of vulgar, dogmatic caricatures of marxism."[30]

On the strategic problem of building class alliances, Rowley goes on to define the two historical alternatives as follows:

"The first is where labour moderates and weakens its militancy and restrains its demands against capital. This is the 'weak' solution, and the only possible alliance to result would be one of mutual subordination to capital. It is a bourgeois and not a socialist strategy. The 'strong' solution is that, although the working class must provide the backbone of the movement, it can never restrict itself to 'sectional' working class demands, but must concern itself with leading the struggle against injustices wherever they occur, must agitate and organize on all fronts and must try to isolate and weaken big capital whenever possible."[31]

It is in relation to this theoretical dilemma and this strategic choice that the post-war history of the CPA, and the diverging tendencies it now contains, are to be understood.

For reasons that have been elaborated earlier in this article, the 1971 split left the CPA with a strategic conception which, however much it pointed in a new direction, was undeveloped in crucial areas. The extent of this undevelopment was the extent to which the post-split consensus was more apparent than real. Two of these crucial areas were the party's analysis of the predicted ALP government, and its role in the international communist movement. The latter, far from being a trivial question of protocol, is forcing the party to face its own substantial differences with the mainstream of international communism. The fact that conflicting views on these issues were held by the leadership (and especially among those who had done most to steer the CPA on its new course), together with the perceived need for unity after the party's misfortunes, meant that these problems were disposed of with vague and ambiguous formulations, and where possible, they were skirted altogether. Indeed, the emphasis placed on militancy and confrontation with "capitalist values" amounted to a form of ideological reductionism which distracted attention away from strictly *political* issues and obstructed the achievement of greater programmatic clarity.

From the split up to the latter half of 1973, the main criticism of the party's theory and strategy came from intellectuals who joined after the split. In many cases, they had been involved in revolutionary politics long before their contact with the CPA. While no strict political homogeneity can be ascribed to this grouping, Louis Althusser's influence on it has been pronounced. Some of these intellectuals are editors of the independent marxist journal *Intervention*, which has attempted to stimulate and publish analyses of Australian society and theoretical discussion on issues raised by Althusser. This is clearly not the place to evaluate the latter's originality and general contribution to marxism: suffice it here to note the potential corrective implicit in both Althusser's main ideas and the timeliness of their intervention in the CPA.

For that party, despite the peculiarities of its development, has been heavily influenced by the successive theoretical trends in international communism. Indeed, its susceptibility in this regard is a measure of the historical underdevelopment of marxist theory in Australia. In common with its fraternal parties in Europe, it embraced first economic determinism, then stalinist dogma. After the CPSU Twentieth Congress and the Sino-Soviet split, the theoretical vacuum was filled by "creative marxism", which in the event covered a haphazard collection of concepts and theories, both survivals of earlier trends and new rationalizations for revisionist policies. It was small wonder, then, that in the late sixties, as the party became involved in movements led by radical intellectuals and New Left elements, it was unable to resist or critically evaluate their ideology. "Creative marxism" gave way to "humanist marxism" which, in its more crass expressions, took the form of unconsidered radical rhetoric and simplistic ethical critiques of capitalist "irrationality". This trajectory was more a succession of trends than a progress of theory, for new currents were rarely justified by a serious and sustained critique of the old. All these currents, moreover, shared a reductionist problematic which systematically obscured the complexity of social determinations. If the CPA was to use marxism for analysis rather than just mobilization, this reductionism had to be overcome.

The "Althusserians" within the party at first joined issue with the "humanist" trend on a fairly theoretical level, arguing for the need for a strategy which recognized the irreducibility of levels of struggle and criticizing the collapse of political perspectives into an undifferentiated ethical struggle against "capitalist values". They have insisted on the need for an exact knowledge of Australian society to inform strategy and to prevent its degenerating into abstract moralizing which fails to confront the complexities of each conjuncture on the one hand, and a populism which fails to differentiate class interests on the other.

But it was not long before two new fronts were opened up, as the group grew more impatient with the party's continuing ambivalence towards the new ALP government and soft-pedalling of its already-established differences with the international communist movement. The groups's most contentious contribution has been its critique of the frontism and parliamentarism of the major western European and Chilean communist parties, a critique based on the classical marxist theses on the class nature of the state and the impossibility of wielding it as an instrument of socialist transformation. On these two fronts, the group has drawn a good deal of fire from right-wing elements within the party, but not from the major part of the leadership, whose differences with the group's political stance are limited to matters of emphasis and tactics.

Althusser's own membership of the PCF and orthodoxy in relation to the "official" international communist movement is motivated by a belief in a single indivisible international workers' movement that Blackburn and Stedman Jones have aptly compared to Erasmus' conception of Christendom. They point out that, in spite of this, his ideas have led to the formation of left currents in European Communist parties and have, as well, provided the conceptual framework for a complex materialist analysis of the postition of particular oppressed groups, such as women, homosexuals and blacks, in a way that relates their liberation movements to the revolutionary struggles of the working class[32]—an area in which the major communist parties are notoriously backward. This Althusserian paradox has recently become particularly evident in the CPA, in which a number of serious attempts to analyse the weaknesses of the international communist movement and to lend theoretical coherence to the party's involvement in diverse liberation struggles have borne a distinctly Althusserian stamp.[33] The group's thinking certainly suffers from the usual shortcomings of any set of ideas originally conceived at a considerable remove from working class struggle, and it has often expressed itself in academic terms that hardly confront the day-to-day preoccupations of militanus in the party, but it has been moderately successful in precipitating debate on major issues. The controversies it generated were pushed into the background, however, by a resurgence of the "international problem".

In October–November 1973 talks were held in Moscow between the CPSU and the CPA to explore possibilities of "normalizing" relations between the two parties. From the CPA's point of view, the only advantage to be gained was sufficient Soviet recognition to allow it to maintain its credentials in the international communist movement. The CPSU for its part appeared to entertain hopes for the CPA's return to the fold, a desirable result in view of the SPA's abysmal record. In the first part of these "frank discussions", Laurie Aarons recapitulated earlier criticisms of the USSR's treatment of minorities and dissidents, its lack of democratic institutions and its manipulative interventions into the affairs of other parties, especially into those of the CPA. The Soviet delegates interjected with a mixture of abuse, threats and platitudes about "Soviet achievements".[34] However, in the subsequent session, the other two CPA delegates tacitly opposed Aarons' position and agreed to work for the CPA's acceptance of the CPSU's terms for "normalization": recognition of the Soviet bloc as "socialist" rather than "socialist-based", unqualified support for Soviet foreign policy (especially détente policies which had been attacked in *Tribune*) and cessation of criticism of the USSR in CPA journals. From that point, differences within the leadership were openly acknowledged.

When the right wing[35] of the leadership took its stand at the subsequent National Committee meeting, it did so on issues far wider than the Soviet one. In its attacks on the "left-adventurism" of the builders' labourers, "sectarianism" towards the ALP and overseas communist parties as much as in its pro-Soviet apologetics, it demonstrated its tacit disapproval of the "strong solution" with which the Aaronses were identified. The right's isolation in the National Committee, which unanimously rejected the Soviet terms, was followed by a spate of polemics between the party leaders, ostensibly in the form of contributions to discussion leading up to the Twenty-fourth Congress in 1974. That the real issue in the debate over internationalism is whether the CPA is to revert to orthodox gradualism is clear from a "symptomatic" reading of John Sendy's contribution.[36] It poses the basic question, "Is the party going to develop as a responsible, Communist political organization?", and comments on the international question:

"A number of leading comrades consider that our links with the world communist movement are in fact a hindrance to us and that most CP's, with the notable exception of the Vietnamese, are 'no bloody good' . . .

"It is curious that the party leadership has never in recent times defended the Chilean, Italian, French and other CP's which frequently come under attack in Tribune articles and letters. Nor does it wave a demurring finger (publicly) at such things. The reason is obvious. Some comrades have come to the same conclusion as Ted Hill came to in 1962—that largely the CP's in capitalist countries are being contained by capitalism, are maintaining it and abrogating the development of revolutionary struggle—that we are living in a situation surrounded by a sea of revisionism as Hill put it then."

He goes on to conclude that the party is "well on the way to a left line which can isolate us and ruin the Party for years to come".

Since the chances of a reversal of the party's "new policies" are remote, the dissolution of the former unreal consensus may have the positive result of clarifying the issues raised in this controversy. Another desirable result could be the serious posing of the questions raised by the Labour government and its impact on capitalist development and consolidation in Australia.

In the late 60s the ALP, under Gough Whitlam's leadership, underwent a thorough-going transformation. The old, populist rhetoric gave way to a new image, one much more akin to those of European social democratic parties. Whitlam promised not equality but growth, not nationalization but planning, not a workers' government but a régime of efficient administrators whose trade union affiliations allowed them to guarantee what the liberals never could— industrial peace. Technocratic labourism may have occasioned little response to the labour movement, but its birth was celebrated by the more progressive elements of capital and the financial press. The enthusiasm with which they supported the ALP's successful bid for office in the December 1972 elections was to a great extent a response to the bankruptcy of the Liberal-Country Party government after its twenty-three years of unbroken rule. Many economic sectors called for the decisive intervention that the Liberals could not make. Subsidization and protection of inefficient industries constituted a continuing heavy burden on other sectors. A lack of government planning and co-ordination perpetuated misallocation of resources and uncertainty of markets. The fact that the coalition parties were tied to sectional (especially rural) interests meant they had no room to manoeuvre to overcome these economic problems. The growing absenteeism, job dissatisfaction, high labour turnover, recurrent labour shortages and strikes pointed to the need for "rational" man-power and integrationist policies which could only be introduced by a government that the labour movement could "trust". Liberal foreign policy, based on containment of communism in Asia and "forward defence" collapsed in the failure of Australia's military adventure in Vietnam—an adventure which had seriously weakened social cohesion at home. In foreign policy, the Liberals now offered nothing but a barrier between Australian exporters and the enormous untapped markets of communist Asia.

The economy which the Labour government inherited, though superficially stable, had serious structural weaknesses. The normal features of an advanced capitalist economy—high wages, monopoly control and large-scale secondary industry—co-exist with low productivity and a comparatively low growth rate. The balance-of-payments had long depended on favourable terms of trade for agricultural exports. The decline in this sector during the sixties was compensated, not by the export of uncompetitive Australian manufactured goods, but by mineral exports whose share of total export income rose in this period from 8 to 29%. Dependence on non-industrial exports goes hand-in-hand with a continuing dependence on overseas sources of capital and technology: a third of Australian industry is overseas controlled, while only 14% of new products are developed locally. Australia's heavy dependence on Britain, Japan and the USA is a particular cause of concern.

Australia joined the OECD in 1971, and the following year that body produced a survey of the economy which contained a comprehensive plan for overcoming these weaknesses, and above all, for producing a high and stable growth rate.[37] The new government has followed this plan with extraordinary fidelity. In particular, it has attempted to offer a package deal to the labour movement: in exchange for the latter's acceptance of wage restraints, it is offered improved social benefits (including a national health scheme), workers' participation in management and inclusion of trade union leaders on government planning boards. Since the new social benefits are to be financed by per-capita levies, and the workers' participation schemes leave the traditional prerogatives of capital untouched, the new régime is hardly a burden on the capitalist class. On the contrary, the latter is the beneficiary of the new medium- and long-term planning, the already significant achievements of recent trade delegations to China and North Vietnam and the new government assistance to Australian enterprises establishing subsidiaries in South-East Asia. Dislocation of the work force was hardly a consideration in the progressive abolition of subsidies to inefficient industries and an across-the-board 25% tariff reduction in July 1973, but again, the financial press hailed this reversal of hallowed Labour policy in the interests of economic "rationalization" as an "act of true statesmanship"

While the new régime has certainly proved that it is "good for business confidence", its standing in the labour movement has become somewhat precarious. It has presided over a boom period in which profit increases have demonstrably outstripped wage increases, and the latter are rapidly undermined by a 14% rate of inflation. A redistribution of national income in favour of the working class has no place in the ALP programme, but present trends point to an actual decrease in the proportion going to that class. In these circumstances, the government's prices and incomes policy met with bitter opposition from major unions. One year after its taking office, the government held a referendum to give the Federal Parliament power to introduce a prices and incomes policy. Many sections of the labour movement campaigned against it, and it was overwhelmingly defeated. The proposed introduction of "workers' participation", "job enrichment" and productivity bargaining have met with an equally sullen reception from left-wing unions.

The CPA's response to the new régime has been a studied refusal to see in its programme an integrated and coherent plan to increase and stabilize growth (and therefore profit) rates, and to that end to tie the work force more closely to the interests of capital at the point of production, in the board room and on government planning panels. Its critique of the ALP government, which starts with the assumption that the latter is a "merely reformist" régime, deals with the items in its programme in a piecemeal fashion, supporting the "progressive" measures and attacking those which it sees as opposed to the interests of the working class (especially the incomes and "industrial relations" policies). The setbacks suffered by the CPA through its "sectarianism" in the Third Period and in the 1949 Coal Strike are repeatedly invoked in aid of this approach. Finally, most communists see the ALP as a "working class party" by reason of its mass electoral base in that class and its institutional links with the trade unions. It hardly needs to be pointed out that this sociological reductionism is flatly contradicted not only by the rationality of technocratic labourism, but also by the whole genesis and history of the ALP itself. Nevertheless, the conclusion is often drawn that the CPA should *always* give high priority to preserving Labour's electoral base.

It can be said in defence of the present CPA approach to Labour in office that it at least counters illusions that the ALP is potentially a socialist party or that socialism could be achieved by a left Labour government. The CPA's total opposition to class collaboration and insistence on mass activism is at least a partial mobilization against the new threat posed to the independence and effectiveness of working class organizations. Failure to situate the several actions of this government in their wider context, however, leads to a consistent misperception of those actions, a dangerous non-perception of their overall thrust, and the CPA's resulting lack of strategic coherence.

At the core of this analytic failure is the absence, referred to earlier, of an autonomous notion of political struggle (including a conception of the state that goes beyond a narrow institutional definition) in the CPA's theoretical framework. For an understanding of the ALP is to be sought not in its electoral base but in its relation to the state and the latter's articulation of the interests of capital. Positing an expressive relationship between the trade unions and the ALP is no less misleading: even the most "tame-cat" unions are directly involved in day-to-day class confrontations at the point of production, such that, in the economic sphere at least, they must remain sensitive to working class interests in spite of their subordination to the state. This failure to appreciate the ALP's structural independence from the trade unions also underpins the CPA's blanket inhibitions against "sectarianism". In fact, the political arraignment of the ALP is hardly a bar to unity between communist and Labour militants on the shop floor.[38]

The recent isolation of the right in the CPA may clear the way for a more rigorous approach to the Labour government. The issue is still very much alive in the internal party debate, and its outcome will determine the party's capacity to produce a coherent strategy for the labour movement for the remainder of the decade.

*   *   *

This period may well be decisive for the development of an effective revolutionary movement in Australia. The growing industrial militancy of the last few years, expressed particularly in the combativity towards the arbitration system, has led to a weakening of traditional restraints on working class initiatives in economic struggle. But the now widening gap between the ALP and its working class electoral base is likely to have even more significant political consequences. As well, the ascendancy of technocratic labourism, the abandonment of the ALP's traditional (if purely ideological) identification with the underprivileged and its active courting of the urban middle class has made its links with the trade unions particularly tenuous, as the latter's often hostile reception of key government policies has illustrated. The incompatibility between technocratic labourism and the growing class consciousness in the labour movement is becoming increasingly obvious.

The restraints on working class mobilization referred to would be taxed still further in the event of an economic downturn. And there is every possibility that the next few years will reveal the fragility of the Australian economy, dependent as it is on three major markets and sources of capital and technology: Britain, Japan and America. As recent events have shown, all three are facing difficulties—although to different degrees—in maintaining stable growth rates and their international competitiveness. Should the British or American government attempt to alleviate their serious balance of payments problems by restricting imports into, or the flow of capital out of, their countries, their actions could lead to stagnation and unemployment in Australia. Whether such a recession eventuates in the mid-seventies or not, the structural imbalance of the Australian economy, its low growth rate and the low productivity of its secondary industry, will not be easily eradicated by all the OECD-inspired wizardry at the government's command. And Australian "mini-imperialism", its attempts to establish markets and investment outlets in South-East Asia, will inevitably meet with more and more formidable opposition from US and Japanese imperialism.

Australia in the seventies, then, offers considerably brighter prospects for revolutionary working class and mass mobilization than at any time since the thirties. The CPA's strategic thinking in this new situation suffers from some crucial weaknesses, many of them associated with the difficulty of overcoming its own past. But it remains the only existing political organization capable of implementing an overall socialist strategy for the labour movement and of forging the class alliances essential to the success of the socialist project. This is not simply an observation on its working class and mass links, but also on its independence from the constricting perspectives and political constraints imposed by the "official" international communist movement on its orthodox sections. More positively, it is an observation on its adoption of the "strong solution" which requires that it continue to mobilize around the most advanced demands rather than attempt to dampen and restrain mass upsurges in the name of a " 'unity' which buries principles".

But the immediate obstacles before the Australian left are internal ones: the absence of a productive left debate that could only emerge out of a polycentric political movement, and the CPA's own theoretical backwardness in key areas of strategy.

NOTES

1. For a more detailed discussion of the development of capitalism in Australia, see Kelvin Rowley, "Pastoral Capitalism", *Intervention*, no. 1 (1972), and "The Political Economy of Australia Since the War" in J. Playford and D. Kirsner (eds.), *Australian Capitalism* (Penguin, Melbourne, 1972) and Bruce MacFarlane, "Australia's Role in the World Capitalism" in the same volume. The genesis of the labour movement is analysed in Humphrey McQueen, *A New Britannia* (Penguin, Melbourne 1971).

2. "Socialism and Labourism" in Richard Gordon (ed.), *The Australian New Left* (Heinemann, Melbourne 1970), p. 55.

3. A useful factual account of the CPA's history is Alastair Davidson, *The Communist Party of Australia* (Hoover, Stanford, 1969).

4. (Australian) *Communist Review*, September 1948, pp. 270–1. See also in the same issue "Reply of the CPGB" and "British CC's Reply Rejected". The effect of this dispute on the CPGB is recounted in Edward Upward's novel *The Rotten Elements*. The relevance of the issues raised in this debate to the later Sino-Soviet dispute was referred to in an interview between CPA leaders and Mao Tse-tung in 1960: see the transcript of this interview in E. F. Hill, *Australia's Revolution: On the Struggle for a Marxist-Leninist Communist Party* (CPA (M-L) publication), pp. 249–254.

5. See ibid., pp. 187–223 for Hill's speech to the CPA Central Committee in February 1962. Hill was the leader of the pro-Chinese faction and has led the CPA (M-L) since its foundation.

6. Significantly, almost all the Chinese-trained cadres remained in the CPA.

7. This incident, described in Eric Aarons, "As I Saw the Sixties", *Australian Left Review*, no. 27 (October–November 1970) reveals the CPSU's heavy-handedness in dealing with fraternal parties—a quality that was again to the fore in the 1973 CPSU-CPA talks, referred to later.

8. The fact that Gramsci's writings were contained in occasional articles, correspondence and unedited notebooks makes the problem of interpretation difficult in any event.

9. *Australian Left Review*, no. 4, 1968.

10. *Tribune*, 24 July, 1968.

11. "Czechoslovakia and the USSR: Why?", *Tribune*, 4 September 1968.

12. "On Self-Determination," *Australian Left Review*, no. 5 of 1968, p. 44.

13. Industrial action in solidarity with overseas movements was not new to the CPA. Action had been successfully promoted during the Spanish Civil War, against export of pig-iron to Japan in 1938, and in support of Indonesian and Vietnamese struggles for independence, 1945–8 and 1954 respectively.

14. A clear comparison between the minority's and the leaders' views on industrial

questions was published in pamphlet form by the party in November 1969 under the title "Two Views of Modern Unionism". The pamphlet was made up of an exchange of letters between Frank Purse and Laurie Aarons.

15. Geoff Sorrell, "The Arbitration System" in Playford and Kirsner, op. cit., p. 255. This is true in an institutional sense, quite apart from the widely held view that trade unions are structurally tied to the state.

16. "Statement of Aims, Methods and Organization", "Modern Unionism and the Workers' Movement" and "Charter of Democratic Rights". Since their adoption, these documents have remained part of the official CPA programme.

17. "Modern Unionism", op. cit., p. 10.

18. *Discussion*, no. 1 of 1970, p. 20.

19. Ibid., p. 29.

20. Ibid., p. 30. The minority's extraordinary fetishism of governmental power that went hand in hand with its faith in the ALP was shown in their opposition to black bans on war materials bound for Vietnam: ". . . the decision to withdraw the trips must be made by a govt. and not by some queer form of workers' control". (*Australian Socialist*, no. 2.)

21. See *New Times*, no. 36 (9th September 1970) for an abridged version of the *Rude Pravo* article, and *New Times*, no. 1 (1 January 1971) for the main Soviet attack.

22. Detailed information on events leading to the split are contained in two CPA publications, "What's Happening in the CPA?" (1970) and the Letter to Fraternal Parties of 16 December 1971. As a result of Soviet interference in the CPA's internal affairs, letters were sent to the CC, CPSU, requesting that Soviet representatives in Australia refrain from discussing with, advising or otherwise assisting anyone in the CPA opposing its decisions and that the CPSU refrain from attacking the CPA in discussions with members of delegations from mass organizations visiting the USSR. The CPA further requested a return to the pre-1968 practice of inter-party consultation about the relation of trade union and other delegations to the USSR.

23. The charges and "evidence" are elaborated in W. J. Brown, "What Happened to the Communist Party of Australia?" (Socialist Unity Committee publication, November 1971). Aarons' defence is contained in a contemporary CPA pamphlet, "For a United Revolutionary Party". And see *Tribune*, 22 September 1971.

24. Workers even took over the construction of the Sydney Opera House in 1972 and thereby forced sub-contractors to concede the stringent demands made by the two unions involved, in both of which communist influence was strong.

25. A detailed account of this union's development and activities is P. Thomas, *Taming the Concrete Jungle: the Builders Labourers' Story* (BLF publication, Sydney, 1973).

26. Ibid., p. 65.

27. A good critique of these parties in general is contained in *Il Manifesto's* "Theses", translated in *Politics and Society*, Vol. 1, no. 2 (August 1971). There is a good deal of similarity between the positions taken up by *Il Manifesto* and the CPA. Also see Bill Warren's "The Programme of the CPGB: A Critique" in *New Left Review*, no. 63 (September/October 1970).

28. "The Chilean Revolution", *Australian Left Review*, no. 42 (December 1973), p. 8.

29. Approximate memberships are: CPA 2,300, SPA 600, CPA (M-L) 200, main trotskyist groups 200.

30. "The Political Economy of Australia", op. cit., p. 321.

31. Ibid., p. 323.

32. "Louis Althusser and the Struggle for Marxism" in Dick Howard and Karl E. Klare (eds.), *The Unknown Dimension: European Marxism Since Lenin* (Basic Books, New York, 1972), pp. 382–4.

33. In December 1973, the group produced an 85-page discussion document as part

of pre-Twenty-fourth Congress discussion. In spite of a good deal of wordiness and derivativeness, this document makes some theoretical headway on the issues of strategy, liberation movements, internationalism, the nature of Soviet society, the Australian economy and the vexed question of the ALP. A reading of this and other contributions of the group shows it to be selective in its application of Althusser's ideas.

34. While this anti-CPA apoplexy was being enacted in Moscow, Laurie Carmichael (Assistant Commonwealth Secretary of the AMWU and CPA National Executive member) was receiving a pointedly enthusiastic welcome in Hanoi. The long-standing warmth of VWP-CPA relations was based on the Vietnamese' high estimation of the Australian anti-war movement and the CPA's mobilization of material support for the war effort and post-war reconstruction. The Vietnamese' comments to Carmichael (*Tribune*, 30 October 1973) suggested, however, that the two parties also shared a distaste for interference in their internal affairs and grave doubts about détente politics.

35. It would be simplistic to identify this group as it first emerged with any coherent position beyond a retreat from those adopted by the party since the mid-sixties, and an admiration of the size and achievements of the larger western communist parties. It is curious that two of its most prominent members, John Sendy and Bernie Taft, played a large part in promoting the new policies. The latter, who was singled out for attack in the 1971 *New Times* article (footnote 21), was the most prominent advocate of appeasement in the 1973 Moscow talks. More recently, it has attempted to re-interpret the existing party programme so as to present it as an expression of conventional frontism and the revolution-in-stages schema. Thus they include the ALP in the "coalition-of-the-left" and "socialist-based" is made synonymous with "socialist", etc. Their line strongly echoes that of the minority prior to the split, even though it is expressed with more sophistication and European urbanity.

36. "The Real Issues before the Party and the Congress" (CPA publication, November 1973).

37. For analyses of this plan and the government's adherence to it, see B. Catley and B. MacFarlane, "Labour's Plan: Neo-capitalism Comes to Australia", *Intervention*, no. 3 (August 1973) and three articles in *Arena*, nos. 32–3 (1973) sub. nom. "Technocratic Labour in Office". See also Bill Warren, "Capitalist Planning and the State", *New Left Review*, no. 72 (March–April 1972), for an excellent analysis of capitalist planning.

38. For many militant trade union officials, membership of the ALP is no obstacle to co-operation with communists, participation in advanced actions or even opposition to ALP policy. Bob Pringle, N.S.W. President of the BLF is a prominent example of this phenomenon.

STRUCTURALISM—SCIENCE OR IDEOLOGY

Raoul Makarius

FREAK or genius? Opinion with regard to Lévi-Strauss has wavered persistently between these two extremes. The question is personal and quite irrelevant to anthropological theory. That it is raised, however, is symptomatic of the bewilderment of those who avowedly do not understand him, when confronted with the ecstatic transports of those who professedly do. All, of course, recognize signs of intense cleverness in his writings; but cleverness, as felt by many, borders perilously on sheer artfulness.[1] It is therefore not surprising that his writings should always have been received with diffidence by British anthropologists. Obviously, before such distrust could be overcome, wide acceptance of his views, in Britain, was hardly to be expected.

For a long time, Lévi-Strauss's books were available solely in French, and thus were read only by a minority of British social anthropologists who, as Professor Leach remarks, were "put off by what may be called the oracular elegance" of his style.[2] Indeed, even when translated into English, passages of Lévi-Strauss "seem almost meaningless". Are they more meaningful in French? Difficulty in understanding him has been reported not only by his English readers, but by . . . Lévi-Strauss himself, when re-reading his writings.[3] Yet if we are to follow Leach, the cause of the trouble is due not so much to the "verbal obscurity" surrounding the "profundity" of Lévi-Strauss's thoughts, as to the peculiar subtleties of the French tongue and the general subservience of his English readers to traditional British empiricism. If, therefore, they are uneasy and uncomfortable before a Lévi-Straussian script, the fault is all theirs (they are biased . . . their French is not up to standard etc.), and have no one but themselves to blame.

Now the interesting thing is that *Les structures élémentaires de la parenté*, on which Lévi-Strauss's celebrity rests, is among the least nebulous of his works. In some parts, it does indeed make very hard reading, and often when the author ought to be explicit he becomes ambiguous; but these difficulties are due to the nature of the subject, and perhaps to a certain amount of precautionary restraint exercised by the author, not to any affectation of style, or other preciosities peculiar to French. So that if that work, in spite of its much-vaunted merits, did

189

not meet with immediate response in Britain, the reason was not linguistic. In France it did not fare better. Serious attention was paid to it only in the mid-sixties (the book appeared in 1949), although outside of social anthropology the champions of structuralism justified their conversion to the new doctrine on the grounds that it had passed the severe test of scientific scrutiny, precisely in that discipline, and that its principles and methodology could be applied successfully in the *sciences humaines* generally. It was only after structuralism had come into fashion that the *ethnologues* realized that they, the most concerned, were badly out of step. Eager students and belated scholars—but also their plodding and more prudent seniors—then started discovering the hidden virtues of structural analysis, and vying with one another to bask (and shine) in the reflected light of its inventor's fame.

It was not, therefore, to his work as an anthropologist, or "scientist" that Lévi-Strauss owed his success, but to other factors, such as his merits as a writer. His one readable book, *Tristes tropiques*, published in 1955, at once commended itself to the public and won him literary fame. Unfortunately, in his other more anthropological writings, instead of drawing on his exceptional talents to elucidate complex problems, which usually defy clear formulation, he strives to achieve the opposite and perverse result of completely befuddling his reader with oblique references and unnecessary innuendo, even when dealing with plain and simple ideas. Excelling, as he does, in marshalling an imposing array of words and phrases with unshaken assurance, he contrives to create uncertainty as to the real meaning they are intended to convey (thus opening avenues of safe retreat), while at the same time implanting conviction regarding the impeccable logic by which they are ruled. In short, he has raised to a fine degree of perfection the art of saying anything and getting away with it.

Another factor which contributed to build up his reputation relates this time not to form but to content. In developing the concepts of "structure" and "structuralism" along new lines, he provided the ideological framework needed to justify the operational methods of modern processes of production and control, at a time when their alienating effects were being increasingly denounced. As an ideology ultimately consists of a distortion, if not a misrepresentation of reality, and must therefore rest on warped premises, its makers are faced with the task of giving these a deceptive appearance of verity. This they succeed in doing all the better when they share the illusions they strive to propagate. In the case of "structuralism", as a framework, or basis of ideology, formulated in terms of anthropological theory, form and content join hands in happy complicity under Lévi-Strauss. For in his case, the price of literary virtuosity is incapacity to resist its temptations and forego the delights which the production of "harmonious ambiguities" helpfully procure.[4] Willingly or unwillingly, as far as he is concerned, the involutions of his style, with the ambiguities they contain, dovetail, as it were, into the gaps left by inconsequential reasoning and inconsistencies. Fallacies of argument, which would stand out conspicuously in a plain and straightforward exposition of ideas, are blurred out of significance and escape detection. As ambiguities, with their magma of associated ideas, often depend on the language in which they are formulated, they are liable to disappear in translation, leaving a residual meaning manifest in all its nakedness; deformity of thought and absurdities then stand exposed. That is why passages by Lévi-Strauss appear "quite preposterous when translated into English", as Leach observes, and not because English is different from French.[5]

Lévi-Strauss's equivocations have the further advantage of allowing his readers to read different meanings in his texts; so that each, according to his particular conception of structure and structuralism, may, with a little effort, interpret his words so as to make them fit them. As curiosity about structuralism waxed, book after book appeared, purporting to explain it to the layman. Naturally, the presentation of Lévi-Strauss's ideas varied considerably from one to the other, but in most of these books, social anthropology was treated as just one discipline—albeit a privileged one—out of many, in which structuralist methodology and approach were considered operative and yielding positive results. Without realizing it, their authors were showing that structuralism represented a new development in the *ideology* of contemporary society. Obviously, structuralism could not be a new philosophy, although rooted in a certain brand of philosophical thought, since it did not set out to *interpret* or *explain* the world, but to introduce a new way of *looking at* it, and therefore ultimately of determining judgements and conduct with respect to the things of the world and society. For in spite of the different and even conflicting interpretations of structuralism given by its exponents and popularizers, there was common agreement amongst them on at least a number of its more conspicuous aspects. The ultimate reference was, of course, inevitably Lévi-Strauss, not only because he occupied the leading position in the field, but also because his discourse on the subject was flexible enough to fit into widely different interpretations.

But however elusive Lévi-Strauss may be, it is not impossible to pin him down to what one is tempted to call certain basic articles of faith, provided care is taken not to fall victim of the deceptive statements which abound in his works, nor, above all, to draw hasty conclusions from what he seems to be implying, but never commits himself to say. For instance, on the basis of oft-repeated declarations, he has been described as a Marxist, or near-Marxist; an adept of Hegelian dialectics;

a representative of the French traditional school of anthropology; a continuator of Marcel Mauss; a confirmed materialist, etc., etc., when in actual fact the full weight of his works is directed against the marxist interpretation of history; his criteria of reasoning are rigorously mechanistic; his anthropology is an elaboration of Robert Lowie's, with secondary borrowings right and left; while in his role as continuator of Mauss, he is so in so far as he contradicts the latter's fundamental position on the nature of social phenomena. Lastly, it is difficult to see by what standards he has been described as a materialist. [6]

Structural Analysis and Combinatory Logic

It is possible to approach Lévi-Strauss's system of thought from various angles, precisely because it presents an appearance of logical coherence. The system cracks up and the incoherences appear when it is strained beyond breaking point to fit the facts. Before setting out to examine it, however, it is necessary to say what it is not, and remove certain initial ambiguities.

Contrary to what the word seems to imply, structuralism, as presented by Lévi-Strauss, does not propose to study social structures, or the structure of social phenomena. That was the object, in a general way, of the structuralists, properly so called, who preceded him and who, in Britain for instance, made valuable contributions to social anthropology in spite of a certain onesidedness due to their anti-historical bias. The terms "structuralism" and "structuralists" as currently used today must therefore be understood as broadly referring to Lévi-Strauss's school of thought and to his followers, unless the context makes it clear that it is otherwise. As used by modern structuralists, the word "structure" is applied indiscriminately to a variety of phenomena not necessarily of the same order. Sometimes it is used in the traditional, classical sense; sometimes it refers to "mental structures", or "structures of the unconscious", not in the Freudian, or even general psychological sense, but in a sense left to the reader's better judgement to decide. At other times it refers to what some authors regard more properly as ideal models of social phenomena. Lévi-Strauss sometimes uses the term as though it referred not even to such models, but to a logically inter-locking set of rules capable of manifesting themselves empirically, but not necessarily doing so. So that, in fine, while social phenomena are viewed as made up of component elements, it is not the structure of these phenomena which the structuralist studies, but what he regards as the rules whereby their component parts may or may not be joined together.

That a social phenomenon is a whole embracing the totality of its parts is, of course, a tautology. That it may be studied and therefore understood in terms of the rules governing the relations among its parts,

follows logically enough, and to some will commend itself as methodo-
logically economical and advantageous, since the results of a study of
rules and relationships, necessarily carried on an abstract level, will be
comprehensive in its scope and apply to the various individual manifestations of the phenomenon concerned. To many, however, this approach
will appear dangerous and unreliable precisely because carried on at an
abstract level; for however carefully concrete facts are translated into
abstract language, there can never be any certainty that elements of
meaning foreign to the former will not slip inadvertently into the latter.

At first sight, the difference between the study of a social phenomenon
in its abstract expression to grasp its significance directly at that level,
and the empirical and comparative examination of the various particular forms which it assumes in the world of reality in order to draw
generalizations from that basis, may seem to be simply a difference of
method; and indeed structuralists often insist that structuralism is not
a doctrine or philosophy, but simply and quite modestly a method.
However, it is more than that, and would have scarcely provoked wide
discussion if it had not been.

Now, if a given phenomenon is the sum (or more) of its component
parts, this is proof that these parts are capable of combining to form a
whole. But what if these same parts, or elements as we shall call them,
are combined differently? If the order or conditions under which they
combine are relevant, each new combination will produce theoretically
a new form of variety of the phenomenon under study. Thus, given a
certain number of elements, it will be possible to work out mathematically the total number of combinations into which they may enter,
and therefore the number of distinct forms in which the phenomenon
concerned may manifest itself. In these conditions, quite a small
number of elements will suffice to account for a relatively considerable
sum of combinations. In many, if not in most cases, however, it will
happen that owing to the properties of these elements, or to other
factors, a large number of combinations will be ruled out, leaving a
really very limited number that can be easily dealt with conceptually.

Suppose, by way of illustration, we consider "first cousin marriage".
Each marriage will consist of a combination of two *cousins* (elements)
of *opposite* sexes. Now, the different mathematically possible combinations between two cousins, *irrespective* of sex, are those between

1) two sons of two brothers
2) two daughters of two brothers
3) a son and a daughter of two brothers
4) two sons of two sisters
5) two daughters of two sisters
6) a son and a daughter of two sisters

7) two sons of a brother and sister
8) two daughters of a brother and sister
9) a son and a daughter of a brother and sister

The total number of possible combinations is thus nine. However, out of these nine combinations, only a third, or three, are between cousins of opposite sexes and therefore marriageable, representing the different possible types of first cousin marriage. The other six are ruled out.

This by way of example to illustrate one type of structural analysis. Structuralism, of course, does not stop at this level of simplicity. In the case of cousin marriage, which presents no mystery, the analysis would be pointless. It is otherwise when the object to be analysed is not clearly understood, for then the purpose of the analysis is to make it comprehensible. A case in point is that of totemism, where on the basis of the analysis made, far-reaching conclusions have been drawn concerning the nature of the phenomenon.

Totemism refers to a peculiar association, in most cases between the animal world and the world of man, familiar to field-workers, who have described it with a wealth of details, both as a system of social organization and a system of beliefs. When examined "structurally", all of its sociological manifestations are ignored, as though inexistent, and only its formal, external aspect is considered in terms of *mechanical* relations between two *distinct* abstract concepts: the "collective" and the "individual". These are supposed to be the "elements" to which both the animal world and the world of humans may be reduced, and which through their combinations in all the mathematically possible ways, construct so many different types of totemism. The resulting combinations are four in number, giving four types of totemism:

1) between animals as a *collective* entity (a species) and humans as a *collective* entity (a clan)
2) between animals as a *collective* entity (a species) and a human as an *individual* entity (a particular person)
3) between an animal as an *individual* entity (a particular animal) and humans as a *collective* entity (a clan)
4) between an animal as an *individual* entity (a particular animal) and a human as an *individual* entity (a particular person)

Every known case of totemism should fall under one of these four categories, since they logically exhaust all possible combinations, provided, of course, that the basic assumption is correct, namely that the phenomenon in its total manifestations is composed of the different combinations of the elements mentioned above.

Now, as long as the phenomenon itself (totemism) is very imperfectly understood, there can be no decisive way of determining whether or not the exhaustive classification proposed according to the criteria postulated (individual and collective entities) is not after all purely arbitrary and the result of clever manipulation. Lévi-Strauss, who is the author of the classification, claims that the examples which he adduces to illustrate the four categories thus defined, represent genuine examples of totemism as commonly, though very imperfectly understood. [7] Yet his claim, precisely because totemism is imperfectly understood, is open to challenge on perhaps more valid grounds than those on which he substantiates it. Be that as it may, the weakness in his interpretation is that with regard to at least two of the four categories concerned, known cases of totemism are extremely rare. We shall see presently how he meets this objection. Assuming, for the present, that the four categories are correctly defined, recognition of the fact does not in any case reveal the nature and significance of totemism, although it does enable us to view it from a new angle.

In the case of structural analysis applied to totemism, it stops short (at least in Lévi-Strauss's book on the subject) of a further development which he carries out sometimes in the case of kinship systems and myths. In the case of totemism, two binary oppositions are clearly perceptible, though not designated as such: one between "individual" and "collective" entities in the case of animals, and another in the case of humans, not to speak of a third opposition between the animal world and the world of humans.

In the case of cousin marriage, we also come up against binary oppositions. Proceeding a step further in the analysis, we find that marriage between a son and a daughter of a brother and sister (type 9) may be of two kinds, either marriage of the son of a brother to the daughter of his sister, or marriage of the daughter of a brother to the son of his sister. We thus obtain four types of cousin marriage in all and not three. These represent two binary oppositions, first that between marriage of the children of two brothers and marriage of the children of two sisters; and second that between the two kinds of marriage described above. These two binary oppositions, being opposed to each other, may also be said to represent a third opposition at a higher level, namely that between marriage of cousins whose related parents are of the same sex, and marriage of cousins whose related parents are of opposite sexes.

The final purpose of structural analysis is to show that all forms of social thinking (ex. in myth) and social behaviour (ex. in kinship systems, ritual etc.) are ultimately so many different types of combination of binary oppositions. For if so, then the reason must be that they borrow their structure from the same source, namely the human mind. In other words, binary oppositions represent a structure or matrix of the mind, so that all thinking that filters through it is moulded or structured accordingly. As all behaviour is operated by the mind, any fixed pattern of behaviour must reproduce its binary structure.

When applying structural analysis to myth, Lévi-Strauss proceeds in a variety of ways. In analysing the Oedipus myth, for instance, he finds on examination that according to the story[8]

1) Cadmus sets out in search of his sister Europa, ravished by Zeus;
2) Oedipus marries his mother, Jocasta;
3) Antigone buries her brother, Polynices, although this is not allowed.

He also finds that

1) the Spartoi annihilate one another;
2) Oedipus kills his father, Laius;
3) Eteocles kills his brother, Polynices.

These two series of events are part of the story told by the myth. Through a process of abstraction, they are raised to a higher level of generality and each series is shown to carry the same general meaning. We thus obtain two generalizations that are then said to form a binary opposition. Thus, each of the three events in the first series "concern blood relations, whose relations of proximity are so to speak exaggerated; these relatives are made to manifest behaviour of greater intimacy than countenanced by social rules". They represent "overrated kinship relations". Conversely, the second series, where in each case a blood relative or more are killed, concerns once again blood relations, but this time carrying the opposite sign. They represent "underrated kinship relations". In the first series exaggerated solicitude is displayed between blood-relations, in the second exaggerated repulsion. Thus six episodes belonging to the myth are shown to represent a binary opposition. It is unnecessary to comment here on the highly fanciful way in which a brother looking for his sister is viewed as exhibiting overrated kinship relations, and a massacre is given as an example of underrated relations. According to structuralist theory, all the events recounted in the myth may be resolved in this way into binary oppositions.

The difficulty in subjecting myth to such treatment lies in first successfully aligning a number of items and showing that through some common trait, detected by the analyst, they may be regarded as a single component "element" of the myth; of doing the same with another series of items, and then showing that the resulting pair of "elements" are in some way contrary to each other and therefore form a binary opposition.

With a little imagination, the analyst will always get out of any difficulty. If, for instance, in a given myth mentioning a coyote, a mist, scalps, clothes and ashes, he wishes to show that all these items refer to one and the same thing and represent the same "element", he will say that the "coyote (which feeds on carrion) is intermediate between grass-eating and flesh-eating animals, in the same way as a mist is intermediate between heaven and earth, a scalp is, between warfare and agriculture (a scalp is a war 'crop') . . . clothes, between 'nature' and 'culture' . . . ashes, between the hearth (on the ground) and the roof (image of the heavenly vault)". [9] In other words, by showing that they display a common trait (in this case, occupying an intermediate position), different items (objects or acts) mentioned in a myth may be said to be mere repetitions or expressions of the same basic element or component part. However, as any two objects may always be shown to possess a trait in common, the method as a "method" turns into a caricature of itself. All objects may be regarded as occupying intermediate positions, because every object *is* in an intermediate position between two other objects, physically if not metaphorically. That would be too ridiculously simple, and Lévi-Strauss usually looks for more sophisticated "common traits" and devotes much space to trace (or invent) the tortuous routes which would presumably link up together various mythical facts, or items, or themes, in order to show that they are equivalent and fill the same structural function in myth.

When we come to the next step in the structural analysis of myth, reliance on purely subjective and arbitrary judgements becomes still more evident. The first step, as we saw, consisted in bringing together several items of a myth under a single abstract formula. The second consists in finding which pairs of such formulations stand in binary opposition to each other. In practice, the two steps go together, with the imaginative operator juggling with the items provided by a myth until he finds a number of them which, to his mind, may be fitted into one or other of two opposite formulas. In some cases, the first step may simply be omitted, as when these items are strung together along two lines and paired off in couples of opposites.

Thus, to analyse mythical thinking, Lévi-Strauss on one occasion examines two groups of myths, each group consisting of versions of the same myth. All these variations are thus reduced to two basic myths which, he tells us, are opposite to each other. To demonstrate this he summarizes the story told by each myth in his own words, and sets forth each summary in the form of a series of sentences, each sentence in each series corresponding to one in the other, but with the opposite meaning. [10] Thus, the opening sentence in one myth, namely: "A *step-brother* (affine), irritated by a *boy*, abandons him *definitely*, so he believes", is opposed to the following in another: "A *mother* (kin), irritated by a *girl*, abandons her *temporarily*, so she believes". *Step-brother* and *mother*, *boy* and *girl*, and *definitely* and *temporarily* are thus opposite pairs, and each sentence is the inverted image of the other. The stories contained in the two myths are recounted in this way till the end, and the analysis is then completed.

The arbitrary character of this procedure is self-evident. A number of facts are picked up from two myths, while other facts, deemed irrelevant, are ignored. Then the facts selected are lined up opposite to each other and worded in such a way as to show oppositions between the two. If a different selection of facts is made, the general pattern of the myths and the oppositions that will emerge will obviously be different.[11]

Now, Lévi-Strauss need not necessarily deny the arbitrary nature of such analysis. It would be quite sufficient for his purpose, as we shall see, to show that in some way or other, myths are made up of combinations of binary oppositions, and mythical thinking the process of combining such oppositions. The important thing is to show that a piece of mythical thinking may be thus split up into constituent oppositions, whether the ones he points out in a given instance are the real ones or not. If they are, so much the better; if not . . . "so what?" For instance, "it amounts to the same thing", he says, "whether the thinking of South-American Indians takes shape when my thinking operates on it, or when their thinking operates on mine".[12] The important thing is that irrespective of what the thinking is about, it is constructed by means of binary oppositions.

Anthropologists, however, cannot be satisfied with a method of investigation whose purpose is not really to shed light on the significance of the phenomenon analysed, but simply to demonstrate that it is structured on the basis of binary oppositions whatever their meaning. Nevertheless following Lévi-Strauss's lead, quite a number of anthropologists in France, Britain and elsewhere, working mainly in the field of myth and ritual, have undertaken, at the cost of great painstaking effort, to show that this or that set of ritualized practices, or mythical representations may be ordered in such a way as to reveal series of combinations of binary oppositions. Quite apart from the fact that the results obtained are always exposed to the charge of being at bottom arbitrary and the fruit of the operator's imagination (as some have been shown to be), they are inevitably bound to prove barren and disappointing, since they add nothing to our knowledge of the object analysed, nor are they intended to. The novelty of structuralist analysis made it attractive for a while, and in the process of analysing a myth, interesting and suggestive aspects relative to its meaning could reveal themselves; but that would be incidental to the final purpose of the analysis which is to reach the ultimate stage where all that remains of the myth, after successive abstractions have been made, are binary oppositions between *plus* and *minus* signs—abstract units devoid of factual meaning. In short, when structural analysis expresses its full meaning as a method, it is meaningless in its results.

Structural Analysis and Marxist Interpretation

In *Les structures élémentaires de la parenté* kinship systems are represented as so many modes of effecting an exchange of women between different groups. Through the marriage of a man and a woman, the group to which the former belongs is "wife-taker" as opposed to the woman's group, which is "wife-giver". In its turn, the "wife-taker" group becomes "wife-giver" relatively to the other, which then becomes "wife-taker". Thus, an exchange of women takes place between the two groups whereby each is alternately "wife-taker" and "wife-giver", while the other is "wife-giver" and "wife-taker". (The situation is more complicated, but the principle of exchange is maintained when group A gives its women to group B, group B to group C, and group C to group A.) From the structuralist point of view, exchange is not the result of marriage, but its condition. In marrying a woman, a man "takes" a woman. Owing to the binary structure of his mind, the act of taking cannot be separated from the opposite one of giving. This opposition rises to consciousness in the form of the "notion of reciprocity" described by Lévi-Strauss as a structure of the mind; so that the act of taking a woman is felt as having to be "reciprocated" by that of giving another in exchange.

Reasoning along these lines, Lévi-Strauss comes to advance a peculiar theory to account for the prohibition of incest, a phenomenon of universal application that has been the subject of considerable discussion in anthropological literature. In the absence of such a prohibition, a man would be allowed to marry a woman of his own group, a kinswoman, a sister. From the point of view of the group, no woman would have to be "given" to an outsider in order to "take" one from outside. The individual marrying a woman (a sister) in his group would be "taking" a woman without his group's "giving" any woman away. The "notion of reciprocity" would thus be baulked and, in practice, marriage and the family would be meaningless. In seeking to fulfil itself, the "notion of reciprocity" brings into being the rule prohibiting incest, that is forbidding marriage with women of one's group. All existing women are thus divided between the forbidden women of one's group, and the permitted women of other groups, so that the latter may be "taken" only by "giving" the former in exchange. The exchange between two groups exhibits on the social level the result of the binary opposition structured in the mind. This opposition expresses itself in consciousness as the "notion of reciprocity" which is thus itself, as Lévi-Strauss says, a structure of the mind. In practice, it expresses itself in exchange—a form of communication—and in

marriage, the opposites are two groups whose oppositeness results from
the prohibition of incest that marks their women with opposite signs
relatively to each group, and renders their exchange possible between
the two groups.

As an outer expression of inner binary oppositions, exchange is
fundamental for Lévi-Strauss, and not only for exchanging women.
Anthropological evidence, however, points the other way and indicates
that it is secondary in relation to social requirements. The prohibition
of incest, of marriage within the kin-group, by obliging its male and
female members to seek wives and husbands in other groups, leads
automatically to what has the appearance of a deliberate exchange of
women (or of men). That marriage eventually is viewed as such, and
women are equated to merchandise, is a subsequent development, and
it is that development which gives rise to the notion of reciprocity and
not *vice versa*. Lévi-Strauss's chain of reasoning from mental structures
to a notion of reciprocity, to the emergence of the prohibition of incest
as a rule governing marriage, to the resulting *exchange* of women, to
human marriage rests on no evidence whatever, is not even expressible
hypothetically in terms of psychological or physiological processes, and
finally stems from a purely imaginary assumption (not unrelated however to a philosophical view-point). This assumption leads him to
contend that the sudden appearance of the incest prohibition in a
non-human mind made it just as suddenly human, marked the passage
from "nature" to "culture", or rather *was* that passage, made marriage
possible, nay inevitable, instituted the family and started the whole
historical process going.

The bulk of *Les structures élémentaires de la parenté* is devoted to a
demonstration that certain highly complex, exceptional and still
unaccountable systems of kinship are really particular cases of the
exchange of women. To do this, Lévi-Strauss does not attempt to trace
their development from simpler or better understood systems, not on
the grounds that such a historical reconstruction is well-nigh impossible,
but because in his view kinship systems are not determined by any
process of historical development. Given the particularities of local
conditions and other contingent factors, the unconscious structures of
the mind, with their matrix of binary oppositions, elaborate kinship
systems that will meet these conditions; while fulfilling the requirements of exchange, the prohibition of incest and the notion of
reciprocity.

It is here that Lévi-Strauss strikes at the root of the marxist interpretation of history and sets out to discredit it. His attempt has been
hailed by Nur Yalman, an American anthropologist, as "a superb
attack . . . against the marxist position".[13] It marks, in fact, a new
departure in that discipline—anticipated by Robert Lowie, it is true—

in that the attack is "theorized" for the first time, whereas until now, Marxism was combated indirectly. As Yalman further points out; "We can now more clearly understand that Lévi-Strauss's encylopedic examination of cross-cousin marriage was really undertaken to undermine the assumptions of materialist anthropology." Things could hardly be stated more plainly and acquire added significance when made by a non-Marxist. Among intellectuals of the Left, Lévi-Strauss's anti-historicism and references to unconscious structures of the mind called forth some reservations and caused uneasiness, but all that was quickly explained away as inevitable lapses into idealism by a bourgeois writer who, at any rate, had expressed admiration and approval, though distant, of marxist thought. The temptation was too great not to represent him as a fellow-traveller and share in the prestige he enjoyed. Books and articles appeared, reconciling marxism and structuralism, demonstrating their complementarity, and even suggesting that Marx's method, after all, was really structuralist. After 1968, and except for the Althusserians, the popularity of structuralism among the left declined steadily for a variety of reasons: its barrenness as a method in anthropology; increased criticism of Lévi-Strauss's work on technical grounds; increased awareness—though hazy—that structuralism with its emphasis on "synchrony" was more conservative than progressive etc.; but its profoundly reactionary character and the ideology and theoretical premises from which it stems were not yet fully apprehended.

In Lévi-Strauss's view, then, if kinship systems, myths, ritual and even odd unsystematized practices and beliefs, as manifested at different periods in history and in different parts of the world, are similar in essence, the reason is that everywhere and at all times the binary oppositions in the human mind are at work. Social phenomena are not to be regarded as products of historical processes, subject to the maturation of the appropriate material conditions and governed by laws of development. His standpoint thus offers the very appreciable advantage of relieving social scientists of the formidable *problématique* which constantly dogs their footsteps, namely that of accounting for the facts they study by tracing their development to historical antecedents. The search for historical causality is eliminated at a stroke. Henceforth, they may dismiss such concern with a light heart: social facts are determined by structures of the mind, and all that remains to be done is to identify the pattern of symmetries and oppositions that underlies them.

Such an impoverishment of scientific research is not presented by Lévi-Strauss as a theoretical imperative of structuralism, for that would bring upon it immediate discredit, but as a practical necessity imposed by the limitations of science itself. To the question "Why are societies structured differently?" his reply is not that they are not structured differently in essence; on the contrary, it is that such questions "are most relevant, and we should welcome the possibility of answering them. In the present state of knowledge, we can consider ourselves in a position to do so only with respect to precise and limited cases".[14] This expression of scientific modesty is such as to disarm the critic and at the same time to mislead him completely as to the real implications of structuralism. The question of why, for instance, do kinship systems differ so much from one another, is never answered squarely, it being given to be understood that the question betrays incredible naivety. Outward circumstances and events, as so many contingent forces, come into play and affect the way in which the ubiquitous unconscious structures of the mind will project themselves outwardly, and that is all. Yet it is precisely this area of reality, which supposedly belongs to the realm of contingency and historical hazard, that Marxism, and not only Marxism, regard as the area where historical necessity reveals itself as governed by laws of development that account for the appearance of social institutions and explain their sociological significance.

As a doctrine purporting to interpret social facts not in terms of their development, but in terms of mental structures—of accounting in anthropology for, say, the prohibition of incest in terms of these same structures and not of the material conditions that imposed it etc., structuralism will have to face the test of time as any other doctrine. It is in its pernicious effects in the field of anthropological research and ideology that its reactionary nature becomes manifest.

The Linguistics Fallacy

Its effect in anthropology is the systematic destruction of anthropological facts. This follows from its basic premises and is substantiated in practice by the successive positions taken by structuralists on various theoretical questions. By destruction of anthropological facts is meant the denial that they possess specifically intrinsic and objective meaning in respect to primitive societies. The reduction of anthropological facts by structural analysis to pure, abstract logical oppositions strips them of their specificity, and their ascription to properties of the mind deprives them of objective basis. In practice, the destruction of facts proceeds piecemeal at the hands of structuralists who are seldom aware of the implications of what they are doing.

Lévi-Strauss's reductionism with regard to social facts is achieved *via* linguistics, linguistics providing him with a ready-made model, logical and coherent, on which to operate. Studied structurally as a system of signs devoid of intrinsic meaning, language reveals the underlying logical network of relationships which structuralism in anthropology would fain extricate from the disorder of social facts. In this respect, structuralism is said to lag far behind linguistics, the system of relationships underlying social facts being in no way as easily discernible. Linguistics is supposed to prove that what matters is not so much the facts (signs) of language as the system of relations binding them. Structuralism adopts this view with regard to social facts, and leans heavily on linguistics to justify it.

What all this really boils down to is that linguistics shows that it is possible to study a system of relations independently of the terms which these relations bind together. The terms are said to be devoid of intrinsic meaning, their position in the system of relations, only, giving them meaning. The same is supposed to apply to social facts. It is the system of relationships to which they belong that gives them meaning, according to their position in that system, and it is therefore the system which constitutes the proper subject of study, and not whatever meaning comes to be derivatively attached to the facts. Again, just as the structure of a language is not apprehended by its users, but is situated at the level of the unconscious, so also the structure of social systems (of thought or behaviour) is rooted in the unconscious part of the mind, that is in the binary oppositions of the unconscious. Linguistics offers the model for the reduction of observable facts to the invisible oppositions of the mind.

It has been said that tragedy is a beautiful deduction killed by an ugly fact. The ugly fact in Lévi-Strauss's "deduction" is that social phenomena, unlike linguistic signs, *do* possess intrinsic meaning and are rich in sociological content, independently of their position in a system of relationships, although they are not unaffected by it. Analogies between linguistic and social phenomena may be made, provided the essential difference that separates them is borne in mind. Lévi-Strauss remembers it sometimes. He points out, for instance, in the case of kinship systems, that while women are signs, like words, they are also producers of words; "therefore, they cannot be reduced to the condition of symbols or mere tokens".[15] However, it seems that the recognition of this difference between women, in their social function, and words, is made, in the present case, in anticipation of the objection that will arise when he does not choose to recognize it, in order to remove that objection beforehand. Thus, although women cannot be reduced to the condition of symbols, yet kinship systems, he claims, "because they are systems of symbols, open up to anthropology a privileged terrain on which its endeavours may almost (and we insist on the word 'almost') join with that most developed of all the social sciences, namely linguistics".[16] Furthermore, "a system of kinship is a language", and "in another *order of reality*, kinship phenomena are of the same type as linguistic phenomena". The parallelism between the world of social facts and the world of words is drawn so tight, in spite of the insistence on the word "almost", that the essential difference between the two is simply smothered out of existence.

This is particularly evident in Lévi-Strauss's treatment of myth. Here again, the same precautions are taken, and he is at pains to explain that myth is not to be identified with language. It turns out, however, that the difference between the two does not bear on their essence. We are told, in a summary to a long disquisition on the subject, that (A) if a myth has any meaning, it is derived from the way its constituent parts are combined together (a fundamental tenet of structuralism, applied not only to myth, as we saw); (B) myths belong to the same order of phenomena as language, they are an integral part of language, although language as used in myth possesses specific properties; (C) these properties of language manifest themselves at a high level of expression and are of a more complex nature than usually met with.[17]

The essential difference between language and myth having thus been "abstracted" away, the one may now be reduced to the other without much difficulty. How this reduction is effected is summarily stated under (A), above. The assertion made there is of paramount importance for the structuralist position, because its validity is made to rest upon it. Untenable, gratuitous and unsupported by any evidence, as they may be, the basic assumptions of structuralism (as relative to the binary oppositions of the mind, their role in determining social structure etc), may be legitimately advanced, though with less pretentiousness, as hypotheses to be verified subsequently. The reduction of social phenomena to binary mental structures *via* linguistics (on the far from acceptable supposition that language is thus also reducible) is supposed to be demonstrated in the case of myth, and so confirming the validity of the hypotheses made. The demonstration is crucial for structuralism, and therefore deserves some attention.

First of all, it purports to show that "in accord with modern linguistics . . . content [of myth] never has a meaning in itself . . . it is only the way in which the different elements of the content are combined together which gives a meaning".[18] Now linguistics, we are told, teaches that when taken separately, phonemes have no meaning, but when combined to form words, they have. What Lévi-Strauss omits to say is that it is for this reason that the meaning of words is arbitrary. It is otherwise when we come to myths. The elements that go to form a myth carry an intrinsic meaning of their own. Combined in the myth, they acquire a new, different meaning, but this meaning is determined by their individual intrinsic meanings. It is therefore not arbitrary. The same applies to social facts when combined. It is to linguistics that it does not always apply.

The analogy drawn between myth and language easily leads to confusion, because myth, like language, consists in conveying a message, and like language also, does so by means of words. Whence the wrong conclusion that as in the case in linguistics, "meaning cannot depend on the separate elements which enter into their composition, but on the way they are combined".[19]

If, however, myths are not to be confused with language, then their meaning will not depend exclusively on the way their elements are combined, but also on the separate meaning of each. If it is true that a myth, like language, conveys meaning by the use of words, its meaning however is not the textual one given by the story it tells in words. The story is symbolical and contains a message to be unravelled when its symbolism is deciphered. Furthermore, it acquires its global symbolical meaning from both the symbolical meaning of each of the events it relates, as from the way they are combined. Lévi-Strauss takes advantage of the fact that when this symbolism is not understood, the myth appears as a meaningless tissue of incoherence and often of nonsense— so that "anything may happen in a myth", he thinks[20]—to claim this as proof that its component parts are themselves devoid of meaning. Actually the argument turns against him. For if a myth, when not understood, may seem nonsensical, it is not at all because the separate events which make it up are so, but because their combination is— exactly the opposite of what Lévi-Strauss contends.

According to him, a myth, like language, is made up of constituent elements, to be called *mythèmes*, and which play the same role in myth as *phonèmes* in language. They differ however from phonemes, as he admits, in that they are already loaded with meaning at the level of language expressed in words. They are words, "but words with a double meaning: *words* of words, which work on two levels, that of language when they continue to have meaning each on its own, and that of meta-language (myth) when they intervene as elements endowed with the super-meaning which their union produces".[21]

Except for the last end of phrase, this passage expresses in characteristically unsimple language what was stated just before. For if it can be suggested that myth is a meta-language, it is because while in language a sign (word) refers to its meaning, in myth this meaning refers in turn to what it symbolizes, namely the hidden meaning of the myth which makes of it a myth and not the amusing or horrifying or nonsensical story it tells. It does not follow however from the relation between meta-language and language that the mythemes in myth have the same characteristics as the phonemes in words, that although loaded with meaning they play the same role as phonemes which possess none. Lévi-Strauss does not ask himself whether the meaning with which he says they are loaded does not play a part in determining the meaning of the myth. This leads him into a fallacious reasoning and a wrong analysis. A fallacious reasoning, because if phonemes play no part in determining the meaning of the words they form, it does not follow that mythemes, which possess meaning, do not in the myths they build up; and a wrong analysis, because, as a matter not of inference but of fact, neither in myth nor in language is meaning engendered exclusively by the combination of their constituent elements. In the case of words, these elements or phonemes, combine sounds which then receive a meaning extrinsic to them. That is why the same combination of sounds have different meanings in different languages (and often even in the same language). In the case of myth, the combination of mythemes will engender a new meaning, the meaning of the myth, but this meaning will arise from within and will depend on the individual meanings of the constituent mythemes. That is why also, in opposition to a combination of phonemes, they cannot have different meanings in different languages.

The truth therefore is exactly the opposite of what Lévi-Strauss supposes. It is because phonemes are devoid of meaning that the meaning of words is arbitrary—in fact, has to be; and it is because mythemes have meaning that the meaning of a myth is not arbitrary, so that not "anything may happen in a myth". Nor is this all. Lévi-Strauss's purpose in assimilating mythemes to phonemes really defeats itself on another level also. For mythemes are identified by their meaning. To be fitted into a matrix of binary oppositions, they have to convey opposite meanings. If in the process of abstraction, which aims at reducing them to their simplest expression, as abstract units, marked only with *plus* and *minus* signs, their meaning is eliminated, they disappear altogether, leaving nothing behind, no residual units on which to pin *plus* and *minus* signs. (In the case of the opposition man/woman, for instance, these two terms when divested, conceptually, of specific sexual connotations, subsist, at a higher level of abstraction, as "human beings", capable of being marked with opposite signs standing for the sexual attributes that have disappeared. But then the opposition between man and woman is real (and not only in so far as the binary oppositions of the mind conceive it to be so).)

The argument from linguistics is intended to demonstrate the validity of structural analysis. If it is grounded in fallacy, the entire theoretical justification of the latter collapses.

Reductionism and Computer-logic
To give credibility to structuralist reductionism on the model of linguistics ("language may be regarded as a foundation destined to receive structures which sometimes surpass it in complexity, but which are of the same type as its own, and which correspond to culture when viewed under various aspects") [22] Lévi-Strauss points out that "marriage and kinship rules serve to ensure the communication of women between groups, just as economic rules serve to ensure the communication of

goods and services, and linguistic rules the communication of messages. These three forms of communication are at the same time forms of exchange"[23] (and exchange, as we have seen, is motivated by the notion of reciprocity due to the binary oppositions of the mind). If these types of communication differ from one another, it is with regard to "the strategic level" at which they operate. "They are not of the same dimension".[24]

The word "communication", here, should cause no worry. In ordinary speech it carries so many associations that it meets admirably the conditions of ambiguity, for although it has a different sense according as to whether it is applied to words, women or goods, it verbally ties them all together to any concept that might be associated to it in some way, to exchange, for instance, or to the general theory of communication itself. The recourse to this theory, for instance, is very helpful for it provides a material, functioning model of reductionism as structuralism conceives it. This model is the digital computer which handles information that has been broken down into binary oppositions. It should afford experimental proof that social facts are reducible to binary oppositions. All that remains to be done is to show that these facts are facts of communication.

Now this can be easily shown by straining somewhat the meaning of the word "communication". A body moving from point A to point B may be said to represent a form of communication. It is itself communicated from A to B, and through it they are put in communication and communicate. But if so, it is not even necessary for it to *move* from A to B. It is enough that it should lie between them, occupying an intermediate position, joining (or separating) them. We saw earlier that a coyote, a mist, a scalp, clothes and ashes also occupy intermediate positions, so that they also may be said to provide communication between grass-eaters and flesh-eaters, heaven and earth, warfare and agriculture, "nature" and "culture", the hearth and the roof, respectively. Since every existing (or even imaginary) object occupies some intermediate position (spatial or metaphorical), all objects are elements of some system of communication.

This, of course, we knew all the time, and is what enables a computer to handle information. For Lévi-Strauss, the analogy with the computer also offers the advantage of both simplicity and sophistication, in addition to being fashionable and modernistic, etc. On the other hand, it shows that structural analysis really consists in the translation of a set of observed facts, understood or not, into another language *not understood* this time—comparable to a code—just as the information to be fed into the computer has to be translated through a series of languages before it can be digested by it. Once the facts have been finally put into the same code, it becomes possible to combine them at will.

It is this avowed aim to codify social facts that betrays the ideological, mystificatory character of structuralism, since the purpose is to reduce little understood facts to still less understandable language, if understandable at all. By divesting social facts of their empirical qualities, in order to codify them in simpler terms, structural analysis effaces all traces of their interconnections with the material world surrounding them. At that level of abstraction, they cannot be studied in terms of the specific causes that gave rise to them, because causal relations are no longer visible. Instead of being a method opening new ways of approach to an understanding of social phenomena, structural analysis actually eliminates those available.

Having reduced a set of social facts to their component elements, structuralism proceeds to combine these in all the mathematically possible ways. One or more of these combinations will restitute the original set of facts; but the remaining will represent all the possible variations of these facts, existing but having escaped detection, or simply inextant.[25] In the latter case, their absence will have to be accounted for, unless reasonably imputable to contingent influences.

By way of example, Lévi-Strauss refers to a form of marriage known as the crow-omaha system. In this system the number of different marriage combinations possible is so high that he turned to "mathematicians to translate, so to speak, the crow-omaha system in terms of elementary structures."[26] The results showed that in the case of intermarriage between, say, seven clans, the number of possible combinations was 23,436. In the case of 30 clans, the number was no less than 297,423,855.

A much more manageable result was obtained in the case of totemism. Here we saw that the number of different combinations possible between animals and humans, in terms of binary oppositions, was four, alleged to represent four types of totemism. "Logically speaking", says Lévi-Strauss, "the four combinations are equivalent, since they are produced by the same operation".[27] We should therefore expect to find that, on the whole, the four types are more or less represented in equal numbers. The trouble is that they are very far from being so. By and large, the majority of known cases of totemism come under one (or two) only of Lévi-Strauss's four divisions. Before Lévi-Strauss, totemism was regarded as the result of a process of development, and the relatively rare and doubtful examples, which Lévi-Strauss would class under the minority types, were taken to represent either early phases, or vestiges of totemism.

Lévi-Strauss will have none of this. For if totemism were a social phenomenon possessing objective reality (that is meaning) then indeed it would have to be regarded as a product of historical development, passing through successive stages, accountable in terms of its development and inaccessible to structural analysis. To be reduced to the binary oppositions of mental structures, the objectivity of totemic phenomena had to be shown to be illusory, they had to be disconnected, as it were, from their relationships with other social phenomena, and shown to be the product of the inner workings of the mind and not of any sociological process. On this view, what goes by the name of totemism manifests itself whenever the binary structures of the mind are capable of expressing themselves accordingly, each reported case of totemism being therefore a projection of the mind. On this view also, totemism should be represented equally in the four types defined. If it is not, that is because by some perverse twist of the anthropological mind, the "semantic field" to which totemism belongs has been "distorted", so as to mark out certain of its aspects "at the expense of others, in order to endow them with an originality and oddity intrinsically foreign to them. They are thus made to appear mysterious by the mere fact that they are excluded from the system of which they form an integral part and constitute so many transformations."[28] In other words, pre-Lévi-Straussian anthropologists had narrowed down the term "totemism" deliberately, so as to leave out a number of totemic phenomena and make them look mysterious and fascinating. As to their insistence on regarding totemism as a real phenomenon, characteristic of primitive society, it is due to "a certain taste for the obscene and the grotesque" on their part.[29]

Lévi-Strauss, as stated earlier, has developed the art of saying anything and getting away with it; and here we have a typical, though at the same time exceptional example of his proficiency in the art. For surely, it is a rarity in scientific literature for an author to charge practically all his predecessors with the "distortion" of what he calls the "semantic field" to which the phenomenon under study belongs, out of an erratic desire to endow them with an exotic fascination of some sort. What defies explanation is that such reputed anthropologists as Leach and Needham, though visibly enraptured by Lévi-Strauss's structural anthropology, should nevertheless condone, by their silence, such an expression of declared contempt for earlier anthropologists. No one, after all, as much as Leach has so admiringly expatiated on the virtues of Lévi-Strauss's anthropology; while Needham is none other than the translator of his book on totemism. Both of them having "worked" on that book, it is incredible that both, so critical in other circumstances and with other authors, should prove so insensitive to Lévi-Strauss's reflections on the alleged mental aberrations of his predecessors. Equally incredible, in this context, is the fact that they should have had nothing to say regarding the flagrant misquotations and unabashed garbling of clear and unambiguous statements (by Tylor, Radcliffe-Brown, Boas, Radin, Durkheim and Mauss) appearing in the same and other books.[30] Such practices, that would earn a schoolboy a severe rapping on the fingers, are highly prejudicial to social science when committed by a leading figure in the field, and yet the veil of discretion that covers them is securely maintained.

The structuralist treatment of totemism is revelatory. The purpose is to deny its objective nature as a social fact, reduce it to a subjective manifestation of the mind (its objectivity is therefore illusory) and trace its origin conceptually to the binary oppositions in the unconscious. If when the phenomenon comes to be reconstructed by the combination of opposites, the results as we saw, are not borne out by the facts, the fault is with those anthropologists who, until Lévi-Strauss, were motivated by all sorts of intentions and morbid tastes etc.

The Strategy of Structuralism and its Critique

Social phenomena may be classed under several heads. Lévi-Strauss has dealt mainly with myths, kinship and totemism. The first problem in each case consisted of translating the facts into a language visibly made up of oppositions. The justification for so doing was that these oppositions emanated from the unconscious structures of the mind. In this enterprise, Lévi-Strauss thought that the field of myths would prove the rewarding one to explore, since myths have to obey no other constraints but those of the mind. In other words, they were not subject, at the level at which they expressed themselves, to any limitations imposed by the outer world. In the case of kinship, it was otherwise. "In *Les structures élémentaires de la parenté*, I had chosen a field which . . . I tried to show was reducible to a very small number of significant propositions. Yet that first experience was insufficient because in the field of kinship, the constraints are not of a purely internal order. I mean by that that it is not certain that their origin is exclusively in the structure of the mind: they might be the result of the necessities of social life, of the ways in which social life imposes its constraints on thought. The second stage which will be entirely devoted to mythology, will try to circumvent this obstacle, for it is precisely, it seems to me, in the field of mythology, where the mind appears to be freest to abandon itself to its creative spontaneity, that it will be interesting to determine whether it is governed by laws."[31]

The admission that in the case of kinship systems some constraints could be external really opens a fatal breach in the logical defences of structuralism. For if kinship systems are liable to be determined in part by objective necessities, why not entirely? The primacy of the mind, or at least its independence of any kind of social determinism is implied in all of Lévi-Strauss's works, although it runs counter to the anthropological view that the human brain, while being a biological organ, is nonetheless a social product; so that if the mind exercises constraints on conduct, these constraints ultimately express social needs. From the structuralist point of view, however, the binary oppositions of the human mind constitute a physical condition of the brain, which man shares with the animal world, and which, at a given instant in the course of biological development, emit the notion of reciprocity, introduce the incest prohibition, marriage, the human family and culture. There is no room here for any social causality.

Be that as it may, in *Les structures*, Lévi-Strauss undertakes to show that all forms of marriage are ultimately reducible to the opposition introduced by the incest prohibition. Expressed in a different way and with certain qualifications, this proposition would not be unacceptable, because all sexual life in primitive society is governed by the law of exogamy, whereby sexual intercourse with members of one's group is prohibited and regarded as incestuous.

In saying that all marriage systems are reducible to the opposition between permitted women and forbidden women, and constitute systems of exchange, Lévi-Strauss is therefore saying nothing new, although he is formulating the problem in an unusual way and straining the meaning of some of the concepts used (as, for instance, when stating that kinship systems *are* systems of exchange, simply because they may be viewed or used as such). When he comes to demonstrate in detail how the properties of some highly complex kinship systems are deducible from his theory of exchange, his demonstration fails to carry conviction. His basic postulate being that kinship systems are different ways in which exchange works, he will not take into consideration the action of social factors—factors external to the structural premises of kinship systems—as being other than contingent. Now, kinship systems are not governed exclusively by structural principles; so that any attempt to account for their variations exclusively in their terms is bound to fall short of its aim.

Les structures, as was natural enough, interested students of kinship with its technicalities. As is evident in the light of Lévi-Strauss's other works, its significance, as that of his work on myth, lies in showing how in the field of kinship, human conduct is moulded by the binary oppositions of the mind. Anthropologists are not particularly interested in this aspect of the question. They are more interested in the details of his analyses of particular systems, and students of primitive mythology in the analysis of particular myths. Yet the impact of structuralism outside the field of anthropology and its ideological implications relate to its basic theoretical postulates; furthermore, it is doubtful whether Lévi-Strauss would have devoted so many years to study first kinship systems and then myths, if he were not motivated by the desire to illustrate a philosophical position in some way, and anthropology offered him the opportunity to do so. For in spite of his career in social anthropology, both as writer and lecturer, his thinking is not really anthropological. Leach reminds us that his prime training was in philosophy and law: "He consistently behaves as an advocate defending a cause rather than as a scientist searching for ultimate truth."[32] At any rate, he makes it abundantly clear that nothing interests him as little as the sociological significance of facts. His interest lies elsewhere, and there is no reason why it should not. That is why so much of what comes under structuralism seems so utterly alien to anthropology, and why it could happen that an "anthropologist" should work out a system destined not to explain sociologically the facts he studies, but to disqualify all explanation of these facts by denying their intrinsic sociological significance.

Paradoxically enough, it is in the field of mythology, where structuralism for the reasons given above, is supposed to deploy its full force, that the results obtained are of least worth, in spite of the loud applause of the "literary claque", as Needham would say. For when all is said and done, the detection of oppositions in this field is an illusionist's performance, since a difference may always be manipulated so as to appear as an opposition.[33] Lévi-Strauss would have been in a much stronger position if his analyses of myths received confirmation from their meaningful content. His claim that what matters is not what myths say, but the way they say it, is simply a verbal flourish to make a virtue of incapacity. For after insisting so much that the meaning of a myth arises from the combination of mythemes, irrespective of their meaning, the least that could be expected of him was to show how the combinations of mythemes in the cases he analyses engenders meaning and what that meaning is.

In his analysis of the Oedipus myth, he singles out three events which, he says, express "underrated kinship relations"; but this is simply an abstract formulation of what each murder is supposed to illustrate in the story of the myth, as a story—it is not their allegorical, or mythical, or symbolical meaning. Lévi-Strauss avoids posing the question, expected of the student of myths, namely what does the textual meaning of the myth—assuming it is the overrating of kinship relations—really refer to? He seems suddenly to forget all about seeking the meaning of myth at a higher level than that of ordinary language. In actual fact, the story told in the myth cannot reveal its hidden meaning when formulated in abstract terms, because its hidden meaning is contained in the specific terms in which the story is told; for each detail figuring in the story has also an ethnological meaning which it is the mythologist's task to unravel, and which is left out when the story is told in the abstract. Viewed ethnologically, the murder committed by Oedipus is not to be associated with the two other murders related in the myth, but with other acts performed by him and reported in other parts of the myth, defining him in the role of a violator of taboos. The repetition of such acts is necessary to mark his character as that of violator. As such he is king, cultural hero, possessor of unusual magical powers and capable of solving the riddle that baffled others before him and caused their death. His capacity to answer the question put to him by the Sphinx is thus explained and justifies his encounter with the monster. So also does his violation of taboo, through incest with his mother, which has been identified as the central theme of the myth. The ethnological interpretation of the myth links up all the apparently disconnected and unrelated events of the story and shows that they form a coherent, interlocking whole, giving the meaning of the myth, and Oedipus's role in it. In Lévi-Strauss's analysis not only is Oedipus's incest palmed off as just another example of overrated kinship relations, but the drama that has left such a deep impression on public imagination and which unfolds as Oedipus runs to meet his tragic fate, driven by the acts he performs to avoid it, is entirely neglected. It had to fall to the anthropologist who placed the incest prohibition at the centre of his system, to empty the most celebrated of myths of its human content and rob it of its anthropological and psychological implications.

In the case of myths, the failures of structural analysis are not as apparent as in other fields. In their expression, myths belong to the world of the imaginary. Erratic and unreal as they are, any suggested interpretation of their content or form, however absurd and far-fetched, will be less erratic than they are, and therefore, on the face of it, more or less plausible. Thus the analysis of an apparently incomprehensible myth will always create the impression that it has rendered it less incomprehensible. It can be refuted in two ways only, one negative, by showing that it involves inconsistencies, distortion of facts and bad reasoning; the other positive, by showing that another reading of the myth renders it much more comprehensible.

When we move to kinship structures and other social phenomena, like totemism, or even ritual, which involve human activity and are not limited in their manifestation to the realm of the mind, criteria of objectivity come into play, and the absurdities resulting from structural analysis become more easily perceptible, especially when the phenomena concerned are not so totally incomprehensible as in the case of myths. Thus the structuralist permutatory interpretation of totemism, described above, ridiculous as it is in its imputation of mental perversity to anthropological workers, appears doubly so when the process giving rise to the phenomenon is understood in terms of its development in answer to social needs.[34]

In the case of ritual practices, performed to obtain tangible results, the structuralist interpretation appears even more ludicrous. The Hidatsa, a North-American tribe of Indians, are given to eagle-hunting for the purpose of obtaining eagle-feathers. The hunter crouches inside a hole he has dug in the ground, and covers the opening with leaves and branches on which a bait has been placed. As the eagle flying overhead sees it, swoops down to carry it away and, alights on the branches, the hunter grasps it by the legs and captures it.[35]

How did the Hidatsa come to invent this method of hunting? Not by observation and experiment, says the structuralist, but thanks to the binary oppositions in their mind. For the eagle flying *overhead* constitutes the term of a binary opposition of which the other term is something that lies, or should lie, *below* or *underneath*. The first term evokes the second by "reciprocity", and the Hidatsa eagle-hunter is impelled by a nondescript inner urge to give it material shape by going *down* into the hole and placing himself *below*, in opposition to the eagle *above*. Through the mediation of the bait, the bird comes *down*, whereupon the hunter raises his arms *up*. The distance between the hunter and the hunted shrinks to nought, and as the fingers of the former close on the legs of the latter, the opposites meet, the binary opposition is resolved and the bird is captured!

The first step in structural analysis, then, whatever "fact" it is applied to, is to view it in terms of oppositions, an operation which is always possible, since differences can always be resolved into "oppositions" relatively to a suitable frame of reference. Sometimes this requires quite an effort of the imagination, at other times no effort at all, because oppositions do exist objectively. But in the latter case, a difficulty of another kind arises, for the structuralist now has to show that the objective nature of the opposition is really illusory, or rather results from an ordering effected by the binary oppositions of the mind. In the case of kinship systems, these are all based on the objective socially determined division of society into two basic exogamic groups— groups, that is, which are differentiated by virtue of the incest prohibition. The structural dichotomies investing social conduct and often extending to myths and beliefs, may be shown to be but prolongations of this structural division, and therefore having nothing to do with any hypothetical oppositions within the mind.

The reductionist operations of structural analysis can be justified only on the assumption that on the concrete specific level, social facts have no significance. But when reduced to binary oppositions, to mathematical points or abstract units, represented by *plus* and *minus* signs, they have no meaning either, except the mathematical and abstract one of constituting oppositions. How then do they acquire their meaning? Through the combination of their component oppositions, is the structuralist answer. But no structuralist has ever shown how by their combination, abstract units, or elements acquire meaning and what that meaning is.

The truth of the matter is that the so-called structural analysis of social facts, their reduction to their basic component units (binary oppositions), followed by their reconstruction by the combination of the latter are operations carried out independently of their content and of whatever meaning they might have. To pretend the opposite is simply to give proof of the mystificatory character of structuralism. Yet structuralists cannot do otherwise without disqualifying their method. Their argument therefore is that social facts acquire their meaning from the combination of their basic elements, and that to understand that meaning, they have to be broken up into these elements and built up again from their combination. As long as the social facts concerned are not understood, as we saw in the case of myths, any meaning attributed to the combination of their constituent elements, according to the unconscious structures of the mind, has a chance of passing for being logically plausible. When, however, the facts concerned are explained and understood, the fictitious character of structural analysis becomes manifest. The only way left, in these circumstances, to save the structuralist position, is to declare the explanation false, or better still, illusory. This is precisely what Lévi-Strauss does when dealing with totemism, describing it as an illusion, while at the same time reducing it to combinations of elements. His purpose in that particular case is "not to understand totemism, but to abolish it", as one writer aptly put it.[36]

It follows from all this that structural analysis cannot be applied to social facts that are to be understood without mutilating them, since a given phenomenon is understood to the extent to which its necessary connections with other phenomena have been determined, while its reduction by analysis requires such connections to be severed in order to "free" its component elements and allow them to be permutated. We saw, in the case of the Oedipus myth, that once it is realized that the parricide committed by Oedipus is necessarily connected to other events—such as his incest with his mother—in that they build his character as a violator of taboos, endowing him with the magical powers that will enable him to solve the riddle of the Sphinx, the myth acquires meaning. Compared to this, the structuralist assimilation of Oedipus's parricide to other cases of murder on the basis of a factual analogy, followed by their forced reduction to "underrated kinship relations" to be opposed to "overrated kinship relations", appears as a puerile exercise of the imagination. It is simply because the necessary connections and the meaning of the myth were not understood by Lévi-Strauss, that searching for an opposition by reshuffling the items of the myth to fit them into a symmetrical pattern, he finally managed to invent one, which however explains nothing.

Structuralism as an Ideology

It must be clear that a doctrine which by its aims, methods, and results obstructs scientific enquiry and leads student and investigator astray, renders an immense service to the forces of reaction in the field of ideology and social science, where these forces have no greater enemy than the revelation of the nature, function and significance of social facts.

These forces have always been hostile to the development of the social sciences as *sciences*. They have not been opposed to their development as *methods* for collecting, analysing and classifying information. Such information, manipulated and processed, has managerial and technical value in reducing waste in production, promoting more refined methods of exploitation, and even increasing productivity. The aim of social science is thus perverted in order to apply it not to the discovery of the sociological or causal explanation of facts—which is dangerous—but to their manipulation for the purpose of serving economic ends—which is profitable. Structuralism fits in perfectly with this scheme, since it fulfils the double purpose of disqualifying the search for explanation and substituting for it fact manipulation. This is not accidental. Structuralism represents the culminating point of a theoretical trend in social anthropology that goes back to the years immediately preceding the first World War. The previous period had been dominated by the idea of evolution. Historical development was then still viewed as part and parcel of the general evolutionary process at work in nature, and was explanatory. By the beginning of the 20th century, social evolutionism, with its condemnation of the capitalist form of production and its socialist anticipation of the future, could no longer be tolerated. This placed it under "severe attack"; and in anthropology, the attack was carried out with extraordinary violence.[37]

Commenting on this "attack", Leach relates it to developments in the physical sciences. The connection between the physical sciences and social evolutionism is visibly remote; yet it undoubtedly exists and explains how structuralism came to acquire its particular character and assume an ideological role today. Obviously, it was not the physicists who were going to take up arms for or against social evolutionism. They come into the picture, however, in that their discipline being the least historical, as it were, of all the sciences, a philosophy inspired by its subject-matter would be the most likely to provide general concepts uncontaminated by historicism and evolutionism, as required, and applicable to the social sciences. This is precisely what happened.

It was Ernst Mach who, perhaps more than any other physicist, drew philosophical conclusions from the new physics. His declared aim, to substitute functional analysis for causal analysis, did not fall on deaf ears, and was enthusiastically acclaimed by Robert Lowie, a personal friend and fervid admirer (Mach was "the dominant influence of my maturer days"; "the founder of a new and real scientific liberalism"), who made it the corner-stone of his anthropological teaching.[38] Indeed, no one applied himself as diligently to the task of outlawing—the word is no exaggeration[39]—the idea of evolution in social anthropology, through his attacks on L. H. Morgan.

The offensive against Morgan provides an interesting and illuminating chapter in the history of social anthropology. That evolutionism was combated on purely methodological grounds, as in the case of Lowie and others, is no doubt true. But it is no less true that other motivations were also involved which were to turn the offensive into a real crusade. "The Marxist and Communist adoption of nineteenth century evolutionism, especially of L. H. Morgan's scheme, as official dogma, has certainly not favoured the acceptability to scientists of the Western nations of anything labelled 'evolution' ", wrote J. H. Steward, an American anthropologist.[40] As evidence of this, one may quote Malinowski: "Evolutionism is now the wholly accepted anthropological creed in the Soviet Union, in which form, of course, it ceases to be scientific."[41] As Eleanor Leacock shrewdly remarks, "since Morgan's works was used as the basis for Engels' 'Origin of the Family, Private Property and the State', arguments about Morgan are often veiled arguments about Marx."[42] To sum up in the words of yet another anthropologist, "the adoption of the evolutionary thesis, in general, and Morgan's theories, in particular, by Karl Marx and the socialist and working class movement, has raised the powerful opposition of the capitalist system. Thus, antievolutionism has become the *credo* of certain sectors of society . . . a philosophy bringing its support to the Church, private property, the family and the capitalist state."[43]

Lowie's explanation of the popularity which evolutionism enjoyed in the 19th century was that "the belief in social progress was a natural accompaniment of the belief in historical laws, especially when tinged with the evolutionary optimism of the seventies of the nineteenth century".[44] By the same token, the spread of "synchronic" theories (functionalism, structuralism) in the 20th century ought to be "tinged" by the pessimism accompanying the social and ideological crisis of that century, and indeed pessimism is well reflected both in Lowie's writings and more so, significantly, in those of Lévi-Strauss. Similarly it should not be impossible to find "sociological" explanations of the popularity of "synchronic" theories in the 20th century.[45]

"Sociological" interpretations, however, are not enough to account for the development of the trend that has led to modern structuralism, though they may account for its success. That is why the reference to Lowie here is not incidental. For if Lowie was deeply influenced by Mach and applied the latter's methodology to social anthropology, he was also to become the friend and *maître à penser* of none other than Lévi-Strauss. The filiation of ideas running from the world of physics to that of philosophy (ideology), to that of anthropology and structuralism is remarkable and could not have been more direct. It could, in fact, be described as genetic, for the structuralist approach developed by Lévi-Strauss is already contained in Lowie's methodology. Lowie's classification of kinship systems, for instance, (into four groups) based on combinatory logic, is of essentially the same type as Lévi-Strauss's later "classification" of totemic phenomena (also into four groups), and suffers from the same defects and for the same reasons. It is thus an error to see in Lévi-Strauss a representative of the traditional French school of anthropology, simply because he works in France and writes in French, and poses as the continuator of Mauss.

The error is understandable. Much less understandable is the other error of regarding him as an adept of Hegelian dialectics. Lowie was under the influence of Mach's neo-positivism, not Hegel's dialectics. The development of physical science and of technology reinforced the "scientific" justification of neo-positivist thought and the depreciation of causal in favour of functional analysis. Translated into sociological terms, this meant the rejection, in the field of social (and anthropological) studies, of historical and evolutionary interpretation, whether Hegelian or materialistic, in favour of the "functionalist" approach. For Lowie, for instance, "laws" in social anthropology could at best refer to invariable correlations, excluding all idea of "necessity". The same idea is expressed by Lévi-Strauss, for whom " 'understanding history' will have to be given up in order to make of the study of different cultures a synchronic analysis of the relations between their constituent elements in the present".[46]

Dialectical methodology has been attributed to Lévi-Strauss owing, among other things, to his constant references to the "contradiction" between the so-called binary oppositions of the mind, supposedly at the bottom of all structural inversions and symmetries. But "contradiction" occupies as important a part, negatively, in formal logic as, positively, in dialectics. In structural analysis, the contradiction manifested in a binary opposition is totally inoperative unless understood in its absolute, anti-dialectical sense. Structuralism takes into account only that aspect of contradiction whereby the terms in opposition sharply exclude each other, for whatever bears on the unity and the interdependence of contraries does away with the essential condition of structural analysis. Structuralism cannot go beyond the limits of formal logic and is essentially anti-dialectical.

That is why the concept of society as a living organism in process of constant change and development is abhorrent to structuralists and seldom, if ever, appears in their writings. Society they prefer to view as "something mechanically assembled, allowing for all sorts of arbitrary combinations between a variety of social elements", to use Lenin's words directed at his opponents of the day, but admirably suited to characterize modern structuralism.[47]

The structuralist view of society, which chooses to ignore the revolution in men's thoughts brought about by the theory of evolution in the 19th century, revives the mechanistic world-view of the preceding period. It constitutes a *regression*, which had already been envisaged as a possibility by Engels, not to the crude though historically justified mechanistic philosophy of that period, but to a mechanistic philosophy of the same type, expressed in the language of modern technique by "automatic control" and represented by the digital computer.

The air of modernity which thus pervades Lévi-Strauss's structuralism is largely due to his use of the terminology and concepts of present-day cybernetics. Social facts and relationships, expressed in terms of "messages", "information", "communication", "patterns", "combinations" etc., lead down ultimately to the abstract units of "binary oppositions". It is here that the hard core of structuralism fully reveals itself. For the structuralist permutatory reconstructions of social facts from these basic units, on the model of the combinatory yes-no logic of the digital computer, takes the mechanical contradiction between the terms of binary oppositions as the basic *unit of articulation* between necessarily *discrete* elements. The ultimate result of structural analysis, which consists, as stated before, of washing away the specificity of social phenomena by reducing them to combinations of their component elements, also implies that the latter, whatever their degree of abstraction, are discrete. Growth, development and change, as dialectical processes carried through by virtue of inherent contradictions working themselves out, are not viewed as such. They are viewed as the outer appearance which different combinations of standard elements present when appearing in succession.

Thus, when dealing with ritual as a social phenomenon (magical), Lévi-Strauss is at pains to break it down into its constituent elements without destroying it in the process. A rite appears functionally as a continuous whole, and the structuralist problem is to show that it is really discontinuous, consisting of a chain of discrete elements. Ritual practice, according to Lévi-Strauss, consists of "words uttered, gestures performed and objects manipulated".[48] Since "gestures" and "objects" fulfil the office of words by other means, they may be assimilated to them. Brought down to a common denominator, they are all thus permutable. At the same time, the strict, scrupulous observance of prescribed gestures and movements in their minutest details, on the one hand; and their constant repetition in ritual on the other, show, first, that each detail is identified as a distinct infinitesimal element; and, second, that through their repetition in succession such details fall in to form a single sequence. "Differences which have become infinitesimal tend to coalesce and virtually to achieve identity; and so we come once more to that figure evoked by the film strip which decomposes motion into such small units that their successive images become indistinguishable and seem to repeat one another."[49] Thus, "starting from discrete units", ritual "reaches out for the continuous and strives to attain it" but always fails to, as, structurally, it must; whence the touch of frenzy and exacerbation which always accompanies it.[50] The argument is ingenious though unconvincing; if put forward at all, it is to emphasize that the elements entering into combination must be discrete, otherwise, by computer-logic, they cannot combine. The mechanistic character of structural analysis is thus implicitly asserted.

In viewing social change not dynamically, as the expression of social development through the development of the forces of production, economic and political struggle etc., but statically, as the expression of different combinations of unchanging elements, structuralism represents history as a chronology of the reshufflings and re-alignments of the inner structures, institutions and cultural acquisitions of human societies, in order to maintain them in equilibrium and ensure their survival. "Men", says Lévi-Strauss, "have always and everywhere set themselves the same task and fixed before themselves the same objective. . . . In the course of their becoming, only the means have changed; through succeeding millenia, man has only managed to repeat himself."[51]

In this refusal to recognize that historical change is a process of development, in favour of the combinatory interpretation of social facts,[52] structuralism provides the operational justification for the hostility which conservatism, as stated, manifests towards the social sciences. For if, in the course of structural analysis and reduction, social facts lose their specificity, nothing remains of the subject-matter of these sciences. With the destruction of social facts, as *social* facts, the sciences that study them cave in and vanish. Lévi-Strauss does indeed suggest something of the kind, though in a different way in order to grant them a temporary respite, as it were. The real answers to social problems, according to him, are to be provided by the physical and natural sciences. However, as these sciences are yet incapable of supplying them, there is room for the so-called social sciences to play their role as "shadow" sciences, in order to "assuage the craving for immediate knowledge with approximate answers, and to offer the physical and natural sciences an anticipatory but often useful simulacrum of the truer knowledge which it will be their lot one day to articulate".[53] The present role of the social sciences is therefore not entirely useless. They act, though imperfectly, by proxy, as it were, on behalf of the physical and natural science, until such a time when these are ready to assume their full responsibilities.

It is evident from Lévi-Strauss's many remarks that when speaking of the physical and natural sciences in this connection, he has in mind information theory. "Society can only be understood through the study of the messages and the communication facilities which belong to it", is a remark by Norbert Wiener, whom Lévi-Strauss is fond of quoting; but this has to await future developments of communication or Information theory before the physical and natural sciences can take over from the "social sciences".[54] All this, of course, is calculated to validate the scientific character of structuralism, which entails the effacement of social specificity in its analytical reductionist procedures, prefiguring the effacement of the social sciences themselves.

This again betrays the mechanistic nature of structuralism, incapable of recognizing the qualitative specificity which matter acquires at each different level of organization. The reductionist attempt to interpret objective phenomena in terms of those which conceptually appear as at the most fundamental level—for instance, the physical, or mechanical —is not new. Its failure is due precisely to those qualitative distinctions which render phenomena belonging to one level irreducible to another, and not to any theoretical weakness or insufficiency. If, for instance, biological phenomena depend on physical and chemical processes, these, when integrated in the living organism, exhibit properties particular to the latter which are irreducible to purely physical and chemical interpretations. However operationally powerful Information theory may prove to be and useful in the analysis of social action and reaction, it can therefore never become a substitute for the sociological interpretation of social facts, that is for their interpretation in terms of the dialectics of historical development. Still, once again, the ideological character of structuralism reveals itself as not only springing from its anti-dialectical approach, but as aiming, further, at eliminating from the field of investigation the method of historical analysis which gives the explanation of social facts in terms of their own development—in terms of the *social* forces that give rise to them, and the *social* purposes which they are called upon to serve—not in terms of phenomena belonging to other dimensions of reality, such as "messages", "information" etc.

Whether it is through its reductionism, the recourse to combinatory logic in its operations, or through the utilization of the technological terminology of information theory, structuralism presents social phenomena, relationships and processes in terms of the concepts introduced by that theory. Sociological laws—as natural laws of society—thus appear as technological necessities; while technological necessities appear, conversely, as possessing the force of natural law. In other words, as nature and society are increasingly interpreted in terms of information theory or cybernetics ("signals", "communication", "feedback" etc.), the application of the teachings of that theory to the organization of society must seem natural and necessary. The latter follows from the former. Ideologically, structuralism prepares for obtaining acceptance of the social order, modelled by technology, as the natural order of things; while on the scientific plane, it prepares in its field of operation—anthropology—for the effacement of that discipline. The question naturally arises: Is structuralism, then, Science or Ideology? The validity of its claim to be the former is challenged in the preceding pages. To give an answer more in line with structuralist style, let us suggest that if Science and Ideology may be said—rightly or wrongly, structurally it does not matter—to form a "binary opposition", it is in the ideological "message", not the scientific, that structuralism, in fine, puts its "information".

NOTES

1. "Some readers even suspect that they are being treated to a confidence trick."—E. Leach, *Lévi-Strauss*, London, Fontana, 1970, p. 8.
2. E. Leach (ed.), "Introduction" in *The Structural Study of Myth and Totemism*, London, Tavistock, 1967, pp. xvi–xvii.
3. Cl. Lévi-Strauss, *Les structures élémentaires de la parenté* (1949), Paris, Plon, 1967, p. xiv. "There is little evidence that many French critics understand him (or succeed in reproducing his ideas in detail) more clearly than those overseas do." G. S. Kirk, *Myth*, Cambridge University Press, 1971, p. 59.
4. Leach, "Claude Lévi-Strauss—Anthropologist and Philosopher", *New Left Review*, 1965, 34:27.
5. Leach, "Mythologiques: *Le cru et le cuit*", *American Anthropologist*, 1965, 67:776.
6. See our "Présentation" and "Introductions" in L. H. Morgan, *La société archaïque*, Paris, Anthropos, 1971.
7. Lévi-Strauss, *Le Totémisme aujourd'hui*, Paris, PUF, 1962.
8. Lévi-Strauss, *Anthropologie structurale*, Paris, Plon, 1958, pp. 235–7.
9. Ibid., pp. 249–50.
10. Lévi-Strauss, *Du miel aux cendres*, Paris, Plon, 1966, p. 215.
11. Cf. R. and L. Makarius, *Structuralisme ou Ethnologie*, Paris, Anthropos, 1973, p. 295 n. 5.
12. Lévi-Strauss, *Le cru et le cuit*, Paris, Plon, 1964, p. 21.
13. Nur Yalman, "*La Pensée sauvage*", *American Anthropologist*, 1964, 66:1181.
14. *Anthropologie structurale*, p. 373.
15. Ibid., p. 70.
16. Ibid., p. 41.
17. Ibid., p. 232.
18. G. Sterner, "A Conversation with Claude Lévi-Strauss", *Encounter*, 1966, 26:32–38.
19. *Anthropologie structurale*, p. 232.
20. Ibid., p. 229.

21. Lévi-Strauss, "La structure et la forme", *Cahiers de l'Institut des Sciences économiques appliquées*, 1960, 99:35.
22. *Anthropologie structurale*, p. 79.
23. Ibid., p. 95.
24. Ibid., pp. 326–7.
25. "In the version of Lévi-Strauss, the essence of 'structuralist' method seems to be in the construction of deliberately abstract models by the artificial breaking down of the object under study and its subsequent reconstruction in terms of essentially relational properties," W. G. Runciman, "What is Structuralism", *British Journal of Sociology*, 1969, 20:257. The author misses an essential point. The aim is not just the reconstruction of the object under study, but the construction of all possible "objects", of which the one under study is a particular case.

Some of these ideas were expressed by Lévi-Strauss as long ago as 1950, referring to Mauss: ". . . for the first time in the history of anthropological thought an effort was made to transcend empirical observation and reach deeper realities. For the first time, things social ceased to belong to the domain of pure quality . . . and appeared as forming a system revealing connections, equivalences and interdependence between its component parts. Such are first of all the products of social activity: technical, economic, ritual, aesthetic or religious—tools, manufactured goods, foodstuffs, magical formulas, ornaments, songs, dances and myths —admitting comparison between each other by virtue of that character, which they share in common, of being transferable through processes which may be analysed and classified and which, even when they seem to be welded to certain types of values, are reducible to general, more fundamental forms. These products of social activity not only admit comparison, but are also interchangeable, insofar as different values may replace one another in a single operation. It is moreover these operations themselves, however diversified they may appear when seen through the events of social life, such as birth, initiation, marriage, contract, death and inheritance, and however arbitrary with respect to the number and distribution of the individuals they involve, whether as fellows, intermediaries, or donors, which always permits a reduction to a smaller number of operations, groups or persons, where, in fine, one again finds only the basic terms of an equilibrium diversely conceived and differently realized, according to the type of society concerned. Those types may thus be defined by these intrinsic attributes, and compared to one another, since these attributes are no longer ordered qualitatively, but according to the number and disposal of elements which are themselves invariable for all of the types concerned . . ." (Lévi-Strauss, "Introduction à l'oeuvre de Marcel Mauss" in M. Mauss, *Sociologie et Anthropologie* (1950), Paris, PUF, 1966, pp. xxxiii–xxxiv).

This laboriously worded passage is a good sample of Lévi-Strauss's style, when he chooses to make it deliberately tortuous and involuted. It would have been simpler to express the simple ideas it contains in simple words, but that would have perhaps made them less impressive. The general tone and long-winded sentences conspire to suggest that profound truths are being uttered. But the "transcending of empirical observation to reach deeper realities" is just another way of saying that social facts are to be expressed in the general terms to which they are reducible; and the succeeding sentences are to indicate that these terms, when they are not identical and merge into one another, are at least of the same order and therefore permutable. In 1962, Lévi-Strauss gave a more succinct description of his method:

1. define the phenomenon under study as a relation between two or more terms, real or implied;
2. draw up a table of possible permutations between these terms;
3. regard this table as the general subject of an analysis conducive, at this level

only, to necessary connections—the empirical phenomenon, initially considered, being one possible combination out of many which, together, form an
all-comprehensive system to be reconstructed beforehand (*Le Totémisme
aujourd'hui*, p. 22).

26. *Les structures . . .*, p. xxvii.
27. *Le Totémisme aujourd'hui*, p. 24.
28. Ibid., p. 25.
29. Lévi-Strauss, *Anthropologie structurale II*, Paris, Plon, 1973, p. 38.
30. Cf. *Structuralisme ou Ethnologie*.
31. Lévi-Strauss, "Réponses à quelques questions", *Esprit*, 1963, 11:630.
32. Leach, *Lévi-Strauss*, p. 20.
33. Cf. *Structuralisme ou Ethnologie*.
34. R. et L. Makarius, *L'Origine de l'Exogamie et du Totémisme*, Paris, Gallimard, 1961.
35. *Structuralisme ou Ethnologie*, pp. 235–76.
36. P. Worsley, "Groote Eyland Totemism and *Le Totémisme aujourd' hui*", in *The
    Structural Study of Myth and Totemism*, p. 142.
37. Leach in R. Firth (ed.), *Man and Culture*, London, Routledge & Kegan Paul,
    1957, p. 120. Cf. "Présentation" in *La Société Archaique*.
38. R. Lowie, *R. H. Lowie, Ethnologist*, Berkeley and Los Angeles, 1959, p. 60.
    M. Harris, *The Rise of Anthropological Theory*, London, Routledge & Kegan Paul,
    1961, p. 345.
39. This applies particularly to the period extending from the First World War till
    about 1959. "In 1939, when I discussed 'Evolution in Social Anthropology' at
    Association meetings in Chicago, I had been warned by a social scientist, who
    was by no means extreme in his views, that 'evolution' was a dirty, dangerous
    word, and urged one to replace it by the word 'development'." (A. Lesser, "Social
    Fields and the Evolution of Society", *Southwestern Journal of Anthropology*, 1961,
    p. 40). In 1940, as Radcliffe-Brown could confirm, "in certain anthropological
    circles the term 'evolutionary anthropologist' is almost a term of abuse". (*Structure
    and Function*, London, 1956, p. 203.)
40. In A. Kroeber (ed.), *Anthropology Today*, Chicago: Univ. Press, 1953, p. 315.
41. *A Scientific Theory of Culture*, Chapel Hill, 1944, p. 17.
42. "Morgan and Materialism," *Current Anthropology*, 1964, 5:110.
43. L. White, "The Concept of Evolution in Cultural Anthropology", in B. Meggers
    (ed.), *Evolution and Anthropology*, Washington, 1959, p. 109.
44. *Primitive Society* (1921), New York, 1947, p. 440.
45. Thus R. C. Lewontin: "Like all revolutions the bourgeois revolution gave way
    slowly to a period of consolidation. . . . Once the new classes had gained power, it
    was clearly to their advantage to prevent the evolution from going further. . . .
    Liberal democracy of the twentieth century has a vested interest in maintaining
    the world social order. . . . It is not remarkable, then, that evolutionary theories
    of the twentieth century are marked by a concern for equilibrium conditions and
    dynamic stability, a playing down of progressivist and perfectionist elements, and
    a general reliance on the principle that *plus ça change, plus c'est la même chose*."
    ("Evolution" in *International Encyclopedia of the Social Sciences*, 1968, vol. V, p. 209.)
46. *Anthropologie structurale*, p. 13.
47. V. Lénine, *Ce que sont les "amis du peuple" et comment ils luttent contre les social-
    démocrates* (1894), Moscow, 1966, p. 55.
48. *L'Homme nu*, Paris, Plon, 1971, p. 600.
49. Ibid., p. 602.
50. Ibid., pp. 607–8.
51. *Tristes Tropiques*, Paris, Plon, 1955, p. 424.
52. Lowie had clearly expressed this position: "Neither morphologically nor dynami-
    cally can social life be said to have progressed from a stage of savagery to a state of

enlightenment. . . . The renunciation of historical laws does not imply the renunciation of uniformities, *independent of the time factor*, and veritably inherent in the very essence of social existence . . . empirically it turns out that the several types of social units are combined in a purely capricious fashion." (*Primitive Society*, pp. 440, 436, 430.)

53. *L'Homme nu*, p. 573.
54. *The Human Use of Human Beings*, London, Eyre & Spottiswoode, 1950, p. 9.

CLASS STRUGGLE AND THE INDUSTRIAL REVOLUTION

John Saville

John Foster: *Class Struggle and the Industrial Revolution* (Weidenfeld and
Nicholson. pp 346. £6.00)

THIS is an important book by a marxist historian which will have a
considerable influence upon the work of social historians in the future.
In a number of ways, this is a pioneering work, and its use of sophisticated quantitative techniques for the dissection of urban social
structures will serve as a model for subsequent research workers. It is,
however, a difficult volume to read; for one thing it is awkwardly organized around the experience of three towns—Oldham, Northampton
and South Shields, with the greatest amount of space and attention
being given to Oldham; and for another the analysis is densely argued
but discontinuous, so that one has to jump from one section to another
to obtain an overall understanding of the author's approach.

The theme of the book, in the words of E. J. Hobsbawm who con-
tributes a Foreword "is an enquiry into certain central features of
British industrial development, and into the nature of both the Victorian
bourgeoisie and the working class. More generally, it is an attempt
both to clarify and to provide analytical and preferably quantitative
methods for investigating the concept of 'class consciousness'." In
the author's own words (p.1), "the main problem with which the book
is concerned, [is] the nature of the change which English capitalism
underwent in the middle years of the last century. Many terms have
been used to describe it. It has been made to represent 'liberalization',
the achievement of mass citizenship, the arrival of a mature industrial
society. And from another viewpoint, the coming of social imperialism,
the emergence of a labour aristocracy and a decisive shift within the
economy from the export of commodities to the export of capital."

The three towns he studies were chosen because they represented
different forms of economic organization and a different tempo of
economic and social change. Oldham, "the central town of the study",
was an important segment of the cotton industry, the earliest factory
sector in the British economy:

"Politically, it had a continuing history of radical activity from the 1790s to 1848. It
was one of those areas where the United Englishmen had a mass base in the 1800s

226

and during the guerrilla campaign of 1812 it was the scene of a two-day battle between armed workers and troops. Throughout the second quarter of the century the town was more or less permanently under the control of the organized working class; much of its local government was subordinated to the trade unions, the new poor law was unenforced for well over a decade, and radicals like Cobbett and Fielden were elected as MPs. This situation did not change much until the end of the 1840s when the town moved remarkably quickly towards class collaboration and a 'labour aristocracy' type of social structure" (pp. 2–3).

By contrast, Northampton and South Shields, with industrial structures still for the most part technologically unrevolutionized and a range and depth of poverty greater than Oldham's, had a working class that never achieved anything approaching the degree of radical intervention in local politics that obtained in Oldham; and Foster uses these towns as "controls" against which to set Oldham's experience. His analysis before the late 1840s is concerned with the emergence of working-class consciousness, and its varying ideological content, and after 1850 with the argument "that liberalization was in fact a collective *ruling-class* response to a social system in crisis and integrally related to a preceding period of working-class consciousness" (p.3).

*   *   *

He begins, in chapter 2, with a brief but useful account of Oldham's "entry" into industrialization, making, *inter alia*, two important points. The first, that the early generations of mill-owners came from families who already had money; and the second, that Oldham at least provided no basis for the argument that Nonconformity was the entrepreneurial driving force behind the shift into industrialization. The controversial section in this chapter relates to Foster's short analysis of the origins of English industrialization, and although this is not central to the book's main themes, it will be commented upon here as an example of certain general weaknesses in Foster's approach. One of these is the narrow base of secondary source material on which he relies. A refusal by any historian to produce a book from other historians' writings is to be welcomed, and in any case Foster's own study of Oldham is inevitably grounded in original sources, and these he has explored in great depth. But as will be remarked upon later, his reluctance to place his own work in the context of previous writing has led him into error in some parts of his analysis, and nowhere is this more strikingly illustrated than in the brief discussion of the pre-conditions for the development of industrial capitalism in Britain. To come to the point, it is Marx whom Foster ignores and the classic analysis of British industrial origins in the concluding section of Vol. I of *Capital* finds no echo in his pages. Since most marxist historians in this country (with the outstanding exception of Maurice Dobb) have also ignored the greater part of Marx's analysis as it relates to the 18th century in particular, it is worth pursuing the matter further through Foster's own approach. He sums up his general thesis:

> "England's pioneer industrialization seems, then, to have involved the following elements. Underlying the whole process, but not explaining it, were the general factors common to all Europe: the slow, spasmodic advance of agricultural productivity; the recurrent but abortive bursts of merchant capitalist production; and the new type of colonial surplus. Then, providing the necessarily devious escape route, came the factors that put England ahead. First, there was the out-of-step pattern of population growth that brought a boom in cheap labour, capitalist production and bourgeois revolution. Next, there were the conditions that enabled the capture of Europe's colonial surplus, the long-term maintenance of capitalist forms of organization and continuing industrial and agrarian innovation. Then, finally (after the over-investment in colonial primary production had brought a collapse in colonial profits) one gets the massive switch of investment back to the home industrial sectors in the 1770s and 1780s: back in order to exploit the crucial super-profit techniques developed in the previous two generations. At this point, with all three basic preconditions fulfilled (labour, raw material and market) industrial revolution could begin" (p. 18).

Foster, in fact, gets half-way to a Marxist analysis. In the paragraph which follows the quotation given above he notes (a) that industrialization did not bring about any fundamental change in social structure, for that change had already occurred and (b) in general, before industrialization began, "all essential capitalist institutions were already old". What he misses is Marx's central concept of primitive accumulation by which Marx was referring to the emergence of new forms of both capital and labour as the fundamental prerequisites for industrial development. Using British experience for his model, Marx's pre-conditions involved the expropriation of the agricultural producer from the soil—"the basis of the whole process"—*and* the concentration of property into relatively few hands, with its conversion into capital for industrial development. It is the elimination of the peasantry from the social structure of the countryside that is one of the central dynamic factors in British economic development; the emergence and growth of a capitalist, market-orientated agriculture being a product of the same historical process of change. Marx's analysis is set out clearly and coherently in Part VIII of Vol. I of *Capital*, and in all its essentials the model that he presented has been confirmed by later research. Foster's own analysis is jejune; he makes use of concepts such as "lucky breaks" to explain the differences in internal development between Britain and Europe. Whatever its merits—and many of the points he makes will be fully acceptable to most kinds of historians—his theoretical analysis is not that of Marx.

*   *   *

The fourth chapter in this volume and of central importance to the whole work is titled "Economics of Class Consciousness". It is preceded by a chapter which describes the ways in which the working class community in Oldham secured control in certain key sectors of local politics, notably the police and poor law administration, and developed a "labour community" which was "closely related to extra-legal unionism and involved a massive cultural reorganization of the working population" (p.72). It is the shift into "a deeper political awareness"—from a labour consciousness to a class consciousness—that forms the theme of Chapter 4. Foster uses "class consciousness" in a very special and narrow meaning, as a synonym for "revolutionary consciousness". This is what he says:

> "Obviously one cannot make the same tests for class consciousness as one could for a living population. But one can get some measure of the *process* by which, if it was class consciousness, it must have come about. If Oldham's militancy was indeed of this nature—the result of a mass realization of demands for a total change of the social system—then it could only have developed in very special circumstances; those in which the community's revolutionary vanguard was able to break out of its structural isolation, get access to labour as a whole, and convince people that radical political change was the only solution to their problems. And this, to an extent, is something we are able to test" (p. 74).

"A total change of the system", "the revolutionary vanguard", a mass conviction of the need for radical political change: obviously it is possible to define class consciousness in these ways, but it must not be assumed that these are the only ways. There is the "economist" consciousness that Lenin was writing about in *What is to be Done* and there are degrees of class consciousness which stop at varying distances from revolutionary consciousness. This last is a fairly rare phenomenon; limited normally to a minority even in critical historical situations; hence Lenin's well known conditions for a successful revolutionary uprising. But there can be no objection to Foster's definition, once it is clearly understood, and we turn now to his analysis of how this (revolutionary) class consciousness came into being, and what was its precise intellectual and political content.

There were two main periods in Oldham which radicalized the workers. The first was down to about 1830 when the handloom weavers were still larger in number than the factory workers. The "repeated and deepening crises" of the weaving trade and the general technological imbalances within the cotton industry as a whole radicalized the Oldham working class at least to the point of what Foster describes as a labour consciousness. It should be remarked in passing that Foster never makes specific what the content was of this pre-1830 ideology. It is notable, for example, that although it is clear from the text that the handloom weavers were a central group in the pre-1830 years, exactly what their ultra-radicalism consisted of is never examined. But the second phase of the processes of radicalization after 1830 had a quite different background (p.80). The numbers of handloom weavers were now fast declining and the whole industry was rapidly becoming mechanized within an economy that was still technologically under-developed. It was this basic contradiction between the advanced technology of cotton and the very much slower technological rate of change outside the cotton sector that provides the background for the crisis in which the industry found itself. While investment and pro-ductivity made rapid progress in cotton, "the effect was merely to reduce the exchange value of the industry's output without any balancing reduction in the labour cost of inputs from other sectors, especially food and machine goods" (p.80). The consequences for the cotton industry were a long-term decline in the rate of profit and a series of worsening crises. In the 1820s, Foster notes there was only one bad year of depression (1826), while there were four in the 1830s (1831, 1836, 1838–9) and five in the 1840s (1841, 1842, 1846, 1847–8); and during these periods "anything up to 30 per cent of the labour force would be out of work". Over the whole period from 1830 to 1850 there was "an almost uninterrupted drop in the real wages of the largest section of adult male mill workers, the cotton spinners", who found themselves "the principal victims of the industry's almost suicidal economics". In a later comment Foster generalizes the situation as "the hard, intractable *trend to crisis* into which the cotton industry became locked after 1830" (p.109). He sums up:

> "This, then, was the experience of the 1830s and 1840s: deepening crisis; repeated employer attacks on living standards and conditions; lengthening periods in which the whole basis of industrial society appeared to be breaking down" (pp. 83–4).

It is necessary to look closely at Foster's understanding of the cotton industry in the second quarter of the century for it is indeed crucial for his later analysis of social consciousness. There are two separate but related problems to be considered. One is the facts of the cotton industry's situation as they affected working class living standards, and the second is the historical evaluation of the cotton sector within the general framework of the British economy at this time. Were its economics "almost suicidal"? and was the industry trapped within a "hard, intractable *trend to crisis*", and what happened to the crisis?

But first, the facts of life of the cotton operatives, and here there is no disagreement. As against the large number of apologists for these decades, Foster provides a careful statement of the trends in real wages, housing and living conditions and the incidence of sickness. His family and household analysis taken from the 1851 Census schedules is especially notable, and offers a new dimension to the study of urban poverty in the mid-century. Living standards—as a broad general-ization—were worse in Northampton and South Shields than in Oldham, but in all three they were appalling. "While in Oldham the proportion of working families below the subsistence line at any one time was about one-fifth, the proportion in Shields was over one-quarter and in Northampton over one-third" (p.96). The striking feature of the cotton industry is the decline in wages during the thirties and early forties, and the fact that in some years—1841–2 especially—unemployment was very high. There is no doubt, therefore, of the material oppression and the stresses and strains that were imposed upon the cotton operatives during these decades; and in the context of the political evolution of the British working people from the 1790s, the growth and deepening of a radical consciousness was only to be expected.

When one turns from living standards to the wider historical evaluation of the cotton industry, there are serious criticisms to be made of Foster's judgements. The generalizations that he gives us—"a deepening series of crises" (p.80); "the industry's almost suicidal economics" (p.82); "lengthening periods in which the whole basis of industrial society appeared to be breaking down" (p.84); "the hard, intractable *trend to crisis* . . . after 1830" (p.109); "the classic sequence of industrial capitalist crisis" (p.124)—all suggest that the cotton industry in particular, and perhaps industrial society as a whole, were rapidly approaching the abyss of total breakdown and collapse.

The first comment to be made is that anyone using language of this kind to describe the cotton industry of the 1830s and 1840s has grave difficulties in explaining the remarkable, and relatively smooth, expansion of the industry after 1850. If the cotton industry was subject for so long to "the classic sequence of industrial capitalist crisis" how did it come about that it solved its problems so rapidly at the end of the 1840s? Foster might have addressed to himself the question which Marx put to Engels in 1857, after the crisis of that year:

"I must say all the same, however, that the way the mass of overproduction which brought about the crisis has been absorbed is by no means clear to me; such a rapid ebb after such a violent flood tide has never occurred before." (*Correspondence* (1934 ed.), p. 116.)

Except for the declining rate of profit argument—which is admitted —Foster offers no serious account of the inner crisis of the cotton industry between 1830 and 1842, the period with which he is mainly concerned; and his general treatment of the economics of the industry is perfunctory and superficial. What he misses—and misses completely —is the paradox of crisis and growth co-existing during the same years; the presence of serious contradictions, including the heavy social costs, within a framework of rapid development overall. These paradoxes reside in the nature and character of the cotton industry within the general context of British industrialization during the first half of the 19th century; and it is a history which goes much beyond the simple categories which Foster himself uses. The growth of the industry in the second quarter is very remarkable and the fact cannot be reconciled with Foster's apocalyptic statements. Some basic data are set out below:

EXPORTS

	Raw cotton imports (million lbs.)	Piece goods (million yds.)	Thread (million lbs.)	Nos. employed factory workers (000s)
1820	152	251	0.4	126
1830	264	445	1.2	185
1840	592	791	2.8	262
1850	664	1,358	4.4	331
1860	1,391	2,776	6.3	427

(From: B. R. Mitchell and P. Deane, *Abstract of British Historical Statistics* (1962) pp. 180, 182, 187.)

These are not the statistics of an industry locked in insoluble crisis, although to be fair to Foster he uses the word "intractable" rather than "insoluble". Not only were foreign markets growing fast during the first half of the century, but so was the home market, and the ability to switch from one to the other (as in 1839 for example) acted as part cushion to the industry. This is not the place to enter into a discussion of the cost structures of cotton firms which brought about a high level of investment, rapid growth of output and employment against a background of falling profit margins, but the materials for analysis are abundant; and the published works of Matthews, Blaug and S. D. Chapman, to mention only three of the leading writers of the last twenty years, provide a coherent explanation of the apparent paradoxes involved. There is, however, a comment of a general kind to be made relevant to the wider considerations of social history in these middle decades of the century: the paradox of the cotton industry writ large in terms of British society as a whole. What is at issue here is the nature, character and dynamic of industrial society in the first sixty or seventy years of its existence. After 1800 industrialization developed in extremely jerky, uneven ways; the institutional framework within which the new industrial relations expanded was weak at many points, and in particular in the banking sector, a continuing source of instability until the 1850s. The contradictions of growth in new sectors or technologically revolutionized sectors, and decline or extinction in others—all within a total context of very rapid overall development—produced the economic and social tensions with which all historians of these decades are familiar. The social and human costs of early industrialization were immense, and no one has documented them in more bitter detail than Marx in *Capital;* but this immense human suffering occurred within a society that was growing economically at a very fast rate; and one of the central problems of 19th century history—the social, political and intellectual changes around 1850—can only be understood if the full complexities of the first half of the century are appreciated.

* * *

Foster's narrow and in part inaccurate account of the cotton industry does not, however, vitiate the general argument he is making. The "social being" of the mill workers of Lancashire was such that it produced a consciousness of class, an hostility to the established order, a desire for change that was all part of the wider national shifts in consciousness of the years to 1850. As E. P. Thompson has described the process:

> "In the years between 1780 and 1832 most English working people came to feel an identity of interests as between themselves, and as against their rulers and employers. This ruling class was itself much divided, and in fact only gained cohesion over the same years because certain antagonisms were resolved (or faded into relative insignificance) in the face of an insurgent working class. Thus the working-class presence was, in 1832, the most significant factor in British political life."

It is Foster's argument that before 1830, the working people of Oldham developed what he calls an "occupational solidarity" or a "labour consciousness"—what E. P. Thompson understood by "an identity of interests as between themselves, and as against their rulers and employers"; but that after 1830 this labour consciousness deepened into a class consciousness which in Foster's definition is a synonym for revolutionary consciousness. This is the issue. Certain of the key passages in the argument have been quoted above. Foster relates this qualitative change to the worsening economic crisis in the cotton industry after 1830. The new factor in consciousness is an "intellectual conviction" of a different kind from that which obtained before 1830; and he believes it to have been consciously willed. "If it can be shown", he writes "that the development of a mass movement was in fact closely linked to the careful, conscious process by which the radicals guided mass understanding from one level to another, then we will be well on the way to establishing the key element of intellectual conviction" (p.109). To establish his general thesis that an intellectual conviction of a new kind came to be part of the political thinking and attitudes of working people, he selects two episodes from Oldham's history: the first, the events of 1834, and the second, the general strike of August 1842.

On 25 November 1833 a conference at Manchester founded the Society for National Regeneration. It represented a coming together of Robert Owen and John Fielden, the latter the Todmorden cotton master who was such a valiant supporter of the Ten Hours movement. The Manchester Conference accepted five resolutions which ended with a call to establish the eight hour day on 1 March 1834. Fielden persuaded William Cobbett—his fellow MP for Oldham—to publish the scheme in the *Register*, and the committee appointed by the Conference included George Condy, proprietor and editor of the Tory *Manchester Advertiser*, Philip Grant the radical journalist, and John Doherty. The last named was the most important personality in the movement, for it was he who had the confidence of the Lancashire cotton operatives and trade unionists. The Regeneration Society met with considerable support in Lancashire but with opposition elsewhere, especially in the West Riding, where the leaders of the Ten Hours movement were hostile on the grounds of the political impractibility of the scheme. These Yorkshire leaders were highly sceptical of the use of industrial action to achieve a shortening of hours, because of the absence of mass support, and in the event they were proved correct. While there is still much research to be done on this short-lived movement, it would seem that Oldham was the locale where the most militant confrontation took place with the authorities. Two trade unionists were arrested on the evening of 14 April 1834, and by the 20 April the town had become a military camp. The Oldham operatives, according to Foster's account, went on strike for two weeks in support of the Regeneration Society's demand for an eight hour day, but elsewhere action was ragged and partial, and the whole movement soon collapsed. For Foster the episode is central to his general thesis:

"It plainly reveals the ease with which radical leaders could move from industrial to political struggle *without losing* their mass support and also gives an unusually sharp focus to their ultimate objectives. What it may not establish as fully as one would like is the element of mass conviction. In view of the sequence of events, it could be plausibly argued that the wider mobilization sprang more from the attack on trade union rights than any belief in a new social order" (p. 114).

With this last argument Foster is more than half-way towards throwing away his case; and the whole episode needs to be assessed in the context of the period in which it occurred.

First, the ideology of the Regeneration Society. Late 1833 and the first half of 1834 represented a point in time when various strands in the national movement came together to provide the dynamic for mass activity on a very large scale. The conjuncture of militant trade unionism and Owenism, inspired by a range of political and industrial ideas which included Benbow's advocacy of the General Strike, the advanced politics of the *The Poor Man's Guardian*, and the syndicalism of *The Pioneer*, had brought the working class movement to new levels of consciousness and mass action; but anyone coming fresh to Foster's account of this period in Oldham would have no understanding of the national background to the Oldham events, since it is simply ignored. The central phenomenon of this period: the astonishing rise and fall of the Grand National Consolidated Trades Union is not mentioned (nor is the name to be found in the index); the seminal discussions in *The Pioneer* on the part which the unions could play in the achievement of a new social order are similarly missed; and in general what happens in Oldham takes place in a national vacuum. But neither the events in Oldham nor the ideology of the Regeneration Society can be understood without reference to the history of the Ten Hours movement or to the ferment of ideas which provided, not a symbiosis, but a temporary union, between Owenism and industrial class politics, and which, by the summer of 1834, had collapsed. The quotation which Foster gives from a speech of John Doherty (*Herald of the Rights of Industry*, early April 1834) is an excellent example of this mixture of militant unionism and Utopian ideas:

> "We have now arrived at a most important crisis. . . . You are to be the artificers of your fortunes. Philosophers may write, politicians may struggle and your friends labour in vain. Unless you yourself now put your hands to the work in good earnest all will prove unavailing. If you are not emancipated now, *immediately*, the fault is your own. We say solemnly and emphatically Strike! . . ." (p. 111).

And so on. Foster suggests that the ideas of the Regeneration Society were at once "practical" and "totally subversive". It all depends, of course, upon how one defines "practical". Eight hours a day would not have ruined British industrial society in the 1830s, although it would certainly have materially slowed down the rate of capital accumulation; and John Fielden's other ideas of investment boards and control of output were also not beyond a theoretical application. But "practical" meaning politically practicable is quite a different matter, the point in doubt being the readiness or otherwise of the factory workers in general to withdraw their labour in support of the eight hour day. It was just on this issue that the Yorkshire left-wing radicals like Peter Bussey joined forces with Parson Bull in opposing the plans of the Regeneration Society. The totally subversive argument is also difficult to sustain. In the sense that all such programmes, however Utopian, were totally subversive, stemming as they did from a total opposition to the existing order, the term can, rather guardedly be accepted; but it can hardly be accepted for the actual programme of the Regeneration Society which is limited in its aims and objectives and silent on such key questions as the nature of state power and the political agencies by which control of the state may be obtained. In a later discussion Foster half recognizes the point which is being made here, when he refers to the "somewhat unsystematized economic analysis" and the "lack of Leninist rigour about state power" (p.148); although it must be said at once that the use of "Leninist" is anachronistic and unhistorical.

It is, in fact, impossible for the reader to evaluate and assess the "mass conviction" of the Oldham workers in the early months of 1834 and during their two week strike because Foster provides no evidence of what their ideas were, or of the events themselves. Was it really a mass mobilization of Oldham workers during this two week strike? (which incidentally the Webbs and Cecil Driver state was a strike of one week). There is not a single incident quoted during the strike period itself except for a meeting on 18 April which Doherty and others addressed; and the lengthy reports in the *Times*, which the Webbs referred to, or from the *Leeds Mercury*, are not noted in the sources used.

The second episode that Foster uses to confirm his approach is the general strike in the industrial north of August 1842, usually referred to as the Plug Riots. This is a well known story; it took place against the background of widespread economic depression; and it represents a high point, probably *the* high point, of mass action during the Chartist period. The national context within which the events of 1842 took place is only very briefly touched upon in Foster's text and again no one without previous knowledge would be able to appreciate the complexities of working class politics as refracted through the Chartist movement at this time; and for Oldham the information is even more meagre. Foster admits that "we only know a very little of what was said" by Oldham radicals during the crucial days of August 1842 (p.117), but this does not prevent him from being categorical about the nature and purposes of the strike in the town:

"It was clearly a political one to gain what amounted to State power. Support had to be won on these terms beforehand and the process of achieving it plainly involved discussion and argument on a mass scale. What is more, it is also clear (as it should be if we are really dealing with class consciousness) that the success of such arguments was closely linked to the immediacy with which the cotton industry's economics reflected—and could be shown to reflect—the contradictions of the overall system" (p. 117).

Now some of these points are acceptable from what is known of the national debates within the Chartist movement, although the general understanding of state power and political agency among working class groups seem to me to fall a good way short of Foster's confident generalizations. But he is concerned with Oldham and the political consciousness of the Oldham working class, and one is bound to repeat once again that his readers are not provided with the facts upon which his generalizations are founded. There is indeed throughout his discussion of labour or class consciousness a sharp contrast between the imprecision in terms of the evidence offered and his positive and often dogmatic generalizations about their meaning.

There are other matters that must be briefly touched on in this present context. One is the political character of the two Oldham MPs in the early 1830s, Cobbett and Fielden. Foster has only a brief discussion (p.69ff.) but the implications of his text suggest that both men were sympathetic towards, indeed were almost integrated within, the developing class consciousness of the Oldham workers. In certain important matters (factory legislation, opposition to the New Poor Law, hostility towards the new police forces) there was, of course, a complete rapport between the Oldham radicals and their MPs. But there is a good deal more to be said about both Cobbett and Fielden, and it would have illuminated some important parts of the "consciousness" thesis to have explored in detail the relationships between the Oldham working class and Fielden, the great humanist mill-owner, and the extraordinary, marvellous and inconsistent bundles of ideas that united themselves within the personality of William Cobbett. In these middle years of the thirties both men were certainly articulating the hopes, aspirations and general oppositional attitudes of Oldham working people; but neither was "class conscious" in the sense that Foster uses the term. And who were the "vanguard" of the Oldham working class between whom we are told close contact was maintained with their MPs in London? (p.69).

Chapter 5 of this volume, "Class Struggle and Social Structure" is largely devoted to the description and delineation of Oldham's working class leadership. What Foster is concerned to prove is the presence of a "revolutionary vanguard [which] was able to break out of its structural isolation, get access to labour as a whole, and convince people that radical political change was the only solution to their problems" (p.74). This, omitting the use of the term "revolutionary vanguard", fits exactly the achievement of the Chartist leadership in the later thirties and forties. Feargus O'Connor was its outstanding representative, and O'Connor is mentioned only in passing in the text and will not be found in the index; another example of the way in which Foster refuses throughout his book to connect the events in Oldham with the movement in the country as a whole. What we are given in this section on Oldham's working class leaders is detailed but limited statistical information on occupation, political and industrial activity, support for this movement and that, which when put together provides the bare bones of political biographies. It is the result of patient and intensive research, but the conclusions which can be drawn from all this work are by no means clear. Foster establishes a high level of continuity of radical action throughout the first half of the century; he shows that Oldham working people of different occupational backgrounds had a considerable degree of "social closeness" (pp.125–31); and he attempts to describe and define the radical leadership. It is in this last section, central to his argument, that the impressionism of parts of his analysis—despite the apparent hard-headedness of his approach—shows itself most clearly. There are several important sections of this book where a straightforward chronological history would greatly help readers to assess the evidence for themselves, and the lack of a continuous argument is often very confusing.

Let me discuss in some detail the leadership question after 1830. This is the period which sees the shift to class consciousness and as noted above Foster concentrates on the two events of 1834 and 1842. In his words, a "new political unity" emerged after 1830: "three distinct social groupings can be distinguished . . . the continuing group of working-class radicals, the shopkeepers and publicans, and a number of small employers" (p.133); but within this leadership the working-class radicals "largely dictated" the terms on which radical politics were conducted. Foster discusses at some length the shopkeeper/publican group and the small manufacturer group; but there is almost no analysis of the working class radicals. We are told who they were: "The key men remained roughly the same throughout: Knight, Fitton, Haigh, Mills, Swire." These (with the exception of Mills) are among those listed in Table 8a on pp. 151–2 which includes the main working class leaders from 1795 to 1830; and the names appear again in the much longer list in Table 8b on pp. 154–9 which relates to the post-1830 years. Both Tables provide minimal biographical details. Knight was a small manufacturer who became a schoolmaster; Fitton was a weaver; Haigh a cotton spinner and later a small shopkeeper; and Swire a clogger and trade union leader. We are given a short biography of Knight (p. 139) but of the others we have nothing save the bare details in the two Tables mentioned above. Foster admits that he lacks "complete information", and therefore:

"any attempt to build up coherent groupings of working class leaders by matching particular campaigns and slogans . . . can really only be used as a rough backing for more impressionistic findings" (p. 131).

This lack of any information does not, however, prevent him from insisting in a number of places that a "Vanguard" did exist; that an intellectual commitment was "the really decisive factor"; and that while the movement's theory was "somewhat unsystematized economic analysis [and lacked] Leninist rigour about State power—the key point is that it worked" (p.148).

This really will not do. We are offered nothing which helps us define the political ideas of this working-class leadership, and the two quotations from Knight could have been spoken by any advanced radical of these years; there is no indication at all of the place and role of these working-class leaders in the radical movement of Oldham except the unsupported assertion that they dominated it; if they did form a vanguard in the usual sense of the word we can only take this on trust from the author, for no facts are provided; and the repeated insistence upon a class consciousness of a revolutionary kind remains, as noted already, wholly unproved. Indeed, from the confused history in this chapter it looks as though Alexander Taylor of the shopkeeper group was one of the outstanding personalities in Oldham during the 1830s and 1840s. He was apparently very close to John Fielden, but we have no basis of fact to judge the relationship between Taylor and the group of working-class radical leaders. Who led whom in these twenty years remains undisclosed.

That there *was* a competent and continuous leadership in Oldham seems to be established at least on *a priori* grounds. The radicals' control of the police and poor law administration, and the extensive and successful use of exclusive dealing as an extra-legal weapon of coercion, could not have come about without an organized radical commitment of a high order; but its social definition, structure, and change over time will not be discovered from this text.

*   *   *

This review has concentrated upon some parts of the Oldham story before 1850. It would be unfair to the author not to make clear that there are many aspects of this book which have not been touched upon, and which are of great interest. There is a fascinating chapter on the Oldham bourgeoisie, and the discussion in the last chapter of the fall away from the pre-1850 consciousness after the middle of the century provokes many questions for this reviewer but no fundamental disagreement. The argument of this present essay is not to deny in any way the existence of a definable class consciousness before 1850, but to dispute the hard, dogmatic categories which Foster seeks to impose upon his material. There were elements of revolutionary attitudes within the general class consciousness of working people, and some of their leaders, both before and during the Chartist period, but this has long been recognized. What there was not was a single strand which can be defined as a "revolutionary class consciousness" and applied as a blanket term upon a single movement at any one point in time. In theoretical terms Harney and Ernest Jones get nearest to it after the failure of the movement in 1848. Certainly for Oldham, for which town Foster has proved his case as an ultra-radical centre, the argument for the shift to mass revolutionary attitudes, inspired and led by a proletarian vanguard, cannot be accepted—on present evidence at least; and his insistence upon this analysis makes it all the more difficult to understand the changes of the late 1840s "when the town moved remarkably quickly towards class collaboration and a 'labour aristocracy' type of social structure" (p. 2).

Marxist historians will welcome the renewed emphasis which Foster's book will encourage on the definition of "social being" as the necessary starting point for the more complicated analysis of social consciousness. But while many of the questions he asks will at once enter the discussions of historians of this period, the immediate answers he has given will not, unfortunately, command universal agreement. His analysis of the economics of the cotton industry is no more than partial; his understanding of the dynamics of industrial capitalism in Britain during the second quarter of the century is severely limited; and the analytical jump that he makes from social being to social consciousness conceals a large gap which the evidence presented wholly fails to bridge. Foster quotes with approval the Russian scholar Porshnev who insisted that "it is language—the particular social codes which determines what information is (or is not) acceptable—which forms the keystone of any culture" (p.124); but it is precisely the failure to define and then to examine language and ideas that makes Foster's argument for a mass revolutionary consciousness in Oldham so unconvincing.

Class Struggle and the Industrial Revolution is a book that will deservedly be much debated among 19th century historians. It will stimulate a much needed shift towards local and regional studies of a new kind: far removed from chronological antiquarianism. Foster's use of quantitative techniques in the analysis, for instance, of "social closeness" or of inter-class relationships are valuable pointers to what can be done with local records. The arguments, and the tone of the arguments will be heard in all future discussions, for the emphasis upon "hard" social facts will prove a very necessary corrective to much of the writing that passes for intellectual and cultural history today. The dialectical relationships between social being and social consciousness are among the central concerns of the historian, and this present volume makes a vigorous, controversial and interesting contribution to the debate.

WORKERS' CONTROL AND REVOLUTIONARY THEORY

An Appraisal of the Publications of the Institute for Workers' Control

Richard Hyman

THE organizational existence of the Institute for Workers' Control (IWC) dates from the eventful spring of 1968, but a decade has passed since the first of the series of workers' control conferences out of which the IWC was formed. The eighty participants at the inaugural conference, convened in April 1964 by the *Voice of the Unions* newspaper, were mainly socialist journalists and academics, and the discussion concentrated largely on general issues. The two conferences held in 1965 attracted a larger attendance, with significant numbers of rank-and-file trade unionists; seminars were held on specific topics; and the work of local study groups in Sheffield and Hull led to the formulation of concrete plans for workers' control in steel and the docks. The 1966 conference was co-sponsored by *The Week* and the Centre for Socialist Education, and drew 200 participants; the following year numbers rose to 300, about a third of these trade unionists. The sixth conference in March 1968, which established the IWC, had 500 delegates and for the first time a majority of trade unionists. In 1969 and 1970—in many respects a high point of IWC activities—over a thousand attended. The next national conference was not held until March 1973, when there were some 500 participants.

The functions of the IWC, according to one of its leading spokesmen, are "to act as a research and educational body, to co-ordinate discussion and communication between workers' control groups and trade unions, to provide lists of speakers and to publish important materials on the subject of industrial democracy and workers' control".[1] Hence the publications which I have been asked to review may be regarded as a significant element in the work of the Institute. Up to the end of 1973 these consisted of a series of 38 pamphlets;[2] a bulletin, of which ten issues were published in booklet form between 1968 and 1973,[3] and which then appeared in October 1973 in the format of a monthly magazine;[4] a report on the 1968 conference;[5] and two symposia entitled *Can the Workers Run Industry?* and *The Debate on Workers' Control*.[6]

It is necessary to indicate four problems which confront the reviewer.

241

In the first place, the subject-matter of the Institute's output is extremely wide-ranging and heterogeneous, and the level of analysis and argument varies considerably—a point to which I return. It is scarcely possible to identify a common theme or approach: even workers' control, in any clearly defined sense, is far from a universally integrating theme of the pamphlet series. It follows that any survey which attempted to discuss each publication in detail would be disjointed and confusing. For the sake of thematic coherence I therefore focus on a number of general issues which emerge from a reading of the IWC output as a whole, and do not claim to do justice to each and every item.

The second problem is related to the first. Since the IWC function is defined in part as a forum for discussion, it does not claim to propagate a single and integrated body of doctrine. Thus the debates which have occurred within the Institute are reflected in the varying and even opposing viewpoints expressed in its publications. In order to sharpen the focus of my own analysis, I will be obliged at times to neglect this diversity and to write as if there were a greater uniformity of perspective within the IWC than is actually the case. In defence of this simplification it should be said that one specific group, with a relatively clearly defined common viewpoint, has in fact proved dominant in shaping the policy of the Institue. This group, with Ken Coates as its most prolific publicist, formerly produced *The Week* and now publishes *The Spokesman*; it is also closely involved with the Bertrand Russell Foundation, with which the IWC shares an office and secretary.

Most of those associated with this group were involved with the *Voice* newspapers in the period when the first workers' control conferences were convened. Subsequently a differentiation has occurred. Walter Kendall, the best known of those currently identified with *Voice of the Unions*, shares many of the perspectives of the former group but disagrees with certain of the policies of the IWC—advocating, for example, the pursuit of a wider working-class membership and more agitationally oriented publications. Other left-wing groups have participated in the workers' control conferences, but without significant influence on IWC policy. There are others—"broad Left" (i.e. Communist and left Labour) trade unionists, Tribunite MPs and "unattached" academics—who have been prominent in the councils of the IWC, but again without a determining role in policy formulation.

Insofar as there exists an "orthodoxy" of the IWC, its principal exponents are unquestionably Ken Coates, Tony Topham and Michael Barratt Brown. No other individual has figured more than twice as author of an IWC pamphlet. Moreover, these three have collaborated extensively in writing on social, economic and political issues, and may be said to have generated a comprehensive common viewpoint on questions of workers' control. There can be little serious objection to regarding them as the prime exponents of the Institute's position.

A third problem is the absence of any clear principle determining whether or not the writings of the leading members of the Institute appear under its imprint. A number of their important writings have been published elsewhere: for example Coates' *Essays on Industrial Democracy;*[7] the collection of readings compiled by Coates and Topham,[8] and more recently their *New Unionism;*[9] the three volumes of the *Trade Union Register;*[10] and various *Spokesman* pamphlets.[11] Since such publications are, so to speak, from the same stable, I will take some account of them in this review.

Finally, I am conscious that this appraisal demands to be fraternal as well as critical. The IWC, and the conferences which preceded its formation, have played an important role in the revival of theoretical debate on the issues involved in workers' control. The vital question of the relationship between workers' current struggles in capitalist industry and possible forms of self-management in a socialist economy has become a subject of discussion within the mass labour movement, even if still only at the margins. The slogan of workers' control was of course one of the demands of a variety of socialist organizations long before the contemporary movement commenced—indeed, it was from the political "fringe" that the early conferences were primarily constituted—but few of these have sought to explore systematically and in detail the meaning of this commitment. Forthright criticism of those aspects of IWC analysis which appear incomplete or inadequate can only benefit the further development of the theory and practice of the workers' control movement. This is a point which Coates and Topham have clearly asserted: "the question of reform in the power structure itself, the issue of control and of extensions of democracy in the industrial field, requires, of all subjects, the most rigorous testing in the light of the belief that most reforms are ambiguous".[12] It is an important element in my argument that in its central perspectives the IWC has failed to transcend this perilous ambiguity. Yet critics of the IWC must surely accept that theoretical defaults on this score are our common responsibility.

Current Struggles and the Problem of Totality

The heterogeneity of IWC publications has already been noted: in particular, the pamphlet series ranges from structural blueprints for individual industries, and discussions of specific and immediate problems confronting trade unionists, to a compilation of speeches at a memorial meeting for Bertrand Russell, and a reprint of some of Gramsci's *Ordine Nuovo* articles of 1919–20.[13] Within the Institute itself there has been some criticism of the character of publications. Thus Kendall has argued that "IWC pamphlets are high-priced and of limited interest to working people. Our IWC seems to lack any coherent publishing policy, pamphlets are produced in a great rush, without adequate prior consultation and are not representative of the views of the movement as a whole."[14] More charitably, it might be said that the quality of IWC publications—whether in terms of intellectual calibre or of agitational bite—is uneven. For example, the first two pamphlets—Hugh Scanlon on *The Way Forward for Workers' Control* and Tony Topham on *Productivity Bargaining*—provide careful and thoughtful analyses; while *The Dockers' Next Step* and Brian Nicholson's *UCS Open Letter* make agitational points powerfully and economically. But there are many pamphlets which are less than impressive on either score.

Despite the wide variety of subject matter, a substantial proportion of IWC publications focus on topics of immediate concern to trade unionists: proposed control structures in particular industries; such general issues as unemployment, industrial relations legislation, incomes policy and productivity bargaining; and notable ongoing struggles (the Upper Clyde work-in, in particular, was the subject of four pamphlets). Roughly two thirds of the pamphlets come within these categories; so does much of the content of the Bulletins (including the two issues on the docks and the motor industry which were reprinted as special booklets); while the bulk of the symposium *Can the Workers Run Industry?* has a similar focus. This orientation towards immediate problems, or proposals for individual industries, has characterized most of the seminars which, almost from the outset, have formed an important part of the workers' control conferences; and indeed, many of the IWC publications are reprints of seminar papers. Comments made by Coates and Topham on the work of the seminars also bear, by implication, on the orientation of IWC publications:

> "The IWC seminars are composed of dockers, miners, steelmen, grappling with the real problems which confront them. They represent a serious effort to elaborate programmatic solutions to these problems which can become the property of the whole trade union movement. Already the dockers have had a national strike about the issues spelt out by one such seminar, while the campaign for parity in the motor industry took an important step forward at the motor workers' seminars convened by Stan Newens and others for the IWC. All this is working-class democracy in action, uniting members of different political organizations and outlooks in a practical effort to find a common platform upon which to fight."[15]

This argument, which neatly encapsulates the dominant IWC perspective, has political implications which deserve close scrutiny.

No serious socialist would dispute the premise that any initiative to transform capitalist society must start from the problems experienced by workers themselves and from the struggles and strategies thrown up by the organized labour movement. The only alternative is the sterile isolation of the sect, substituting its own revolutionary imagination for the self-activity of the class. But conversely, no serious socialist imagines that the "spontaneous" action of workers engaged in their immediate struggles will lead naturally to workers' control[16] if this is conceived as the positive and comprehensive working-class direction of industry, rather than as merely defensive encroachments on capitalist domination.[17] For otherwise, the *intervention* of socialists and theorists of workers' control in the class struggle would be superfluous. The crucial question is therefore the forms that intervention should take in order to develop the current struggles of the labour movement in a direction that challenges the structure of capitalist society.

Three Strategies

Not all the IWC publications confront this issue: many remain at the level of "pure-and-simple" trade unionism, offering proposals for more vigorous union action, or providing statistical argument to support such action. But the problem of transcending orthodox trade union perspectives is faced in a number of publications, and three main strategies are suggested. The first, the demand to "open the books", has been closely associated with the IWC from the outset, having been advocated at the time of the first workers' control conferences as a suggested response to Labour's incomes policy.[18] In one of the first IWC pamphlets,[19] Michael Barratt Brown suggested areas in which company information should be pursued, and advised on its interpretation and evaluation. The rationale for this strategy was that "every governing class in history has tried to clothe the business of government in mystery. . . . [Most business secrets] have nothing to do with competition but everything to do with confusing the workers." The point is clearly important: real industrial democracy, at the level of the individual enterprise or the whole economy, presupposes extensive sources of information and a sophisticated ability on the part of workers to *use* this information; otherwise the fetishism of the "expert" holds sway. (In this context, Stephen Bodington's discussion of the potential role of computers in collective decision-making in a socialist society provides a valuable contribution to the theory of industrial democracy.)[20] One function of the critical scrutiny by workers of the information and decision processes of capitalist industry would evidently be the development of the confidence and expertise essential in any system of self-management.

Yet the great emphasis laid by the IWC on "opening the books" is normally justified in terms of its immediate relevance for the industrial struggle rather than for its long-run self-educative potential. In this respect, the slogan involves some serious dangers. Documentation of

financial, technical and related information is always helpful in adding
ideological reinforcement to a trade union demand, yet its role is
always subsidiary. Any idea that workers' organizations can win their
struggles primarily through the excellence of their statisticians—a
notion perhaps fostered in a number of recent negotiations—is a
pernicious illusion. It diverts attention from the prime importance of
building rank-and-file militancy and solidarity, and can imply the
elitist supposition that only those who understand "the books" can
properly determine union policy.[21] Moreover, the emphasis placed on
such data can unintentionally reinforce the conventional assumption
that management's own economic criteria necessarily set the limits of
bargaining over wages and employment. It is certainly true that in
some cases, the figures may demonstrate that a particular economic
demand can be easily afforded by a company, or that proposed redundancies or closures are readily avoidable; and by exposing such facts
it is possible to strengthen workers' determination and self-confidence.
But in other cases, "the books" may suggest quite otherwise: union
demands "cannot" be met given existing profit levels, redundancies are
"essential" and "inevitable". It is for this reason, of course, that
managerial sociologists have long stressed the importance of "communications", while enlightened capitalists often consider "opening the
books" in no way terrifying.[22] Their expectation is that, in the typical
situation, making such information available will demonstrate the
constraints within which the individual capitalist enterprise or industry
operates; and that this will weaken militant aspirations and even prove
demoralizing in major conflicts. So long as these constraints are themselves unquestioned, this estimate may well be correct. To combat such
a tendency, it is essential to emphasize that the economic position of
the individual company is only of secondary importance, and that the
irrational criteria of capitalist economic "rationality" represent the
key issue.

Barratt Brown is clearly conscious of this problem. In his pamphlet on
the topic he emphasizes the need to take account of those social costs
and benefits of company activities which are suppressed in market
valuations and conventional capitalist accounting:

> "It will be clear from the emphasis on the social implications of company policy that
> something wider is being proposed here than an improved bargain between workers
> and management in industry. What is being proposed is the establishment of
> Workers' Control Groups that would act as social audit groups for their particular
> factories. The reasoning behind such a proposal is that without bringing in such
> wider social questions workers' control groups attempting to extend their power will
> very soon come up against the rigid framework of existing social and economic poli-
> cies within which firms operate. The corollary of an extension of workers' control
> into social audit is that individual workers' control groups will need both a centre for
> exchanging information and a wider political arm for challenging the existing frame-

work. A chain of workers' control groups in many different firms and industries throughout the country could begin to afford to finance a Research and Information Exchange Centre. From this it would be a natural extension to set up National Social Audit Groups, consisting of engineers, scientists, accountants and workers' representatives which could bring pressure to bear on Parliament and Government."[23]

This perspective has been elaborated in subsequent IWC publications, most notably in endorsing the miners' resistance to pit closures and the struggle of the Upper Clyde workers.

Yet the greater the emphasis placed on the social costs and benefits of industrial policies which are ignored in capitalist book-keeping, the more misleading the original slogan: for the primary goal is not to open the books but to transcend them. In this context, the fundamental task of the workers' control groups proposed by Barratt Brown would appear to be one of enhancing political understanding and awareness. In the abnormal circumstances of an Upper Clyde crisis the agitational yield of the social audit is obvious; but in the more routine context of the day-to-day workplace struggle its immediate relevance is far less apparent. It is thus far from clear that the slogan "open the books" can function as an effective bridge between routine workplace trade unionism and broader and more ambitious aspirations for control.

A second strategy to provide such a bridge is centred around proposals for trade union representation in management decision-making. IWC literature has always emphasized the dangers inherent in such proposals, the typical rationale of which is "participation" rather than workers' control, the collaboration and incorporation of worker representatives within a framework of policy determined by purely capitalist priorities. The classic example is the role allotted to worker representatives in the German system of *Mitbestimmung* ("co-determination"), through the institutions of works councils and worker-directors. Coates and Topham refer to "the well-known fact that . . . workers' representatives at local level have become absorbed in the routines of management and now constitute a privileged and isolated grouping, quite alienated from their constituents. The workers' leaders are in this way incorporated into a structure which remains no less hostile than ever to the interests of the work force as a whole."[24] Yet while insisting that a clear distinction must be made between the perspectives of participation and control, they add that it is necessary to "avoid a purely negative response".[25] The argument is that "the very ambivalence that employers rejoice in, when they settle for participation schemes, leaves a whole number of questions wide open. . . . The ambiguous element in 'participation' as an employers' strategy can, perhaps, backfire, and help to arouse the very demands it was designed to forestall."[26]

The notion that "control" demands may be pressed in a form which exploits the ambiguities of "participation" would seem to underlie the specific structural proposals of the IWC for such industries as steel, the docks, and public transport; such procedures as 50% worker representation on managing boards or veto power over specific managerial decisions may differ only in degree from conventional participatory mechanisms, yet it is suggested that the implications are qualitatively radically different. More generalized blueprints for worker representation which have been warmly received by IWC spokesmen are the Belgian trade union response to the projected extension of co-determination throughout the Common Market countries,[27] and the TUC *Interim Report on Industrial Democracy* of July 1973.[28]

Endorsement of such representative machinery involves a nice balance of dangers and potentialities. It would be facile to suggest that any strategy which compromises trade union independence should be eschewed, for compromise is of the essence of trade unionism. (As I argue below, it is characteristic of trade unionism to straddle the shifting and uncertain borderline between "participation" and "control"; historically, all trade unions which have sought to preserve revolutionary integrity by spurning contracts, treaties or agreements with employers have disintegrated or else quietly abandoned their inflexibility.) Yet the pursuit of specific forms of worker representation does give rise to two distinct types of problem which demand more explicit discussion than they have received from the IWC.

The first is the need for a clear assessment of the *practical* changes in the balance of industrial power to be expected from such representative machinery. At times, Coates and Topham appear to regard their blueprints as classic "transitional demands"—targets ultimately unattainable within the framework of capitalism, but for that very reason a means of enhancing consciousness. Thus they write that "it is a pipe-dream to hope, as some industrialists and politicians appear to be hoping, that the climate in Britain is ripe for 'participatory' reform in which the workers might be coaxed to accept some of the illusions and trappings of authority as a substitute for the powers they have already determined to secure. The appetite will grow with eating, and the demands for real industrial democracy will become all the more insistent with every ruse which is applied in the intention of fending them off."[29] Previously, in responding to the Labour Party Working Party Report on *Industrial Democracy*, Coates and Topham criticized its primary concern with "how *things* should be *changed* to extend industrial democracy". "The real problem", they argued, "is that of how *people* should be *stimulated* to demand such an extension. The purpose of any proposals for reform will be overborne by the established power-structure, without any real trouble, if this lesson is not learnt."[30]

Yet simultaneously, the IWC also offers a rather different perspective, regarding far more optimistically the possibility of a stable and significant shift in the balance of power through such representational mechanisms. John Hughes, a member of the Labour Party Working Party, is an active participant in the IWC. Jack Jones, the chairman of the Working Party, is one of the most prominent union leaders associated with the IWC; his writings express the assumption that industrial democracy is attainable by institutional reforms within capitalist industry which extend collective bargaining into forms of "joint control" over traditional managerial prerogatives.[31] Coates and Topham themselves imply partial endorsement of this view, writing of the possibility of "a major structural reform which can *institutionalize* workers' rights of veto over closures, investment decisions, mergers, takeovers and the like, just as traditional collective bargaining has already institutionalized joint determination, or mutuality, in so many lesser decisions".[32]

A third perspective admits the possibility of a real shift in the balance of industrial power through such representative mechanisms, but regards such a shift as inherently unstable: for it trammels capitalist decision-making without transcending it. This is the view of Ernest Mandel, whose theories appear to have exerted a significant influence on the Belgian trade union movement. In his IWC pamphlet he points to the ambiguity inherent in the notion of "structural reforms", a notion taken over by Coates and Topham. "The formula of 'structural reforms' can be interpreted in two diametrically opposite ways: either it can mean *a reform of capitalism whose purpose is to ensure that the economy will function more satisfactorily* or it can mean 'reforms' extorted by the working class struggle, completely incompatible with the normal operation of any kind of capitalist economy. These latter inaugurate a period in which there is a duality of power, whose conclusion must either be a defeat for the working class (in which case the 'reforms' are destroyed) or a defeat for the bourgeoisie (in which case the 'reforms' are consolidated by the conquest of power by the proletariat and the socialization of the means of production, democratically managed by the workers themselves)."[33] (To this it should be added that, as the whole history of the British labour movement demonstrates, reforms achieved only through immense working-class struggle and against bitter bourgeois resistance have proved perfectly compatible with capitalist economic relationships.)

It is surely vital that the workers' control movement should approach the insidious problems of worker representation with clear perspectives: are representational blueprints primarily a means of raising consciousness, the source of a viable extension of workers' control, or the means to provoke a crisis of dual power? Each perspective demands wholly

different strategies; yet within the IWC literature the issue appears
fudged and confused. The lack of clarity on this point, it seems to me,
reflects a more general ambivalence on the issue of reform and
revolution: a topic which I discuss below.

A second, and in some ways related, problem associated with proposals for worker representation in managerial control structures is the
danger of "officialization" of the largely informal and spontaneous
controls constructed by workers' shop-floor organizations. For the
Labour Party Working Party, the principle of a "single channel of
representation" was axiomatic: control should be exercised through
the orthodox trade union machinery. John Hughes laid great stress
on this principle:

> "The basis for any extension of industrial democracy in Britain can only be that of
> the organized workers, that of representation and accountability through the Trade
> Unions. We argue, very strongly indeed, the need for a single channel of representa-
> tion, a Trade Union channel of representation, because there is no other way, not
> only of securing that particular workers are representative and are accountable, but
> there is no other way also of linking plant level problems with regional, industrial
> and national problems and the pressures that may need to be exerted to deal with
> them. So that we are saying, very firmly indeed, that we start out on the basis of the
> need to strengthen the position of organized workers and we do not want to see the
> development of forms of so-called participation and industrial democracy which try
> to by-pass or artificially separate this from the organized workers and their Trade
> Union organizations."[34]

In their discussion of the Working Party report, Coates and Topham
do indeed criticize this insistence, but their comments are mild and
marginal. "The trade unions should certainly be responsible for the
election of such councils or representatives. But there is nothing im-
practicable or unreal in the idea that workers should elect two sets of
representatives to carry out two different functions—the traditional
defensive role of the trade union bargaining machine, and the new
offensive forms of workers' control over management."[35]

Leaving aside the point that, in many unions, the full-time staff of
the union bargaining machine are *not* elected by the workers, these
brief remarks are less than adequate. The principle of the "single
channel" raises vital issues which deserve detailed discussion: for its
implication, as Coates and Topham hint, is the subordination of
potential agencies of self-management to the existing priorities of
collective bargaining. This is, in my view, a certain recipe for the
emasculation of the workers' control movement. As Gramsci insisted,
in a series of articles which are reprinted by the IWC but appear to
have exerted little influence on its thinking, workers' management
presupposes "a type of organization that is specific to the activity of
producers, not wage-earners, the slaves of capital".[36] The functions and

composition of the "Factory Councils", he argued, were quite distinct from those of the trade unions; and it would be disastrous to subordinate the former to the latter. What is remarkable in the publications of the IWC is the failure even to consider the question of the "officialization" of worker representation from this perspective. This, as I argue in a later section, appears indicative of a serious theoretical deficiency.

Closely related issues are involved in the third strategy advocated by the IWC: the "control bargain". This notion was originally elaborated by Tony Topham, in one of the first IWC pamphlets, as part of a counter-offensive to managerial "productivity bargaining".

> "A major breakthrough could be achieved if the advanced sectors of the shop stewards movement took a leaf out of the tactical book of management, and *reversed the whole process*. Instead of a productivity bargain, why not a 'control bargain'? The first stages would be conducted by the stewards and unions themselves, in a particular firm or plant or industry. Detailed discussion and careful preparations would be conducted, setting the goals and the minimum demands. What aspects of workers' control do we want to advance, what areas of managerial authority do we wish to challenge and acquire for the workers, what reductions in top executive salaries do we seek and what restrictions on information do we wish to challenge? What wage structure and overall wage increase will we settle for? What research into the firm's profits, structure, monopoly links, and alliance with the state, is needed?
>
> "After the goals are settled—a process which must involve a thoroughly democratic debate for the whole trade union membership in the firm or industry—the demands should be presented. The initiative rests now with the workers. Their demands must be explained and disseminated throughout the labour movement; they are utterly reasonable, for they begin from a premise of *equality of status* between the contending sides of industry. They aim to achieve, however, a dominance for the *majority* in industry; the workers by hand and by brain. (Attention should be given to the role of the white-collar workers, particularly the draughtsmen and technicians, not only because these are organized in militant unions, but because they normally have access to specialised knowledge of a firm's affairs.) The bargain then proceeds, until or unless the proposals are rejected by the representatives of the employers—i.e. the representatives of the small, wealthy minority in our society which 'owns' the firm or industry.
>
> "Imagine such a bargain. Imagine what happens if the workers' proposals are rejected. Assuming a real industrial democracy, with complete equality with management, what would the workers do? What do the employers' representatives do in today's circumstances? If the trade union refuses to meet them on their productivity proposals, management responds by predicting and threatening redundancies and dismissals, or reduced wages.
>
> "If the shoe was on the other foot, how many redundancies amongst directors would the workers decide upon? How, indeed, could workers continue to maintain production in the face of such stubborn refusal to co-operate on their proposals?"[37]

The notion of a "control bargain" is clearly imaginative; and it stems from a valid appreciation that management attempts to neutralize informal shop-floor restrictions on its authority—to "regain control by sharing it"[38]—cannot be overcome by a purely negative response but require a counter-offensive. In another IWC publication, Ray Collins has offered an interesting appraisal of this strategy: "there are obvious dangers in this approach but it offers the opportunity of encroachment by mutuality and veto; ultimately it requires linking with political challenges to the power structure, but without activity below there will be none higher up".[39] Yet what are these dangers, so obvious as to necessitate no explicit discussion? On the one hand, there is the risk that the more ambitious control objectives proposed by Topham may represent little more than rhetoric. Within a capitalist political economy, the employer exercises both *de facto* and *de jure* domination; the power wielded by workers' organizations is essentially reactive and defensive. Hence Topham's premise of "equality of status" is essentially unrealistic: a slogan of aspiration, not a recipe for practical action in the context of current workplace struggles.[40] Hence the specific responses offered by the IWC to one-man operation on the buses[41] or measured day work at Chrysler[42] do not involve demands for managerial redundancy but are far more modest in their control objectives. And here the second danger is, once again, the problem of "officialization": that the weight of the union's authority is attached to a compromise in a control bargain the parameters of which derive mainly from managerial initiative, and on terms far less advantageous to the workers than those imposed by their own informal shop-floor militancy. Precisely because the "counter-offensive" proposed by Topham lacks immediate relevance, it fails to provide a safeguard against the dangers inherent in productivity bargaining and may even serve to obscure the main issues.

Thus there are serious weaknesses in all three strategies proposed by the IWC to link immediate trade union struggles to the long-run objectives of industrial democracy. In consequence, it is necessary to question the emphasis placed by the IWC on specific short-run issues and the problems and perspectives of individual industries. "Socialism in one industry" is an illusion because each industry is a component of an environing *political economy*, a structure of political and economic domination. Whatever control structures are attained on a local or sectional level are subject to virtually irresistible pressures to accommodate "realistically" to the coercive demands of market forces or government requirements. Yet the perspectives of trade unionists confronting the problems of their own industry or enterprise do not lead naturally to a focus on the questions of state power or of capitalism as a total system: and a lack of attention to these questions is a characteristic of many of the IWC publications. It is true that Michael Barratt Brown has written important analyses of the structure of British industry and the control of the economy; but these analyses have not generated proposals for working-class action at the level of the whole economy.

Indeed, the space devoted to demands and blueprints for single industries contrasts notably with the dearth of attention in IWC publications to the possible structure and the major problems of a *self-managed economy*. The most explicit attention to this question by Coates and Topham arises from their examination of the Yugoslav experience, and in particular the harmful effects of the subordination of conscious control to the anarchy of the market;[43] the lesson repeatedly emphasized is the need to combine comprehensive planning with grass-roots autonomy. Yet how this vital synthesis is to be achieved—perhaps the central problem of socialist theory and practice—receives scarcely any detailed attention within IWC publications (the one significant exception is provided by Walter Kendall,[44] whose views almost certainly diverge from those of other leading IWC members, yet have failed to provoke any debate).[45] The lack of discussion of such *general* problems of workers' control—problems which so clearly transcend the perspectives of day-to-day trade union action—is a notable lacuna in the preoccupations of the IWC.

The Problem of Reformism

The failure to attend systematically to the need to transcend capitalism *as a system* is linked to a reluctance to confront explicitly the question of the limits to reformist adjustment of the industrial control structure and hence the extent to which the ultimate objectives of workers' control are revolutionary in character. The revolutionary perspective is, indeed, at times unambiguously asserted. Thus Coates has castigated the assumption "that an unbroken continuity of democratic advance stretches between the imposition of a Trade Union veto on dismissals and the ultimate overcoming of capitalist property relations. This is a naive view, because it completely ignores the deforming power of these property relations in the generation both of ideology and of social forces beyond democratic control."[46] To achieve real solutions to the problems generated by capitalism, Coates has argued, "the reforms must not be *within*, but *of* the power-structure. Its dismantling is the prior necessity, outside which lesser reforms are all too apt to come to grief, or even to aggravate the problems they were designed to solve."[47] Within this perspective, Coates and Topham have suggested that the extension of workers' control within capitalism leads ultimately to a revolutionary crisis of dual power[48]—the stark choice, in Gramsci's words, between "the conquest of political power by the revolutionary proletariat . . . or a tremendous reaction by the propertied classes and the governmental caste".[49]

Yet on closer examination, the notion of "dual power" employed within the IWC seems somewhat less cataclysmic than in its normal socialist usage. "Nobody", Coates writes, "thinks that unions can simply encroach all the power in industry until they can run the whole show. Sooner or later, and sooner rather than later, workers' control in the trade union sense comes up against the barrier of the private ownership of industry, and that barrier will only be surmounted by political action, by a change in the law, socializing industrial property."[50] Thus while the need is admitted for a political transformation of capitalism to achieve the qualitative leap from workers' control as a negative and defensive process to the positive exercise of self-management, this transformation is conceived in essentially reformist terms: as Coates has recently insisted, parliamentary action and the Labour Party should be assigned central strategic significance by the workers' control movement.[51]

The belief that revolutionary social transformation is attainable through the medium of established political institutions is not a novel doctrine: its classic name is centrism. To apply a label is not, of course, to controvert a thesis; and Coates correctly emphasizes that "it is not at all true that the socialist ideas which are appropriate to defeat late capitalism were all formulated, intact, fifty or a hundred years ago".[52] But if, as Coates implies, the arguments of Marx and Engels or Lenin and Trotsky possessed considerable validity when they were developed, it is surely necessary to analyse systematically in what ways subsequent changes have diminished their relevance. Yet—to take the most obvious example—the Leninist conception of the role of the state and the need for an organizationally distinct revolutionary party (which must not, indeed, eschew parliamentary action but should regard this as no more than a subsidiary tactic) is not merely dismissed as outdated; the analysis on which it rests is simply neglected. Similarly, Coates takes issue with Ralph Miliband's conclusion, in *Parliamentary Socialism*, that the social and institutional pressures on any primarily parliamentary party oblige it to conform to the structural constraints of capitalism; but he gives scant attention to Miliband's detailed argument in that book, and wholly ignores his *State in Capitalist Society*.

The same is not true of Michael Barratt Brown, who includes a brief section on the theory of the state in his *From Labourism to Socialism*. Miliband, he argues, "recognizes only two parts of the state system—the *repressive* and *ideological*—and ignores an increasingly important third part. This is made up of institutions which have a *conformative* role, which contain and moderate the conflicts inside capitalist society. Marx and Engels, in more places perhaps than Ralph Miliband concedes, seem clearly to recognize this role." It is possible, he continues, on the basis of the independent strength of the economic organizations of labour, to achieve a duality of power within society such that the state is obliged to detach itself partially from the interests of capital and make significant concessions to the working class.[53]

Such a perspective was, indeed, implicit in some of the writings of Marx and Engels (most notably, perhaps, the *Inaugural Address* of 1864). But any conception of "duality of power" must be employed with great caution; and in particular it is dangerous to assume that such a situation can be achieved merely on the basis of a militant and control-oriented trade union movement backed by a revitalized Labour Party. Because, as I argue below, even militant trade unionism does not put in question the fundamental principles of a capitalist political economy or the power and privileges of those who own and control industry, the latter "are rarely driven to call upon their reserves of power in any overt and public exercise. Only the margins of power are needed to cope with marginal adjustments. . . . Labour often has to marshall all its resources to fight on these marginal adjustments; capital can, as it were, fight with one hand behind its back and still achieve in most situations a verdict that it finds tolerable. Only if labour were to challenge an essential prop of the structure would capital need to bring into play anything approaching its full strength."[54] In what does this "full strength" consist? Not only the "special bodies of armed men, etc." (though in the aftermath of Chile the potential centrality of their role should surely not be ignored), but also the "sturdy structure of civil society . . ., a powerful system of fortresses and earthworks" through which the hegemony of bourgeois ideology and culture is *deliberately* inculcated. If labour develops the industrial strength and assertiveness to challenge seriously the economic dominance of capital, without the corresponding capacity to undermine the social, political and cultural dominance of the exploiting class, the appearance of dual power is an illusion.

The classic case for a revolutionary party rests on the recognition that the hegemony of the ruling class derives from a more or less integrated totality of a complex variety of social institutions and processes (among which the coercive role of the state is of considerable but not always supreme importance). To combat effectively, and ultimately to overturn this sophisticated structure of domination demands an organization of similar sophistication, with a clarity of theoretical perspectives and a dedication of membership which alone can enable a conscious, comprehensive and integrated challenge to the multifarious foundations of capitalist society. Such issues appear remote from the concerns of the IWC. The conception of the capitalist *enemy* who "sooner than lose the things he owns . . . will destroy the whole world" is proclaimed on the cover of the paperback *Workers' Control*, but rarely surfaces within the pages of the Institute's literature. Hence the question "how far can the structure meet our demands?" receives a diffuse response—as in the pamphlet with that title, a summary of one of the main discussions at the 1973 conference. The main point to emerge from the arguments of Wedgwood Benn (who takes up the bulk of the space)[55] is that Labour's parliamentarism reflects not abstract dogma but a belief in the need "to advance by persuasion".[56] What is to happen if the minority who control industry *refuse* to be persuaded to surrender their power is not discussed. Nor is the broader question whether economic domination sets stringent limits to the policy objectives which, both practically and ideologically, are "realistic" within the framework of bourgeois-democratic institutions. More generally, within the literature of the IWC the whole conception of the *transition* to a self-managed society is extremely hazy. Hugh Scanlon's pamphlet *The Way Forward for Workers' Control*[57] discusses various current industrial issues and also refers briefly to some problems of self-management, but does not examine the process leading from the former to the latter. "Towards Self-Management", the concluding chapter of the recent book by Coates and Topham,[58] is likewise misleadingly entitled: problems of transition are not discussed. This reticence, again, helps avoid an explicit choice between the perspectives of reformism and revolution.

A decade ago, Tony Topham wrote in this *Register* that incomes policy proposals drafted by John Hughes and Ken Alexander were "over-optimistic concerning the institutional prospects for their reforms".[59] Insofar as it adopts a clear position, the same is true of the IWC today. There is no serious examination of the possibility that the acts and omissions by Labour governments which are castigated as "errors" and "betrayals" are in fact a natural outcome of the logic of reformism; and that this logic is inherently antipathetic to working-class mobilization, the aggressive extension of workers' control, and the ultimate attainment of industrial democracy. The faith that it is possible "to reclaim the Labour Party for socialist policies"[60] writes off, without serious consideration, the argument that such a logic exists. Similarly, the aspiration to create under the umbrella of the Labour Party a band of "socialist activists in Parliament to work in concert with other socialist activists in factories, trade unions and neighbourhoods"[61] ignores the possibility that undemocratic practices within the Party may be structurally generated.[62] How, for example, would such parliamentary "activists" avoid subordination to the authoritarian discipline of the reformist party? (Historically, precisely this problem drove the Independent Labour Party—the last significant example in this country of a political group adopting the strategy today advocated by the leaders of the IWC—to secede from the Labour Party. The parent body will expel, isolate or absorb individual dissidents, and will not tolerate an organized party within a party.)

The main consequence of the approach current within the IWC is to encourage illusions on parliamentarism and social-democracy. The

comments of Michael Barratt Brown and Ken Coates on the relevance
of legislation to workers' control are significant in this context: "a
fully-fledged system of self-management, of truly co-operative association, cannot be legislated overnight. Indeed, it cannot be *legislated*
at all. What can be done legislatively is to open the doors, to advance
new standards and ideals, and to legitimize and encourage that truly
social initiative which is so ruthlessly suppressed in our working people
today." [63] The implication is surely that demands for legislative reforms
should be subsidiary to and derivative from rank-and-file organization
and pressure. Moreover, it could be added, it is precisely the balance of
forces *outside* Parliament which principally determines how far any
government (Labour or otherwise) accedes to demands for fundamental
structural reforms. All this is to suggest that the classic revolutionary
perspectives still possess a large measure of *prima facie* validity, which
propagandists of the IWC have barely attempted to overturn by
reasoned analysis. To argue thus, it must be added, is not to suggest
that parliamentary action is irrelevant, that socialists should ignore
the Labour Party, or that the pursuit of reforms within capitalism is
pointless or undesirable (though IWC spokesmen often imply that their
critics are victims of precisely these well-known infantile disorders).
There is an alternative to infantile sectarianism on the one hand, and
reformism on the other: the tactical use of parliamentary action, while
simultaneously seeking to reduce popular mystification by parliamentary institutions; involvement in the Labour Party because this is
the major party of the working class, while simultaneously seeking to
destroy working-class illusions in Labour; participation in the struggle
for reforms, because these dominate workers' present perspectives and
because victories help create a stronger and more confident working
class, while simultaneously seeking to expose the limits to reformism.
Such strategies derive from a revolutionary tradition which most of
those who write for the IWC do not appear to share yet do not confront
explicitly or directly. To evade the implicit theoretical debate is no
service to the workers' control movement.

The Problem of Trade Unionism

The problem of reformism impinges in different form in the context
of the attitude of the IWC towards trade unionism: the second main
gap in its theoretical foundations. This general question may usefully
be approached by pursuing in more detail a specific issue on which I
have already touched: the "officialization" of workers' control into
formal trade union channels.

The source of the problem lies in the essential ambivalence of trade
unionism: on the one hand a protest and defence against the economic
and human deprivations imposed on workers by their role in capitalist

industry; on the other a means of accommodation to the political economy of capitalist industry. This in turn reflects the contradictory pressures inherent in trade union organization and collective bargaining activity: on the one hand the expression of the basic conflict of interest between employers and employees on matters of pay, conditions and control; on the other the development of a stable and compatible bargaining relationship. Hence the curious phenomenon of "antagonistic co-operation" discerned by many students of industrial relations: the constant interpenetration of conflictual and collaborative aspects of trade unionism. [64]

This ambivalence can be highlighted by raising the question: how can trade union negotiations and agreements be categorized within the definitions of participation (a collaborative and subaltern role of worker representatives vis-à-vis management) and workers' control (an independent and oppositional role)? [65] The answer must be that neither the concept of workers' control nor that of participation can be applied without qualification. The fact that collective bargaining institutionalizes industrial conflict, generating rules, conditions and procedures which are mutually agreed, entails that the oppositional and negative quality which is intrinsic to the notion of workers' control is in large measure sublimated. But the organizational separateness of the union, and the possibility that disagreement may be articulated through overt conflict, entail that analysis in terms of participation is not wholly appropriate. It is precisely this contradictory character of trade union action which gives rise to extensive academic debate on the nature of collective bargaining and the proper categories for its theoretical analysis. [66] Some writers (especially in the United States) have laid overwhelming emphasis on the participatory aspects of industrial relations, conceiving collective bargaining as a form of joint management. [67] Such an approach involves an illegitimate generalization (embraced by many theorists of "mature" industrial relations) from the highly collaborative disposition of American trade unionism in a particular phase of post-war history. The function of management is to attempt the accommodation of a variety of conflicting interests, and the satisfaction of employee aspirations is far from its primary responsibility; hence a trade union can become a partner in "co-management" only through the abdication of its own primary function of representing its members' interests. This is of course an unstable basis for trade unionism.

By the same token, to view collective bargaining as a basis for industrial democracy—the position of the Webbs in their classic study, and more recently associated with Hugh Clegg—is to exploit to the limits the imprecision inherent in the latter concept. [68] For within a capitalist political economy, employees can at best achieve marginal adjustments to (or at worst acquiesce in) decisions which reflect a structure of power and interests hostile to their own. The currently popular concept of "joint regulation", though indicating that union-employer negotiations focus on the detailed application of rules rather than the fundamental direction of company policy, also diverts attention from the one-sided societal power structure within which the formally equal and possibly collaborative bargaining relationship takes place.

It would be absurd to dismiss the importance of trade union achievements in collective bargaining. Hence I am not attempting to suggest that "trade unions are a millstone round the neck of the working class", a view that Ernie Roberts somewhat unfairly attributes to Perry Anderson in criticizing the latter's slightly mechanical elaboration of the theories of Lenin and Gramsci. [69] It is of vital significance for the working class that unions win material improvements for their members and impose limits on the arbitrary powers of employers. Yet while ameliorating the *terms* of workers' subordination to managerial control, they do not and cannot contest the *fact* of this subordination: for to do so would be to challenge the very social order from which trade unions derive their function. And conversely, collective bargaining forms a means whereby sophisticated employers can qualify and contain workers' own *autonomous* exercise of control so as to render the problems of labour management more tractable. Wright Mills' familiar description of the trade union function as the "management of discontent" indicates this ability of collective representation to domesticate the dangerous (to employers) potential of employees to impose unilateral controls on managerial prerogative. [70]

The exercise of control *over* employees through the very process by which unions win improvements *for* them was one of the key insights of Gramsci in the articles which the IWC has reprinted. The essence of trade union achievement, Gramsci argued, is the establishment of a form of "industrial legality" which guarantees certain concessions by capitalists to employee interests. This achievement, however, though "a great victory for the working class", nevertheless represents the continuing preponderance of employer power over that of employees and their organizations. "Industrial legality has improved the working class's material living conditions, but it is no more than a compromise— a compromise which had to be made and which must be supported until the balance of forces favours the working class." [71] The development of cohesive and self-confident workplace organization, able to apply pressure directly at the point of production, is a key factor in shifting the balance of forces and permitting further inroads into the prerogatives of capital. By contrast, from the perspective of official trade unionism the established relationships and the established balance of power are a basis of order and stability; and the negotiation and re-negotiation of order and stability are central to the trade union function. Gramsci's description of the Italian scene half a century ago has a familiar ring: "the union bureaucrat conceives industrial legality as a permanent state of affairs. He too often defends it from the same viewpoint as the proprietor. . . . He does not perceive the worker's act of rebellion against capitalist discipline as a rebellion; he perceives only the physical act, which may in itself and for itself be trivial." [72] Such a disposition on the part of union officials is not to be explained primarily in terms of their corruption by soft living (though this doubtless occurs at times). Nor is the main reason the fact that on elevation out of the workplace the full-time official becomes socially and in consequence ideologically isolated from those he represents (though this is a tendency that has long been recognized). [73] By and large, the average trade union representative (lay or full-time) tends to be more progressive in his outlook than those he represents. The basic problem is one of *function*. The ordinary employee, perpetually subject to the oppressive and exploitative relations of capitalist wage-labour, is always liable to overturn some aspect of the existing "industrial legality". The union representative, however, has an additional concern: to "keep the faith" with those with whom he negotiates, to regard each conflict as a "problem" to be resolved within the framework of possibility defined by the prevailing political economy. It is precisely at the point when existing structures of capitalist domination are under pressure, when the frontier of control is being forced forward, that the potentially conservative role of official trade unionism as the defender of industrial legality is a most serious danger.

The specific implications of this argument for the debate on workers' control are threefold. In the first place, it suggests the possibility that the formalization of a "control bargain" may actually *reduce* the effectiveness of worker control over the dehumanizing consequences of capitalist production, where informal work-group controls are extensive. The oppositional exercise of control, it might be argued, is inseparable from the emergence and development of employee organization which is autonomous both of the employer and of external agencies with close commitments to the employer. To a large extent, such control is rooted in the employer's dependence—despite the imposing scope of his formal authority and prerogatives—on workers' active co-operation, ingenuity and initiative; seriously disaffected employees can effectively sabotage the objectives of organizational managers. [74] There is much evidence that the relatively informal and spontaneous forms of employee organization limit managerial autonomy most effectively. The range of employee controls documented by Goodrich in his classic study were primarily of this character. [75] More recent industrial relations analysis has of course placed special emphasis on the significance of informal shop-floor trade unionism and the influence of "custom and practice": it is the activities of the unofficial organization, rather than of official trade unionism, which because of their *de facto* erosion of managerial control have been shrilly identified as the central industrial relations "problem".[76]

The role of the official institutions of trade unionism in the application of control is often more ambivalent: for union organization tends to lose some of its autonomy, to absorb some of the dimensions of "participation", the more formalized its collective bargaining relations. The enthusiasm for productivity bargaining and the "reform" of procedures, the subject of so many industrial relations homilies and textbooks in the 1960s, reflects in part an appreciation that managements can blunt the disruptive edge of employee controls over such issues as manning, job allocation and work standards by making them the explicit subject of collective bargaining. Richard Herding's detailed study of industrial relations in the United States offers important lessons.[77] He shows how union achievements in negotiating contract clauses on "control" issues relate primarily to the "rationalization" of personnel administration or to the containment of certain forms of inter-worker competition. In both these contexts, the interests of employers and workers run, if not in parallel, then not fundamentally in opposition. But in the context of the organization of production—where the employers' interest in maximum exploitation of labour conflicts frontally with workers' interest in humane working conditions—the achievements of control bargaining have been minimal. Indeed, the formal involvement of unions in negotiations on such issues has been associated with an actual *decline* in the real ability of shop-floor trade unionism to control the dehumanizing effects of company production decisions.

The moral is that what may appear, on paper, as notable advances in workers' control may represent in fact an erosion and diminution, a reinforcement of the hand of management—"regaining control by sharing it". Coates and Topham have paid some attention to the dangers, at national level, of the "incorporation" of trade unions through their relationships with governments and employers; the same danger at the level of plant or company has been less extensively discussed.[78]

A second implication bears on the attitudes of trade union officials to workers' control. There would seem to exist a powerful tendency to favour "institutionalized" mechanisms which are consistent both with the prevailing authority structure within the unions and also with stable bargaining relationships with employers and the state. A preference for the "single channel of representation" is no accident, for this principle reinforces the status and authority of the union, whereas the elaboration of workplace-based structures not formally integrated into the official union may weaken them. Just as it is natural for Labour politicians to interpret socialization of industry in terms of state control, so it is natural for union officials to conceive industrial democracy in terms of trade union control. In both cases, such conceptions match the organizational preoccupations of their bearers; but those who believe that industrial democracy must be based on grass-roots self-activity are bound to enquire: who will control the controllers themselves? "No man is good enough to be another man's master," is a phrase of William Morris often quoted by Ken Coates. Quite apart from the objections already raised against the "single channel" of representation, it is therefore necessary to emphasize that the question of industrial democracy must extend to include that of trade union democracy. The latter is in part an issue of the formal structure of representation, election and decision-making within trade unions, and the impact of the rules on the "civil liberties" of the members; but it also involves the *de facto* distribution of influence, expertise, involvement and control over organizational resources, factors which are themselves profoundly affected by the structure and character of union-management relations. Attention to these problems within the publications of the IWC is surprisingly limited. In one pamphlet there is a useful discussion of demands which should be made in respect of formal union structures;[79] but the problems of low membership involvement, of oligarchic concentration of control, even *despite* formally democratic constitutions (problems which have exercised not only the latter-day epigones of Lenin and Trotsky, but also a weighty tradition of academic enquiry dating back to the Webbs and Michels), seem barely recognized as of relevance to the movement for workers' control.

Just as the "officialization" of control is commonly preferred by union officials because of its congruence with existing authority relations within the organization, so it is also favoured as a form of "democratization" which does not jeopardise the established external relations of the union. The problem of reform and revolution, on which the IWC appears to equivocate, is unambiguously treated in several official union formulations: "workers' control" can be established through institutional mechanisms which involve no fundamental challenge to capitalist relations of production or to those who benefit from them. On this point the Labour Party Working Party was uncompromising:

"We believe that the extension of industrial democracy is important both because of its likely beneficial effects on the well-being of individual workers and because of the contribution it can make to the overall efficiency of industry by removing many of the existing obstacles to a genuine collective effort in industry by both management and workers. Both factors urge us in the same direction, and we do not choose between them. They are of equal weight."[80]

Yet the question inevitably arises: if, as Coates and Topham at times suggest, the development of workers' control will lead eventually to a crisis of "dual power", what will be the reaction of those who conceive of "workers' control" in essentially collaborative terms? Surely it is less than certain that they will remain allies of the IWC. Ominous evidence is provided by the pamphlet *Plant Level Bargaining*, produced by the Transport and General Workers' Union in 1970 (drafted, one suspects, by some radical in the research department without close vetting by the union leadership), which was forthright in its support of workplace militancy and its condemnation of capitalist wage relationships. This pamphlet, Coates and Topham report, "produced a howl of protest from the press and employers"; and a second edition was printed with significant deletions and bowdlerizations.[81] Coates and Topham merely comment that "it seems a great pity" that these changes were made. Similarly, in their muted criticisms of Jack Jones' collaborative conception of industrial democracy they suggest that "perhaps here his tongue is in his cheek".[82] Likewise, in the general appraisals of the Labour Party and TUC statements on industrial democracy, a fundamental issue is evaded: that the structural situation of trade union officialdom leads logically to an effort to contain the movement for workers' control within channels which do not threaten the stable role of trade unionism as the permanent mediator between wage-labour and capital. The publications of the IWC devote scant attention to this possibility, let alone to proposals to overcome it.

This points to a third and more general implication: that when stable industrial relations are threatened, union officials may be expected to react in ways which *restrict* rank-and-file self-activity. The strength of such tendencies does of course vary situationally. In the post-war period, suspicion and hostility towards rank-and-file initiative and unofficial organization was a built-in reflex for many union leaders; recent years have seen the emergence of leaders who insist that the membership has a right to direct involvement in union decision-making, and who are prepared to associate themselves openly with the idea of workers' control. This is an important development with significant consequences for the internal life of trade unionism; in particular, more ambitious and militant aspirations on the part of union members receive valuable practical and moral reinforcement. Yet even in such favourable circumstances, the relationship between union leaderships and membership militancy retains elements of the older, more authoritarian pattern. Huw Beynon, in his study of the Ford plants at Halewood, documents the intervention of Jack Jones and Hugh Scanlon to settle the 1971 strike—an intervention over the heads of the shop steward organization and the representative negotiating machinery, which virtually shattered the delicately constructed basis of a sophisticated, militant and responsive system of shop-floor representation. In 1973, at Chrysler in Coventry, the sensitive relationship between militant shop stewards and their constituents was similarly devastated when the same union leaders advised their members to cross the picket lines of electricians on strike in defiance of Tory pay policy, and to work on machinery maintained by blackleg labour. In coal-mining, during the extensive unofficial strikes of 1969, Lawrence Daly, newly elected General Secretary on a left-wing platform, joined with Lord Robens in calling on the men to return to work. Jim Oldham and a group of miners responded bitterly: "if you don't support the very actions you've encouraged, then you've said it, 'we become ineffective and discredited as a union'. Over 100,000 men on unofficial strike understood what you meant. Did you?"[83] A final example: following the judgements of the Industrial Relations Court in 1972, the TGWU printed on its shop stewards' cards the warning that "shop stewards are not authorized to initiate or continue industrial action on behalf of the Union". As *Voice of the Unions* commented, "without any fanfare, the union quietly but effectively seems to have gone a long way towards meeting the requirements of the Industrial Relations Act".[84]

It is unnecessary to accumulate further instances of actions by union leaders associated with the IWC which in fact contradict the Institute's own objectives and perspectives; and not all such actions can be explained by the fact that individual leaders may be tied by executive or conference decisions of which they personally disapprove. Occasionally such actions are noted with regret in the Institute's own publications; and Coates and Topham disclaim any intention of implying that "the new leaders have been beyond criticism".[85] Yet criticism presented in any but the most muted and apologetic fashion is liable to be denounced as sectarian, as character-assassination or as an attack on the very institution of trade unionism. No doubt some critics do display these traits. Yet without impugning the sincerity or goodwill of such leaders as Jack Jones, Hugh Scanlon or Lawrence Daly—whose advocacy of workers' control can only be welcomed—it remains possible to insist that any defaults by progressive union officials on the principles of workers' control should be carefully studied, not merely dismissed as embarrassing accidents. It is essential to seek *structural* causes. As Moss Evans is reported to have said in relation to the 1971 Ford settlement, "once you've been a full-time official you realize that certain things are part of an agreement which the Executive have committed the union to and you are empowered to carry out.

You're obliged to follow it. It's out of your hands as it were. You know, it's the system I suppose. The system we work to. It's like everything else, you've got to give some order to it."[86]

"The system we work to": the words of a radical union official, sympathetic to the goal of workers' control, capture succinctly the point I have been trying to argue. The contradictions inherent in the reformist practice of trade unionism, in the commitment to "industrial legality", entail that official trade unionism is *necessarily* an ambiguous ally for the cause of workers' control. At certain points, and particularly at times of rank-and-file offensive, even the best and most honest official by his very function will typically feel constrained to *suppress* forms of self-activity which from the perspectives of workers' control are healthy and desirable, and indeed an essential part of the forward movement. Appreciation of this fact cannot but affect the relationship which the workers' control movement adopts towards official union leadership.

Implications for IWC Practice

The argument developed above is one which spokesmen of the IWC display an extreme reluctance to confront; as I have already noted, discussion of these issues is almost wholly absent from IWC literature. Nor is this altogether surprising, for from the outset a major objective of the IWC has been the cultivation of left-wing leaders as vice-presidents of the Institute, speakers at its conferences, and authors of its pamphlets. In itself this aim is perfectly reasonable: such influential leaders can powerfully aid the propagation of workers' control ideas within the labour movement, and add legitimacy to arguments which might otherwise be unthinkingly dismissed. Yet identification with specific union leaders is desirable only insofar as this does not cut across more fundamental aims of workers' control. In three distinct respects, the IWC risks subordinating its primary goals to the tactical requirements of the goodwill of influential labour leaders.

In the first place, these tactical requirements encourage the conception of the propagation of workers' control ideas as an essentially *intellectual* process. It is possible to envisage two alternative models of the development of socialist consciousness, of the transition from partial and sporadic revolts against specific aspects of capitalist domination to the articulate pursuit of self-management. The process may be conceived as one of primarily individual conversion and education through exposure to speeches, pamphlets and conferences; or as one of collective learning through self-activity and struggle. Workers' control groups may be conceived as educational circles engaged in more or less abstract and future-oriented discussion; or as centres of ongoing struggle against existing authority (including, at times, official trade union authority). These two perspectives are not, indeed, mutually exclusive: but in practice one or other must be assigned primacy. It has always been central to the Marxist epistemological tradition, as against bourgeois-rationalist theories of knowledge, that the development of consciousness is a *collective* and *active* process; and this implies that aspirations for self-management must develop through collective struggle. This has, indeed, been explicitly asserted by many of those associated with the IWC; yet in practice, the cultivation of influential leaders has tended to inhibit the encouragement of grass-roots self-activity, whenever this has risked offending these leaders. In the early days of the IWC, Michael Barratt Brown argued that "the challenge to Trade Union bureaucracy as well as to employers' authority . . . is not going to make the movement for Workers' Control a popular one in those quarters whose authority and bureaucratic ways are challenged".[87] But in fact, the IWC seems to have gone to considerable lengths to avoid the unpopularity of its eminent patrons.

The second danger follows directly from this. In their anthology of readings on workers' control, Coates and Topham quote part of the 1912 unofficial manifesto *The Miners' Next Step*. "Leadership implies power held by the leader. . . . This power of initiative, this sense of responsibility, the self respect which comes from expressed manhood, is taken from the men, and consolidated in the leader. The sum of *their* initiative, *their* responsibility, *their* self respect becomes his. The order and system he maintains, is based upon the suppression of the men. . . ."[88] The syndicalism of which this manifesto was an expression exaggerated its case: purely spontaneous collective action is an illusion, leadership of a kind is essential within the labour movement. Yet the syndicalists were correct to recognize a "bad side of leadership": the persistent tendency for the mass of members to abdicate, or the leaders to usurp, collective rank-and-file involvement which is a prerequisite of effective control from below. Loyalty to leaders, in some respects the natural concomitant of solidarity and pride in the union, can (as Michels so devastatingly demonstrated) easily degenerate into virtual hero-worship.[89] Any trace of sycophancy towards leaders must therefore be combated as a necessary part of the process of encouraging the self-confidence and self-respect of the rank and file. This is an inherent part of the objective of workers' control; and in addition, if encroachments of control are seen as leading ultimately to a crisis of dual power, it is vital to prepare the basis for the active *mobilization* of the mass of the class when the crisis arises.

Yet the attitude of the IWC itself towards some of the left-wing union leaders verges on the sycophantic. Hugh Scanlon's speech to the 1968 conference, published as the first IWC pamphlet, receives a eulogy from Ken Coates which reads like a bid for canonization.[90] Jack Jones is the subject of several pages of *The New Unionism* which are little short of obsequious.[91] The persistent name-dropping of union leaders in the pages of IWC publications is no service to a movement of industrial democrats, in which the humblest should deserve no less respect than the greatest. The words of Jack Murphy might be well recalled: "real democratic practice demands that every member of an organization shall participate actively in the conduct of the business of the society. We need, therefore, to reverse the present situation, and instead of leaders and officials being in the forefront of our thoughts the questions of the day which have to be answered should occupy that position."[92]

The third danger stems clearly from what has already been said: that in presenting prominent union officials as allies of workers' control, without any serious suggestion that their support is (or in critical situations may prove to be) ambivalent, is to underwrite illusions. The parallel is uncomfortably close with the stance of the National Minority Movement which the Communist Party launched exactly half a century ago. It is a familiar story that the Minority Movement encouraged reliance on left-wing union leaders whose revolutionary rhetoric accorded less than completely with their actual practice within their own unions; as a result, the militants were ill prepared for the collapse of the General Strike when their champions joined the rest of the General Council in abject surrender. This is not to suggest that another 1926 is round the corner in which the trade union patrons of the IWC will assume the roles of Hicks, Purcell and Swales: history does not repeat itself so neatly. But a theoretical analysis of the role of trade union officialdom, such as I have tried to develop above, implies that the endorsement of and reliance on any union leader, however progressive, should always be highly qualified. A balanced approach demands that praise or support must be coupled with a warning of the limitations inherent in the very function of union leadership, an encouragement of the development of *independent* organization and initiative on the part of the rank and file, and a readiness (should the need arise) to offer unsectarian but forthright criticism of erstwhile allies and to applaud action which bypasses or even opposes their leadership.

Those with most influence in the IWC are indeed aware that their position has been criticized along lines similar to those above; and Coates and Topham have offered a reply. In 1970, they write,

"at the Birmingham Conference, some comrades put forward the rather extra-ordinary view that 'bureaucracy begins with the shop stewards'. The implications of such a view are that trade unions themselves corrupt the workers. Few would subscribe to it in this extreme form, but there are many more whose programme and whose analysis of trade union bureaucracy make sense only as part of a separatist strategy. They are implying, whether they recognize it or not, that the shop stewards should organize outside the unions—which is of course where isolated and abstract intellectuals would like them, more easily accessible to the *a priori* reasoning of detached moralists and the freemasonry of the socialist groups. This is a path trodden by many sectarian groups in the history of the socialist movement in Britain. The most interesting and instructive parallel is with the 1910–14 period, during which two rival strategies for trade union radicalization emerged. One was led by Tom Mann, who taught consistently that the workers must operate on the institutions which were to hand, and transform them from within, and by amalgamation. His efforts and inspiration were directly or indirectly responsible for the creation of the NUR, the T & GWU and the AEU, which between them led the battles of the twenties, and which took the TUC to a position of militant socialism. There were defections, there was Jimmy Thomas, there was the heavy hand of Bevin's authoritarianism—there was indeed a period during which Mann himself was General Secretary of the Engineers, and so presumably in sectarian terms rendered himself indistinguishable from any other bureaucrat. That is, to put the matter in more rational terms, there was *contradiction*. Strength, unity, and the authority to weld masses of workers into a fighting force, require large organizations, and that carries with it the danger of bureaucratization. But any sane comparison between the achievements of Tom Mann, and the arid and ineffectual products of the school of the Socialist Labour Party—insofar as the latter influenced trade union structure at all—must recognize the futility of a policy which asks the stewards and militants to break away and start all over again. Of course the industrial unionist movement and the SLP produced some fine and influential individual militants, just as the groups do today. But it produced no structures in which those militants could operate effectively—in order to make their full contribution, they had to break with the 'pure', that is the abstract, half true, doctrine in which they were trained.[93]

In this passage (as elsewhere in their writings) Coates and Topham stack the cards by presenting a false dichotomy. The choice is not *either* to work within the official trade union machine *or* to work outside it (any more than that the same stark alternatives apply to parliamentary action or working within the Labour Party). It is possible *both* to work within the sphere of official trade unionism, *and* to seek to construct independent rank-and-file organization.

In this respect, their historical example is singularly ill-chosen. Tom Mann was a remarkable revolutionary trade unionist, perhaps the greatest militant the British labour movement has ever produced, and any criticism must be made with humility.[94] But if one considers the whole decade 1910–20 it is far from obvious that Mann was of more importance than the "sectarians" of the SLP. His main involvement in the pre-war years, the industrial syndicalist movement, struck terror into the breasts of the bourgeoisie and established labour statesmen alike, but collapsed as suddenly as it had arisen; syndicalism lacked any coherent theoretical foundation and represented a fleeting mood as much as any solid organizational basis. During the wartime industrial crisis, Mann's role was strangely obscure; he spent most of the period as a full-time union official, for some of the time assisting the arch-patriot Havelock Wilson. There is little evidence of his active involvement in the key wartime struggles against militarism, against conscription, against the Munitions Act, against deteriorating working-class living standards. Tom Mann was indeed more prominent in the Amalgamation Committee movement, which deserves much of the credit for the formation of the AEU in 1920.[95] But the new amalgamated union, like the old Amalgamated Society of Engineers, was dominated by the orthodox and "responsible" J. T. Brownlie; Mann's brief interlude as General Secretary left no lasting consequence of any significance, perhaps because his election was unrelated to any basis in independent workshop *organization*. In his last years as an active trade unionist, Mann did indeed work closely within the official structures of trade unionism; so closely that he was effectively absorbed.

By contrast, it is grotesque to write off the significance of the SLP. In the pre-war period it was indeed, because of the sectarian inflexibility of its theoretical purism, an ineffectual and self-isolated grouplet. But its critique of union bureaucracy, absurdly one-sided in its immature formulation, was to play a vital role when the Clydeside SLPers found themselves at the head of a spontaneously generated wartime shop stewards' movement. When trade union officialdom abdicated the defence of their members' living standards and established working conditions, the analysis of the SLP was applied to make the crisis comprehensible and to provide guidelines for action: and the central lesson was the need to work within the official union structures, but to do so from a base of independent rank-and-file organization. Those who, like Mann, worked merely for amalgamation of the official union structures found themselves on the sidelines of the main wartime struggles of the class; and Murphy's comment was telling. Such schemes, he wrote, "sought for a fusion of officialdom as a means to the fusion of the rank and file. We propose to reverse this procedure."[96] The *primacy* of the rank-and-file organization, as the only basis for working within the official institutions without being absorbed or suppressed, was the keynote of the inaugural manifesto of the Clyde Workers' Committee:

> "We will support the officials just so long as they rightly represent the workers, but we will act independently immediately they misrepresent them. Being composed of Delegates from every shop and untrammelled by obsolete rule or law, we claim to represent the true feeling of the workers. We can act immediately according to the merits of the case and the desire of the rank and file."

This principle—a critical and independent, but not abstentionist, attitude towards the official institutions of trade unionism—was the vital contribution of the SLP to the theory of revolutionary activity in industry, and to the practice of the highest point (to date) of socialist militancy in Britain.[97] It is a lesson which, it is clear, must be learned anew.

Forward

My final task is not to draw conclusions so much as to consider the way forward. Stephen Bodington has summarized his own conception of the role of the IWC in setting out a plea for

"more people to give a higher priority to developing the movement for workers' control, to giving it a more tangible organized existence. This means making a clear political commitment to it. It does not mean seeing it as an alternative to other organizations such as Trades Councils, political parties, Women's Lib. Workshops, Trade Unions, Community Action groups of various kinds and so forth. On the contrary, what is needed is an organization that links people in different jobs, engaged in different activities, involved in different socialist organizations and so forth. It is an attempt to reduce dependence on centralized organization through charismatic leaders and to substitute a multiplicity of brains and a multiplicity of experiences discovering alternatives close to the feelings of the people and developing co-ordination that turns a multiplicity of socialist actions into a political force."[98]

This is an appeal which demands a positive response from all socialists; it is impossible to contest Bodington's emphasis on "the importance of clearing ideas and developing consciousness". Similarly, Coates and Topham's notion of "mental policemen" captures succinctly the profoundly debilitating influence on the labour movement of the hegemony of bourgeois conceptions of industrial normality. Yet when the Shrewsbury pickets languish in gaol it is difficult to accept without qualification the argument that "it is a mental police force, first and foremost, which holds the trade unions in a subject role".[99] From such a proposition stems an unwarrantably *voluntaristic* conception of the labour movement which pervades the publications of the IWC. Thus Mandel asserts that "it is above all the subjective factor which plays the key role in deciding whether or not the workers' movement makes use of the opportunity which neo-capitalism provides for an anti-capitalist strategic offensive".[100]

The familiar "problem of consciousness" cannot be properly discussed in the space available. Suffice it to say that in reacting against the mechanical determinism of some of the crasser distortions of Marxism, such voluntarism commits the error of the opposite extreme. It is not necessary, for example, to accept Kautsky's argument that socialist theory must be brought to the workers by the bourgeois intelligentsia in order to question the following assertion of Ernie Roberts:

"it is primarily through *their own practical everyday experiences* that the workers will learn about the nature of the capitalist state, and how to consolidate and extend their control over various aspects of their working lives. As a result of their experiences, they will evolve a theory and practice which will lead to the complete overthrow of the existing order and its substitution by a worker-controlled state."[101]

It is interesting that, as if to underwrite such a faith in the spontaneous development of revolutionary consciousness, the one section of the Gramsci pamphlet reprinted in another IWC publication is the passage in which he writes that "the actual unfolding of the revolutionary process takes place subterraneously, in the darkness of the factory and in the obscurity of the consciousness of the countless multitudes that capitalism subjects to its laws".[102] But the Gramsci of 1919–20 clearly exaggerated the potential of spontaneity; and one consequence was the defeat of the Italian revolution and Gramsci's own years in Mussolini's dungeons, spelling out the key importance of state power and of the very tangible institutions and processes which sustain bourgeois hegemony. Moreover, even in his *Ordine Nuovo* period he insisted that developing working-class consciousness must be given coherence and direction by independent workplace-based organization—"proletarian institutions of a new type: representative in basis and industrial in arena";[103] and he also stressed the vital role of the revolutionary party, "in a position to give real leadership to the movement as a whole and impress on the masses the conviction that there is order immanent in the present disorder, an order that will systematically regenerate human society".[104]

Why this emphasis on independent organization and the revolutionary party? Because the forces which lead to an accommodation between the labour movement and capitalist forms of industrial organization are material as well as ideological. Because, in other words, "consciousness-raising" must go hand-in-hand with the organization and articulation of a *physical* challenge to capitalist domination: neither can succeed in establishing socialism without the other. The argument that I have developed is that trade unionism as such, because of its very function of negotiation and accommodation within industry *as it exists*, cannot be revolutionary. Hence trade unionism itself—necessary as it indeed is to the working class—is in practice (whatever the rhetoric of the conference platform) one of the agencies which help maintain a belief in the normality of capitalist industry. Hence independent industrial organization and a revolutionary party both have an essential role in the development of the conscious aspiration for self-management: the one in co-ordinating militancy against the often constraining intervention of the official union hierarchy; the other in maintaining permanently a perspective which transcends what is immediately possible within capitalism, and in consciously organizing for working-class self-emancipation.

On the eve of the formation of the IWC, Tony Topham warned that attempts would be made "to institutionalize workers' representation in both private and public industry, in ways which may confuse, mystify and head-off the drive for independent workers' control".[105] Contemporary socialists operate, as Edward Thompson has so eloquently argued, in an "infinitely assimilative culture"; in consequence, he insists, "one must make one's sensibility all knobbly—all knees and elbows of susceptibility and refusal—if one is not to be pressed through the grid into the universal mish-mash of the received assumptions of the intellectual culture".[106] The IWC is clearly right to refuse to pose as a revolutionary party; but in apparently denying the *need* for revolution-ary organization, it facilitates the incorporating embrace at which Topham hinted. By confronting explicitly and in detail the classic arguments of the need for a revolutionary party, by asserting un-ambiguously the revolutionary character of the goal of industrial democracy, and by cultivating scepticism of *all* existing authority—in these ways the IWC could develop its "knees and elbows", and ensure the vigorous independence essential for the movement's success.

NOTES

1. Ken Coates, Pamphlet 14. See also Constitution of the IWC, Bulletin 1, pp. 104–105.
2. The pamphlet series comprises the following:
   1. Hugh Scanlon, *The Way Forward for Workers' Control*, 1968
   2. Tony Topham, *Productivity Bargaining and Workers' Control*, 1968
   3. Michael Barratt Brown, *Labour and Sterling*, 1968
   4. Michael Barratt Brown, *Opening the Books*, 1968
   5. Ken Coates and Tony Topham, *The Labour Party's Plans for Industrial Demo-cracy*, 1968
   6. Bob Harrison and Walter Kendall, *Workers' Control and the Motor Industry*, 1968
   7. Sheffield Steel Workers' Group, *The Steel Workers' Next Step*, 1968
   8. *Industrial Democracy and the National Fuel Policy*, 1968
   9. Tom Fawthrop, *Student Power*, 1968
   10. Ernest Mandel, *A Socialist Strategy for Western Europe*, 1969
   11. Antonio Gramsci, *Soviets in Italy*, 1969
   12. Hull and London Port Workers' Control Groups, *The Dockers' Next Step*, 1969
   13. Jack Ashwell, *Four Steps for Progress (Workers' Control and the Buses)* 1969
   14. Michael Barratt Brown and Ken Coates, *The "Big Flame" and What is the IWC?*, 1969
   15. Ken Coates and Tony Topham, *The Law versus the Unions*, 1969
   16. Ray Collins, *Job Evaluation and Workers' Control*, 1969
   17. *GEC-EE Workers' Takeover*, 1969
   18. John Hughes, *A Hope for the Miners?*, 1969
   19. Ken Coates, Lawrence Daly, Bill Jones, Bob Smillie, *Bertrand Russell and Industrial Democracy*, 1970
   20. Nick Hillier, *Farmworkers' Control*, 1970
   21. Richard Fletcher, *Problems of Trade Union Democracy*, 1970
   22. Hugh Scanlon, *Workers' Control and the Transnational Company*, 1970
   23. Scunthorpe Group, *The Threat to Steel Workers*, 1971
   24. *Trade Unions and Rising Prices*, 1971
   25. John Eaton, John Hughes, Ken Coates, *UCS—Workers' Control: the Real Defence against Unemployment is Attack*, 1971

26 *UCS: the Social Audit*, 1971
27 Brian Nicholson, *UCS: an Open Letter*, 1971
28 Ken Fleet, *Whatever Happened at UCS?*, 1971
29 Michael Barratt Brown, *Public Enterprise Defended*, 1971
30 Ernie Roberts, *The Fight against Unemployment*, 1972
31 Michael Barratt Brown, *What Really Happened to the Coal Industry?*, 1972
32 Brian Nicholson and Walt Greendale, *Docks III: a National Strategy*, 1972
33 John Eaton, *The New Society: Planning and Workers' Control*, 1972
34 Paul Derrick, *The Incomes Problem*, 1972
35 Walter Kendall, *State Ownership, Workers' Control and Socialism*, 1973
36 Tony Benn, Walt Greendale and others, *Workers' Control: How Far Can the Structure Meet Our Demands?*, 1973
37 Ken Coates and Tony Topham, *Catching Up with the Times: How Far the TUC Got the Message about Workers' Control*, 1973
38 Michael Barratt Brown and Stuart Holland, *Public Ownership and Democracy*, 1973.

3. The original Bulletin was nominally a quarterly, though it appeared somewhat less frequently. Two issues were republished as special booklets: *Democracy in the Docks* and *Democracy in the Motor Industry*.

4. At the time of writing (early 1974) it is unclear whether this monthly basis is to continue.

5. Ken Coates and Wyn Williams (eds.), *How and Why Industry Must Be Democratised*, 1969.

6. Ken Coates (ed.), *Can the Workers Run Industry?*, Sphere, 1968; Bert Ramelson, Ken Coates, Tony Topham, Charlie Swain and Bill Jones, *The Debate on Workers' Control*, 1970 (reprinted from *Marxism Today*).

7. Ken Coates, *Essays on Industrial Democracy*, Spokesman Books, 1971 (essays previously published in 1965 and 1967).

8. Ken Coates and Tony Topham (eds.), *Workers' Control*, Panther, 1970 (previously published as *Industrial Democracy in Great Britain*, MacGibbon and Kee, 1968).

9. Ken Coates and Tony Topham, *The New Unionism*, Peter Owen, 1972.

10. Ken Coates, Tony Topham and Michael Barratt Brown (eds.), *Trade Union Register*, Merlin Press, 1969 and 1970; Michael Barratt Brown and Ken Coates (eds.), *Trade Union Register 3*, Spokesman Books, 1973.

11. For example, Michael Barratt Brown and Ken Coates, *Workers' Control in the Nationalised Industries*, Pamphlet 26, 1972; Ken Coates, *The Quality of Life and Workers' Control*, Pamphlet 27, 1972. Other relevant Spokesman publications include Ken Coates, *The Crisis of British Socialism*, 1971 and Michael Barratt Brown, *From Labourism to Socialism*, 1972.

12. ''Participation or Control?'' in *Can the Workers' Run Industry?*, p. 227.

13. The latter had previously appeared in *New Left Review* in 1968.

14. Walter Kendall, *Voice of the Unions*, April 1973. For a rejoinder see Bill Jones and Ken Fleet, May 1973.

15. "A Reply to Some Critics", Bulletin 8, p. 32.

16. Faith in the spontaneously revolutionary character of working-class struggle is confined to such anarcho-syndicalist groups as *Solidarity*—though elements of such an assumption appear in the writings of some of those associated with the IWC.

17. It is true that Coates and Topham have often insisted, following continental usage, that the concept "workers' control" should be applied solely to negative restraints on capitalist power, whereas working-class decision-making within socialized industry should be termed "workers' (self-) management". While this distinction is of vital importance, the use of "workers' control" as a label for *both*

processes is embedded in the traditional terminology of the British labour movement; and the title of the IWC itself, as well as the usage in many of its publications, indicates this duality.

18. See for example Ken Coates, "Incomes Policy: a Strategy for the Unions", *Socialist Register*, 1965.

19. No. 4.

20. E.g. "Socialism, Democracy and the Computer" in *Can the Workers Run Industry?*

21. On these grounds an orthodox American academic long ago insisted that "trade union wage policy is inevitably a leadership function. The reason is not that the leadership has wrested dictatorial power from the rank and file, but that it alone is in possession of the necessary knowledge, experience and skill to perform the function adequately" (Arthur M. Ross, *Trade Union Wage Policy*, California University Press, 1948, p. 39). While the IWC aim may indeed be the development of a *mass* capacity to handle what are currently specialist tasks, in the short run it is only a small minority who are likely to attempt to master the tasks of information gathering and interpretation listed by Barratt Brown in his pamphlet.

22. Hence, for example, the proposal in Labour's notorious White Paper *In Place of Strife* for the "disclosure of management information to trade union representatives"; and also the legislation on this question in the Common Market.

23. Pamphlet 4.

24. "Participation or Control?" in *Can the Workers Run Industry?*, p. 232.

25. P. 235.

26. *The New Unionism*, pp. 208–9.

27. See Ken Coates (ed.), *A Trade Union Strategy in the Common Market*, Spokesman Books, 1971; and *The New Unionism*, pp. 209–13.

28. Pamphlet 37.

29. Ibid., p. 13.

30. Pamphlet 5. Unless otherwise specified, all emphasis in quotations is in the original.

31. See for example *The Right to Participate: Key to Industrial Progress*, TGWU, 1970, gently criticized in *The New Unionism*; and "No Top Hats for Shop Stewards", published without critical comment in IWC Bulletin, October 1973.

32. Pamphlet 37, p. 10.

33. Pamphlet 10, p. 8.

34. 1967 Conference Report, p. 28.

35. Pamphlet 5.

36. Panphlet 11, p. 11.

37. Pamphlet 2.

38. Allan Flanders, *Collective Bargaining: Prescription for Change*, Faber, 1967, p. 32. Flanders' much-quoted phrase has obvious implications for my arguments on the "officialization" of workers' control: in the context of formalized agreements, those with whom managements share control are not the same, and do not have the same interests and perspectives, as those from whom they regain control.

39. Ray Collins, "Productivity Bargaining after Aubrey Jones", Bulletin 8, p. 49.

40. Moreover—as is perhaps hinted in Collins' remarks—Topham's prescription appears to echo some of the illusions of "encroaching control" propagated by the Guild Socialists over half a century ago. The whole question of state power is ignored in Pamphlet 2: remarkably in view of the impetus which the productivity bargaining offensive received from government policy during the 1960s.

41. Pamphlet 13.

42. *Democracy in the Motor Industry* (Bulletin 3).

43. See in particular *The New Unionism*, pp. 224–30.

44. In particular "Workers' Control and the Theory of Socialism", 1968 Con-

ference Report, and Pamphlet 35. The title of Pamphlet 33, which implies a focus on problems of this order, is misleading; the pamphlet is almost exclusively concerned with current struggles.

45. Kendall, whose analysis would seem to derive from Schachtman's theory of "bureaucratic collectivism", reacts particularly negatively not only to current East European structures of industrial control but also to the whole Soviet and Communist tradition. This leads him to assert that a "socialist market" should be the centrepiece of a self-managed economy, that the anarchy associated with capitalist commodity production is separable from market institutions. This issue deserves detailed critical attention, which I intend to put forward in a forthcoming publication; but precisely because Kendall's analysis on this score appears unrepresentative of most IWC writers, I do not pursue this here.

46. *Essays on Industrial Democracy*, p. 9.

47. "Introduction", *Can the Workers Run Industry?*, p. 14.

48. *The Debate on Workers' Control*, pp. 34–5; *The New Unionism*, p. 56. See also Ernest Mandel, Pamphlet 10, cited above.

49. Pamphlet 11, p. 31.

50. "Introductory Review", *Trade Union Register 3*, p. 27.

51. Ibid. and "Socialists and the Labour Party", *Socialist Register*, 1973.

52. *Socialist Register*, 1973, p. 160.

53. *From Labourism to Socialism*, pp. 67–71. There is also a brief discussion of the question of the state in Ernie Roberts, *Workers' Control*, George Allen and Unwin, 1973; Roberts' involvement with the IWC is probably the most intimate of any full-time union official.

54. Alan Fox, "Industrial Relations: a Social Critique of Pluralist Ideology" in John Child (ed.), *Man and Organization*, George Allen and Unwin, 1973, p. 211.

55. Indeed the pamphlet reads rather like a public relations exercise for Benn, whose enthusiasm for workers' control formed part of the cultivation of a left-wing image from 1971. The stalwart of the workers fighting redundancy at Upper Clyde Shipbuilders and Rolls Royce was the same Wedgwood Benn who as minister in the 1964–70 government pursued policies of capitalist "rationalization" which helped contribute to the subsequent crises in those firms. See Ernie Roberts, *The Solution is Workers' Control*, Spokesman Pamphlet 19, 1971, and *Workers' Control*; Roberts also points out that Benn's subsequent conversion to workers' control has been less than unqualified.

56. Pamphlet 36, p. 15.

57. Pamphlet 1.

58. *The New Unionism*, Ch. 15.

59. "Incomes Policy: Background to the Argument", *Socialist Register*, 1965, p. 168.

60. Ken Coates, *Trade Union Register 3*, p. 42.

61. *The New Unionism*, p. 185.

62. For details of such practices see, for example, Ernie Roberts, *Workers' Control*, Ch. 11.

63. *Workers' Control in the Nationalized Industries*, p. 3. See also Ian Mikardo, "The Scope and Limits of Legislation" in *Can the Workers Run Industry?*

64. I have developed these points at length in *Marxism and Sociology of Trade Unionism*, Pluto Press, 1971.

65. For these definitions see Coates and Topham, "Workers' Control as a Strategy of Socialist Advance" in *The Debate on Workers' Control*.

66. For a sophisticated example of this genre see Allan Flanders, "Collective Bargaining: a Theoretical Analysis", *British Journal of Industrial Relations*, 1968.

67. See for example Neil W. Chamberlain, *Collective Bargaining*, McGraw-Hill, 1951.

68. Sidney and Beatrice Webb, *Industrial Democracy*, Longmans, 1897; Hugh A. Clegg, *Industrial Democracy and Nationalization*, Blackwell, 1951 and *A New*

Approach to Industrial Democracy, Blackwell, 1963. For a critique of the latter see Paul Blumberg, *Industrial Democracy: the Sociology of Participation*, Constable, 1968.

69. *Workers' Control*, p. 214. Roberts is criticizing Anderson's article "The Limits and Possibilities of Trade Union Action" in Robin Blackburn and Perry Anderson (eds.), *The Incompatibles: Trade Union Militancy and the Consensus*, Penguin, 1967.

70. C. Wright Mills, *The New Men of Power*, Harcourt Brace, 1948.

71. Pamphlet 11, p. 15.

72. P. 17.

73. Even in the last century the Webbs noted (*The History of Trade Unionism*, Longmans, 1920 edn, p. 469) that once an official left the shop floor "the former vivid sense of the privations and subjection of the artisan's life gradually fades from his mind; and he begins more and more to regard all complaints as perverse and unreasonable". In *The Workers' Committee* (1917; reprinted Pluto Press, 1972, pp. 13–14), J. T. Murphy pointed out that "a man in the workshop . . . feels every change; the workshop atmosphere is his atmosphere; the conditions under which he labours are primary; his trade union constitution is secondary, and sometimes even more remote. But let the same man get into office. Those things which were once primary are now secondary. He becomes buried in the constitution, and of necessity looks from a new point of view on those things which he has ceased to feel acutely."

74. Many recent sociologists have stressed that those in charge of a wide variety of hierarchical institutions are in practice dependent on some degree of voluntary co-operation from subordinates or inmates, even though the latter may be in theory absolutely powerless. The functioning of any complex organization requires some measure of co-operation and initiative from even the most menial participants. Nowhere is this more true than in industry. Thus Reinhard Bendix (*Work and Authority in Industry*, Harper and Row, 1963, p. 204) cites a study of inmates in Nazi concentration camps, forced to perform wartime factory work, who "sabotaged the production effort by consistently asking for detailed instructions on what to do next". In more typical industrial situations, of course, the scope for sabotage by employees is immensely greater.

75. Carter L. Goodrich, *The Frontier of Control*, Bell, 1920.

76. See for example the Report of the Royal Commission on Trade Unions and Employers' Associations (the *Donovan Report*), HMSO, 1968, with its notion of the "two systems" of British industrial relations.

77. Richard Herding, *Job Control and Union Structure*, Rotterdam University Press, 1972.

78. The dangers of incorporation at national level are discussed, for example, in "Participation or Control?" in *Can the Workers' Run Industry?* Not all leading members of the IWC share this caution; in the same volume, John Hughes ("Democracy and Planning: Britain, 1968") advocates a system of "tripartite bargaining" the collaborative implications of which have been all too clearly revealed in the Heath-TUC-CBI talks of 1972 and the "social contract" of 1974. Probably the most detailed discussion of the problem of incorporation at workplace level is provided by Tony Topham in "New Types of Bargaining" in *The Incompatibles*: he warns (p. 137) that at this level the working class is "at a point where the levels of class and political consciousness of its different sections and tiers are so unevenly developed, and so often in conflict with each other, that the outcome could still be a new accommodation between capital and organized labour". Yet his discussion of the aftermath of the 1960 Esso productivity agreement (he writes that "the role of the stewards at Fawley has been enhanced, and in a most interesting way") fails to confront adequately the danger that the formal involvement of shop stewards in negotiations over conditions and control

may in some circumstances intensify the contradictions experienced by stewards as "honest brokers" between shop-floor and management, and may serve to contain the autonomous forms of workers' control at the point of production. Similarly Topham seems over-optimistic in writing (p. 152) that "the intensification of work—speed-up—cannot but lead to an intensification of class struggle— even in the relative backwater of Fawley". As Huw Beynon has sensitively demonstrated (*Working for Ford*, Penguin, 1973), the struggle against intensification of work—even when led by a militant shop steward organization, responsive to the experiences of the rank and file—generates *in itself* no more than a "factory consciousness", not class consciousness and class struggle. "Tied up in the perpetual negotiations with the superintendents of capital on the factory floor", compromise and accommodation over control issues is inevitable.

79. Richard Fletcher, Pamphlet 21; see also his article "Trade Union Democracy: the Case of the AUEW Rulebook", *Trade Union Register 3*. Ernie Roberts discusses similar questions in *Workers' Control*, Ch. 10. By contrast, the most prolific writers of the IWC (Coates, Topham and Barratt Brown) almost wholly ignore problems of union democracy.

80. P. 17. A similar collaborative perspective pervades a recent Fabian discussion: "managers in many enterprises who recognize the value of good union organization should be able to work more constructively with the unions over a wider range of issues under the TUC proposals" (Jeremy Bray and Nicholas Falk, *Towards a Worker Managed Economy*, Fabian Society, 1974, p. 5). This comment in turn indicates the ambivalence of the TUC proposals themselves.

81. *The New Unionism*, pp. 79–80. One example is the comment in the original pamphlet on the slogan "a fair day's pay for a fair day's work": "this paternalistic concept is the very opposite of all the union's objectives. There can never be anything fair about a master and servant relationship. All that any agreement ever achieves is a 'temporarily acceptable day's pay for a temporarily acceptable day's work'. Both are always re-negotiable". The revised version reads: "this generalized slogan can confuse the practical situation at work".

82. P. 202.

83. "The Miners' Strike", Bulletin 4 and *Trade Union Register*, 1970.

84. "TGWU—Troubled Giant", *Voice of the Unions*, June 1973.

85. *The New Unionism*, p. 178.

86. *Working for Ford*, p. 300.

87. Pamphlet 14.

88. Unofficial Reform Committee, *The Miners' Next Step* (1912), Pluto Press, 1973, p. 19.

89. See Robert Michels, *Political Parties*, Hearsts, 1915.

90. 1968 Conference Report. Coates devotes three pages of his brief introduction to praising Scanlon, while in winding up the conference he declares that Scanlon's speech "was one of the most revealing, one of the most far-sighted statements to come from any trade union leader for 50 years; for 50 years!" (p. 218). Despite the merits of the speech, such language is surely extravagant.

91. Pp. 177, 198–202.

92. *The Workers' Committee*, p. 14.

93. "A Reply to Some Critics", Bulletin 8, p. 30.

94. I have attempted a brief assessment of Mann's career in an introduction to his pamphlet *What a Compulsory 8 Hour Working Day Means to the Workers* (1886), Pluto Press, 1972.

95. Though Coates and Topham exaggerate in suggesting that the formation of the NUR and TGWU are in any significant respect attributable to Mann's efforts; in both cases, pressure for amalgamation of the competing sectional unions dated back to the period when Mann was still in Australia, and was approved by many

who were in no way syndicalists (including, of course, the leaders of the new amalgamated unions). Moreover, even the creation of the AEU perhaps involved a less momentous transformation than Coates and Topham imply: it took its basic structure, and over two-thirds of its membership, directly from the old Amalgamated Society of Engineers.

96.   *The Workers' Committee*, p. 18.
97.   For this interpretation of the significance of the SLP I am wholly indebted to James Hinton; for a detailed analysis see his *The First Shop Stewards' Movement*, George Allen and Unwin, 1973.
98.   "Workers' Control as a Movement", Bulletin 10, p. 66.
99.   *The New Unionism*, p. 217.
100. Pamphlet 10, p. 11.
101. *Workers' Control*, p. 59.
102. Pamphlet 11, p. 6; Bulletin 1, p. 81.
103. P. 7.
104. P. 31.
105. Introduction to 1967 Conference Report, p. 9.
106. E. P. Thompson, "An Open Letter to Leszek Kolakowski", *Socialist Register*, 1973, p. 91.

THE MULTI-NATIONAL CORPORATION:
A CHALLENGE TO CONTEMPORARY SOCIALISM

Walter Goldstein

THE emergence of the multi-national corporation (MNC) has fundamentally changed the pattern of trade flows and international finance
in the last twenty years. Worldwide enterprises such as General Motors,
Imperial Chemical Industries, Royal Dutch Shell, the Bank of America,
Nestlé, Siemens, Hitachi and Fiat have grown rapidly in number and
power. They now account for one-eighth of all international trade flows;
but in 1980 they will control one-quarter. Mobile and powerful, they
can threaten, if they so choose, the sovereignty and the viability of the
nation state. The régime of Allende in Chile commanded less economic
power or disposable cash flow than ITT. The nine nations of the
European Common Market (EEC) found in last winter's petroleum
crisis that they could neither expose nor control the cross-national
transfers effected by the eight largest of the MNC oil "majors". It now
appears that the MNC will serve as the agent necessary to develop
contemporary capitalism to the "next stage" in the concentration of
international wealth and political authority. It yet remains to be
determined how socialist theory and socialist movements will adjust to
this fundamental development.

In the space of one generation the MNC has carved out for itself a
novel role in international affairs. Financed and controlled by parent
company HQs in North America, Europe, or Japan, the MNCs have
ranged across the world's markets as if national frontiers, currency
differentials and tariff barriers were of little consequence. Six hundred
of the largest MNCs have established manufacturing affiliates or
subsidiary plants in dozens of countries simultaneously. Combining
total asset values worth almost one trillion dollars, these global enterprises have overcome the economic defence works of the nation state
and revolutionized the dynamics of international capitalism.

Previously it had been assumed by liberals that the national economy
would be fully controlled by the sovereign state. Theorists on the left
shared this assumption when they committed themselves to the formula
of "socialism in one country at a time." Both liberals and socialists
failed to recognize the extent to which the leading export and technology
industries of the advanced economy were so intricately tied to the

international trading system that it was no longer feasible to think in terms of statist autonomy. Following upon the tumultuous expansion of the MNC it is not realistic for the left to plan the collectivization of any nation's economy *in toto*. Too much of it today is in the ownership or control of foreign based MNCs.*

The global communications and management networks of the MNC are directed more often than not from parent HQs in the skyscrapers of New York, London, Rotterdam or Tokyo. The leading MNCs have utilized their global scanning capabilities to transfer enormous values investment capital, production components and Research and Development (R and D) between the home and the host countries in which their affiliates operate. Decisions have been made by the Ford Motor Company (in Detroit) to build auto assembly plants in Belgium and France; or by the British Petroleum company (in London) or General Electric (in New York) to close down major facilities in Italy; while new production capacity has been deployed by Olivetti or by Fiat in the United States and in the Soviet Union. These deployment decisions have allowed MNCs to capture major markets, to optimize the profitability of investments, to achieve sizeable economies of scale and timing in manufacturing, and to consolidate their oligopoly grip over critical world prices.

The employment and the welfare of millions of people have been forcibly changed by the MNC's creation and transfer of wealth. Between 1971 and 1973 the leading MNCs secured windfall profits by converting billions of dollars in company reserves into German marks, Japanese yen or Swiss francs. But their action also precipitated a sequence of crises in national money markets. Their momentous transfers of short-term liquidity helped force the devaluation of the dollar (in some cases by nearly forty percent) and to erode the Bretton Woods pattern of world monetary stability. Treasurers of the MNCs anticipated sudden exchange fluctuations by selling short against the dollar in Frankfurt or borrowing heavily in francs in Zurich, thus sparing their share-holders from appreciable exchange losses. As a consequence of their respectable business of monetary speculation they undermined several governments and several national currencies. They also taught the Chancellor of the Exchequer and the oil-rich sheikhs of OPEC that monetary speculation was ethically acceptable so long as it was justified as a fiscal "sub-optimization" strategy.

Suspicion and fear of the multiple product-division and production transfers of the MNCs have become so intense that the United Nations has been asked to prepare a detailed appraisal of their growth and

---

* For the sake of clarity this analysis will focus only upon the role of the MNC in the developed or advanced capitalist economy. The role played in the socialist, developing or retarded economies is so different that a wholly separate enquiry is required.

strength. The first report in 1973, *MNCs in World Development* (ST/ECA/ 190, henceforth cited as the *UN Report*), noted that 650 of the largest MNCs record a combined turnover worth 773 billion dollars a year. 213 of these firms do more than $1 billion business outside the banking or financial sectors (i.e., mainly in manufacturing and extractive industries) of the capitalist economy. Their aggregate worth exceeds the value of any nation's GNP in the world except the USA and the USSR. Of the 213, 127 are American in origin and legal domicile. Of the total of 650 MNCs surveyed in the *UN Report*, 358 are American 74 are Japanese, 61 are British, 45 are German and 32 French. It is worth noting that many of the largest MNCs do more than 50% of their production in other nations' economic structures. This allows them to operate freely outside their home environment and to push for growth wherever opportunities appear most promising.

Economists on the left and on the right have been slow in adjusting to the new phenomena of multi-national corporate activity. Conservative politicians have welcomed the inflow of productive wealth, technology and sophisticated management that the MNC has brought to host countries. But they have also been disturbed by the threat that the MNC can pose to the administrative and regulatory capabilities of the nation state. The automobile and the computer industry in Britain, for example, is now dominated by the affiliates of giant American MNCs. Germany, Italy, and France experienced a comparable invasion, especially in the computer, aerospace and telecommunication industries. Across the Atlantic, Canada saw nearly 63% of its industrial and mineral assets pass into foreign control and Australia has now reached a figure of 35%.

Though the MNCs have helped boost the export and industrial performance of host economies, even the advocates of *laissez-faire* capitalism have grown uneasy about their free-ranging power. In all of the 23 wealthy nations that belong to OECD, conservative econo- mists and Ministers have expressed their misgivings over the influence wielded by firms of foreign parentage. So, too, have Labour or Social Democrat critics in Canada, Britain, India, Australia or Scandinavia. Harold Wilson warned ten years ago that Britain must not become a "helot to the sophisticated apparatus of American business". Though he did little to arrest the growth of MNC influence, his counterparts in Ottawa, Paris or Tokyo attempted to introduce a few pieces of regulatory legislation. They sought to force the publication of sub- sidiaries' account books, to manipulate the tax liability or to restrain the labour practices of the incoming MNC. But it cannot be said that these regulatory tactics have deterred or deflected the expansionist drive of the MNC.[1]

There has been a rather striking failure among parties on the left to understand the extent to which the MNC has invalidated the limits of economic nationalism. Perhaps because their expectations of the collapse of capitalism were geared to the dialectic of class strife, the Communist parties of France and Italy virtually ignored—until recent years—the threats posed by the MNC. Armed with surplus value formulae derived from Lenin's theories of monopoly capitalism and imperialist struggle, they failed to comprehend the strategic expansion of the MNC. They saw its attempt to dominate local industries but not its need to internationalize their production processes. Indeed, one Communist official, from Austria, worried by the loss of local capitalist control, warned that the

> "interlocking of capital and the establishment of co-operation with foreign organizations [i.e., MNCs] must not be tied to conditions which endanger either the property or the independence of Austrian factories."[2]

The dilemmas placed by the MNC before the socialist movement can no longer be ignored. Parties on the left in the OECD countries have narrowly planned upon capturing the "commanding heights" or the territorially based structures of the national economy. This might now prove to be a costly mistake. Unless the socialist parties can synchronize their take-over of all MNCs that specialize in cross-national production they might wreck the international sector of their own economy. Were the left to take office in one country at a time they would surely smash their own productive and out-going affiliates (like ICI or Rhone-Poulenc) or in-coming subsidiaries managed from Tokyo or New York. It is not so much the legal issues or the capital-ownership difficulties that need deter left parties from grappling with the MNCs that so largely determine economic growth patterns and the nation's export earnings. It is the potential mobility of the MNC that must worry the left. American affiliates in the UK account for nearly one-quarter of Britain's balance of payments. Were they to be expropriated, nationalized or simply scared away, the freedom of manoeuvre remaining to a socialist government in London would be drastically curtailed.

It will later be noted that MNCs have concentrated their deployment *only* in those strategic sectors of the host economy that are programmed to the iron-clad laws of comparative advantage in international trade. None are to be found in the profitless, in the ageing or in the labour-intensive industries that are nationalized—usually without protest—by conservative or liberal régimes. By contrast, Olivetti in Scotland, Ford in Cologne, Matsushita in Ireland and the Banque de Paris in Rome could not easily be held hostage by a determined socialist government once it came to power. These major affiliates could either relocate their capital assets and their firm-specific technology to a more "favourable investment climate" (in Spain, or Greece or Belgium). Or they could utilize the subtle procedures of transfer pricing to undermine *dirigiste* controls. In doing so they would negate any socialist designs to re-schedule production planning, capital outflows or full employment.

A fundamental paradox will have to be resolved by left movements as the capitalist system moves further toward a pattern of international inter-dependence. The desired or the "acceptable" limits of socialism in any country will no longer be determined by trade union militancy or by electoral mobilization. Nationalist planning and one-country socialism will become increasingly untenable. Unless the total system of international trade is changed outright, no single régime can dare seize the MNC organs that figure so largely in its ability to compete in world trade.

The logic of the situation can be simply stated. Automobile, petro-chemical, electronics and computer industries cannot survive by simply servicing the domestic market. Nor, were they to be nationalized, could they compete with MNC subsidiaries in financing expensive R & D, or in tapping Euro-dollar resources or in deploying production overseas. Each of these vital activities depends upon a global management in order to realize economies of scale and a full mobility of capital resources. Were they ever to be deprived of their foreign plant as a result of the nationalization of the parent company, Volkswagen, Rio Tinto Zinc or Unilever would be worthless and shrunken entities. They would be forced to rely upon exporting home-finished products—unlike their multi-divisional MNC competitors—in a world disfigured by tariff barriers, import surcharges and aggressive trade wars. Their residual worth to a socialist régime would be short-lived and of paro-chial value.

The gravity of this argument can be measured by evaluating the export trade of the advanced economies of Europe. British, Dutch and Swiss MNCs earn four or five times more through manufacturing overseas than can be gained by marketing home-based exports. Uni-national firms like the British Aircraft Corporation, British Leyland Motors and International Computers Ltd. are puny competitors to their MNC rivals. They are inadequately capitalized, they have penetrated too few foreign markets and they have had to pay high licencing fees to tap into the MNCs' worldwide technology base.

At first sight, therefore, it appears that any left party can acquire industrial power or implement collectivist planning only up to the point that the MNCs have chosen to leave the means of production and distribution under local control. Any encroachment beyond that point will drive a socialist régime into forcible confrontations with either the out-going or the in-coming affiliates of the MNC. Judging from the recent failure of the Italian Government to arrest the investment withdrawals of General Electric or British Petroleum, there is little reason to believe that a socialist government could prevail in such a confrontation of bargaining power. In the less developed countries (the LDCs) it is still feasible to nationalize the mining and drilling facilities of the MNCs in extractive or raw materials industries. In the OECD world, to which this analysis must limit itself, the options for socialist action are considerably reduced. For IBM, ITT or Bayer to relocate its physical and financial assets is so painless that host governments have cause to tremble.

Conventional wisdom holds today that the "acceptable" limits of socialism must be determined by the MNCs' requirements to manoeuvre across the fast-changing conditions of international competition. Nationalist sentiment and pride of ownership are no longer viable constraints. No wonder then that the managers of British Petroleum (49% of which is owned by the UK government) have argued that the extraction of oil and gas from the North Sea must be preserved from national controls. Were the Labour government to nationalize North Sea fields, they have claimed, BP's rigs on the North Slope of Alaska and its extensive retail outlets in the American midwest might be put in jeopardy. Worse, its multi-national ability to "swap" crude shipments with Mobil in Japan, to enter refinery joint ventures with Gulf in Kuwait, or to observe oligopoly pricing rules would be impaired worldwide. Instead of earning billions of dollars (on *Britain's* behalf) nationalization would reduce BP to the minor league status of such non-MNC oil companies as ENI in Italy or Gelsenberg in West Germany.

Strikingly, not a single socialist party in the OECD countries has determined what should best be done with the MNC. In some countries (e.g. Germany or Holland), the trade unions have demanded that MNCs must concede the right to collective bargaining or to co-determination councils. In others (e.g., France and Japan), the left has called for the control of *some* in-coming MNC affiliates but not necessarily of the out-going units implanted overseas. Given the expansion of MNC activities in the Soviet Union (by Fiat, Mercedes-Benz or Renault), or their "turnkey contracts" in East Europe (i.e. contracts to build manufacturing facilities that are then turned over to the host country intact), it may be that the European left can conceive of no viable formula. Before so cynical a conclusion is reached, however, it might be wise to take a closer look at the MNC and at the novel form of free trade imperialism that it has promoted.

I. The MNC and Contemporary Imperialism

The motives that drive various types of MNCs into foreign economies have been investigated by Marxist scholars (such as Ernest Mandel and André Gorz), by economic nationalists looking to Europe as an industrial "third force" (such as Servan-Schreiber and Christopher Layton), and by innumerable professors of business or economics (Raymond Vernon, Jack Behrman and Charles Kindleberger, to name only three).[3] The conventional conclusions of the MNC literature have been summarized by a notable creator of liberal mythology, Arthur Schlesinger. In his foreword to the best seller of M. Servan-Schreiber, *Le Défi Américain*, he explained the triumph of the American MNC in Europe:

"The secret does not lie, as de Gaulle (and Lenin) would insist, in the pressure of surplus American capital for investment outlets abroad; M. Servan-Schreiber argues that nine-tenths of American investment in Europe is financed out of European resources. Nor does it lie in American plans for political dominion; M. Servan-Schreiber rejects conspiratorial explanations. Nor does it lie in American scientific and technological superiority. . . . The disparity lies rather, M. Servan-Schreiber contends, in the 'art of organization'—in the mobilization of intelligence and talent to conquer not only invention but development, production and marketing. . . . American industry spills out across the world primarily because of the energy released by the American system . . ." (p. ix).

The sentiments aroused in 1967 by *Le Défi Amércain* have quietened down in the wake of devaluation alarms and the energy crisis. MNCs of European origin have successfully emulated and competed with the expansion strategies of their American rivals. After the dollar weakened on the world's money markets in 1971, the American practice of cheaply taking over European companies or of implanting local subsidiaries appreciably slowed down. No longer can it be said, as M. Servan-Schreiber had prophesied in 1967, that:

"Fifteen years from now it is quite possible that the world's third greatest industrial power, just after the United States and Russia, will not be Europe, but *American industry in Europe*. Already, in the ninth year [1967] of the Common Market, this European market is basically American in organization."[4]

Powerful forces drive the giant MNCs to build a major position for themselves in the affluent and technologically advanced economies of the world. If they are to maintain a dynamic growth they must straddle more and more frontiers. In their relentless pursuit to improve their multi-product marketing, their economies of technology and scale, and their profitable specialization in component manufacture, they must enter *all* advanced economies simultaneously.[5] It is through such strategic scanning and manoeuvring that they can administer world prices, promote their product differentiation and reinforce their oligopolistic control over the export sectors of the penetrated economy. Conservative economists notwithstanding, it is difficult to believe that their "wealth input" (as the MNC managers put it) and the pursuit of corporate profit is co-incident with or co-equal to the host country's best interests. Though business elites may welcome the enrichment that the MNC can bring them, they also regret to some extent the ensuing loss of political sovereignty. Like socialism in one country advocates, though for different reasons, they believe that control over the leading or export sectors will still remain in the host economy.

The resentment generated by alien MNCs is occasionally of grave concern to government officials and small business interests. Political criticism has been levelled in most capitalist countries against the dominant position taken by MNC affiliates of American, European or Japanese parentage. The subversive behaviour of ITT, in offering the US Government $1 million to assist in the early overthrow of the Allende régime in Chile, revived widespread fears of the MNC and its wealth-generating activities. Radical and nationalist critics argued that only a chance exposure in the Washington press had uncovered the ITT subversion proposal; but that many other conspiracies involving MNC banks, defence firms or insurance syndicates would surface one day in Rome, Paris or Moscow. Naturally, the MNC managers claim to be bound by a "code of good citizenship" in their overseas business roles but critics on the left insist that they can only serve imperialist or colonizing interests. With good reasons the left believes that the massive entry of MNCs into the capital-intensive or science-based sectors of a host economy will generate both political conflict and a sharper inequality in wealth distribution. The market domination secured by RCA, Royal Dutch Shell, SKF or Mitsubishi may thrill business journalists and evangelical industrialists but they acutely disturb liberal politicians, bourgeois nationalists, trade union bureaucrats and the small business men who resent the sympathetic treatment that their own government often extends to the powerful MNC. That the MNC will enlarge corporate profits for the parent company rather than for the welfare of the host economy is believed alike by left critics and right-wing patriots.

Three distinctive arguments have been advanced by the MNCs most determined critics. First, it has been alleged that the gigantic scale of the MNCs' operations, especially in the oil, chemicals and automobile industries, is acutely menacing. The power of GM, Ford, Exxon, GE and Dupont in Britain or West Germany affects millions of jobs and their export capabilities. The deflection of investment capital or production runs from either country on the part of any six towering MNCs could imperil that nation's trade balances or inflation policy overnight. The factor of size is especially vital to the MNC. It allows the firm to bargain on a basis of equality with other giant oligopolists and to match their market innovation and expansion cycles at their own convenient pace. It is not surprising that the average turnover of the larger MNCs should exceed $1 billion a year; or that their intra-affiliate transfers can account for 25 or 30% of the export trade of either a home or a host government. Small firms (like Plessy or Elliot Automation) or uninational firms (such as Machines Bull or Montedison) cannot afford the product differentiation or the capital deployment practices of the MNC. They are caught in the technology bind of contemporary capitalism: without worldwide economies of scale they cannot finance vast R&D and investment programmes; but without such programmes they will never become large enough to operate multi-nationally. [6]

Second, it is argued that the MNCs tend to concentrate their holdings in those few industries where high-technology or extensive sums of capital are of critical importance (such as micro-circuitry, nuclear engineering, aerospace, insurance, banking and computer leasing). Though they employ relatively few people these sectors determine the growth curves, the profitability rates, the technological accomplishments and the labour productivity of a "post industrial" society. Whether they choose consumer products, nuclear reactors or syndicate banking, the MNCs' concentration upon the "commanding heights" of the capitalist economy allows a small number of firms to wield a disproportionate influence over its international trade. [7]

The third accusation of the critics of the MNC is of the closest concern to this analysis. It has been claimed that the power amassed by the MNC depletes the economic authority and the political sovereignty of the nation state. For example, the movement of $6 billion in MNC funds from New York to Frankfurt or Zurich early in 1973 helped spread inflation across the Atlantic, thus forcing Europe to pay for the last remaining costs of the war against Vietnam. As a result, unemployment began to increase, welfare and public sector expenditures were cut, and tariff protections were raised to shelter prized national industries. Only the MNC treasurers controlled the massive blocs of capital that could suddenly be moved from one currency to another. Only the MNCs knew how to convert their tax liabilities into a devalued currency while converting forward reserves and accounts receivable into harder denominations. MNC managers, who customarily advertise their virtue as "good citizens" of the world business community, realized windfall gains from these speculative exercises. As in a zero-sum game, however, whatever they gained the nation state had to lose in investment and employment opportunities.

Capitalist governments can rarely triumph in a confrontation with the mobility and oligopoly capacities of the MNC. [8] As the interdependence and competitiveness of national economies grows apace, however, the collisions will become more frequent and intense. In that case the discretionary power of the MNC can only expand. But as the opportunity to exploit oligopoly and mobility advantages in world trade become more highly prized, the MNC will insist that it should be released from all national or collectivist controls. When it is finally shorn of its power to regulate the profitable, the science-based and the export sectors of its economy, the state will be left with few functions to perform other than to service the infra-structure requirements of the MNC. It will be charged with pacifying the work force, maintaining an orderly market mechanism and a reliable subsidy for the hopeless industries (such as coal, railways and docks) that the MNC prefers to leave under statist control.

II. Public Versus Private Power

The principal constraints faced by the MNC stem from the consequences of its own success. Had it not succeeded so well in revolutionizing the thrust of international trade, and had it not acquired such an unprecedented mobility of resources, it would have generated less criticism and abuse. The enviable profits and the ubiquitous influence of the MNC are too visible to be ignored. Even the bureaucrats and bankers who determine EEC policy in Brussels have come to recognize that *laissez passer* will no longer do. The Gaullist vision of a *Europe des patries* has been replaced by the vertical integration and the frontier-crossings of the MNC. The realities of the new Europe are to be found not in agricultural price supports and tariff waivers but in the network of petroleum and chemical pipe lines across the continent that are owned by a handful of monolithic MNCs.

Today the MNC is viewed with either suspicion or envy by the managers of power in both the public and the private sectors of the capitalist state. As local nationals, the managers cannot relocate their public revenues or their venture capital to a nearby economy. No matter how faltering may be their return on investments or their productivity ratings, they are locked in by the frontiers of the national economy. If they resent the incoming MNC they have no choice but to combat its bargaining manoeuvres. Even if they need to repair a short-term imbalance of payments they must accede to the MNC's transfer of funds, licence fees and dividend payments. It is not often that they dare summon the formal authority of the state to shut out, or close down, or curb the transfer arrangements of powerful affiliates. Were the state managers ever to do so firmly the MNCs would merely announce that a favourable climate for investment could better be found elsewhere. [9]

The economic logic of the MNC is impressive in concept, in its profitability and in its mode of operation. By contrast, the political logic of the nation state is static and parochial. Bourgeois nationalism has been so obsessed in the era of Cold War with military budgets and the salving of political pride, it seems, that little attention has been given to the fading sovereignty or to the permeable autonomy of the "free market" nation state.[10]

The most dramatic consequence stemming from the spread of MNCs is the increasing division of labour between national economies—rather than between firms. The MNCs' global transfers have helped destroy both the mechanism and the justification for economic nationalism. They have overpowered the defence works of the industrial state by seizing control over its finance and technology capital. This has left the European states dependent upon the MNCs' promotion of their most cherished export firms in order to finance their costly fuel imports and to stem the crush of two-digit inflation. The effects produced by the MNCs' implanting of wholly-owned affiliates in the export and growth sectors have been remarkable. In Belgium, for example, the MNCs provide 30% of the nation's exports (as against 24% in the UK), 18% of its industrial employment and 70% of the new jobs created between 1964–8. It is thus of little concern whether Belgians elect a left or a right-leaning coalition government.

Protectionist responses to this new pattern are pointlessly deplored. There is little hope that a world trade revolution or that a united socialist Europe will emerge in the near future. In his provocative work, *The Left against Europe?* (New Left Review, 1972), Tom Nairn provides a timely and apposite quotation from Isaac Deutscher:

> "The nation-state decays and disintegrates whether people are aware of it or not. . . . Like any organism that has outlived its day, the nation-state can prolong its existence only by intensifying all the processes of its own degeneration."

There are only two important choices that can still be made by national political elites. Should they encourage deflation and the threat of unemployment; or should they relax exchange and investment controls and welcome the inflationary pressures generated by the MNC and the international economy? Since both choices are unpalatable, governments have come to regard the MNC as a disruptive—if not a politically irresponsible—agent of change. Large firms have been reluctantly bought out by MNC conglomerates (such as ITT or British-American Tobacco); or their local affiliates have suddenly been closed down on orders from overseas HQ (as happened to Remington Rand in France or Raytheon in Sicily) before the host government could even be warned. In a competitive world market, ripe with inflation, few governments can pretend to control the actions of the MNC. They therefore enjoy no option but to live with its imperious mobility.[11]

In coping with the MNC it is obvious that home and host governments must move with caution. In some countries, including the USA, the value of the MNCs' turnover exceeds by 400% the total value of the nation's export trade. In others, the capital or the technology supplied by the MNC are well-nigh irreplaceable. No uni-national enterprise could hope to duplicate the research patents or the vertically-integrated assemblies of Siemens, Ciba-Geigy, or Texas Instruments. Thus host governments cannot lightly resort to nationalization or to legislative controls to regulate the actions of the MNC. At all costs the MNC needs to preserve its freedom of action, to relocate component or assembly schedules from one country to another, to reassign its management cadres or to redeploy its cash reserves. ICI achieved a phenomenal growth by doubling its turnover and its new plant outside the UK; Volvo and Volkswagen, appalled by the inflation of wage levels at home, put their capital into new installations in the Western hemisphere; Matsushita and Bayer are desperately following suit to prepare against the day when their exports to the USA are saddled with high tariff and import surcharges. In the face of such pressures what can governments do but collaborate with the MNC entrepreneurs?[12]

At this stage it might be useful to consider the two arguments that are customarily cited to justify the claims of entrepreneurial capital in general and of the MNC in particular. Both arguments are based upon conservative interpretations of economic theory.

The first posits that an optimum efficiency in world trade will only be attained after a full-scale equalization of factor costs has been implemented on a global basis. In other words, countries that are fitted to specialize in one industry (such as aerospace or computers) must concentrate their energies where best they can and stay away—as must their neighbours and rivals—from what they cannot do cheaply or well. A "natural" division of labour must distribute work between free market economies. Its outcomes will be freely determined by the laws of comparative advantage. The belief in the equalization of factor costs, as a transnational imperative, assumes that all (or most) nations will follow the dictates of global market forces. Following this thought, the UK would abandon its tariff-protected and government-subsidized computer industry. It should concede that a leading MNC, like IBM or Honeywell, will always deploy a superior technology or sell better and cheaper machines. In fact, as globally integrated firms, both Honeywell and IBM have built huge plants in Scotland to revive respect for economic doctrine—and also to drive British and European competition out of the UK market.[13]

The second argument closely resembles the first. This posits that consumers must be free to follow their own purchasing preferences regardless of the consequences to the national economy. If consumer sovereignty is to prevail, it is argued, consumers must be allowed to buy cheap German cars, Japanese television sets or British turbogenerators. They must not be forced to buy a domestic product that is cheaper simply because discrimination against foreign goods has overladen them with heavy import taxes. In catering to mass tastes the MNC claims that it knows better than government authorities what customers really want. Moreover, the MNC takes great start-up risks when it establishes new plant or expensive new product lines. It cannot afford to be penalized by host governments or protectionist trade groups, such as EEC. Even if protection is invoked for the laudable cause of boosting local employment or balancing an excessive payments outflow, this will eventually impede the equalization of factor costs (by protecting domestic industry) and cheat consumers of the satisfaction of buying yet another saturation-advertised detergent product.[14]

The thrust of these two arguments can quickly be grasped. Both presume that the free play of market forces will promote a cross-national division of labour, an optimum utilization of resources and the fullest regard for consumer preferences. Conservative economists and corporate executives have urged that the MNC will provide the best vehicle to implement these axioms of international trade. Unfortunately, they tend to overlook critical imperfections in the working of the capitalist economic order:

1. Even if governments withheld all subsidies, tariff charges and regulatory controls the oligopoly structure prevailing among MNC-intense industries will thwart market competition. Barclays Bank, Philips, Union Carbide or Petrofina can exploit their oligopoly position in several host economies simultaneously. If they wish, they can often ignore or bend the requirements of a local market in order to delay the introduction of new technologies or to manipulate oligopoly price competition. The imperfect competition in which MNCs thrive thus invalidates the "laws" of comparative advantage and of factor equalization that pietists perceive in the international market place.

2. The welfare needs of a host economy cannot always be subordinated to the dictates of conservative economic doctrine. Even if it is strongly inadvisable for the UK to subsidize its computer firms or for the Japanese to protect their aerospace industry, infra-structure requirements frequently oblige political elites to modify the MNCs' most lucrative deals. Moreover, there are grave risks in relying on the vertical integration or the imported technology of a foreign oligopoly. Many nations are not ready to sacrifice their pride and future growth prospects so that MNCs can freely move in (or out of) their economy in pursuit of further corporate profit. That an MNC, such as Nestlé or Chrysler, will implement the best division of labour or allocation of resources is doubted even by Ministers of trade or of finance with corporate careers of their own on the side.

3. The myth of consumer sovereignty is hard to dispel. Radical

critics or liberal economists have assaulted the myth either from the perspective of controlled supply or of manipulated demand. Their findings appeared to be over-stated until this year, when the MNC oil "majors" revealed the killings to be made in the exploitation of tied-up franchises, refinery processes and administered prices. As in other oligopoly industries, the producers (other than the OPEC sheikhs) determined where they wanted to locate and price their goods; but it was the managers of public power who had to protect consumer interests against the MNC.[15]

4. The welfare utilities of capitalist society cannot be left to the tender mercies of market forces, no matter how competitive or oligopolist they might be. In all industrial economies consumer-electors look to the state managers to curb inflation, to guarantee full employment, to protect new industries or to balance the nation's payments. In most countries centrist governments have foresworn the dogmas of private enterprise to police business activities and to protect the economic infrastructure from outright piracy or fraud. However, the opening of national frontiers to any MNC, indiscriminately, threatens to waste scarce resources, to squander hard currency, to impair employment opportunities and to stifle home-based R & D. Not one instance can be cited of an advanced capitalist state that has yet dared to deal with the threats posed by the MNC in an aggressive or resolute manner.[16]

5. The managers of public power are held accountable, at least in theory, to representative government and political processes. The managers of the private powers incorporated in the MNC are not. There are many occasions on which the retention of national economic controls will be preferable to the free floating benefits that *might* be imported by the MNC. But by surrendering its regulatory authority to control the MNCs' behaviour the capitalist state can only increase its dependence upon their resource and marketing decisions. Neither the economic wealth nor the political stability of the EEC will be secure if the MNCs continue to expand at the rate of nearly 20% a year—as the EEC now estimates—and if the Japanese should increase their $250 million holdings to $8 billion within ten years.[17]

III. The MNC and the Nation State

The phenomenal expansion of the MNC has aggravated the political anxieties of the advanced industrial economies which it has penetrated. In an era of runaway inflation and towering payments deficits the MNCs' lack of political accountability has begun to appear highly menacing. So far no major attempt has been made to cope with this problem; or to reconcile the divergent interests of uni-national states and multi-national enterprises. Nor have convincing solutions been proposed to repair the breach.[18] That the breach is widening and will widen further is accepted by all parties. The cause is obvious. The MNC has become a powerful actor in international affairs. As the MNC banking consortia in the City of London discovered, the logic of inflation and credit manoeuvre is especially distasteful to those political elites that fail to share in the expansion of monetary benefits or commercial paper.

The ability of any economy to seal itself off from foreign competition and penetration has greatly decreased in recent years. National governments have tried valiantly—but ineffectually—to insist that they and not the MNCs should serve as the arbiters of interdependence.[19] The MNC is accountable to its parent shareholders and directors, most of whom reside in a foreign environment and all of whom are anxious about minimizing tax liabilities, repatriating dividends and increasing patent royalties. On the other hand, the nation state is supposed to be attuned to local needs and to the popular determination of policy priorities. Its claim to pre-eminence is difficult to contest—and even more difficult to implement.

Parliamentary régimes, apolitical trade unions and social democrats are extremely apprehensive about applying sanctions against the MNC distributors of industrial wealth. First of all, their sanctions might be counter-productive. If popular protest should ever intensify and if restrictive legislation should be called for, the MNCs could either relocate their component production and R & D to another country; or they could deflect their new investments and short-term funds to a more hospitable business climate. This could be done in a rapid and covert manner. By borrowing short and lending long, or by utilizing "leads and lags" in intra-affiliate payments, the MNC can evade capital export controls and import restrictions. By channelling cash reserves through tax havens and the $100 billion Euro-market the MNC can utilize transfer pricing strategies that could knock any uni-national or nationalized competitor out of its key international markets.[20]

Second, were parliamentary régimes to abuse the MNC as poor corporate citizens, sharper criticism might be directed against *all* corporations, indigenous or foreign. Were this to occur, a collectivist drive to regulate oligopoly activity might gain popularity and the resentment generated by the MNC might be turned against other forms of corporate capitalism. At this point the MNCs would be tempted to cast the economy out of the pale of the free market world, as they did to the Allende régime, or they might engineer a counter-revolutionary change in order to protect their affiliates' local investments.

These conflict potentials are not marginal to or easily removed by the capitalist state. Nor are they likely to disappear with the passage of time. The political imperative to defend its economic autonomy and legal sovereignty is vital to any state, no matter how left or right-leaning its government might be. On the other hand, the huge investment power, the technology imports and the employment opportunities brought by the MNC cannot be under-estimated or ignored. As the asymmetry increases between the power of the MNC and the state, the latter will perceive that it can no longer compete in specialized and demanding markets without the assistance and the willing compliance of the MNC.

At the present time there is a vague supposition among conservative politicians and the liberal mass media that no nation should intervene against another's MNCs lest a full-scale retaliatory war should be triggered. Moreover, it is widely believed that:

> "The instrumentality of multinational business is man's best hope for achieving political unity on this shrinking planet."[21]

This reflects the elitist and managerial views that prevail among parliamentary régimes. It is basically believed that giant corporations are politically neutral in their quest for profit; and that their cadres of trained managers are wiser than national electorates or elected governments in harnessing national resources to the engine of world trade. It is assumed, too, that free competition will equalize factor costs, that oligopoly equilibrium will provide a reliable mode of market planning (as in the oil industry), and that mass societies will gear their living standards to the productivity ratings that they can attain in the international market place.

The first glimpses of scepticism have begun to emerge in the wake of the ITT scandal and of the hostility generated by the MNC oil companies. For example, Professor Raymond Vernon of the Harvard Business School has suggested that if the MNCs were to flourish unchecked by state power, governments would "be obliged to convert issues they had once thought domestic into issues of international concern." He added that:

> "the basic asymmetry between multinational enterprises and national governments may be tolerable up to a point, but beyond that point there is need to re-establish balance. . . . [There must be MNC] accountability to some body, charged with weighing the activities of the multinational enterprise against a set of social yardsticks that are multinational in scope. . . . If this does not happen some of the apocalyptic projections of the future of the multinational enterprise will grow more plausible."[22]

At this time no state or grouping of states has yet learned to cope with the challenge offered by the MNC. There is no sign that EEC will ever correct the asymmetry that Professor Vernon fears. Nor is it likely that international capitalism possesses the self-righting mechanism needed to avoid domestic strife and trade warfare. Thomas Jefferson noted of the business leaders of 1800 that:

> "Merchants have no country. The mere spot they stand on does not constitute so strong an attachment as that from which they draw their gains."

It is from this perspective that a new critique must be built on the left. The MNC must be correctly seen as the logical "next step" in the maturation of international capitalism. It contains within its network of tentacles the greatest contradiction that has so far emerged in a world of economically insecure and intensely competitive nation states. Locked into a zero-sum struggle with the managers of state power, the MNC is not likely to forfeit its global capital or to wither away before the onslaught of economic nationalism. It is more likely to succeed in pitting one state against another than to succumb to the puny weapons —of tariff barriers, capital controls and export subsidies—that capitalist states can mobilize against it. As the late Steve Hymer put it, fragile nation states will surely fragment long before the mobile and flexible MNC falls to pieces.

There is no apparent or straight-forward resolution that the left can devise in dealing with the MNC. Certainly, the dogmatism must be avoided that is all too frequently found in socialist literature. It is courageous but not necessarily realistic to insist that:

> "the growth of the multi-nationals must be stopped; the surplus value which feeds [their] growth must be directed to national enterprises instead. If this cannot be done under capitalism as Canada's experience strongly suggests that it cannot, a further answer follows: national independence and capitalism are not compatible, whereas national independence and socialism are."[23]

A brief review of two industrial factors—the level of skills and the export earnings of advanced economies—suggests that since neither can be raised rapidly this prescription is fundamentally erroneous. Unless the deeply rooted patterns of world trade are revolutionized *in toto*, it will pay no socialist régime to resort to the nationalization or the forced feeding of its national enterprises. It would simply impose upon them the fate of Rolls Royce. Dismal as the conclusion appears, the fact remains that an industrialized economy depends upon its technology and its capital-intensive industries to maintain a growth momentum and aggregate national income. It can safely resort to the collectivization of the primary sectors (such as agriculture, coal, steel and transport—all of which operate within national boundaries, and often without profit) and it can intervene heavily in the service sectors, too. But it is likely that the key export units will be stifled if they are forced to operate *exclusively* within the domestic milieu.

This is to suggest that a new formula of technological change must be articulated by those on the left who still look for socialism in one country—or at least, one at a time. The choices available are daunting and complex. If Telefunken, Pechiney, Courtaulds and Montecatini Edison are to be nationalized outright they will probably lose control of their foreign subsidiaries, forfeit the benefits of transfer pricing, renounce the cross-national economies of integrated production and scale, lose valuable sales to their former oligopoly competitors, and thus abandon the revenues required to finance their formidably expensive R & D programmes. Alternatively, if they remain in private hands— somewhat like BP, ICI or ICL, which are in part owned by the UK Government—then they will surely export investment funds, jobs and new product lines to those capitalist countries in which their affiliates are not constrained by socialist priorities or collectivist planning.

The gravity of this choice must be everywhere apparent. No society in the advanced industrial world could afford to rely upon the home-based export trade that would remain once its in-coming and out-going affiliates had passed into socialist control. Even if a drastic redistribution of domestic income took place, the earnings available to the home community might fall by 50% or more. New R & D would have to be acquired (e.g., in aerospace or nuclear generators) from the foreign MNCs that lead the technology race. Worse yet, employment might have to be expanded by sub-contracting (like Taiwain or Hong Kong) to foreign firms that had acquired both the capital and the market position needed to enlarge their assembly runs. Hungary, Rumania and Poland might yet follow this dubious pattern. They are sliding toward the affluence of a "post-industrial society" by sub-contracting with such warmly welcomed visitors as Krupp, Saint Gobain, International Harvester and Pirelli.

"Damned if you do, Fleeced if you don't" is the MNC view toward nationalization and socialist control outside the third world. (Within the third world their views are altogether different, as they are within the Soviet bloc, too; for the sake of clarity, both areas have been excluded from this analysis.) It would admirably suit the purposes of Dow Chemical Hoescht or Sumitomo if its British or French competitors were to be nationalized. Though a few of their own affiliates might be hurt, too, they could partly regain through added patent fees and licences what they had lost to a newly socialist régime in sequestered production investments. Alternatively, were the régime to nationalize everything *except* the MNC sectors, the MNC managers could bargain from strength with a new government of the left. In addition, they could threaten the currency values, the anti-inflation controls and the full employment policy of a socialist régime—unless, of course, they were bought off with the tax favours and the labour "discipline" that Yugoslavia now offers to its MNC guests.

Regrettably, the conclusion of this essay must be somewhat inconclusive. Socialism in one country (at a time) is no longer a viable strategy for an advanced economy. In his effective debunking of left-wing nationalism, *The Left Against Europe?*, Tom Nairn raised the question of what should be done in a system in which "capitalist forces of production long ago outstripped the confines of nation-states . . . and inter-imperialist conflicts". Should the MNC sectors, that are based upon international finance-capital, be allowed to build their own monopolist enclave or "off-shore island" (as he put it), in the midst of a socializing economy? Or should a left régime deprive itself of the powerful "invisible export" gains that the MNCs in the City of London bring to the UK economy by collectivizing such powerful bastions of finance-capital?

The question is difficult to answer in the short term. A socialist government in London that abandoned the UK's leading position in the Euro-dollar market, where the MNCs transact their usurious business, would be reduced to stark penury. Large segments of the population would be forced to surrender the security of their life styles were this nationalization to go through; and the most dynamic sectors of the UK's export industries would weaken in the markets of "free trade imperialism" in which the nation's aggregate income is earned. On the other hand, if the City and the MNC oligopolies were not nationalized, the national thrust of British socialism would soon be blunted.

Tom Nairn ignores these critical short-term difficulties by urging that Britain could resolve the dilemma in the longer run by entering EEC. "For the revolutionary left entry into the Common Market," he believes, would increase "the chances of effective political opposition to capitalism because it weakens the traditional hegemony of the ruling class . . .; [it would] increase the tempo of revolutionary politics, and further diminish the role of social democracy".[24] But his advocacy, certainly in the short run, would not remove the two-edged threat posed by the MNC. And it is in the short run, as the Allende régime discovered, that the destiny of socialist movements is largely determined.[25]

There is no easy formula, therefore, to answer the question that Lenin asked while still in exile: What then is to be done? The nationalization of the MNC could cripple the national survival of a left régime. But the failure to nationalize the MNC banks, oil "majors" and technology leaders would reduce socialist policy to a mere reformism. For a national movement to pit its strength against the world market strength of the MNC would lead to disaster. But to leave the MNC to its own devices would lead only to the dismembering of socialism in one country. This is the material circumstance of industrial technology that must force the left to articulate a new strategy.

NOTES

1. My preliminary attempts to evaluate the clash between the MNC and the capitalist state appear in James Kurth and Steven Rosen (eds.), *Testing Theories of Imperialism* (Lexington, Mass.: D. C. Heath, 1974); and in the *Yale Review*, Vol. LIX, No. 2 (December 1969).

2. The delayed and blunted perception of the MNC on the part of the Communist parties of Europe can be gauged from the reports submitted to a conference of Party representatives held in London in 1971: *The International Firms and the European Working Class* (London, The Communist Party of Great Britain, n.d.), p. 8.

3. Ernest Mandel, *Europe versus America? Contradictions of Imperialism* (London, New Left Books, 1970); André Gorz, *Strategy for Labor: A Radical Proposal* (Boston, Beacon, 1964); Jean-Jacques Servan-Schreiber, *The American Challenge* (New York, Atheneum, 1968); Christopher Layton, *Industry and Europe* (London, Political and Economic Planning, No. 531, October 1971); Raymond Vernon, *Sovereignty at Bay* (New York: Basic Books, 1971); Jack N. Behrman, *National Interests and the Multinational Enterprise* (New Jersey, Prentice-Hall, 1970); and Charles P. Kindleberger (ed.), *The International Corporation* (Cambridge, M.I.T. Press, 1970).

4. Op. cit., p. 9. It should be noted that a modest start has been made by EEC to curb MNC activities by imposing anti-trust constraints against the chemical dye giants, against Continental Can and against various joint venture and marketing arrangements. But most of these constraints are very limited in effectiveness.

5. 23,282 affiliate companies of American MNCs were listed in 1966 and 65% of them were located in developed market economies. In a different calculation (for 1968–9) this figure was put at 74.7%. The concentration of affiliates of British MNCs in the richest markets was 68.2%, while the German, Swiss and Swedish MNCs recorded about 83%. *U.N. Report*, pp. 143–7.

6. The factor of organizational "size" is a determinant of the oligopoly interests of the MNC. The companies that play a mammoth role in the home market are those that also exert the largest influence in host economies overseas. The firms that appear at the head of the *Fortune* listing of the Top 500 corporations in America or of *The Times* 1,000 in Britain are the same as those (with a few remarkable exceptions) that set the pace in many of the export and growth sectors of other countries' economies. Several attempts have been made to explain why giant companies at home are quick to expand their operations overseas. Among the more interesting are Robin Murray, "The Internationalization of Capital and the Nation State," *New Left Review*, No. 67 (May–June 1971), pp. 84–109; and Stephen Hymer and Robert Rowthorn, "MNCs and International Oligopoly: The Non-American Challenge," in Charles P. Kindleberger (ed.), *The International Corporation* (Cambridge, M.I.T. Press, 1970).

7. The heavy concentration of MNC investment in manufacturing and petroleum industries is emphasized throughout the *U.N. Report* (pp. 10–15 and Tables XIII–XVIII); these industries absorb 75% of MNC investments in most developed or "mature" economies. Admittedly, the combined investments of the incoming MNCs rarely surpass 5% of the host country's gross domestic product (GDP). But the careful selection in the location and concentration of this capital allows foreign affiliates to dominate Japanese aerospace, British automobiles, French engineering, German lease-financing, Belgian electronics, or Italian oil refineries. The motives of the MNC in pursuing this pattern of concentration are examined in John M. Stopford and Louis T. Wells, *Managing the Multinational Enterprise*, and

THE MULTI-NATIONAL CORPORATION

in Raymond Vernon, *Sovereignty at Bay* (New York, Basic Books, 1972 and 1971).

8. A valuable criticism of the literature on oligopoly theory and MNC expansion appears in Theodore H. Moran, "Foreign Expansion as an 'Institutional Necessity' for US Corporate Capitalism: The Search for a Radical Model," *World Politics*, Vol. 25, No. 3 (April 1973), pp. 369–86. The emphasis upon economies of scale, market control and extensions of the "product life cycle" theory explains, in Moran's view, the new form of industrial imperialism practised by the MNC.

9. The conflict between the de Gaulle régime and General Motors in 1962 deterred Ford from entering France until the Gaullists decided to revise their restrictionist policy. In the meantime, Ford located new assembly plants in Belgium and expanded their installations in West Germany. It also took the decision to build the Pinto engine in Britain, and then cancel it, but it made little effort to consult the British government or trade unions while doing so. The Ford managers knew that they could relocate major projects out of the UK without trouble; and that British authorities could not go to Detroit to protest.

10. Relations between states and MNCs vary greatly. A review of recent studies and of the testimony given before Congressional and business groups appears in Hugh Stephenson, *The Coming Clash: the Impact of MNCs on National States* (New York, Saturday Review Press, 1972). The author fails to note Professor Kindleberger's awesome conclusion that "the nation state is just about through as an economic unit", in *American Business Abroad* (New Haven, Yale University Press, 1969, p. 207). Both authors note that MNCs are growing at a rate of 10% or more each year while few national economies expand at even 5% annually.

11. A strenuous defence of contemporary nationalism is attempted in David P. Calleo and Benjamin Rowland, *America and the World Political Economy* (Blooming-ton, Indiana University Press, 1973). They argue that nationalism is the only force that can satisfy "the psychological hunger for identity in a bewildering world" of economic turmoil and environmental catastrophe. For all of its imper-fections, therefore, the bourgeois state is the only agency that can still pretend to a popular control over the surge of market forces and oligopoly capital.

12. That social and political elites are likely to collude with corporate interests, rather than to constrain them, is convincingly argued in Ralph Miliband, *The State in Capitalist Society* (London, Weidenfeld and Nicolson, 1969). Since many Cabinet Ministers have quit the conservative or Social Democrat governments of Europe, Japan, and North America to join the directors Board of prominent MNCs, their reluctance to sell out national interests to foreign capital should not be taken too seriously.

13. A similar "rationalization" planned by Olivetti in the 1960s required the closing of its Underwood subsidiary in Connecticut and the relocation of its manufacture of portable typewriters to Barcelona. Its new plant in Pennsylvania produced expensive desk-top calculators and electric typewriters while manual machines were made for the US market in Glasgow. Nine plants in Italy specialized in manufacturing just one or two product lines; and the Glasgow factory (which exported 80% of its products instead of supplying the UK market) was greatly enlarged. An identical regard for differentials in labour productivity and wage rates has been shown by Singer. Its cheaper sewing machines are mass produced in Italy or the UK, largely for export; only a few top-of-the-line products are still manufactured in its American home base.

14. Neil H. Jacoby, the Dean of the U.C.L.A. Business School, provides a determined defence of the MNC in *Corporate Power and Social Responsibility: A Blueprint for the Future* (London and New York, Macmillan, 1973). In applauding the contribu-tion that the MNCs can make to the equalization of factor costs he insists that they are:

"leading Europe toward a more egalitarian, homogenous and democratic society. . . . Ultimately, they may facilitate the joining of all Europe in an enduring political and economic union . . . an achievement that eluded Caesar, Charlemagne and Napoleon" (p. 108).

A more sceptical view is revealed in Anthony Sampson, *The Sovereign State: The Secret History of ITT* (London, Hodder & Stoughton, 1973). He cites significant examples of how an MNC can interfere in the policy decisions of elected governments to protect a monopolist market (e.g., in defence contracts) and to reverse the equalization of mass consumer benefits. Nor need one believe that ITT is unique in corrupting public managers or private marketers. It is merely the first that has been energetically exposed.

15. The US Senate was appalled to learn that ARAMCO, though owned by four US oil 'majors', instantly obeyed Saudi Arabia's order to cut off oil supplies to the Sixth Fleet in the autumn of 1973—even before it alerted the Pentagon. When the Senate criticized the oil MNCs for rigging Western markets it still could not bring itself to tax their windfall profit margins. The emphasis placed by "the technostructure" on growth and oligopoly control, rather than on national interests and short-run profits, is usually attributed to J. K. Galbraith, *The New Industrial State* (Boston, Houghton Mifflin, 1967).

16. The concentration of giant firms among MNCs makes it difficult for any state to curb their investment plans or outflows. One study for the US Government, *The MNC: Studies on U.S. Foreign Investment*, Vol. 2 (Washington, US Department of Commerce, April 1973) revealed that 250 to 300 US-based MNCs account for over 70% of all foreign investments; practically all are to be found on the *Fortune* list of the 500 largest US companies. Another study, by EEC, showed that three-quarters of the affiliates in the nine EEC countries are branches of giant MNCs. Thus 29% of the largest companies in Belgium and 47% in West Germany are MNC affiliates; in Italy they tend to be four times larger than the average Italian company. See *European Community*, January 1974, pp. 16–19.

17. The EEC estimates that American MNCs have already invested $80 billion in the nine member states and that they will rapidly increase their capital each year: (a) because they earn a higher rate of return overseas than at home; (b) because their expansion is financed largely from local borrowing, retained earnings and accelerated depreciation; and (c) because the economies of Europe—many of which, like Italy and the UK, face formidable inflation *plus* payments deficits—have little strength left to fight the MNC managers. See *Vision*, March 1974, pp. 73–5; and *The U.N. Report*, Table XXXVII.

18. *The U.N. Report* (pp. 75–105) lists many of the proposed remedies and solutions that have appeared in the academic literature or that have actually been attempted. At most the proposals would be of marginal effectiveness in controlling MNC operations. A set of recommendations is also given in Jacoby, op. cit., pp. 119–21. In the superficial analysis that passes as "corporate social responsibility" he urges MNCs to be "good citizens" and nation states to "liberalize" their trade policies.

19. Two different approaches to the development of interdependence in the world order can be found in Johan Galtung, "A Structural Theory of Imperialism", *Journal of Peace Research*, No. 2, 1971; and David Osterberg and Fouad Ajami, "The MNC: expanding the frontiers of world politics", *Journal of Conflict Research*, Vol. 15, No. 4, December 1971, pp. 457–70. Both review the claim that the MNC can serve better than the nation state as an agent of economic integration; for different reasons, both dispute the claim.

20. Michael Brooke and Lee Remmers, *The Strategy of Multi-National Enterprise* (London, Longmans, 1970) review the performance of the MNC in many different host economies. They describe the range of instruments available to MNC treasurers in redeploying financial resources, the gains that can be sought through

transfer pricing and the additional market leverage that can be applied through cross-affiliate pricing strategy.

21. Jacoby, op. cit., p. 122.
22. Vernon, op. cit., p. 284.
23. H. L. Robinson, "The Downfall of the Dollar", *Socialist Register, 1973*, p. 443. An equally assertive and unrealistic prescription appears in Michael Barratt Brown, *Europe: Time to Leave and How to Go* (London, Spokesman), Pamphlet No. 34 (n.d.). In his concluding section, on Alternatives to the EEC, he insists that a socialist Britain should "establish a state monopoly of foreign trade with power to monitor all transfer prices . . . and to discriminate among imports and exports according to social priorities rather than the dictates of the giant companies" (p. 14).
24. Nairn, op. cit., p. 154. In urging that socialists should repudiate the parochialism of a "moribund nationalism" to enter EEC he aptly quotes Marx from the text on *Free Trade*: "One may declare oneself an enemy of the constitutional régime without declaring oneself a friend of the ancient régime. . . ."
25. Ralph Miliband makes the point in his analysis of "The Coup in Chile", *The Socialist Register, 1973*, that short run changes are terribly susceptible to subversion unless they are moved by a drastic sense of urgency and commitment. In Chile, with its income largely derived from extractive industries, this prescription is highly relevant. In an advanced industrial economy dependent upon the imperialism of free trade it could lead, within a few weeks, to chaos and economic collapse.

AMERICAN HEGEMONY UNDER REVISION

V. G. Kiernan

AT the end of the Second World War the United States was ready—
though the American people was very unready—to take on the
hegemony of the non-socialist world. It had already during the war
assumed the leadership of a large part of it, the saner sectors of capitalism
against the wilder. War accelerated its rise by crippling all the rest; it
was not however crippling capitalism, but rather liberating it from
out-of-date moulds, cutting away its feudal links in Germany and
Japan with military adventure, which for capitalism ought to be only an
adjunct of the pursuit of profit, not its substitute. World capitalism was
left a good deal more homogeneous, more purely bourgeois as in the
United States it had always been. But world capitalism was for the
time being badly shaken by its civil war, and in need of a shepherd;
also of a shining example, a proof that "free enterprise" really could
still work. America possessed moreover a dominance not only total
in the economic sphere but, for the first time, in the military as well.

If it is true that a nation gets the government it deserves, we might
say that the "free world" was getting the kind of leadership it deserved.
But it must be allowed that this was by no means of a wholly bad kind,
even if its better qualities were muffled by its Cold War rantings and
ravings. It ruled out any more wars among the major countries of its
flock. Brief conflicts between more juvenile members, like India and
Pakistan, have occurred, but no such danger threatens as, in the rival
camp, that of armed conflict between Russia and China over their
senseless wranglings. From this point of view it has been an asset to
the "free world" that it contains only one great power. Again, America
favoured a transformation of direct imperial rule into looser, informal
control, of the sort that has come to be known as "neo-colonial". This
represented progress, albeit limited, and it was a misfortune that the
obduracy of some behind-the-times Europeans, worst among them the
French and Portuguese, was allowed to bedevil it. In colonial areas
which did become self-governing, American hegemony had a further
function to discharge, in ensuring that they should be firmly integrated
into the anti-socialist family, and taught the behaviour appropriate to
the station of each of them within it. In course of time the retreat of the
Europeans became almost complete, leaving them, as Kissinger was to

remind them acidly in April 1973, with a political standing merely regional. They and the Japanese and other scattered addicts of free enterprise could have only a small and declining share of influence on what happened outside their own limits, while on the other hand their involvement in world trade was growing, under the American peace, by leaps and bounds. It was another duty of the hegemony to provide coordination, to fit them all into a common framework.

Responsible for the destinies of capitalism everywhere, the US could not simply or crudely dominate: it had to support and sustain as well. Cares of leadership made their demands, as they always must do, and imposed on the US a qualitative change of manners. In the early 1920s Trotsky was predicting that industrial competition from an expanding America would ruin Europe and drive it into communism.[1] He was too hopeful, even for that time, and after 1945 the communist spectre was all too obvious. The Europe of Attlee, de Gaulle, and Franco had to be reinvigorated, and Japanese capitalism ransomed, healed, restored, forgiven. Thus the biggest capitalist complex was in a sense being compelled to behave uncapitalistically.

In another way, the work of restoration helped to promote activity more in accord with Marxist expectation. War had enlarged American production so gigantically that an outpouring of capital investment was bound to take place, and form an integral part of the hegemony. And a good proportion at least of this capital has been constructive, rather than parasitic, in its operations. American capitalism has always been heavily infected with graft and corruption, might indeed be called inseparable from them, and in corners like Guatemala it is quite ready to sink to a merely colonial-parasitic level. Yet it has always remained to a surprising degree faithful to its original ethic of hard work, purposeful effort, the Carlylean injunction to *produce*. British capitalism by contrast has stood midway between it and the pre-war German-Japanese type: it has always suffered from a streak of illegitimacy, of the bar sinister, and from instincts which in recent years have displayed themselves in a morbid thirst for property deals, land-speculations and swindles, a senile relapse into old habits of usury-capital. Lately the head of Leyland Motors observed ruefully that the Stock Exchange valuation of his firm, a linchpin of the entire British economy and balance of payments, was about the same as that of one untenanted block of London offices.

In his Reith lectures at the end of 1973 Alastair Buchan pointed out that the trebled total of world trade since 1960 implied an unprecedented interdependence among "all the political units of the democratic world".[2] By this he meant of course the capitalist world: one of the units mentioned by way of example was Taiwan. It is not socialists alone who have had to resort to forms of "Aesopian" language.

Allowing for this, the lectures were often as realistic and penetrating as a non-socialist commentary on the world and its wife can be. Welcoming the expansion of trade, he sang the praises of the "multi-national" companies, as the vital new factor in economic growth and the flow of export capital. Multinational or transnational companies are not new. They made big advances after the First World War, when already it could be argued that "large-scale corporations with world-wide investments were superseding the national state". The rise of the totalitarian State hampered these "private empires", or "economic states", as the Nazis called them, but they did not go out of existence.[3] Under American auspices they were free again to proliferate, and to revive the flow of capital that Marx, or Hobson, expected to carry industrialization to fresh quarters of the globe.

The shareholder was showing himself readier than the workingman to learn the lesson of "no fatherland". My country is the world, he might have paraphrased Tom Paine by saying, and my religion is to draw dividends. These corporations are, all the same, mostly American, in that their ramifying roots and suckers link them closest to the US. Emancipated though they may be from any humbug of patriotism, they must have some government or governments to call on for help, when the big stick is required, or the silken filaments of finance have to be hardened into iron fetters. It is the US that can wield the big stick most effectively, and this fact must be one of the main attractions that have been drawing capital from other countries into companies with their own discreet "hot lines" to the State Department. An investor is a venturesome yet timorous creature, perpetually racked by Antonio's anxieties about his galleons tossing on distant coasts, beset by water-thieves and land-thieves (the worst of these, the socialists, always panting to lay rude hands on the Lord's anointed, the merchant of Venice was blissfully ignorant of). His ear is vastly comforted, his willingness to risk more of his precious ducats fortified, by the rattle of chains far away, the clang of cell doors, the measured tread of the sentry; the sound of a firing-squad at work now and then, as of late in Chile, raises his spirits wonderfully, in joyful anticipation of a rise tomorrow in the Dow-Jones Average, that *line of life* across the palm of modern civilization.

For developed countries with surplus capital, to export some of it to one another is no novelty, but of late it seems to have been happening on a quite new scale. There was fear for long in Japan—as in France and elsewhere—that too much American capital was pouring in, and might oust the native breed. But now there is uneasiness in America itself about too much Japanese and other foreign capital coming in.[4] All this may appear to betoken a tendency of all capital towards a universal amalgam, logical enough with the removal of any real prospect of war among the major capitalist countries. Yet this merging and mingling are oddly contradicted by an opposite inclination to draw away, both economically and politically. There have been many symptoms of the well-regimented "free world" falling apart. European revolt against American oil and war policies at the time of the Middle East fighting in 1973 only intensified what had been visible considerably earlier. Threatened shortages of raw materials, oil most of all, brought in sight the danger of a scramble, a *sauve qui peut*. There are still contradictions between the "general will" of capitalism and local capitalist interests; in addition, each government has to think of maintaining the standard of living of its own voters.

Since 1945 a generation has grown up under the shadow, or in the warmth, of American domination, or protection, and with a world-picture much unlike its parents'. It has been a very blurred one, gradually in some ways coming into better focus. "The Americans help us, don't they?" a child in a shop at Appleby was heard to ask in August 1966. "There's some doubt about that", was its preoccupied mother's reply. The child might be called a faithful echo of government teaching—Tory or Labour—; the mother, of a public suffering from vague misgivings. Nothing can have done more than their docile submissiveness to Washington, not precisely to *discredit* Whitehall and Westminster, but to deprive them of meaning. Professor Buchan did not draw this moral, but he was very right in saying that nowadays "It is the mass media, rather than our political leaders, which tend to set the agenda of public debate."[5]

London has gone on kowtowing to Washington long after intelligent Americans were realizing that their emperor had no clothes on, or not nearly enough for decency, to say nothing of dignity. In vain did the emperor add Culture to his armoury of self-advertisement, and call in the arts to "counteract Soviet influence", and "correct and humanize the image of the American people held by other peoples, thus to develop a more rounded understanding of the United States, and greater confidence in its leadership in world affairs."[6] The Vietnam war did more than any Muse could to give the world a "rounded understanding" of the hegemony. More completely than the Indian Mutiny for Britain, the mutiny of the Vietnamese people was a traumatic experience, a fundamental denial of both American virtue and American power. It cost uncounted sacrifices, not warranted by any cool logic of socialism, but earning a reward different from the one aimed at—the glory of a supremely heroic resistance to the barbarism of the West, like that of ancient Greece to the barbarism of the East, but a Thermopylae of a quarter-century.

Apart from all this, Europe's economic recovery, and even the feeble approach to political unison represented by the Common

Market and Britain's entry, have been altering the scales between the two sides of the Atlantic. After doing its best for years to push and prod Europe into union, the US now resentfully sees its offspring growing up and questioning parental authority. Australia, which drifted away years ago from the British into the American orbit, has now been breaking away from this too, and looking for a commonsense policy of its own. Australians were conditioned to feel that their survival depended on American protection against China, as formerly against Japan; also that their high standard of living depended on at least token support to their patron in Vietnam, and if this required them to help in destroying a few villages, it was well worth the price. For some time now the idea has been dawning that America's outlays in protecting positions which it would want to protect in any case "are less and perhaps considerably less than Australia's usefulness to some of America's central purposes in the Indo-Pacific region".[7]

In Japan too ingratitude has been rearing its head, and the contradictions between America's role as Atlas upholding the capitalist heavens, and its own mundane interests, have been coming into the open. A group of Congressmen toured south-east Asia in 1970 and protested to the government that while America was spending blood and treasure there Japanese businessmen were quietly moving in to reap the harvest. They were behaving in fact exactly as private enterprise ought to act; between the ideology and the practical working of any system there is always a gap, and the more imperfect the system the wider this is. Professor Buchan was alarmed at the prospect of "a kind of Japanese Gaullism", pointing out that Japan's isolated history makes it harder for it to feel itself part of any combination. He noted that President Nixon during his first term of office treated Japan high-handedly, in a "colonial way", and has since been having to try to make amends.[8] Like Hitler, one might say, he has to make the Japanese feel at home, as "honorary Aryans"; all the rest of the advanced capitalist realm forms an ethnic as well as economic family. Altogether, Buchan's primary preoccupation was that of a European—especially a British—conservatism which found the "Americo-centric world" a very passable one, and wonders uneasily what is going to take its place now that "we are again in the early stages of a new cycle of change", with a possible shift in the balance of power looming up, and for Britain "a new uncertainty".[9]

Before the Second World War capitalism may be said to have possessed no organ of thinking. Its special aptitude is technology, and in matters requiring broader views, comprehension of the science of society, it has been woefully deficient. Painfully and reluctantly it has been learning to think, and the hegemony endowed it with something resembling a central nervous system. What America had to supply, for purposes of ratiocination, was all the same rudimentary. Its world-wide concerns were a good deal more multifarious even than those of the old British empire, which often had great difficulty in making up its mind about them; and they have frequently been contradictory. To evolve policies capable of reconciling them all must be a formidable task, so much so that the very concept of any logical system of American policy may be untenable. What is really happening, how questions are really being decided, has been nearly as hard to make out, even with the help of those spasmodic, irregular disclosures which from time to time offer glimpses into the witches' cauldron.

A capitalist government's policies cannot be in harmony with the long-term welfare of a nation; it may be doubtful whether, in American conditions, they can be in harmony with that of the national capitalism as a whole. America exhibits the reign of capital in purer form, with less admixture of earlier historical elements, than any other country. But capitalism itself suffers from various discrepancies, between its present appetites in one part of the world or another and its more permanent well-being. Businessmen individually are concerned with the profits their next balance-sheet will show, not with collective long-range calculations. Writers like Schumpeter have argued from this that they are not really interested in "politics", or in influencing their governments.[10] The fact is rather that they are mostly content to get their governments to back them, or allow them to go ahead on their own, each in their own province. In return for this, each will let the rest have their way likewise, without asking whether their doings in Guatemala, or Chile, are going to be good in the end for their joint welfare.

Any ruling class must have its impulses translated into action by a governing class, an administrative apparatus, such as American public life is singularly ill-fitted to provide. Growing up far removed from all other big Powers, the country developed only a makeshift diplomatic service. Henry James's Englishman, commenting on the dearth of respectable professions in the United States, added: "American diplomacy—that's not for gentlemen either."[11] During this century it has been overhauled somewhat, but until after 1945 there was no systematized body of aims to give it regular employment. "The nation had no foreign policy to guide it during the historic half-century in which the United States waged three wars", Walter Lippmann once wrote.[12] The Cold War supplied a rough and ready one, under cover of which decision-making, or the appearance of it, could be left in the heyday of American hegemony to a floating mass of individuals, of both parties or no party. They were the lawyers, bankers, officials, academics, whose consensus—as Buchan says—led America into Vietnam, and foundered there.[13] This united wisdom, with its impressive stiffening of pundits from the universities, can be seen now to have been not initiating real policies, but rationalizing American actions. Its function was to bestow what could pass for a philosophy and a programme on a welter of financial pressures. Behind the facade the quantum of serious thought and debate was scanty, all the more so by contrast with the luxuriance of American technology. How many angels can stand on the point of a pin has never been settled, but it would be safe to guess that most of the wise men ever consulted by the White House could find room there. America's actions can be more easily explained in terms of behaviourism than of political theory. Its most successful chairman was Eisenhower, who played golf and read Wild West stories.

Things could go on in this semi-automatic fashion because the real decisions were taken, piecemeal, by powerful bodies able to dictate in particular spheres. America is the homeland of the Lobby, or pressure-group, which in its public life has had the significance of the political party in Europe. Capitalism there is highly concentrated, and can be supposed to function, in moments of crisis or on issues fundamental to it, as a single super-boardroom. More habitually it may be thought of as a congeries of distinct power-centres, many of them with a strongly regional character like those within the Common Market; a federation of blocs of capital, resembling—and to an increasing extent superseding in real significance—the country's federal political structure. American democracy consists in other words of an unlimited arena for wirepulling —which may on occasion make it possible for some good as well as many bad things to be done quicker than they could be in England; measures taken for instance against tobacco-poisoning, or pollution of air or lakes. In terms of American relations with the outside, the result is far likelier to be bad. For a long time after 1948 Far Eastern policy was laid down by the crew of cranks and crooks known as the China Lobby; for longer still Roman Catholic pressure was able to distort American foreign-aid programmes by vetoing aid to population-control: it was one of the pressures to which Eisenhower succumbed most spinelessly.

Big business lobbies work on similar lines. So does an institution like the Pentagon, far stronger and clearer of purpose than the State Department, and closely interlocked with formidable business groups. It has had its own policies in many quarters. "Indonesia", a journalist reported during 1970, "is one of the many countries where the American State Department and the Pentagon wage their silent battles against each other".[14] To keep such rivals in step is as impossible for the White House as it was for the papacy in olden days to smooth out the rancorous discords of Jesuit and Dominican and Franciscan; they too were often intense in the Far East. Presidents are indeed, as we have been taught lately, nearly as free to wage private wars as to conduct secret diplomacy; Johnson's orders for the bombing of Laos which

began in 1967 were not really brought to light until the Senate investigated them in August 1973. Few human beings, even from Texas,
have ever known less about world affairs than L. B. Johnson, and such
presidential decisions must be seen as in effect dictated by the generals.
They imply that Washington has been at times as much under the
military thumb as the Kaiser's Berlin. If America is destined ever to
come under army rule, such as it has helped to impose on so many
other countries, it is likelier to be through a creeping extension of this
ascendancy than through a coup d'état.

Within the Pentagon itself factionalism survives (we may be grateful
for it), despite the post-war unification of the services into a single
"Defence" apparatus, and its further tightening up by Macnamara.
Another feud rages, in the still murkier depths where America's hosts
of secret agents proliferate, between the Central Intelligence Agency
and the more select and secretive Defence Intelligence Agency.[15]
Which of these two is entitled to more credit for the counter-revolution
in Chile in 1973 may be debatable. But in the vast *demi-monde* where
men of the corporations and the agencies rub shoulders, collaboration
must often have been fruitful. They practise similar methods, the
businessmen in their industrial espionage against one another, and
think on the same lines. They confabulated about how to get rid of
Allende, and not by way of a mere intellectual exercise. As for the
State Department, it was left, when Allende perished, in the happy
position of being free to applaud the event without assuming responsibility for it. So we read that in the entourage of Tchaka the Zulu men
were executed at the tyrant's slightest nod.

It is typical of our epoch that both the super-powers rely heavily on
secret practices. Any régime that is growing away from the mass of its
subjects, coming to be alien to them, is afflicted by a sensation of
blindness and deafness, and resorts to these antennae for substitutes,
pseudo-organs of sense. Moreover the publicity surrounding everything American that is not carefully concealed makes it incumbent on
the government to conduct many of its doings through secret channels—

> "Masking the business from the common eye
> For sundry weighty reasons,"

as Macbeth explained to his trio of murderers. But with their prodigious growth and extraordinary ramifications, free from any coherent
supervision, the CIA and its congeners must have acquired a corporate
momentum and authority of their own. The CIA, above all, has come
to represent the authentic, characteristic contribution of capitalist
America to the management of international relations. It has many
features of a state within the State, as armies had in aristocratic

Europe and Japan. It is often reminiscent of the Jesuit Order of old days, weaving its web of conspiracy everywhere. A Jesuit who left the Order a century ago alleged that some of his brethren were prepared to talk of killing a bad (i.e. an anti-Jesuit) pope;[17] it may be assumed that at least as many CIA functionaries would be ready to eliminate a bad president.

Intermittent revelations of their sinister schemings astonish news-paper-readers, and must not seldom astonish the State Department, or the White House. CIA agents in India appear to have induced reactionaries in Tibet to provoke risings against China, so that China could be branded as an imperialist, and India turned against it.[18] The Sino-Indian war of 1962 was the logical sequel. In Greece their complicity in the overthrow of parliamentary rule by the army has been widely suspected. In Thailand in 1973 after the fall of the US-sponsored military régime there was indignation over a discovery that the CIA had been forging reports to deceive the government, and the organization which had been set up in imitation of it was disbanded. South Korea has a CIA of its own, an apt pupil in the occult sciences. Democratic countries too are not always inhospitable to it. A former member of it is reported as saying that "the British Government has been quite content to allow the CIA to construct a headquarters in central London for no other purpose than the steady subversion of the African Commonwealth countries".[19] Such a charge unfortunately cannot be dismissed as incredible.

How many of these plottings and plannings hold out any real gains to America, that is to American capitalism as a present and future whole, would be very hard to calculate, even if there were any responsible organ to undertake the task. Expenditure must be, even for the US, gigantic, an appreciable addition to the overhead costs of the hegemony. Some schemes that have been heard of, academic projects for instance financed by front-organizations, look perfectly childish, money thrown away. It is the instinct of a technological culture to think that anything and everything can be achieved by manipulation. We know too little about what types of individual are recruited into the secret services, but not many of them can be supposed capable of much mental exertion above the level of cunning.

Consensus politics meant agreement on the part of all concerned to pocket their shares of the proceeds without raising awkward questions. It could only last while American destinies seemed transparently manifest, and trade union boss and college dignitary and financier a single happy family, a *Volksgemeinschaft* of the New World, fond like Hitler's of calling itself a "classless society". Since then American scholars have been doing something towards revising their vision of things, and laboriously arriving at more or less realistic views, familiar to the Left a quarter-century ago, about such topics as the Chinese revolution. This revaluation may lead on towards national self-criticism, but only slowly and fitfully. American attitudes to the world cannot change radically until there is a real desire for a change in the structure of society at home. W. A. Williams was putting the cart before the horse when he wrote a dozen years ago that "Once free from its myopic concentration on the cold war, the United States government could come to grips with the central problem of reordering its own society."[20] Liberal criticism has remained too often anaemic, because it has politely reproached American foreign policies only with blunders or miscalculations, not with wickedness. This is the outlook that pervades Galbraith's record of his time as ambassador to India in the early 1960s;[21] it was equally that of Eugene Black, a former president of the World Bank sent by Johnson to tour south-east Asia and talk about reconstruction. Writing in 1969, he was expecting disengagement and peace, to be followed by wonderful economic projects, without any regard to social or political change.[22]

At the height of the protest against the Vietnam war it appeared as if the country really was turning over a new leaf at last, and labour breaking away from its old pro-war leaders.[23] But protest died down abruptly when the war was put on a more long-range basis, with no further call for American conscripts; so abruptly as to throw doubt on the possibility of any big modern country ever having a true change of heart, any more than a sensible foreign policy. Years of campaigning for emancipation left the bulk of Americans still very lukewarm about abolition of slavery when the Civil War started. When Lieutenant Calley was convicted at the end of 1971 for the massacre at My Lai, he was not presented by admirers with a sword of honour, as General Dyer was after his much bigger massacre at Amritsar in 1919, but he met with a great deal of public sympathy. There lurked in it a racialist refusal to believe that killing natives could be a serious misdemeanour, as well as a feeling that Calley was being made a scapegoat for a whole army which had been acting in pretty much the same way for years. The culprit's punishment has turned out to be not much more than nominal; in April 1974 the army discovered or invented "extenuating circumstances", and cut his dwindling prison sentence by half.

This lack of a moral awakening America shares by and large with the rest of the "free" world, its more conservative spokesmen at any rate. There was nothing in Professor Buchan's third lecture, on "The Troubled Giant", to suggest that the American conscience had anything to trouble itself over. Instead he seemed to find it natural, though regrettable, that the US should be labouring under "a sense of living in a thoroughly ungrateful world", where its well-meant efforts to be helpful have gone awry, and like other countries should be turning towards "nationalism", or putting its own interests first.[24] The more paternal of its duties of hegemony no longer appear so urgent: capitalism has its aches and pains, but it looks by no means so frail as it did in 1945, and a return to more normal, i.e. more unfriendly, relations may well seem permissible.

It was inevitable that readjustment of American policies in any more benign form, especially towards the "colonial" world, would be limited and grudging. By the later 1960s readjustment of some sort was becoming a necessity: the question was how it could be carried out, and by whom. Critics who wanted change were apt to want far too much. Bureaucrats wanted too little. Capitalists were least of all qualified to see and do what was necessary, to trim the sails to shifting winds. Businessmen who enter politics with a real sense of vocation can be expected to be those fullest of the inbred dogmas of their class, and to be incapable of the detachment that was now needed. Forrestal was copying out a tragic speech from Sophocles, by a hero rejected and disregarded like himself, just before he committed suicide under stress of anxiety about the red peril. Dulles and Goldwater exhibited a kindred monomania.

Thoroughbred professional politicians, those to the manner born, do not read Sophocles or jump out of windows, and they will be more supple and adaptable, though they may be equally ruthless. Of this species President Nixon has shown himself an excellent specimen, and his landslide re-election in 1972, after four years of experiment and trial and error, was a well-earned tribute to his skill. He may have tarnished his performance by pursuing private gain with the same resolve and the same opportunism that he has brought to the service of American capitalism, and by reckoning himself too much above the law, as his country has so often put itself above international law. We all have our faults, and capitalist society must not expect all its virtues, the solid and the ornamental, combined in one man. An American head of state can hardly afford to be squeamish, or he would get no sleep for thinking of the things perpetrated every twenty-four hours to keep the flag flying. He needs a hide like that of Trollope's politician, proof against fire or steel. This presidential qualification the self-admiring, self-sufficient Nixon can claim in abundance; and if his mentality sometimes appears inexplicable, it may be understood as a compendium of the abnormal or pathological features of his America. He must often have resented his country's ingratitude, as it has resented the world's, and felt that he like Lt. Calley was being made scapegoat for sins as common as daylight. Cosi fan tutti. Within the limits of his mandate, and to the extent of his talents, somewhat of the vulpine order no doubt, he has deserved well of a people content to measure its greatness by the latest figures from Wall Street.

Nixon was the man of the situation, as Spaniards say. In Kissinger he found an assistant equally suited to the work in hand, whom he could make use of to run a *cabinet noir* diplomacy of his own, and circumvent the ponderous State Department, and then to take it over. Individuals of foreign origin have not seldom been employed by régimes facing unfamiliar, baffling problems, as Necker was by the Bourbon monarchy at its last gasp, or Stein by the Prussian monarchy after Jena. Nixon and Kissinger were both, as Professor Buchan said, "by temperament secretive and suspicious".[25] Only such a couple, unimpeded by any hard and fast principles, could have taken charge at such a time, and their twistings and turnings and divings were a necessary response to uncharted currents. They had to give up some things, while giving up as little as possible, but appearing abroad, though not at home, to be giving up more than they really were. The quickness of the tongue deceived the ear; America, which had been hoodwinked and bamboozled into the Cold War, now had to have the wool pulled over its eyes again as it was led out of the Cold War; it had to be led backwards, as it had been led by Roosevelt out of isolation into world power, or as Britain was led backwards out of Africa in the 1960s by flag-waving Tories, or France out of Algeria by de Gaulle. This art of turning horse-shoes back to front, to make a false trail, deserves a high place among the crafts of leadership.

There were many reasons for Nixon to make a *détente* with Russia and China his grand objective. In its pursuit alone he has risen at moments to something like true statesmanship. Deepening disrepute at home sharpened his eagerness for success. He could only make this his aim, however, because there was a prevalent feeling that the time was ripe for it. There was belated recognition that the country is not invincible, and its purse not bottomless. There was also the lure of fresh and boundless markets. Half a century ago the newly-founded Third International pronounced that "The United States sees in China and in Russia (especially Siberia) the markets to satisfy its gigantic need for expansion, and the fields to be won for American capital investment."[26] That need is far more overwhelming today; but there is room for thinking that post-1945 bans on trade with communist China and eastern Europe were disliked by many businessmen from the first.[27] They could not say so in public, for that would have told against the noisy hubbub of anti-communism which from other points of view suited them so well. They left it to the politicians to find a way out of the dilemma, and the politicians lacked the required finesse. They live by their tongues, and are often liable to commit their employers to more intransigent courses than they really desire. Nixon is "no orator", but as the shopkeeper said of his parrot when the customer complained of it not talking much, "he's a devil for thinking".

The Sino-Soviet quarrel helped him to make—or reciprocate—friendly overtures without loss of face. For years every good Maoist had been shouting *Collusion!* if a Russian and an American happened to sneeze at the same time. Mutual suspicions would be fanned by Nixon being on amiable terms with both sides; and while basking in this knowledge he could look forward to posing as leader or umpire of both halves of the world, by playing honest broker between Moscow and Peking, and inviting them to settle their differences out of court. At the same time he would be hoping to induce them both to cut off or cut down their aid and comfort to insurgents in the "free world". Each had shown itself quite willing to be friendly, for reasons of state, with the most repressive régimes, like those of Iraq or Pakistan; perilously willing, from the point of view of socialist principle. This flexibility may well have struck Nixon, as an example to be followed: diplomatic and commercial intercourse with the West might help to soften any doctrinaire antipathy to free enterprise still further.

By other "free" countries the halting movement towards *détente* has been watched with misgivings. The more brutally reactionary their governments, the more undisguisedly hostile these have been, because they owe their existence very largely to the Cold War, and a thaw might melt them. They will obstruct any accommodation with ingenuity and pertinacity, and with the help of the labyrinth of US secret and military agencies, with which they have innumerable links, and for which also *détente* bodes ill. In the novel written by Spiro Agnew after his sad fall from the vice-presidential pulpit whence he was wont to trumpet American righteousness, a band of Iranians intrigue to embroil America with Russia; as a novel it won little acclaim, but this at least was a highly realistic theme. A very convenient weapon of obstruction has been the Zionist campaign of vilification against the USSR. In more reputable quarters too, reservations about *détente* have been expressed. Professor Buchan was notably unenthusiastic. He trusted that Washington would not promote it at the cost of alienating allies who were "open and free societies as the United States herself is"[28]—as usual, without enumerating them, or indicating whether Greece, Turkey, Guatemala, and so on are among these Utopias. He shared the touching concern which the West has been showing for the welfare of Soviet intellectuals, though not for that of intellectuals in Guatemala, Turkey, Greece, and so on. Nixon, to do him justice, has always been able to rise above any sentimental concern with ill-used intellectuals anywhere.

Professor Buchan left Latin America out of his tour of the horizon, as of only peripheral concern.[29] Any admirer of the hegemony does well to leave out Latin America; the cloven hoof has left too many imprints there. Because progressive public opinion has only fitfully made itself felt on the Nixonian handling of external affairs, and because Latin America unlike Asia is remote from any chance of large-scale aid from either Russia or China, no real concessions or new deals have had to be contemplated. There have been some uneasinesses in recent years, with Vietnam undermining respect for the US everywhere, and communism burrowing in Cuba. Firm measures were required, and they have not been lacking. Today a bevy of right-wing dictatorships dominates the scene.

Rule by *caudillo* has old native roots, but the proximity of the US has been a potent factor in keeping it going, and making it more murderously effective, and spreading it from more primitive to more civilized areas, such as Uruguay used to be. It is all the more indispensable because it enables the continent to be kept in order without the US having to interfere too openly or blatantly. What may be called the Nixon amendment to the Monroe Doctrine, as extended since 1945 to cover every part of the globe inhabitable by capitalists, is that a degree of disengagement is required, and more must be left to local régimes able with American aid, material and moral, to hold the fort. This means that such régimes must be lavishly supplied with machine-guns, military advisers, secret police instructors, and the rest of the modern paraphernalia of government, and encouraged to use them "without mitigation or remorse".

As a consequence, government in Latin America has been increasingly militarized. Armies may it is true get out of hand sometimes, and march the wrong way. The Peruvian has for several years been showing a nationalist spirit and a taste for social reform highly unpalatable to Washington, and in April 1974 the Portuguese forces so far forgot their duty as to overthrow one of the most respectably right-wing dictatorships, equipped with the latest and most scientific torture-chambers, whose head had lately lain in Abraham's bosom, or made a state visit to England. As a rule, nevertheless, and particularly in the conditions of South America, armies as upholders of the status quo have furnished an equivalent to the fascist mass movements of interwar Europe. Under the hegemony, South American generals have been brought under regular political indoctrination. Most of those in the saddle in Brazil had a spell of training, clearly not wasted, in the US. Similar instruction has been imparted to receptive police forces; US agents have been convicted of giving lessons in electric torture. Formerly the great inquisitor and pillar of order was the Church; today there is far less need of it, as electricity replaces holy water, the machine-gun the crucifix. Colonial chickens often come home to roost, and Watergate revelations have shown that many of the illegalities familiar in police spying on natives have become part of official practice inside the US. Others can be expected to follow. An ingenious American device for tapping five thousand telephone lines simultaneously has been rumoured; lasers and spy-rays and sky-cameras multiply; there may be a time coming when the myrmidons of the hegemony will listen to and record all the earth's heartbeats. For the experimentation now in train, Latin America provides the best laboratory.

Allende represented a special challenge, because with him Marxism had come into office legally, and it is an essential item of the American creed that this can never happen. It had to be demonstrated that it would not be allowed to happen; but Allende had to be got rid of by, or through, other Chileans. On 16 September 1970, after the election, Kissinger in his "now famous 'off-the-record' press briefing . . . almost openly invited the Chilean armed forces to prevent his accession".[30] They needed more time to prepare; in the meantime economic screws were tightened, and when the generals were ready to act it was with the certainty of US approval, and of financial assistance to follow.[31] Their atrocities have disgusted some of the middle-class sympathizers who welcomed their advent, but not, apparently, any considerable number of Americans; one more symptom of a lagging moral consciousness, and the freedom from ethical restraints enjoyed by Nixon and his factotum. Their whole programme of readjustment rested its appeal exclusively on American self-interest; any awakening of progressive feeling would be an irrelevance or worse, a nuisance to be firmly brushed aside. Any expression of American displeasure at the mass murders in Chile would have halted them; but unlike Sir Richard Burton on his mission to Dahomey, with instructions to protest to King Gelele against human sacrifices, US representatives at Santiago have been silent. It has been too good an opportunity to be wasted for all subjects of the US protectorate over Latin America to be given a terrible warning.

The Chilean junta received constructive help from its Brazilian fellow-usurpers, with a decade's experience behind them of how to deal with opponents; one form it took was a platoon of experts in torture. Brazil has been elevated to the rank of America's trusted foreman, with responsibilities extending outside its own territory. Until shortly before Caetano's fall it was giving firm support to Portugal in Africa, and was enthusiastic for an anti-communist league of southern-hemisphere States, South Africa of course among them.[32] (South Africa is another obvious candidate for a junior partnership: it has been straining every nerve to solicit one, and the Nixon administration has given signs of gravitating towards assent.) An impression has been spreading that in case of Chile, or any other reactionary country in South America, requiring armed aid against subversion, this would be forthcoming from Brazil, which has common frontiers with nearly all of them, with Washington at its back with guns, dollars, and diplomatic umbrella.

From this point of view the supply to favoured armies if such items as submarines or the latest aircraft takes on a more logical aspect. They are useless for internal repression, and have often been sought merely as status-symbols, to tickle the rather childish vanity of the military mind. From early in 1974 it was rumoured that action was being planned in Washington against a now isolated Peru, which was coming under menaces from Brazil and Chile. Britain's Labour government was well aware of this when it decided to sell warships to Chile. One of its arguments, meant to be a clincher, was that jobs had to be made for Clydeside workers. Capitalism offers larger and larger numbers of workers a choice between making armaments, to be sold to any scoundrel with money to buy them, or unemployment. In much the same way society has always offered large numbers of women a free choice between prostitution and starvation. On 17 April the Scottish Trade Union Congress replied by unanimously condemning the sale.

Devolution of authority by the hegemony to a state like Brazil goes with a parallel process on the economic level, a building up of local industry. Brazil is a storehouse of raw materials now in demand, as well as of cheap labour, and European and Japanese capital has been flooding in, in the wake of American. Army rule, besides keeping the workers in their place, has provided a solid framework, or institutional core, round which all propertied or would-be propertied groups can gather and coalesce into an authentic bourgeoisie. By themselves these groups would be too inchoate, too heterogeneous, to sustain an industrial revolution, permeated as they are at one end of the scale with feudal anachronisms, at the other with left-wing intellectualism.

Whether Brazil and a few other chosen lands are destined to emulate Japan and enter the front rank of capitalism, cannot yet be foreseen. At any rate, while most of Latin America continues very backward, there are now quite big industrial pockets here and there, as in southern Brazil and Chile, Mexico and Argentina. Russia before 1914, with its tsarist police and foreign investors, was at a similar stage. To this extent, one socialist thesis is being weakened, namely that only socialist revolution is capable of leading retarded peoples into industrialism and progress. And if the process, on capitalist terms, is a painful one for the majority, socialist construction out of local resources must also be arduous. Industry helps to buttress conservatism in more practical ways too. Whereas over much of the continent, as of Asia, the only clients of the hegemony have been feudal landowners or traders of much the same kidney, industry generates its own more modern-minded affiliates. It creates a working class, a potential base for socialism, but at the same time a new-style middle class, virulently anti-socialist. Classical Marxism greatly underrated both the size of the industrial middle classes, and their significance alike for progress or reaction; the new capitalism is everywhere grasping the importance of humouring them, and enlisting them among its auxiliaries. Thus the more industry a country acquires, the more vulnerable it becomes to US influence, the readier to attach itself to the hegemony.

Contradictions within capitalism, never purely economic, do not vanish when it extends itself into fresh fields and pastures new. When US capital breeds subsidiary industries in its "colonies", its object is to turn out cheaper goods there than it can produce at home, for the local market and others near by. But these markets quickly become inadequate, larger ones are needed, economic requirements may come in conflict with ideology. Brazil has been offering sugar to Russia and China; American-financed firms in Argentina have been clamouring for trade to be allowed with Cuba, so that they can sell cars there. In June 1974 Argentina made a big trade agreement with the Soviet Union. Since America itself is moving in the same direction, it cannot well forbid its satellites to do so. Its reluctant drift towards a lifting of bans on Cuba, not from any change of heart but under this roundabout influence of American capital abroad, is very typical of the country today. It is also testimony that Victorian faith in trade as the great peacemaker, the bringer-together of nations, was not always and altogether mistaken, grotesquely wrong though it has often been.

In 1971 the revolt of East Bengal against the domination of West Pakistan, which had exploited it as a colony ever since the country emerged in 1947, furnished a test of Nixonian prescriptions for Asia. It revealed deplorably little change in the philosophy of repression, but a highly curious dovetailing of it with the new tactic of an understanding with Peking. Erratic and heavy-handed, the new diplomacy imperilled thereby its aim of an understanding with Moscow.

Pakistan had quickly settled down to "stable" rule by army and bureaucracy, of the kind so welcome to America with its Metternichian worship of Order; all the more by contrast with an India disgracefully democratic and tolerant of socialists and non-aligned. Washington took Pakistan under its patronage, liberally bestowed guns and tanks on it, invested in its economy. The alliance never worked well, for reasons that some American commentators have lately explored,[33] and Pakistan made a second, morganatic marriage with China—when such a thing was still anathema. Yet the flow of arms went on, as if by force of inertia, or as if Washington could not find it in its heart to deprive any right-wing dictatorship, however erring, of bullets—it would be like denying holy communion to a fellow-Christian. In 1971 the crisis took it by surprise. Why the myriad-faceted insect-eyes of its innumerable scouts and spies should leave it so much in the dark about what anyone conversant with Pakistan could have told it, must seem strange. But insect eyes do not see clearly, and Americans in Pakistan lived in self-isolating seclusion, with food flown daily from Karachi to Lahore for fear of germs. American dread of germs in Asiatic water, and of political germs in the Asiatic air, must have some common psychological roots.

When East Bengal, led by Mujibur Rahman, finally demanded autonomy, General Yahya Khan—not only by name reminiscent of Swift's Yahoos—turned the army loose in a campaign of frightfulness which may have destroyed half a million lives and driven nine million refugees over the border into India. Ironically enough, Mujib and his followers had thought themselves sure of American sympathy. They were respectably middle-class, with a popularity free from taint of socialism that elsewhere in the "third world" has been so painfully hard to find. It could even be conjectured at the time that the Chinese were egging on Yahya Khan and his butchers because they feared an American design to detach Bangla Desh and turn it into an anti-Chinese base. Nixon was, on the contrary, already meditating an arrangement with China; but in the policies of a country such as America, in the hands of such men as him and Kissinger, the better things are bound to be mixed up with the sordid and brutal. As vice-president, Nixon had been a strenuous partisan of the policy of arming Pakistan to the teeth—or fangs. Possibly in the night-watches he indulged in fancies about Yahya Khan as another Abraham Lincoln, defying secessionist rebels and their foreign abetters. More practically, he was acting in the spirit of his doctrine of devolution. Any strong-arm régime prepared to help itself against subversion would be helped by America; and Pakistan like Brazil was a good specimen of the kind of country he looked to as buttress of order in its own region. Its bosses could easily play on fears that an East Bengal rid of their control would be a vacuum for communism to flow into.[34]

Nixon had to brazen out a swelling chorus of condemnation, in Europe and in America itself where Senator Kennedy made himself the mouthpiece of protest. If Nixon and Kissinger privately thought it hypocritical of Americans, with so many My Lai's of their own behind them, to be making a fuss about massacres in Bangla Desh, they may have had some warrant. All the same, it was a welcome token of American opinion becoming more alive to the realities of power-politics and army rule. It is always easier to recognize sin in others than in ourselves. But a nation cannot find its way to virtue solely by condemning foreign vice. Nixon's crimes of 1971 did not hinder his electoral victory of 1972. And indignation about Bengal had few echoes about Chile in 1973. Meanwhile the doublings and twistings of Nixon and Kissinger in their efforts to evade the pressure on them gave a good view of that pair of artful dodgers in action. The same talents and tricks required to manoeuvre America into some newer and better courses could be utilized to keep it tied up in old bad ones. They contended, with puzzling logic, that if they stopped equipping Yahya Khan with the means of killing Bengalis, they would lose the influence over him which they pretended to be using, or intending to use at some future time, in favour of moderation. It might equally be maintained that by making guns freely available to all criminals at home in the US the government is able to exercise a restraining influence over them, and keep the annual number of murders in Detroit to no more than five times the total in Ulster. On 14 October the Senate Foreign Affairs Committee voted to halt supplies to Pakistan. Nixon had already evaded a resolution of the House of Representatives, and doubtless counted on doing the same with this. The science of democratic government is, after all, knowing how to throw dust in the public's eyes for its own good.

Democratic America was joining hands with communist China to prop up Yahya Khan: elasticity, on both sides, could scarcely go further. Very typical of Kissinger's *modus operandi* was his visit to Yahya Khan at Islamabad, and his furtive trip from there by air to Peking. He like Dulles is always flying about the planet, but whereas Dulles clove the air like a knight of old on snorting warhorse, Kissinger flits to and fro like a witch on broomstick. The announcement of Nixon's forthcoming visit to Peking followed, as if of Birnam Wood coming to Dunsinane. It was designed to make both India and Russia turn pale; it had the opposite effect of pushing them together, despite many reservations on each side. On 9 August they signed a treaty which gave India the guarantee against isolation that allowed it to carry out its intervention in East Bengal in December, and end the reign of terror.

As if they had not done enough to jeopardise *détente* with Russia, Nixon and Kissinger at the last moment made a clumsy move of their own towards intervention, by moving a squadron of the Seventh Fleet into the Bay of Bengal, with an oblique threat of action at Chittagong "to protect US interests". They may well have had in mind the fraudulent Tonking Bay incident which gave President Johnson his pretext for bombing North Vietnam. India ignored the threat, and it fell flat. It threw a forbidding light none the less on the new diplomacy, and on the perils there must be when a super-power's policies are left to be conducted in such hide-and-seek, or hole-and-corner, fashion, because —as happened with the Kaiser's Germany—the country has been able to find no better way of managing them. Clearly the Nixon line of disengagement could turn into its opposite, deeper American involvement. The episode underlined also the undesirability of American naval power being intruded into the Indian Ocean. India and most of its neighbours have continued to dislike this, as calculated to turn one more sea into a cockpit. Just as predictably, Britain has been offering facilities for a US naval base at Diego Garcia island.

Divers Indian princes bore the hereditary title of *Farzand-i-khas-i-daulat-i-Inglisiya*, or Favoured Son of the English Empire. Among Asian rulers who might aspire to a similar American title nowadays the Shah of Iran is prominent, and the rapid growth of his wealth and ambition must help to console Washington for the deflating of Pakistan. He is a despot of the contemporary type congenial to American tastes, no sleepy feudalist but a wide-awake businessman; he is understood to spend large sums on influencing opinion and politicians in the West, particularly in the US. A strong impression has been spreading in Iran and the Middle East that it is the Shah who is being armed and coached as guardian of order in his part of the world, with strong forces ready to quell subversion beyond his borders as uncompromisingly as he has quelled all protest inside them. At Teheran in the summer of 1973 a gathering of vultures took place, a conference of high-ranking CIA men.

Here again Nixonian calculations may be in for some rude surprises. Professor Buchan noted the risks the West is running by its game of flooding the Middle East with weaponry: it might usher in a generation of army officers impatient of antediluvian modes of government, and it might well end in war between Iran and the Arabs.[35] While the advanced states have more or less agreed that fighting among themselves is no longer worth the candle, new aspirants like Iran are ready to take it up. To the Shah and his clique their Arab neighbours, beginning with Iraq, offer more tempting targets than any Soviet windmills; just as Pakistan was always wanting to make a dash at India and Kashmir, instead of keeping its American powder dry for the Russians. There are oil rivalries among Arab rulers too. During 1973, before the war with Israel turned things another way, it looked as though the potentates of the Gulf were getting ready for a fight over undersea oil reserves. This irresponsibility of adolescent feudal-capitalist régimes is compounded by the irresponsibility of their elders and betters in loading them down with masses of what they jocularly call "military hardware". Unable to refrain from this lucrative trade, the US cannot very well try to restrain the others. This is one prime way in which the looseness and laxness of its policy-making stands in the way of the American mission to keep the world safe for capitalism.

It is in south-east Asia that the American hegemony has always met with the most determined resistance, beyond its own strength to subdue. In Dulles' day it tried to mobilize Europe for the crusade, and in the Korean war it did manage to scrape up some small auxiliary contingents. In Vietnam it was left to fight virtually single-handed. Johnson gave the army a free hand, but the resort to unrestricted violence only discredited America, while its failure disheartened Americans. When Nixon took office the war had already gone sour; but he and the Pentagon were still hoping to win it, by widening the battlefield and finding back doors into North Vietnam.

For this the CIA—from whose ranks one could fancy Nixon to have graduated—had long been preparing the ground. Prince Sihanouk's overthrow came at the end of years of restless intrigue against him: in the eyes of the CIA, as of Dulles, the existence of a peaceful neutral Cambodia, owing nothing to their "protection", was something unnatural and indecent. In May 1970 Cambodia was invaded by South Vietnamese forces. Nixon was evidently in hopes that South Vietnam could not only be kept going, but could be made to help in policing Indochina as a whole. This move if successful could have linked up with the secret operations in Laos, the bombings and the enrolment of a mercenary force of hillmen by the CIA. The attempt misfired, however: the attack on Cambodia provoked not only sharp political protests but also, what Nixon would be far more sensitive to, a steep decline on Wall Street. War expenditure was beginning to be felt by the economy no longer as a pleasant stimulus, but as a poison, like arsenic prescribed in excess. Militarily too things went wrong.

There were still diehards in America like Senator Goldwater, who was bloodthirstily bent on war to the end and professed entire indifference to world opinion. He cared nothing about whether America was loved, he declared, so long as it was respected—by which he obviously meant *feared*.[36] But American hegemony could not afford to present itself quite so naked and unashamed. Moreover in 1972 Nixon had to think of getting himself re-elected, and this meant finding a way to extricate himself, or appear to be extricating the country, from a war which some Americans were ashamed of and most were tired of, without admitting defeat. He was obliged to work towards withdrawal of US troops, and reliance on massive air bombardment. This proved unexpectedly successful in preventing the North Vietnam army from overrunning the South. Bombing techniques must have improved very greatly since the Korean war, where also the Americans had complete mastery of the air. They could not suppress guerrillas, but guerrillas could not capture towns. If, therefore, President Thieu were supplied with enough bombs, and could be taught how to use them, Washington might hope to keep him in power indefinitely. It would be a simpler matter to train him to keep the home front under control. In the recesses, as Burke said of Haider Ali, of a mind capacious of such things, Thieu had been devising his own ghoulish modes of dealing with enemies. His "tiger-cages", one of the horrors of our nightmarish century, are said to have been put in shape for him by an American firm of designers, and aptly symbolize the programme of leaving it to native jailors to keep the flag of free enterprise flying.

The limited-liability policy followed the precedent set by Eisenhower, who took office under a necessity of ending the Korean war; he managed to make a draw of it, and then to consolidate South Korea as an American dependency, with a US garrison. Nixon's strategy of "Vietnamization" had to carry Eisenhower's maxim, "Set Asians to fight Asians", further. It went with the decision to abandon conscription in America, as a burden which the affluent society was unwilling to bear, and which was bringing grist to the anti-imperialist mill. No longer would the US send large armies of its own into "colonial" wars. Instead it would conscript more natives, through its local dictators. There has been an echo of the "Vietnamizing" idea in the Rev. Paisley's proposal to "Ulsterise" the war in Ireland, on the ground that "It will take Ulstermen to defeat the IRA."[37]

America was delighted to be left to forget all about Vietnam. In February 1974 a journalist recalled that five years earlier there were 700,000 Americans in south-east Asia, spending six thousand million pounds a year, yet now Vietnam had been "transformed, almost overnight, from a national obsession into a forgotten irrelevance".[38] Nixon and Thieu were equally happy to be left to go on fighting their war. Kissinger had given one of his negotiating displays, and signed something that looked like a peace treaty, which Thieu scarcely pretended to take seriously. It was a fine exhibition of the tactics of making a great show of spring-cleaning, while leaving most of the dust to settle where it was before.

The tacticians could reckon comfortably on the shortness of public memory, but how far their bogus settlement will last is more doubtful. Vested interests have of course grown up round the Thieu government, battening on corruption and the endless golden tide of dollars. But as compared with those accumulated by industrial growth, in a country like Brazil, or even South Korea, they are merely noxious weeds, like those Chiang Kai-shek depended on with such dismal success in the Chinese civil war. Here and in the neighbouring lands, those Balkans of eastern Asia, America cannot, even if it wished to, impose any liberalizing measures on men like Thieu and Park, who can keep themselves in power only by terror. Thailand has made a start at liberalizing itself, with the dismissal lately of the reigning military clique after student demonstrations. In South Korea too there is a militant student movement, largely Christian, whose members face chronic danger; if their country happened to be the Soviet Union, their names would ring round the world. In Laos, by the early months of 1974, America had reluctantly to call off its CIA bulldogs and leave the war to reach an inglorious end; in Cambodia it was having to shore up a puppet régime very much on the defensive.

In the Middle East the Nixon-Kissinger system was to be put to its other grand test. There American hegemony was hampered from the first by one of those haphazard oddities that have often helped to shape imperial history: the presence in Palestine of an intrusive settler-population, an anomaly like the white colony in Rhodesia. Accidents of history determined that Israel should be built up into a warlike State by American arms and money. American prestige came to be tied to its success; and to many Americans, as well as to all Arabs and Russians, it represented a bridge-head of US power in the Middle East. It had many claims to be Washington's first choice as local partner or under-strapper. It showed a penchant for some of America's own methods of self-assertion. In January 1973, just after a massive bombing of Hanoi, Israeli planes were bombing villages in Syria. Before the October 1973 fighting some Israelis were proclaiming the right of the civilized world to take oil by force from Arabs who attempted to withhold it; and it cannot be doubted that the same thought was occurring to the Pentagon, and that there were "contingency plans"—as burglars nowadays call them—with a spirited part reserved in them for the Israeli army.

Unluckily there was the fatal objection that any employment of Israeli troops by the US would unite every tribe and sect of Arabs against them both. A policeman must have at least part of the public he is patrolling on his side. A Brazilian army helping to put down a left-wing revolt in Uruguay would have the wealthier Uruguayans on its side, in spite of some linguistic and temperamental disparity. Between the Vietnamese and their neighbours to the west the gulf is far deeper, a fact overlooked by Nixon when he launched his invasion of Cambodia; but it is trifling compared with that between Israelis and Arabs. By backing Israel through thick and thin, America goaded the whole region into those dangerous thoughts that the mission of its hegemony everywhere was to stifle. Without this, Soviet influence could scarcely have got a footing—a footing that has always been slippery, and not worth having except as a bar to America covering the Middle East with war-bases.

When it came to the point of Nixon seeking a *modus vivendi* with Moscow, American interests suffered afresh, because Zionism like a barking Cerberus stood in the way. In the second half of 1970 Washington was reported to be more and more annoyed at Israeli outcries about alleged Egyptian violations of the last cease-fire agree-ment, because these outcries were taken as an attempt to frustrate any compromise between America and the USSR. If the world wants peace, Mrs Meir once declared, Israel does not intend to be the paschal lamb. The alternative, that the rest of the human race should risk being made the sacrifice for Israel's survival, was evidently quite acceptable to her, and to Zionism. Small tough peoples afire with *sacro egoismo* always try to set one big Power against another, as Serbia did in 1914.

Altogether, America's wholesale, uncritical, and hugely expensive backing of the wrong horse—from the point of view of its own fortunes in the Middle East—has been the supreme example of how a lobby, a sectional interest, can acquire a stranglehold over US foreign policies in its chosen field. The Algerian *colons* had zealous allies in France, the Rhodesian settlers had and have in Britain, but since the days of Sinbad and the Old Man of the Sea there has never been anything equal to the loyal American devotion ensured to Israel by Zionism in America. Its propaganda and influence, through a thousand capillary ducts, have been marshalled with the same redoubtable skill as the Israeli army. As a result, American policy in the Middle East has for many years been Zionist policy, just as in the Far East for years it was China Lobby policy, or in Guatemala United Fruit Company policy. After the 1973 fighting Israel accused Europe, with remarkable effrontery, of letting itself be "blackmailed" by the oil-rich Arabs. In reality it is Israel that has all along, through Zionism, blackmailed the West. In reality also, no policy could have been more unfavourable to Israel, on a broad view of its future.

The latest Middle Eastern war showed America's position blowing up in its face. Nixon and Kissinger went on backing Israel, as in 1971 they went on backing Pakistan: these indiarubber men have been astonishingly rigid and conventional until hard facts have jolted them out of their grooves and forced them to manoeuvre. Again, in all this they faithfully epitomize their country. Threats emanated from Washington, aircraft-carriers and marines were deployed. Finally, on 25 October, all US forces were put on alert, as a menace to Russia. It was a repetition on a more dangerous scale of the crudely theatrical gesture two years before in the Bay of Bengal. World peace was being gambled with in an effort to cover up failure—and, more freakish still, to distract attention from the latest Watergate scandal. Meanwhile America had been making Europe its accomplice in its private war by using NATO bases as supply-dumps for Israel; true, Europe had invited such treatment by letting Portugal use NATO equipment for years for bombing African villages. When European governments jibbed at this flagrant misuse of the hegemony for a totally irrational purpose, they were reprimanded for not standing loyally by their leader. Whatever Nixon and Kissinger have brought into American diplomacy, diplomatic manners are no part of it; they hectored Europe in the same style as if they were dealing with yellow men or black men.

In Britain the Labour party raised no objection to this, but showed the most cheerful alacrity in falling in with the Zionist outcry, and orders from Washington. Its leaders (and the Liberal party's) perorated as fatuously as if Israel were the brightest jewel in the British crown, instead of one of a good many blots on the imperial record, and loudly demanded arms for it. Fortunately (for once in a way) the Tories were in power, and the Foreign Office (to give the devil his due) seems to have a wholesome mistrust of Zionism. But there was an unedifying spectacle of Labour and Liberal spokesmen, and Tory MPs with insecure seats, competing for Zionist votes; it threw into relief one of the weak spots of parliamentary democracy. Campaigning by minority groups has been indispensable for bringing about all kinds of reforms. But Britain is now faced, as the US has long been, with electioneering by multiple national groups, which differ from political or social movements in being concerned, not with principles of right and wrong, but with pushing the claims of some foreign people or State, wrong or right. In 1971 West Pakistanis in Britain were mobilised to demonstrate in favour of the villainous Pakistan government and its terroristic rule in East Bengal. None of our national minorities, from the earliest, the Irish, to the latest, can or should be silenced. But their political interventions ought to be seen clearly for what they are, and none of them should be allowed to speak in the name of British national parties, as was happening last year.

Nixon and Kissinger were left with the task of rigging up some sort of settlement for the Middle East which, like the one in Vietnam, would look like a genuine compromise, while giving away as little as possible. For this school of statesmanship short-term effects, the *trompe-l'oeil* arts of the showman, are the chief stock in trade. Their great asset was the undignified haste of Sadat to find an excuse for breaking with Egypt's old protector Russia, and enroll himself as a campfollower of America; one more reminder that America could have had a very easy time all along in the Middle East, but for its Israeli encumbrance. Kissinger gave a spectacular display of darting to and fro between Tel Aviv and Damascus, a diplomat on a flying trapeze, to rig up a second cease-fire, and Nixon gratefully took a holiday from domestic unpleasantnesses to make a triumphal tour of the Middle East. At Cairo it was a true Roman holiday, with the multitude making the welkin ring with its applause. *If Caesar had stabbed their mothers, they would have done no less* . . . sad proof of how little political education Nasserite rule and Soviet patronage have given the Egyptians in all these years.

The evident aim has been to make it appear, as in Vietnam, that the trouble is over, banished by Richard Nixon the exorcist, and the public can go back to sleep, as it is always so desirous of doing. A lasting settlement of Palestine issues is impossible without considerable withdrawals by Israel; Israel cannot be made to budge so long as the Zionist phalanx in Washington refuses to do so; a president under the shadow of impeachment is very ill qualified to tackle the incubus. Zionism continues to work unchecked against *détente*, as a kind of "revisionism" fatal to its more extravagant demands, by a wild, whirling campaign of anti-Soviet propaganda, and by obstructing the trade agreement due to be made with the Soviet Union. To be sure, the Soviet government's conduct lays it open to some of these attacks; but the "free world" has lamentably little moral right to make them.

Recriminations went on between Europe and America, each resentful of the other acting without consulting it. There were threats to remove American troops from Europe, leaving it to be gulped down by the Russian shark. On 14 March Kissinger made some sort of apology for the vivacity of his diatribes, but left no doubt of his severe displeasure; on 19 March Nixon deplored some indiscreet talk by Congressmen, but added that "there is growing in America a new sense of isolation after Korea, after Vietnam". All this suggested the advent of a "polycentric" management of the "free world", such as the communist camp has been fumbling towards. It would fit the mood of ordinary people, for whom in both camps the idea of any "leading nation" has ceased to carry conviction, in the same way that political leadership inside most countries—socialist as well as capitalist—has lost its gloss.

All the same, the progress of communist governments (as distinct from parties) towards equality of status has so far been unpromising. Western Europe has learned some things from the US, and ought to have some things to teach in return, but it has first to strike out some common outlook, or working hypothesis, of its own,—and not a sterile anti-Soviet one, such as the Chinese showed their hopes of when they welcomed Mr Heath in Peking in June as rapturously as Mr Nixon was welcomed in Cairo, and about as rationally. Europe's united front after the 1973 war fizzled out quickly under Washington's frown. France for a moment emerged as genuine defender of European self-respect; unluckily it has done far too little in other ways to earn European confidence, having been far too egotistic, too petulant, too unscrupulous in its sales of arms. Britain and Germany scuttled, leaving the French in the lurch; and soon Labour was back in Downing Street, in its familiar posture of the yokel pulling his forelock to the Yankee squire. Its flight from Europe may have stirred some memories in Washington of how in 1814, when the US was at war with Britain, there was talk in New England of seceding from the Union and rejoining the Tory motherland.

We are left with an erratic, unreformed America, which has made only a beginning at breaking away from its recent past. In most respects Nixon and Kissinger have done no more than try to plug a leaky hull, by methods as hasty and unsavoury as those of the celebrated *plumbers* set to work in Washington by Nixon to stop leakages of unsavoury information. On the whole the balance-sheet of their stewardship has been a disastrous one, so far as any prospects of a better future are concerned. Capitalism still holds sway over most of its empire, but the cost in repression, violence, bloodshed, grows more enormous year by year. Only an extraordinary blindness allows its apologists to go on talking as if all the tyranny on earth belonged to the Soviet Union.

Against any more radical revision of American policies, the blockages are many. There is some formidable body to bar the way to any and every reform, at home and abroad. All American citizens' lives are at risk because any of them can buy any guns they like: everyone knows it, but it goes on because a strong lobby defends it, and other strong forces do not challenge this because they do not want to be challenged in their own citadels. So long as this "Live and let live"—or *die*— philosophy prevails, the great corporations will exercise something like the power of a feudal baronage over the economy and the national life. We can only take refuge in the thought that American history has not come to an end; and although any prospect of a socialist United States is as remote as ever, there is room within the confines of free enterprise for more sensible and far-sighted choices, as well as less.

If Europe has found itself, to its surprise, better off without its colonies, it may not be out of the question for the US to conclude that it could do better without its present "empire". It *might* decide to help the backlands to grow and prosper, instead of keeping them stagnant. It has in fact begun doing this, here and there, though in a haphazard and politically reactionary style. It was in some such style that better living standards first reached the masses in the US itself, higher wages and police clubbings mixed up together. America did after all pioneer the capitalism of high wages and buoyant home markets, or what might be called "prosperity capitalism" by comparison with the "welfare capitalism" that has been the line of development of a more paternalistic Europe. Capitalism has shown itself capable of variation and evolution much wider than either conservatives or Marxists have been willing to admit. For America to take the lead in raising the living standards and purchasing power of the backlands would be a repetition of that "big leap" on a broader stage; though it could and should be under-taken a great deal more deliberately, and more humanely.

Any such better tendency may be reinforced by expanded commercial intercourse with the communist countries, and—more remarkable, and calling for much new thinking on both sides—large-scale invest-ment of Western capital in the USSR. If this happens, capitalism will be taking on another novel role. It will be learning, willy-nilly, that the communist countries now represent far more worth-while customers than if they were still languishing in their pre-communist stagnation; and possibly coming to admit that socialism may, in some contexts at least, be better qualified than free enterprise to guide backward countries into modernity. Hitherto America has been deafened by its own blood-and-thunder denunciation of communism, unable to recognize its strength as an ideal holding out to many lands the hope of a new life. Marxism, it must be added, was for long equally unable to perceive the continuing productive energy of capitalism, especially in the US where the public esteem that free enterprise enjoys is not wholly the result of indoctrination. Russia is now realizing its want of some of the achievements of Western technology; its government is still reluctant to admit the moral force of liberalism—less surprisingly, seeing how often this is overlaid by Western hypocrisy.

Any speculations about America renouncing imperialism may seem to be ruled out of court by recollection that Earl Browder, then secretary of the CP, indulged in them so hopefully about the end of the Second World War, and was soon proved disastrously mistaken. Even so, the US has gone through a good many chastening experiences since then, and civilization is thirty years older. When it is argued, as by many Marxists it is, that capitalist America is subject to a categorical imperative driving it towards imperialism and war, the more necessitarian element in Marx's thinking is visible, not to say something of Darwin's also. If it was not too bold an effort of human will to set out to transform feudal China into a socialist society, it cannot be beyond the bounds of reason to hope that America may be turned into a peaceful society.

But any effort to foretell, any indulgence in the American pseudo-science of Futurology—or astrology, as it used to be called—grows steadily more hazardous. In our day variables like new technical discoveries may at any time transform situations, as human accidents of birth and death have always done. All that can be attempted is a realistic weighing up of alternative possibilities and their consequences; this, if it can grow into a habit of nations, may make the difference between human survival and extinction.

NOTES

1. L. Trotsky, *Europe and America: Two Speeches on Imperialism* (New York ed., 1971), p. 3.
2. *The Listener*, 22 November 1973, p. 696.
3. G. Reimann, *Patents for Hitler* (London ed., 1945), pp. 16–17.
4. See e.g. *The Guardian* (London, 14 November 1973).
5. *The Listener*, 15 November 1973, p. 656.

6.   C. A. Thomson and W. H. C. Laves, *Cultural Relations and U.S. Foreign Policy* (Indiana University, 1963), p. 125.
7.   H. G. Gelber, *The Australian-American Alliance. Costs and Benefits* (London, 1968), p. 130. Cf. the critique of the alliance in J. G. Gregory, *The West and China, an historical perspective* (Melbourne, 1971), pp. 15ff.
8.   *The Listener*, 6 December 1973, pp. 776, 778.
9.   *The Listener*, 15 November 1973, p. 654.
10. See J. A. Schumpeter, *Capitalism, Socialism, and Democracy* (3rd English ed., 1950), p. 55.
11. Henry James, *The Portrait of a Lady* (1881), Ch. 20.
12. W. Lippmann, *U.S. Foreign Policy* (London, 1943), p. 24.
13. *The Listener*, 29 November 1973, pp. 742–3.
14. *The Guardian*, 21 May 1970.
15. My colleague Mr O. D. Edwards, who knows America well, pointed this out to me. I am grateful to him for reading my draft and giving me many comments and suggestions.
16. E. A. Ritter, *Shaka Zulu* (London ed., 1958), p. 283.
17. Count Paul von Hoensbroech, *Fourteen Years a Jesuit* (English ed., London, 1911), Vol. II, pp. 373–4.
18. *The Guardian*, 31 December 1973.
19. Victor Marchetti, summarized by S. Winchester in *The Guardian*, 14 January 1974.
20. W. A. Williams, *The Tragedy of American Diplomacy* (revised ed., New York, 1962), p. 306.
21. J. K. Galbraith, *Ambassador's Journal. A Personal Account of the Kennedy Years* (London, 1969).
22. E. R. Black, *Alternative in Southeast Asia* (London, 1969).
23. See P. S. Foner, *American Labor and the Indochina War* (New York, 1971).
24. *The Listener*, 29 November 1973, p. 740.
25. Ibid., p. 742.
26. Theses of the Executive Committee, 15 August 1921.
27. This is another point that I owe to Mr O. D. Edwards.
28. *The Listener*, 29 November 1973, p. 742.
29. *The Listener*, 13 December 1973, p. 816.
30. C. Roper, in *The Guardian*, 20 March 1974.
31. Cf. R. Miliband, "The Coup in Chile", in *Socialist Register*, 1973, p. 459.
32. R. Gott, in *The Guardian*, 27 April 1974.
33. See e.g. W. J. Barnds, *India, Pakistan, and the Great Powers* (London, 1972); W. Wilcox, *The Emergence of Bangladesh* (Washington, D.C., 1973).
34. A Pakistani apologist, S. M. Burke, makes use of this argument, in *Pakistan's Foreign Policy. An Historical Analysis* (London, 1973), p. 396.
35. *The Listener*, 13 December 1973, p. 817.
36. Television, 8 January 1973.
37. *The Guardian*, 25 April 1974. On Nixon's idea of disengagement, cf. R. Butwell, *Southeast Asia Today and Tomorrow* (2nd ed., London, 1969), pp. 198ff.
38. T. D. Allman, in *The Guardian*, 6 February 1974.

THE SECOND COMING OF DANIEL BELL*

George Ross

Daniel Bell: *The Coming of Post Industrial Society: A Venture in Social Forecasting* (Heinemann, 1974), pp. 507. £5.50.

The Coming of Post Industrial Society by Daniel Bell is subtitled a "venture in social forecasting". Since the book has been greeted as a major turning point in sociological analysis by many, we might do well to recall for a moment one of Bell's earlier "ventures in social forecasting", *The End of Ideology*. Appearing at the end of the 1950s, *The End of Ideology* was an important document, but hardly because of the astuteness of its "forecasting". In fact, the book's central thesis, that radical ideologies had lost their appeal in the West, was rapidly disproved by events. In retrospect, *The End of Ideology* was significant because it communicated an understanding of 1950s America widely held by the American liberal intelligentsia. In this perspective an economically powerful America had solved, or could solve, the very social problems which had, in earlier times, prompted "ideological" or "utopian" thinking. Because of this in America the social basis of "ideological" thinking no longer existed. This was even more the case because all experiments at acting out "utopian ideologies" elsewhere—and particularly in the Soviet Union—had led to more social unpleasantness than they had originally set out to remedy. As "social forecasting", then, *The End of Ideology* was ideology, the wishful thinking of a generation of intellectuals, scarred by the battles of the '30s and '40s, who had become respected and important figures in the prosperous Cold War America.

When considering *The Coming of Post Industrial Society* we should remember the lessons of *The End of Ideology*. In this earlier book Bell was wrong in his assessment of American society. More important than this, however, he spoke for a caste of American liberal intellectuals who shared his wrong-headedness. This caste perceived their world in the same ways Bell did, a world where capitalism was no longer capitalism, but "industrial society", a world in which the "soulful corporation", disinterested governmental bureaucracies and a democratic pluralist

* The help which came from Charlotte Weissberg was indispensable.

331

political system saw to it that the interests of all were represented and promoted.

The Coming of Post Industrial Society appears after a decade which called all of these liberal certainties into question. The astonished "discovery" of American poverty and racism was followed in short order by Vietnam and the "discovery" of American imperialism. A new American Left emerged to confront the liberal intelligentsia with powerful arguments which claimed that, not only was the American corporation not "soulful", but that, in its search for profits and super-profits it corrupted the very "soul" of American life, destroyed natural environments, polluted air and water, dictated foreign policies which justified any extreme of repression in the Third World and, in general, manipulated politics everywhere to implement corporate goals. *The Coming of Post Industrial Society* is, in its own way, one major attempt to answer these arguments. The contents of *The Coming* may or may not be "scientifically" convincing. This remains for us to ascertain. But, whatever their truth value, they will certainly be influential. The book must also be read, then, as a summation of, and rejoinder for, the 1960s made in the name of the American liberal intelligentsia by one of its most prominent figures, Daniel Bell. As one of Bell's American critics has noted, "when Daniel Bell declares that society has changed, it does not follow that it has done so. But it does follow that many people will think that it has."[1]

I

Before plunging into the substance of Bell's argument, it may help to comment briefly on his method of analysis. Bell suggests that modern societies can best be approached conceptually by dividing them into three separate spheres, the *social structure* (comprising the economy, technology and the occupational system), the *polity*, which "regulates the distribution of power and adjudicates the conflicting demands of individuals and groups", and the *culture*, the "realm of expressive symbolism and meaning" (p. 12). For each of these spheres it is the analyst's task to establish "ideal types" *à la* Max Weber, which will specify their central motivational and structural aspects or, in Bell's terms, their *axial principles* and *axial structures* (the energizing principles from which action flows and the "organizing frame" "around which other institutions are draped" (p. 10).

In *The Coming of Post Industrial Society* Bell does not claim to set up ideal typical maps for all three spheres in modern societies. Rather he is more narrowly concerned with what he calls the *social structural* sphere. He contends that profound changes in this sphere of American society (Bell considers America to be the vanguard of social change elsewhere) began to occur after World War II. He feels that such changes will, once their logic is followed through, cause an entirely new social order to emerge. In other words, for Bell, changes in the "axial principle" and "axial structures" of American social structure have begun which are of such profound import that they will transform America from an "industrial society" into a "post industrial society". In fact, such changes have already gone far enough, to Bell's mind, to permit "forecasting" the shape of things 30–50 years hence, when "post industrial society" will be a full-blown reality. Thus, in much the same way as Marx used evidence from 19th century capitalism to "forecast" changes leading towards socialism, Bell, using evidence from mid-20th century America, is attempting to "forecast" changes leading to "post industrial" society. The success of Bell's endeavour, even in its own terms, depends on his ability to make several different arguments. First of all, he must convince us with hard evidence that the social structural changes he sees as so important are really occurring. He must also demonstrate to us that the changes which he can document actually add up to the introduction of new "axial principles and structures" in the social structures of American society. After all, changes occur constantly in advanced capitalist societies. More often than not, however, they amount to new developments within broader structures which remain essentially the same. Bell must prove that the changes he specifies are "system transcending" rather than "system reinforcing" modifications.

Bell is quick to disclaim that his "forecasting" amounts to either prophecy or prediction. He is building an ideal type analysis on the basis of tendencies which he claims are already unfolding in American social structure. But his "forecasting" is confined to the *social structural* (economic, occupational) sphere. He eschews any precise forecasting for the *political* and *cultural* spheres which, he asserts, have their own "axial principles and structures". In Bell's words ". . . the concept of a post-industrial society is not a picture of a complete social order, it is an attempt to describe an axial change in the social structure (defined as the economy, the technology and the stratification system) of the society" (p. 119). These "axial changes" in social structure will, according to Bell, raise issues and pose questions for both the polity and the culture. But, since these spheres have their own inner logic, in the absence of analyses specific to polity and culture (which Bell does not claim to provide) how political and cultural agents will respond to the social structural changes Bell sees in process can only be a matter for speculation. As we shall see Bell does not hesitate to speculate. For the moment, however, suffice it to note that somewhere in the course of his analysis Bell must supply his readers with a convincing rationale for what appears to be his arbitrary division of the social world into three discrete parts. This is not a trivial methodological point. A conceptual choice to divide up society into three relatively autonomous sub-sectors could, very easily, become an *a priori* assumption that the real world is indeed divided up into three unrelated sub-worlds.

Thus Bell's use of the term *Post Industrial Society* is somewhat in-appropriate. Bell "forecasts" only for one sphere of the total American society. In the absence of "forecasts" for other spheres neither Bell nor the reader can proceed to construct a full model of post-industrial *society*. Indeed, in the absence of some further specification on Bell's part of the interrelationship of the separate spheres of social structure, polity and culture, it is hard to see how Bell can even allow himself theoretically to "forecast" axial change in the social structure to the degree he does. Since both polity and culture may, in Bell's under-standing, "feed back" on social structural developments to modify, or even block their unfolding, the actual shape of any "post-industrial society" must remain unknown. Yet Bell projects tendencies from contemporary American social structure into the next 30–50 years *as if* such tendencies will proceed unchecked and unmodified. It is obvious, however, that even if social structure, polity and culture can be analysed as three separate spheres each with their own specific "axial principles", they can hardly be seen as non-related. In order to be able to make sensible "forecasts", the analyst must be able to say something about their inter-relationship. And there would seem to be two basic possible kinds of inter-relationship. If polity and culture do have relative autonomy to act on the social structure, "forecasting" developments in social structure *as if* the actions of polity and culture will not affect them, might be merely an exercise. If, on the other hand, polity and culture are, in some way, derivative of social structure, the "projections" of the sort Bell makes are easier to justify, with Bell becoming, in process, a social structural determinist.

II

Enough of Bell's method, what of his argument? What is occurring in the sphere of social structure in America which makes Bell believe in the coming of "post industrial society"? Remember, Bell must first present us with evidence that certain things have already happened. Then he must provide us with a convincing argument that on the basis of what has already happened he has the right to "forecast" the unfolding of certain tendencies from the present situation towards the "post industrial society" which he foresees.

Bell begins by calling attention to certain changes which are already occurring in American society. Since World War II there has been a quite dramatic shift in the balance of economic activity from the primacy of goods production towards the production of all sorts of services (transportation, utilities, financial services, health, education, recreation, research, government, etc.). As Bell notes, 50% of the labour force and 50% of the Gross National Product in present day America involves service work. As a result of this shift, and the changed nature of economic activity which comes with it, important modifications in the American occupational structure have occurred. Blue collar domination of the work force (which Bell sees as one important identifying characteristic of "industrial" society) has been rapidly disappearing in the face of a rising white collar/service industry working population. The bulk of this broad group can only be labelled proletarian, and does not interest Bell greatly. The category which draws his special attention is that of "professional and technical persons". As he shows, the numbers of people in this category have increased remarkably since 1947 (doubled between 1947 and 1964, with a similar increase projected to 1975, when the group will include 13 million). This group is, of course, a heterogeneous one, composed mainly of school teachers, technical workers and engineers and social workers, whose only real unifying characteristic is similar educational credentials. Within this broad category Bell is most intrigued by an elite core of scientists and high level technical cadres (roughly those with postgraduate degrees). The source of his intrigue is a belief that this new elite intelligentsia has been the critical variable in the economic growth and change of the past 25 years. Science-based industry and science-based governmental problem solving have been, to Bell, the basic cause of recent economic transformations. And central to all of this has been the stratum of scientists.

Bell's "venture in social forecasting" is built on this new stratum of scientists. Beginning with the assumption that economic growth and change in the future will follow much the same pattern as that of the past 25 years (growing stress on service activities and on science-based techniques of innovating, planning and problem-solving), Bell foresees the eventual emergence of fundamentally new social structural forms. In "industrial society"—a goods producing society—the "axial principle" was "economizing" for economic growth. In recent years, with the expansion in the scientific and technical stratum a new "axial principle" has been creeping into the pores of American social structure, that of "theoretical knowledge". As the shift towards the service sector and towards the centrality of "theoretical knowledge" progresses in years to come, the outlines of a new social structure will become increasingly clearer. "Theoretical knowledge" will replace "economizing" for growth as the "axial principle" of social structural action and become the key source of innovation and policy orientation for both the economy and government. When, at some point in the next three to five decades, the shift towards the primacy of "theoretical knowledge" has been completed, "post industrial society" will have superseded "industrial society".

It is not only the introduction of "theoretical knowledge" as the axial principle of social structure which marks the coming of "post industrial society", it is also the rise to power in the social structure of the occupational stratum which monopolizes the possession of such knowledge. The functional centrality and consequent power of this new intelligentsia in an economy increasingly dominated by science-based methods of production, decision-making and social control will bring decisive changes. Bell asserts that theoretical knowledge, the "axial principle" of post industrial society, is controlled by people with a strikingly different *ethos* (in Max Weber's sense) and institutional base than the presently dominant business elites of industrial society. The *ethos* of the new scientific elite is professionalism, not profit. Its institutional homes are the university and research institute, not the corporation. In the longer run, the effect of such a group moving into key positions of social structural power will be to move post industrial society away from the economizing focus of industrial society (dedication to the optimal allocation of resources among competing ends) towards a *sociologizing* ethos in which profit maximization on the market declines in favour of the calculation of maximal welfare for all.

These are the bare bones of Bell's "forecast", then. Recent changes in the social structure of American society have made theoretical knowledge of crucial importance for economic progress. By projecting these changes into the future, Bell foresees the possessors of theoretical power gaining greater and greater access to the levers of social structural power and influence. Since the new professional-scientific-technical stratum is the carrier of a new social structural ethos, its growing power will involve the progressive infusion of this new ethos into all of social life. When theoretical knowledge assumes its full centrality, when those who monopolize it are consequently propelled into social structural dominance, when their ethos becomes the "axial principle" of social structure, the end product, 30–50 years hence, will be post industrial society.

The careful reader will recognize, hidden under Bell's futurism and Weberian trappings, a very familiar old argument. Bell sees the professional-scientific-technical caste coming to social power in much the same way as many of his American sociological predecessors saw the managers coming to power in the '50s. For this reason it may be worth pausing a moment to reconsider the "managerial revolution" or "ownership-control" arguments. The proponents of the managerial revolution thesis began by granting that Karl Marx had been right, for his time, in connecting private ownership of capital, the exploitation of workers, and bourgeois control over the state. However, decisive changes occurring in the 20th century radically altered the structural reality of capitalist societies, at least according to the managerial revolution theorists. The rise of the modern large joint-stock corporation diffused actual property rights while at the same time a stratum of professional managers developed. Both processes led ultimately to the divorce of ownership (in the hands of large numbers of stockholders and *rentiers*, of whom very few owned enough stock to claim a voice in the firm's direction), from control (now firmly lodged in the hands of the managers). Some versions of the argument were content to stop here, but the more ambitious managerialists had much more to say. To them, since managers were professional administrators and technicians of bureaucracy, the alleged divorce of ownership from control implied a shift in the *ethos* of the large corporation. Profit maximization at all costs was the obsession of the old owner-entrepreneur. The new manager cared much more about growth, performance and size, and even had some concern for communal welfare. In these stronger versions of managerialism the main result of the split between ownership and control was that capitalism ceased being capitalism (having lost the identity of private property and economic power plus the profit motive) and became something new and different, often labelled "industrial society".[2]

The "managerial revolution" thesis is, of course, one of the dogmas of post World War II American liberal thought. This does not make it true however. There is considerable evidence that propertied interests still play a major role in deciding the destinies of major corporations, even if stock ownership has been to some degree diffused. There is also a great deal of evidence that managers of top corporations tend to become large property owners in their own right during their progress towards the tenure of managerial positions. On the basis of a now extensive literature there is presently enough doubt about the validity of the simple ownership/control divorce thesis that the question must be considered still open.[3] That managerialism has led great corporations away from tried and true capitalist goals of profit maximization is not an open question at all. Anyone in the least bit familiar with the workings of American business must be aware that corporate profits are *the* goal of corporate endeavours, whether such endeavours be directed by owners or managers. It may well be that modern large corporations have evolved somewhat different perspectives on how to maintain and maximize profits but the goal of ultimately making as much money as possible remains.

Thus, despite managerialism, capitalism remains alive and easily recognizable. The intellectual lesson to be remembered from the long "managerial revolution" controversy is significant for our present purposes, however. The rise of a new occupational category with a degree of functional indispensability in the social structure (managers) was greeted by many analysts as the harbinger of a new economic ethic. In point of fact, however, the rise of the managerial elite within Western capitalism did not mean the coming to social power of a group with radically different objectives from earlier owner/capitalists. While the structure and administration of capitalist enterprises may well have been changed somewhat at this juncture in Western economic history towards bureaucratic rationalization and routinization (due probably as much to increasing size as to the arrival of managers) capitalism remained capitalism. The fundamental characteristics of the capitalist mode of production remained clearly identifiable. Managers did not transform capitalism. Rather they were absorbed into a system of organization and incentives vastly more powerful than any autonomous ethic which they may have brought with them. The managers were *used by*, and *became the agents of*, monopoly capital. How could it have been otherwise?

All of this is important because Bell's own argument both presupposes, and is analogous to, the "managerial revolution" theory.[4] It is hard to envisage circumstances in which the fate of Bell's professional-scientific-technical vanguard will be much different from that of the managers. Their indispensability as suppliers of theoretical knowledge to the capitalist corporation and state (if, indeed, Bell is correct in his "forecast" that such knowledge will become indispensable) is of the same order as the indispensability of the administrative skills brought to capitalism earlier by the professional managers. In the case of the managers, the indispensability of their skills did not entitle them to a chance to transform society (which they did not want to do anyway!). Likewise, the indispensability of the theoretical knowledge of the new intelligentsia does not mean that it will acquire decisive power or that its particular *ethos* will be enshrined as the dominant ethic of the social structure.

Bell's assertion that the new intelligentsia will come to power and change the ethos of American social structure is, then, a huge sociological *non sequitur*. Bell's failure to recognize that the society which he sees as the vanguard of "post-industrial society" is, in fact, the vanguard of world capitalism is his undoing. The hold of capitalism and its ethic of profit maximization on American society is immensely powerful. American and multi-national corporate giants face an ever more exiguous international environment. This, plus market control, makes greater planning, "forecasting" and, perhaps, the use of theoretical knowledge, both possible and necessary. The same factors have promoted the creation of a bureaucratized and interventionist state. Given the obvious and immense social power in America of huge capitalist economic units the odds are overwhelming that Bell's professional scientific-technical caste will make its peace with advanced capitalism quite easily. Nothing about this group as it presently exists in the USA would indicate the contrary. The pursuit of "theoretical knowledge" in the USA, and the consequent expansion of the stratum engaged in this pursuit has been promoted, encouraged, directed and financed either by the US government, usually with "defence" objectives in mind (connected with a foreign policy designed, in the main, to keep the world free for US corporate enterprise) or by American corporate interests. On the face of its record since 1945, the prospects of the pro-fessional-scientific-technical caste as the carrier of an autonomous, system-transforming, ethic are rather bad. Indeed, throughout most of this period, this stratum has had little difficulty in subscribing to the objectives set for it by American capitalism (although the Indochina war did dampen the enthusiasm of certain sectors in the group, it must be said).

In summary, then, it is quite insufficient for Bell to predict the coming of a fundamental change in American social order simply because theoretical knowledge is becoming more important in American social structure, and that a new occupational stratum with a monopoly on such knowledge is arising. When discussing change in America we are not discussing change in a vacuum. America is a flourishing capitalist order, in which a hegemonic class of property owners, supported by a resourceful stratum of professional administrators, in control of American ideological life and with determinant levers of governmental power is unlikely to see much virtue in ceding its place to a new intel-ligentsia. How will the professional-technical-scientific caste make its way to the top? Here Bell has very little to say. He must do much better than he does to establish that this stratum is indeed the carrier of a new, system-transforming, ethic in the face of the present lack of evidence that the world-view of this stratum is appreciably different from that of the existing American corporate elite. Even beyond this he must prove further that the ethic and institutions of American capitalism are, or will be, ready to give way to such new influences, if they can be proven to exist. There is next to no evidence from America which would indicate this to be true.

Since the USA remains the lynchpin and heartland of the world capitalist system, it would make a great deal more sense, on the basis of Bell's evidence, to "forecast" quite a different scenario. The chances are overwhelming that "theoretical knowledge" will be used in ways which will keep American capitalism intact. Likewise, the chances are overwhelming that the "intelligentsia stratum" which carries and develops such knowledge will end up serving, rather than transforming, American capitalist goals. Faced with the institutional strength and power of enticement of the American corporation and the American corporate liberal state, the independent ethos of the intelligentsia (to the extent that there is one) will, in all likelihood, prove weak indeed. In the absence of a political movement for socialism, to which sectors of this new intelligentsia might well be attracted, this "forecast," and not Bell's, seems most compelling. Bell's vision of the transition from "industrial" to "post industrial" society is, then, not very helpful. It might be in order on the basis of Bell's evidence to argue more humbly for the imminence of a shift from mass production capitalism to a more advanced stage of capitalism characterized by a greater degree of planning and the utilization of more "theoretical knowledge". But Bell does not make this argument.

Whatever one chooses to conclude about Bell's central "forecast", *The Coming of Post Industrial Society* presents the reader with several other dilemmas. We must remember, first, that Bell states clearly his intention to "forecast" only for the sphere of social structure. Yet, as he notes at the outset, the changes which he foresees in the social structural sphere will pose important issues and questions for both the polity and the culture, the other two important spheres in his analysis. His discussions of these issues and questions, and his speculation about the ways in which they will be addressed by the polity and culture, are well worth more detailed attention.

Despite the fact that Bell sees his new intelligentsia making inroads into politics through the penetration of governmental bureaucracies, he also foresees major obstacles to the maturation of "post industrial society" coming from the polity. According to Bell one of the inevitable by-products of the coming of "theoretical knowledge" as the axial principle of the social structure will be that major social choices will more and more be made outside the market economically and outside parliamentary exchange politically. The essence of planning and forecasting in both the economic and political spheres is to promote policy choices which transcend the short-term time perspectives of both the market and liberal parliamentary debate. As Bell notes, the market and parliamentary bargaining both have one great virtue. They lead people to perceive that basic social decisions are being made by "nature" (both the economic market and the pseudo-market of political goods which is liberal parliamentarism lend themselves ideally to the process of mystification definitively analysed by one K. Marx as commodity fetishism). In the emergent "post industrial" situation, such decisions will reemerge from the realm of "nature" and be attributable to identifiable elites, Bell's planners and technocrats making social choices according to consciously decided-upon criteria derived from "theoretical knowledge". The de-reification of major social options following in the wake of advancing theoretical knowledge will, Bell fears, stimulate new political activity among underlying groups. Bell anticipates that post industrial society will be a *communal* society politically. What he means is that collectivities based on occupation and status will be the main political forces. Since not all of these collectivities will possess, respect or understand the expertise of the professional-technical-scientific caste, the risk, according to Bell, is that the full benefits of this caste's superior rationality will be lost in political to-ing and fro-ing.

It is worth stopping on this point. The precise way Bell discusses the political question is very significant. As he puts it over and over, the political danger of post industrial society is "populism", the expressions of "resentment" by the "populace". Readers familiar with American history will be aware of the pejorative connotations of the term "populism". In American parlance, populism is a form of a political philistinism, luddite political activity engaged in during periods of great change by groups who do not understand what is going on, and desire, above all, to hold back the inevitable and, ultimately, to prevent progress. Nowhere in *The Coming of Post Industrial Society* (except perhaps in his *Coda*, where he discusses culture) do Bell's own values come out more clearly. *Bell clearly desires the coming of post-industrial society and believes that the rule of the professional-scientific-technical caste* (of which he considers himself an important member) *will be a benevolent one*. The problem he foresees is that this caste will increasingly make decisions publicly which will determine the fate of underlying groups in the population: these decisions, because they will be based on "theoretical knowledge" and rarified expertise, will not always be understood or approved by these same underlying groups. In short, Bell fears that the intelligentsia in power will face a serious legitimacy problem. Clearly, what Bell yearns for, and what he fears may not occur, is rule by the princes of technocracy. Since there is no real way in which this rule can exist democratically, Bell is faced with a considerable dilemma. He attempts to sweep this dilemma under the rug with a long discussion of meritocracy, concluding finally that a meritocratic society, as long as opportunity to rise socially is really open and equal, is a just society. The difficulty with such a conclusion is that even a true meritocracy need not be a democracy.

Here we needn't subscribe to Bell's "forecasting" about the rise of the new intelligentsia to be sensitive to some of the issues he raises. With the rise of monopoly capitalism and, in connection with it, of the interventionist bureaucratic state, there is a very real tendency for major social decisions to be taken out of the mystifying settings of market and parliament. Economic decisions by huge corporations can be less and less hidden by the market, since it is the essence of monopoly power to be able to by-pass market considerations. Political decisions by the representatives of such corporations and their allies can be less and less hidden by the obsolete liberal myth of a free political market place. In short, with the spread of monopoly capitalism, the economic and political power of big capitalist interests becomes more transparent. Despite the indefatigable efforts of such interests to keep ordinary people in a state of political somnolence, their rule becomes ever more likely to elicit conflictual responses from underlying social groups who feel victimized. Given the narrowing margin of manoeuvre of American capitalism in the world capitalist market it is likely that such responses will be greeted with less and less tolerance by the dominant class as time goes on. Marxists have long "forecast" such a scenario from advancing capitalism, predicting the development of increasingly illiberal political perspectives on the part of monopoly capitalist elites in the face of popular protest.[5] It is interesting to note that Daniel Bell has become aware of some of these possibilities too, albeit from a rather distorted vantage point. It is even more interesting to note the anti-democratic implications of Bell's awareness.

If Bell lives in fear of the deleterious effects of "populism" and "resentment" on the unfolding of post industrial society—of which he is as much an advocate as an analyst, as must now be clear—he anticipates even more trouble arising from the cultural sphere. Although Bell's discussion of the culture is fragmentary (which permits us, in turn, to forego an extensive discussion on the usefulness of using "the culture" as a central analytical concept—what culture, whose culture, what is the role of culture, etc.) it is infused with much passion. Bell finds both the "high culture" and the mass culture of industrial societies appalling. In the realm of mass culture he sees an all-pervasive individualistic and selfish hedonism, which he clearly feels is debasing of the human spirit. He ascribes the historical origins of this hedonism to the shift of capitalism towards the mass production and distribution of consumer goods. With this shift, bourgeois self-restraint gave way to the ethic of *jouissez!* which Bell finds distasteful and anti-social. Bell has even more disgust for the "antinomianism" and nihilism of "modernist" high culture.

In his review of mass hedonism and the "counter" and "anti" culture of the literati, Bell comes very close to a vision of barbarians at the gate. More importantly, he is deeply worried that both phenomena will pose problems for the unfolding of post industrial society. People who want only to satisfy their own desires will hardly be willing to make the communal sacrifices needed to implement the "sociologizing" mode. And literati concerned with an illusory quest for human authenticity are not likely to bless the bureaucratic rule of enlightened techno-crats. What is most interesting about Bell's discussion of the "cultural problem", however, is not his immoderate passion, but the structure of his argument itself. While giving lip service to the notion that popular hedonism originated in the shift of Western capitalism to the mass marketing of consumer goods Bell then conveniently forgets to follow this discussion through, subsequently fixing the blame for the continuation of mass hedonism *on the masses themselves* (after all, the culture is an independent sphere). And, of course, the blame for the antinomianism of the literati belongs with the literati. What Bell seems unable to confront is that the major period of bread-and-circuses consumerism in American social history is precisely that period in which Bell traces the beginnings of the transition to "post industrial society". The very advanced industrial society (read capitalism) pregnant with the new society which Bell sees as so desirable must also be held responsible for discovering the merchandizing utility of manipulating people's private and psychic lives. It is positively grotesque to claim, as Bell seems to, that culture is independent in advanced capitalism, given the barrage of corporate enticements to hedonism which greet us at every waking moment of our lives. Indeed, does Bell consider the large number of his colleagues in the social sciences who use their "theoretical knowledge" to discover new ways of force-feeding consumer goods to the American populace to be members in good standing of his cherished professional-technical-scientific caste? And what of the "theoretical knowledge" of the advertising industry? Approaching things the way he does, artificially dissociating culture from social structure, Bell facilitates the commission of yet another classic error of American sociology, "blaming the victim". Similar points might be made of Bell's disgust with "modernist" high culture. It is hardly surprising to see the most recent practitioners of the arts recoiling more and more strongly in horror from modern consumer capitalism. The flight from classic forms of artistic production into the highly privatized search for authenticity evident in abstract art, musical atonality, even the mocking frivolity of "pop" put-ons, must be seen, at least in part, as a reaction to the appropriation and debasement of more conventional forms of artistic expression by advanced capitalism for the purposes of selling and social control. Without doubt the spread of rule by bureaucrats and technocrats in Bell's "forecast" would further fuel the fires of modernism. Only a sociologist who ignores the connections between culture and social structure can be surprised at such cultural developments. Bell's cultural discussion lacks only a fervent defence of the culture of the professional-scientific-technical caste, the culture of the computer printout.

III

The Coming of Post Industrial Society is a systematic misperception of

American reality. What Bell immodestly claims to be "social fore-casting" is, in fact, his projection backwards to the present from a utopian future—characterized by the domination of the professional-scientific-technical intelligentsia—which he desperately hopes will come to pass. Such a procedure, the evaluation of the present from the per-spective of a future fantasy, is bound to lead to a selective interpretation of things as they are. Because he wants the American future to be "post industrial", he must make the American present "industrial", which leads him to downplay the capitalist core of American life. Relegated to the status of annoying obstacles to the technocratic future (Bell has an interesting literary habit of including evidence which runs counter to his own argument which he then proceeds to ignore) are the deep economic troubles of an America which may have "service-sectored" itself out of part of the world capitalist market already (with layers of excess economic and social fat leading to declining productivity, technological lag in key areas, chronic inflation, balance of payments problems, etc.). Almost completely absent is a comprehensive under-standing of the America we have seen engaged in recent paroxysms of neo-colonial warfare and oppression to maintain the "free world's" "free" access to markets and raw materials by refusing to allow any other people to opt for socialism. [6]

We can only speculate why Bell might have made such an argument. *The Coming of Post Industrial Society* is obviously a self-protecting and self-aggrandizing attempt to legitimate an American intelligentsia of which Bell is one spokesman (while taking the heat off American capitalism in the process). Bell's intelligentsia is a new stratum, as he points out, a product of the great educational research boom of the Cold War years. In a society which has traditionally regarded the adult inhabitants of universities as parasites and *fainéants* it is not surprising to find American intellectuals consumed with status anxiety. Bell's argument, however, ought to be situated much more precisely. The American intelligentsia took quite a beating in the 1960s. Student protest, a more generalized anti-war movement, and finally the militant New Left called attention to some rather disturbing things about American universities and intellectuals. In general, it became crystal clear that American universities were hardly the centres for dispassionate truth-seeking which they claimed to be. Rather they were deeply involved in performing important functions for the American corporate/military establishment. It was not simply that the American intelligentsia was engaged in reproducing the American bourgeoisie, its ideologies, and its trained technical helpers. Beyond this it had con-tracted itself out to America's rulers for small favours such as the development of new weapons systems, or the manufacturing of complex strategies for political and military counter-insurgency (pre-packaged police forces for South Vietnam, for example, or the abortive Project Camelot in Latin America). Indeed, it soon came out that academic leaders in the "social forecasting" field were up to their ears in complicity with American imperialism (a case could be made that between Harvard University—the papacy of the American academic world and Daniel Bell's present employer—and the other institutions of Cambridge, Massachusetts, a goodly number of the main authors of the most infamous "venture in social forecasting" of them all, America's Indochina war, could be rounded up). Finally, it was discovered that many of America's great universities were endowed with investment portfolios which included not only a great many shares in America's largest private corporations, but also holdings in such things as the thriving economic life of South Africa or the oil fields of Portuguese Angola.

The situation which developed was a very uncomfortable one for Bell and colleagues.[7] The sins of the government and its universities provoked a massive student revolt. Irony of ironies, the responsibility for this student revolt was laid by ambitious politicians and part of the public at the door of—who else but—Professor Bell and his peers. This was not because the universities had ventured too deeply into collaboration with the military/industrial complex and thereby prompted rebellion, but because these same universities and their faculties had coddled the young in an overly "permissive" way, even poisoning their minds with foreign thoughts. Memories of this recent period hang like a pall over *The Coming of Post Industrial Society*. In a great many ways the book appears to have been produced from the fear and vulnerability of the very caste of intellectuals which Bell hopes will inherit the earth. For what *The Coming* really attempts to do is to create a new mythology of dispassionate independence for the same group which was caught *in flagrante delicto* in the 1960s with its fingers in the till of American imperialism.

A great deal of turbulent history lies between *The End of Ideology* and *The Coming of Post Industrial Society*. *The End of Ideology* was part of the world of the "Great American Celebration", as C. Wright Mills called it. The intellectual production of that time (including Bell's) radiated social stability, peace, economic growth, legitimated institutions, controllable problems, and, above all, confidence. Politically, pluralist America reigned as the embodiment of democracy (even if the tugging and pulling between different groups for political gains seemed to involve only elite interests, while the low level of participation and commitment to "tolerance and exchange" of ordinary Americans did cause the more astute pluralists to wonder—and worry a bit about—what might occur if the populace began to care about politics).[8]

The world of *The Coming of Post Industrial Society* is a very different, and much less secure, one. Bell can scarcely hide his deep political pessimism, for example. His political world is still pluralist, but afflicted by "populism" and *ressentiment*. The tranquillity of 1950s elite pluralism seems to have been rudely upset by the political claims of all sorts of non-elite groups (blacks, students, women, workers, etc.). While to a naive observer it might seem that such claims would make the American system more open and democratic, Bell fears them and their "un-wisdom". No longer vaunting the virtues of America as democracy embodied, Bell clearly prefers rule by the elites, with, of course, an increase in the political clout of his cherished intelligentsia. Not even his lengthy polemic in favour of a just meritocracy can hide the fact that, politically, Bell has become much more illiberal. And we need say little more of Bell's cultural nightmares. The philistines and barbarians—in the persons of assorted consumer durable fetishists, TV addicts, "counter cultural" erotomaniacs and antinomian abstract painters—already have their feet in the door. Bell's deepest fear is more general. Quite simply put, it is that the elites of "post industrial society" (read advanced capitalism) will have ever increasing difficulties in legitimating their rule. Bell senses that people will tend more and more to withhold consent as their lives increasingly fall under the control of the professional-scientific-technical caste (in particular, we might add, insofar as this caste is merely fronting for monopoly capitalist corporations).

Bourgeois ideology has always advocated democracy and loved the people when the bourgeois ruling class could count on having its own way. Such was the case in the American 1950s. *The Coming of Post Industrial Society* demonstrates how much things have changed by the early 1970s. Bell's pessimism, his open elitism, and his fear of the people, have to be considered the Left's promise. But a promise given is not a promise redeemed. The anxiety of American bourgeois ideology found in Bell's book must also be seen as a warning of turbulent times ahead.

NOTES

1. Norman Birnbaum, *The New York Times Book Review*, 1 July 1973. *The Coming of Post Industrial Society* has been reviewed almost endlessly in the USA over the past year. Indeed, sampling these reviews *and* reading the book would constitute quite a good introductory course in American sociology. For anyone interested, a good beginning would be as follows: Christopher Lasch (polemically Leftish) *New York Review of Books*, 18 October 1973 (with rejoinder by Daniel Bell, *NYRB* 24 January 1974); Robert Heilbroner (liberal pessimist), *Dissent*, Spring 1973; a symposium in *Contemporary Sociology*, March 1974, with reviews by Establishment sociologists Reinhard Bendix and Amitai Etzioni, Marxist Stephen Berger plus

yet another rejoinder by Bell; finally Richard Hill (a solid Left Liberal) does a good job in *The Insurgent Sociologist*, Spring 1974.

2. Bell's own use of the term "industrial" and "post industrial" society are a dead giveaway of his own position in this discussion. "Industrial society" is a category used by those who hold that the commonalities (bureaucracy, technology) of capitalist and socialist industrialized societies are vastly more important than their differences. We must, of course, keep in mind that the use of "industrial society" is not devoid of polemical intent, whatever its scientific value. In American sociology it is designed to separate its "realistic" user from the "ideologues" who insist upon distinguishing capitalism from socialism.

3. The interested reader would do well to consult "Corporate Ownership and Control: the Large Corporation and the Capitalist Class", by Maurice Zeitlin, in *The American Journal of Sociology*, March 1974. Among its other great virtues (lucidity, exhaustiveness and a great respect for hard evidence) this article contains a complete list of references to the long debate on such questions.

4. In a long chapter on "The Subordination of the Corporation" Bell espouses many of the theses of the "Managerial Revolution" advocates. He sees the Western corporation progressively divesting itself of those aspects of its behaviour which justified the label capitalism, becoming a bureaucratic monolith whose responsibility to private capitalist owners is already minimal. Because of this, the motivation to maximize profits is less and less compelling. To Bell, however, profit maximization is still the somewhat atavistic rule. In his eyes, the arrival in power of the scientific-technical-professional caste will provide the needed new ethic to move the corporation away from its last capitalist yearnings. Thus, to Bell, the "managerial revolution" theorists were premature but thinking along the right lines. Mainly they were premature because they chose the wrong group to infuse the modern corporation with a new ethic.

5. One might be tempted to use the term "class conflict" with reference to the protest in question, rather than Bell's chosen term of "populism", which, after all, is a political rather than a sociological term. Bell himself is quite careful not to do so, of course, disposing of the notion of class conflict quite early in his work. Class conflict is a feature of "industrial" society to Bell, part of a situation in which the blue collar work force and the business élite square off. In "post industrial" society, with its declining blue collar work force (which is, apparently, to Bell, the only possible locus of class conflict) the "labour issue" remains, but encapsulated in a routinized industrial relations system with little influence in polity and culture. One wonders whether Bell has not gone a bit too far in generalizing from the American experience of the past 25 years. Had he taken a more comparative perspective which included Europe, he would have had more difficulty in discarding the utility of class conflict. For that matter the concept is not without utility for understanding the USA either, certainly of more utility than "populism".

6. Bell subscribes to a view that the making of foreign policy follows from the ideological and power political concerns of the political executive. He does not deign to dignify with discussion the massive and often convincing neo-marxist literature from the 1960s arguing the connection between economic motives and imperialism.

7. It is only fair to note that the experience of the 1960s provoked a variety of responses from the American intelligentsia. Many intellectuals were forced to choose between support for, or opposition to, American imperialism. A small percentage opted for the Left. One wonders whether Bell would consider Noam Chomsky as a "populist" motivated by "resentment".

8. Pluralism became the great cliché of American political science. The evidence of much pluralist research, that political conflict between élite groups and interests

was rife in America, came as no surprise to anyone familiar with Marxian understanding of capitalist political processes. Since one of the major functions of the capitalist state is to adjudicate disputes between divergent capitalist interests, such conflict was to be expected. One thing which Marxists would not do, however, when confronted by such evidence, would be to suggest that such group conflict amounted to democracy.

THE STATE IN POST-COLONIAL SOCIETIES:
TANZANIA*

John S. Saul

WITH the recent work of Samir Amin and others, Marxist understanding of African economies has begun to progress; political analysis has lagged far behind however. For too long the ground has been ceded, by default, to the ideologues of establishment political science and to their various permutations on the themes of "political modernization" and "one-party states". This comment applies not merely to "radical Africana" of course. A similar short-fall in radicalism's scientific understanding of the political can be noted with reference to Asia and Latin America as well. The problem of "the state" as it presents itself in the context of "underdevelopment" has been undertheorized and little researched. The present essay seeks to contribute to a further discussion of this issue.

Needless to say, it does not do so in a complete vacuum. Most notably, Hamza Alavi has recently provided an important starting point for analysis of "the state in post-colonial societies", premissing his argument

"on the historical specificity of post-colonial societies, a specificity which arises from structural changes brought about by the colonial experience and alignment of classes and by the superstructures of political and administrative institutions which were established in that context, and secondly from radical re-alignments of class forces which have been brought about in the post-colonial situation."[1]

In general, the propositions developed by Alavi in his analysis of Pakistan and Bangla Desh prove most illuminating when applied to the Tanzanian experience—as will be seen in the following pages. At the

* This paper was originally presented in the "Views from the Left" Lecture Series, Toronto, Canada, February 1974. For an overview of the Tanzanian situation which spells out both the country's achievements and its continuing contradictions in much more detail than has been possible here, the interested reader may wish to refer to the author's "African Socialism in One Country: Tanzania", in Giovanni Arrighi and John S. Saul, *Essays on the Political Economy of Africa* (New York and London, 1973), Ch. 6. The present paper is, in effect, a theoretical extension of that earlier essay. There are also the various materials collected in Lionel Cliffe and John S. Saul (eds.), *Socialism in Tanzania: Politics and Policies*, two volumes (Nairobi, Kenya, 1972 and 1973).

349

same time, such a comparison suggests certain qualifications and extensions of his argument which are here discussed tentatively, and fully in the spirit of Alavi's conclusion that "comparative and critical studies are needed before we can hope to arrive at a general theory of the State in post-colonial societies".

There are certain dangers in focusing upon Tanzania to make such points—a possible confusion of the particular for the general for example, a danger which may be intensified with respect to Tanzania because of that country's somewhat atypical post-colonial pattern of development. But there is a compensating advantage of some significance: discussion of the Tanzanian case provides the opportunity to work with an analytical literature of a very high order, a literature which is not widely enough known outside East Africa. Specifically, the past few years have seen the emergence, around the journal *Majimaji*, of an important school of Tanzanian critics of that country's "socialism".[2] The body of work which these writers have begun to produce is rooted in the Marxist tradition and it has provided a stimulating domestic counter-weight to the formulations of President Nyerere, in terms of whose approach to Tanzania much previous analysis has been conducted. As a result, a discussion of "the state" with reference to Tanzanian experience can serve not only as an invitation to others to undertake similar inquiries in a variety of African settings, but also as an opportunity to discuss critically this "*Majimaji* school" of socialist theorists.

I The State in Post-Colonial Societies

There are three points which define the crucial significance of the state in post-colonial societies—two of which can be drawn directly from Alavi. For the first, we may quote at length:

"The bourgeois revolution in the colony in so far as that consists of the establishment of a bourgeois state and the attendant legal and institutional framework, is an event which takes place with the imposition of colonial rule by the metropolitan bourgeoisie. In carrying out the tasks of the bourgeois revolution in the colony, however, the metropolitan bourgeoisie has to accomplish an additional task which was specific to the colonial situation. Its task in the colony is not merely to replicate the superstructure of the state which it had established in the metropolitan country itself. Additionally, it had to create a state apparatus through which it can exercise dominion over *all* the indigenous social classes in the colony. It might be said that the "superstructure" in the colony is therefore, "over-developed" in relation to the "structure" in the colony, for its basis lies in the metropolitan structure itself, from which it is later separated at the time of independence. The colonial state is therefore equipped with a powerful bureaucratic-military apparatus and mechanisms of government which enable them through its routine operations to subordinate the native social classes. The post-colonial society inherits that overdeveloped apparatus of state and its institutionalized practices through which the operations of indigenous social classes are regulated and controlled."[3]

Much about this formulation is exemplary—and immediately illuminates the historical basis of the situation in East Africa.

A second, complementary, point also can be drawn from Alavi, for the state's prominent place in post-colonial society is rooted not only in the colonial legacy, but also in the contemporary production process. "The apparatus of the state, furthermore assume(s) also a new and relatively autonomous *economic* role, which is not paralleled in the classical bourgeois state. The state in the post-colonial society directly appropriates a very large part of the economic surplus and deploys it in bureaucratically directed economic activity in the name of promoting economic development". Since these two features both characterize the East African situation, they also serve there, in Alavi's words, to "differentiate the post-colonial State fundamentally from the state as analysed in classical marxist theory".[4]

There is a third feature, about which Alavi says little. In advanced capitalist countries the state is the "dominant classes' political power centre" and, in this respect, comes to have an important ideological function. For in fact it symbolizes the unity of the social formation, seeming to transcend any narrow class or sectional interest and thus helping to legitimize the *status quo*. It is for this reason that Poulantzas has conceived the state as being "not a class construct but rather the state of a society divided into classes", a fact which does not negate the further reality that such a capitalist state "aims precisely at the political disorganization of the dominated classes".[5] But the state's function of providing an ideological cement for the capitalist system is one which has evolved slowly and surely in the imperial centres, in step with the latter's economic transformation. In post-colonial societies, on the other hand, and particularly in Africa, this hegemonic position *must be created*, and created within territorial boundaries which often appear as quite artificial entities once the powerful force of direct colonial fiat has been removed. Peripheral capitalism, like advanced capitalism, requires territorial unity and legitimacy and the post-colonial state's centrality to the process of *creating* these conditions (like its centrality in "promoting economic development") further reinforces Alavi's point about that state's importance. Indeed, when viewed from a Marxist perspective, this is what all the fashionable discussion of "nation-building" in development literature is all about![6]

These three points, taken together, help define the centrality of the state in the post-colonial social formation. And this centrality, in turn, is sufficient to suggest the importance of *those who staff the state apparatus* within such a formation. In Alavi's terms, the latter are members of "the military-bureaucratic oligarchy", who thus come to play a semi-autonomous role in the situation created by the lifting of direct metropolitan control. The nature and extent of this autonomy—of the state and of those who staff it—from the determinations of other classes more directly rooted in the production process (Alavi identifies these as "the indigenous bourgeoisie, the Metropolitan neo-colonialist bourgeoisie, and the landed classes") is more controversial. And it must be admitted that Alavi's answer to this question is not entirely clear.

He does suggest that the "oligarchy" acts "on behalf of [all three propertied classes] to preserve the social order in which their interests are embedded, namely the institution of private property and the capitalist mode as the dominant mode of production". Moreover, this would seem to be the premise which underpins one of his explanations of the oligarchy's position:

"... a new convergence of interests of the three competing propertied classes, under Metropolitan patronage, allows a bureaucratic military oligarchy to mediate their competing but no longer contradictory interests and demands. By that token it acquires a relatively autonomous role and is not simply the instrument of any one of the three classes."

But what is being claimed here? Does this autonomy arise because these classes balance each other off, thus providing openings for the exercise of leverage by the "oligarchy" in their own interests, or is some different concept at play? In fact, other of Alavi's observations cast doubt on his own use of the term "convergence". Thus he notes on the one hand that "such a relatively autonomous role of the state apparatus is of special importance to the neo-colonialist bourgeoisies because it is by virtue of this fact that they are able to pursue their class interests in the post-colonial societies". Compare this subservient status with the oligarchy's relationship to the "weak indigenous bourgeoisies": here it is the latter who "find themselves enmeshed in bureaucratic controls by which those at the top of the hierarchy of the bureaucratic-military apparatus of the state are able to maintain and even extend their dominant power in society. . . ." Nor is it merely the notion of "convergence" which is called into question by the existence of such gross imbalances between the three classes. What of Alavi's other explanation of the oligarchy's autonomy: its ability to "mediate . . . between competing interests"? "Mediation" scarcely summarizes the oligarchy's drive to "extend their dominant power in society" at the expense of the indigenous bourgeoisie, though this is the situation just described by Alavi. And what, in any case, is the nature of the oligarchy's distinctive interest which any "autonomy" it may win permits it to advance and defend?

East African experience reinforces the importance of these and related questions, in part because the imbalances between the three classes is even more striking there than in South Asia. In fact, the two indigenous classes to which Alavi refers—"the landed classes" and "the indigenous bourgeoisie"—are very much less prominent. This is true, in part, because of the nature of pre-colonial African society. Historically, the colonial state in East Africa became "overdeveloped" not so much in response to a need to "subordinate the native social classes" as a need to subordinate pre-capitalist, generally non-feudal, social formations to the imperatives of colonial capitalism. As a result, there is no equivalent, even today, to "the landed class"; rather, we find a pre-capitalist agriculture which is moving, under the pressures of commercialization, directly towards capitalist relations of production with scarcely any quasi-feudal stopovers along the way.[7] Nor has the "indigenous bourgeoisie" developed even to the degree described by Alavi for Pakistan and Bangla Desh. Primarily confined to retail trade and services, it has been mainly comprised of "Asians" (Indians) rather than Africans, and this fact too has weakened such a class's ability to defend its stake in the system.

At one level, this greater weakness of the indigenous classes might seem to strengthen the positions of those who directly control the state apparatus—Alavi's oligarchy. But, as we have seen, Alavi also emphasized the importance to the latter's power of its ability to mediate *competing* interests. It has therefore appeared to some observers that, under East African circumstances (with weak indigenous classes), the oligarchy falls much more directly under the thumb of the "Metropolitan neo-colonialist bourgeoisie"—the transnational corporations— whose influence may now seem even more imbalanced and unalloyed there than in the case studied by Alavi. In consequence, certain theorists (like Fanon) have presented the new oligarchies as mere transmission belts for these transnationals: "the national middle-class discovers its historic mission: that of intermediary".[8] And Issa Shivji, of whom we shall say more later, was similarly tempted in his first essay on Tanzania to conclude that the real "socio-economic base" of those elements who directly control the state lies "in the international bourgeoisie"![9]

There is, of course, much truth in such an emphasis, but it remains an overstatement. True, Alavi's attempt to premiss an explanation of the relative "autonomy" of those elements which cluster around the state upon the nature of the interplay of other classes in post-colonial society is not entirely convincing, particularly with reference to East Africa. But some measure of autonomy does remain to those elements nonetheless —an autonomy rooted in the centrality of the state in these societies which Alavi's other arguments, cited earlier, do in fact help to illuminate. Indeed, some analysts would strengthen the point by extending the argument concerning the nature of the state's stake in the production process beyond Alavi's rather bland statement that it deploys surpluses "in the name of promoting economic development". Rather, they suggest that the strategic position which the state occupies vis-à-vis the economy, including the privileged access to the surplus which is thus available to the oligarchy, defines the latter's interest as being that of a *class*. Perhaps this is what Poulantzas has in mind when he cites "the case of the *state bourgeoisie* in certain developing countries: the bureaucracy may, through the state, establish a specific place for itself in the existing relations of production. But in that case it does not constitute a class by virtue of being the bureaucracy, but by virtue of being an effective class".[10]

Indeed, in East Africa where other indigenous classes are so relatively weak, the positions articulated by Debray in his discussion of the Latin American "petty-bourgeoisie" may seem to such analysts to be quite *à propos*: "it does not possess an infrastructure of economic power before it wins political power. Hence it transforms the state not only into an instrument of political domination, but also into a source of economic power. The state, culmination of social relations of exploitation in capitalist Europe, becomes in a certain sense the instrument of their installation in these countries".[11] Thus the use of the state—through special financing arrangements, training programmes, manipulation of licences and the like—by newly-powerful elements in post-colonial Kenya to parachute themselves into the private sector at the expense of the Asians is instructive in this respect.[12] Moreover, Shivji suggests that *a very similar logic* leads to a somewhat different result in Tanzania merely because of certain features distinctive to the political economy of the latter country. But on the essential similarity of the process he is quite outspoken.[13] At the same time it must be emphasized that there are others, equally convinced of the relative autonomy of the state in many post-colonial African settings, who would draw rather different conclusions. In doing so, such observers have extended the notion of autonomy far beyond anything conceived by Alavi, arguing that it can actually provide the initial lever for mounting *socialist development strategies* in parts of Africa—including Tanzania! We must now turn directly to these various formulations.

II Models for Africa

Implicitly, some crude notion of the "autonomy" of the state lies at the root of modernization theory for example. Much the least interesting of the three broad formulations we shall mention in this section, it is a model which conceives of those who inherit the post-colonial state as "benign elites"—the "new middle class" or "the modernizers". Their role, within the trickle-down process of enlightenment from advanced countries to backward countries, is naturally, to facilitate the "development", the modernization of their "new nation". In addition, there is a left variant of this essentially benign interpretation—an interpretation which, quite uncritically, sees this new stratum as a force for socialism! Of course, this has been the stuff of much political rhetoric in many centres of "African Socialism", but Green has recently given this argument an academic formulation (albeit with primary reference to Tanzania). Quite aware that "the elite" in many parts of Africa may, in the service of its own self-interest, abuse both its opportunity for service and the trust of the mass of the people, Green nonetheless concludes that, for some unexplained reason, this does not occur in a country like Tanzania. Thus,

> "in the case of Tanzania, it would be fair to say that virtually every general and specific issue raised by university critics had been posed (sometimes in even harsher terms) at least six months (and in certain cases up to two years) earlier by members of the 'neo-bourgeois bureaucratic elite' and that almost all were under active study aimed at evaluating alternative operational solutions both at official and political level. There is no reason to suppose this is a totally unique record even if it may well be atypical in degree. Further, the public sector elite has accepted material rewards substantially lower than those in neighbouring states, and than those prevailing in Tanzania five years ago, with no evident general loss of morale or loyalty. To say that shortcomings can be cited and that the elite is still far above average material standards is fair comment; to argue that it has on any broad scale deliberately obstructed or been unable because unwilling to move ahead on the implementation of the Arusha Declaration is much more dubious. There is no logical reason to assume that because technical competence need not be positively related to political commitment it must always be negatively related."[14]

It is interesting that so close an observer of the Tanzanian scene as Green could come to such a conclusion, but it must also be asserted categorically that his remarks—so sweepingly stated—cannot be squared with the findings of most other students of Tanzanian realities.[15]

At the opposite end of the spectrum from the "benign" school are those who perceive in parts of Africa the crystallization of a fully-formed class around the apparatus of the state—a class with an interest quite distinct from and antagonistic to the interests of the mass of the population. Fanon hints at some such formulation, but it has been given its most vigorous scientific statement by Claude Meillassoux in his important "class analysis of the bureaucratic process in Mali".[16] He focuses on "the bureaucrats", defining them as "a body generated by the colonizers to carry out the tasks which could not (or would not) be undertaken by the Europeans themselves". In this capacity they were entrusted with some of the instruments of power, notably with expertise. In other words, education and government (and business) *employment* are the crucial features.[17] He then argues that in Mali:

> "... having been the instrument of the colonial power, and having turned against it to become the mouthpiece of the exploited Malian peasantry, the bureaucracy was gaining (with its access to power) some of the characteristics of a social class: control of the economic infrastructure and use of it as a means of exploitation, control of the means of repression involving a resort to various devices to maintain dominance. Some of its features are original: its opposite class is not yet socially well defined; it

does not own the means of production on a private judicial basis, but controls them on a constitutional basis. There is no room here for a parliamentary system, regulating conflicts between a great number of private owners or corporations. The situation is better controlled through the single-party machine, within which open conflicts can be reduced to inner struggles between hidden factions. Appropriation of the economic bases of power cannot come from individual endeavour or entrepreneurship, nor from inheritance. It can come through co-operation by the people in position, or as the bargain lot of a *coup d'état*."

Meillassoux's findings parallel those of Alavi in several respects. There is, for example, the subordination to imperialism of this "class": "Given the economic dependence of the country, the bureaucracy is itself a dependent group, and its origin as an instrument of western interests continues to influence its development. Instead of striving towards a real independence after winning the right to assert itself as political intermediaries with the outside world, the bureaucrats are content to return (with a higher international rank) under the rule of the old master." Furthermore, their position is consolidated in contestation with (weak) indigenous classes: in the Mali case, an aristocracy (formerly slave-holders—a class for which there is no equivalent in East Africa) and a fairly well-developed trading-class.[18] However, having gone so far, Meillassoux remains reluctant in the end to call this group a class outright: "it is also crucial that a distinction be made between the class proper and the dependent social elements which are the out-growth of classes, but which may, in specific historical circumstances, assume important historical functions". Others, as we shall see, are prepared to go further in this direction, but for the moment another of Meillassoux' points may be cited. In noting the bureaucracy's attempt "to gain certain positions of control in the modern economy and to eliminate opposition spreading from the Malian historical classes", he comments on their moves "to infiltrate the national economy through the creation of a nationalized economic sector" as follows:

"This was done under the label of 'socialism' which provided them with a convenient ideology to bring the economy under their control, supposedly of course on behalf of the entire population. 'Socialism' permitted them to put the bureaucracy into the position of a managerial board of a kind of State corporation."

This is striking; it is almost identically the analysis that Shivji seeks to document with respect to "Tanzanian socialism"![19]

It also bears a remarkable resemblance to the analysis by Fitch and Oppenheimer of Ghanaian developments under Nkrumah.[20] It is therefore interesting to note that a third model of the role of the oligarchy—he does not, of course, use that term—was articulated by Roger Murray precisely in the context of a brilliant critique of Fitch and Oppenheimer's position.[21] Murray's is a model which falls some-where between the polar opposites of the "benign" and the "class" models sketched above, and, like Meillassoux' argument, is of particular interest because it too foreshadows an approach to Tanzanian develop-ments, in this case an approach very different from Shivji's. Murray is well aware of "the sedimenting of new and gross class and power dis-positions centring upon the state" in Ghana. Yet he is uneasy with Fitch and Oppenheimer's reduction of the socialist impulse there to the status of "*mere* manipulation", suggesting that in so arguing the authors lapse into "pseudo-Marxist determinism". A richer, more complex picture of those who inherit the overdeveloped state in the post-colonial period is needed.

What he sees instead is "the accession to *state power* of unformed classes". Concentrating on the CPP leadership and cadres,[22] he notes that

> "they were drawn from the *petty bourgeois salariat* (clerks, primary schoolteachers, PWD storekeepers, messengers, etc.)—a mixed stratum which concentrated many of the political and cultural tensions of colonial society. It is precisely the socially ambiguous and unstable character of this stratum which helps us to understand its *relative autonomy and volatility* in the political arena. The CPP 'political' class did not express or reflect a determinate economic class."

Murray is trapped, almost inevitably, by the concreteness, the static and undialectical nature, of terminology here for even categories like "unformed class" or "class-in-formation" remain essentially tele-ological.[23] Thus the "political class" to which he refers might really be best considered a "political 'x' " since any other formulation (including the term "oligarchy") will mean that the relative social autonomy and plasticity of the political class-in-formation is lost to view. Yet this is a result Murray obviously wishes to avoid, as his further conclusion demonstrates:

> "The essence of the matter is that the post-colonial state (the 'political kingdom') has simultaneously to be perceived as the actual instrument of mediation and negotia-tion with external capitalism, and as the possible instrument of a continuing anti-imperialist and socialist revolution. In this setting, the 'relative autonomy' of the ruling 'petty bourgeois' (we can see how unilluminating the category is at this point) stratum becomes a critical issue, whose import has to be examined in its *modus operandi* of state power."[24]

In other words, the autonomy of this "x" is real, very real; in this "uncertain historical moment", its members can attempt to opt for different historical alternatives, alternatives which would actually affect in *different* ways their own positions in the production process.

This is not to abandon class analysis. It is merely to highlight the "social *uncertainty* and susceptibility to multiple determinations and influences which make the dimension of *consciousness* so crucial to the analysis—a dimension consistently underestimated by Fitch and Oppenheimer. The contradictory situation and experience of these typically transitional and partial post-colonial ruling groups is mediated through the transformations, incoherences, oscillations, 'false' and illusory representations and reconciliation at *the level of ideology*." Thus, in discussing the CPP's left-turn in the early 1960s—a "new articulation of ideology and organization ... which made socialist Ghana something of a model type in possible postcolonial African development"—Murray mentions as crucial factors not only the economic crisis of the late 1950s but also "the whole *trajectory* of ideological evolution since the 1940s".[25] Nor is this to underestimate the determinations which encourage such elements—harassed by a "frustrated national bourgeoisie", seduced by the easy lure of "bureaucratic consolidation" and alternately tempted and tormented by imperialism—to entrench themselves as an "oligarchy" of dominant "class". Murray states clearly that there are real limits upon what is "historically possible" under such conditions. But he does at least affirm the possibility, in the realm of *praxis*, of a real struggle over the direction which development should take.

It follows that, if such a struggle is possible, it may take place precisely *within* this unformed "x", between those of its members who seek to consolidate the neo-colonial set-up and those who are moved, increasingly, to challenge it.[26] Furthermore, such a model can then be interpreted as providing a scientific basis for one of Amilcar Cabral's most suggestive metaphors. For Cabral, in identifying the "revolutionary" wing of a crucial class in formation which he dubs the "petty-bourgeoisie" (and which is strikingly similar in many of its characteristics to that "political class" discussed by Murray), states that "this revolutionary petty bourgeoisie is honest; i.e. in spite of all the hostile conditions it remains identified with the fundamental interests of the popular masses. To do this it may have to commit suicide, but it will not lose; by sacrificing itself it can reincarnate itself, but in the condition of workers and peasants."[27] As Murray demonstrates, there were no significant sections of the Ghanaian leadership who could bring themselves, ultimately, to "commit suicide" in this sense. Nor did the CPP, the political expression of that leadership, realize any such possibility, failing as it did even to attempt the effective mobilization of that active popular base which could alone have guaranteed forward momentum in the longer run.[28] What of Tanzania? Clearly, Walter Rodney's application of Cabral to the Tanzanian situation is of interest in this respect:

"(Cabral) considers the petty-bourgeoisie not as a decadent stereotype but as a stratum with various possibilities, and he includes himself. Cabral was concerned with evaluating the 'nationalist capacity' of the petty bourgeoisie as well as their 'revolutionary capacity' in the post-independence phase. He speaks about a 'revolutionary petty-bourgeoisie', meaning that section which has joined the Liberation Struggle and is already carrying it forward in the direction of socialist reconstruction in the liberated zones. In other words, the African petty-bourgeoisie stratum includes Shivji, the other TANU Youth League comrades at the University (of Dar es Salaam) and most of the national leadership in Tanzania—irrespective of political convictions. Sections of the petty-bourgeoisie have broken with their mentors, and individuals within the group have at various times wholly or partially opposed the external or local capitalists."[29]

III Socialism and the State in Tanzania

Turning to Tanzania, we may note at the outset that each of the models sketched in Section II has found its echo in the wide-ranging debate about the nature of Tanzania's "socialism". Thus, the "right-benign" interpretation is seen at its most sophisticated in the writings of Cranford Pratt who eventually gives most bureaucrats and politicians in Tanzania high marks as "developers", despite what to him appear as the unnerving hi-jinks of some few "political ministers" and the occasional dangers of a "doctrinaire determination of policies".[30] We have already taken note of Green's "left-benign" variant. Both wings of this approach present much too oversimplified an account to warrant their further discussion here. Rather, the really significant differences of scientific opinion lie between what are, in effect and broadly speaking, the protagonists of the Meillassoux and of the Murray/ Cabral models.

On the one-hand and closer to Meillassoux are "the Majimaji socialists", most notably Issa Shivji, author of two of the most important papers to have emerged from the Tanzanian debate.[31] It is in point to recapitulate his argument concerning the nature of class struggle in post-colonial Tanzania, for it is also a significant statement concerning the nature of the state there. As noted earlier, Shivji's scepticism about the socialist vocation of wielders of state power in Tanzania first found theoretical expression in his attempt to view these elements as quite straightforward agents of the international bourgeoisie. His second paper continues to stress the extent to which such elements service the interests of international capitalism, but he has gone on to develop a much more sophisticated analysis of their own stake in the system.

The class which takes power is, once again, the "petty-bourgeoisie", particularly its "upper level" ("the intelligentsia") identified, rather eclectically, as comprised of "intellectuals, teachers, higher civil servants, prosperous traders, farmers, professionals, higher military and police officers". The inclusion of the (African) "traders" and "farmers" in this class and in the nationalist coalition is not crucial, however:[32] "one of the outstanding features of the petty-bourgeoisie was that they overwhelmingly came from the urban-based occupations, with some education and some knowledge of the outside world".[33] This class spearheads the struggle against the colonial state. In doing so, their interests merely "coincide with those of the broad masses". The same is true, Shivji states, for the next stage of development—the struggle with the Indian "commercial bourgeoisie". The role of the latter class-cum-ethnic group—which has controlled the intermediate sectors of the economy—is analysed by Shivji with great subtlety; in fact, he has provided the first really convincing class analysis of the Asian community in East Africa to date. On the African side he extends his analysis in a manner which is much more controversial.

For the confrontation which Shivji sees to be taking place between petty-bourgeoisie and commercial bourgeoisie for economic power is complicated by a further development, one which emerges precisely with the accession to state power (at independence) of this petty bourgeoisie:

"In an underdeveloped African country with a *weak petty bourgeoisie*, its ruling section which comes to possess the instrument of the state on the morrow of independence, relatively commands enormous power and is therefore very strong. This was precisely the case in Tanzania. . . . The Tanzanian scene . . . comes closer to the 'Bonapartist' type of situation where the contending classes have weakened themselves thus allowing the 'ruling clique' to cut itself off from its class base and *appear* to raise the state above the class struggle. Of course, it is not that the contending classes had weakened themselves in the independence struggle. But a somewhat similar situation resulted from the fact that the petty bourgeoisie was weak and had not developed deep economic roots. This allowed the 'ruling group' a much freer hand. In other words the control of the state became the single decisive factor. For these and other reasons . . . it is proposed to identify the 'ruling group' as the 'bureaucratic bourgeoisie'. Before the Arusha Declaration, this would comprise mainly those at the top levels of the state apparatus—ministers, high civil servants, high military and police officers and such like. One may also include the high level bureaucrats of the Party and the cooperative movement, because of the important role the latter played in the pre-Arusha class struggles."[34]

Shivji does note that the weakness of the petty-bourgeoisie referred to here "is due to the fact that it is still 'embryonic'; the whole class structure is in *the process of* formation". The same *caveat* is introduced with reference to the bureaucratic bourgeoisie. Is it "a class as *distinct* from the petty bourgeoisie"? Not quite. "Suffice to say that the post-independence class struggles (including the Arusha Declaration) were themselves a process leading to the emergence of the 'bureaucratic bourgeoisie'. The process may not be complete." But having noted this, Shivji, unlike Murray, does not draw back from his terms. He is unconcerned with the weight of teleology which they bear. As he proceeds with his analysis, classes-in-formation behave, unambiguously, like fully formed classes. And this is the chief weakness of his argument.

For Shivji, in sum, the "historical moment" is by no means "uncertain". On the contrary, he now uses this conception of Tanzania's class structure—straightforwardly and however much the "structure" may be "in the process of formation"—to explain the history of post-colonial Tanzania: it is the case of "a *non-proletarian class* after coming to political power . . . now trying to wrest an economic base" from the commercial bourgeoisie. Half-measures, like the encouragement of the cooperatives, having failed, "the only alternative, both for further struggle against the commercial bourgeoisie and for further penetration of the economy, was state intervention": "it was thus that the Arusha Declaration was born in 1967". With it, and with the attendant national-izations, a new stage in the class struggle, à la Shivji, is reached:

> "Up until the Arusha Declaration, the 'bureaucratic bourgeoisie' was essentially of the politico-administrative type. Although the state played an important role in the economy it was mostly a regulatory one. With the Arusha Declaration, the state and state institutions (including parastatals) became the dominant actors in the economy. Thus a new and more important wing of the bureaucratic bourgeoisie was created. Political power and control over property had now come to rest in the same class."

Socialism as "*mere* manipulation"—Shivji comes very close to such a position. Nevertheless, he does recognize that there is some difficulty in reconciling this with the Arusha Declaration Leadership Code—a code designed to prevent leaders from involving themselves, profitably, in the private sector. Here Shivji's explanation, in order to save his hypothesis, is that "the ideology had gained the upper hand, for even a rhetoric has its own momentum and can have important effects on concrete measures". This would also appear to be his "explanation" for the very real constraints (certainly as compared with other parts of Africa) on elite income and consumption which have been a part of Tanzania's "socialism". In addition, Shivji states, as if to reinforce his general argument, that the Code has often been flouted since its inception. This, in turn, suggests (quite accurately) that there was a "spontaneous" tendency for "leaders" to overlap into the private sector—as in neighbouring Kenya. Yet such a reality seems to contradict Shivji's emphasis. Why didn't the petty-bourgeoisie use the state to facilitate their own movement in upon the Asians on a private basis—again, as in Kenya—rather than publicly and collectively?

Shivji is aware of this problem, of course, and his explanation is of considerable interest:

> "In Kenya, there were important sections of the petty bourgeoisie—yeoman farmers and traders, for example—besides the urban-based intelligentsia, who had already developed significant 'independent' roots in the colonial economy. Thus the petty bourgeoisie itself as a class was strong and different sections within it were more or less at par. This considerably reduced the power of the 'ruling clique' irrespective of its immediate possession of the state apparatus and kept it 'tied' to its class base—the petty bourgeoisie."

But this does not convince. Even if the entrepreneurial elements were stronger in transitional Kenya, the difference from Tanzania was not so striking as Shivji suggests and in any case these Kenyan Africans' commercial opponents (European and Asian) were themselves much stronger than any counterparts in Tanzania; thus the *relative* economic weight of the African entrepreneurs cannot have been that much different. Moreover, it is quite unnecessary to make such subtle distinctions. As noted, it seems obvious that large sections of Shivji's bureaucratic bourgeoisie continue to cast envious glances at their civil servant and political counterparts in Kenya and at the gross (and rewarding) "conflicts of interest" which serve to characterize Kenyan economic and political life. And, being disproportionately drawn from commercialized, cash-cropping rural areas like Kilimanjaro and Bukoba, they do in fact have intimate (familial) connections with a "yeomanry". Unless contested, such a group would have had Tanzania gravitate in the Kenyan direction, a point made by Nyerere himself on more than one occasion.[35] It is difficult, in fact, to avoid the conclusion that the Arusha Declaration package of policies—the opting for collective solutions to the Tanzanian development problem—represented, first and foremost, an *initial victory* for a *progressive wing* of the petty bourgeoisie (and the announcement of its continuing commitment to the interests of the workers and peasants), rather than some cold-blooded fulfilment of the class interests of that stratum's bureaucratic core.[36]

This difference of opinion requires detailed exploration of a kind that is beyond the scope of the present paper. Suffice to say that for Shivji this kind of "manipulation" also tends to characterize each of the specific arenas of post-Arusha policy-making, while for each such arena it can be shown that this is an oversimplification. Take, for example, the "ujamaa village" programme (designed to promote a Tanzanian brand of agricultural collective), in Shivji's eyes merely a calculated and perfunctory gesture—an expression of "intermittent ideological hostility" to "kulaks"—designed to maintain for the petty bourgeoisie its "popular peasant base". But this was not an immediately popular policy even among much of the peasantry; support for it would have to be *created*, sometimes in a manner (as in Ismani) which challenged the local dignitaries of the party itself. Nor is it entirely true that this policy was "not basically against the interests of the petty bourgeoisie". The fact that in practice bureaucrats often worked hard to defuse the policy by directing it away from the "advanced" areas (Kilimanjaro and Bukoba mentioned above) and towards more defenceless, backward regions (with many fewer kulaks) testifies to their uneasiness. Nor were the extensive nationalizations of 1967 merely a charade. International capitalism was stung and the conventional wisdom of most civil servants visibly affronted. In other words, these and other initiatives represented real achievements in a transition towards socialism.[37] That the full potential of these policies' possible contribution to such a transition has not been realized is, of course, also true, a point to which we shall return.

However, there is one crucial area of inquiry which cannot be passed over here and which also sheds considerable light on the issue under discussion. Thus, Shivji argues that the main contradiction in Tanzania is now between the working-class and the bureaucratic bourgeoisie, and cites the dramatic assertions of Tanzania's working-class in recent years. Indeed, the further investigation of this subject by Shivji's colleague, Henry Mapolu, reveals a level of proletarian action in Tanzania which is virtually unparalleled elsewhere in Africa.[38] As Mapolu writes:

> "By any standards the progress made by the working population in Tanzania in the last few years as far as political consciousness is concerned is astounding. To begin with, at no other time in the whole history of this country have strikes and industrial disputes generally been so much a day-to-day affair as has become since 1970. But more important, at no other time have such strikes and disputes been of such a political nature! . . . It has indeed been a veritable revolution for the Tanzanian workers; within a period of three years they have moved from a state of docility, timidness, and above all disunity to one of tremendous bravery, initiative and class solidarity."

Beginning with the downing of tools and with lock-outs, some Tanzanian workers had moved, by 1973, to the stage of actually occupying factories (both state-owned and private) and continuing production on their own. And the issues were not, by and large, of a conventionally consumptionist nature. Disputes concerned, firstly, "the question of humiliation and oppression on their person by managements" and, ultimately, "issues of general mismanagement and sabotage of the country's economy". Predictably, such initiatives began to earn reprisals from the bureaucracy (including police intervention and arrests), thus polarizing the Tanzanian situation to an unprecedented degree.

But where did such a high level of consciousness come from? This too must be explained, especially when one compares this development with experience elsewhere in Africa. Moreover, the Tanzanian working-class is small, even by continental standards, and, in the past, not marked by notably radical leanings.[39] Once again, the conclusion suggests itself that initiatives taken by a certain sector of the leadership —notably by Nyerere and his supporters—played an important role in bringing about this development and in facilitating the emergence of what Shivji calls "the proletarian line". Unlike their Ghanaian counterparts, such a leadership did sense, albeit haltingly, that "the oppressed" could "alone have provided the conscious support for a socialist path of development"[40] and they therefore sought to create such a base. Initiatives designed to facilitate "workers' participation" (workers' councils) and peasant participation (*ujamaa* and decentralization) reflected this concern, despite the distortion in practice of these programmes by the dead-hand of the bureaucracy.[41] However, most significant in this respect has been *Mwongozo*, the TANU Guidelines of 1971—a crucial document in crystallizing worker consciousness and in legitimizing, *even demanding*, the unleashing of popular pressures against oligarchical tendencies on the part of wielders of state power ("leaders"). Yet the drive for these measures did not come from below. Even Shivji must come part way to meet that reality.

> "In the international situation where capitalism has become a global system and socialism has been established in a large area of the world: where both internally and externally physical and intellectual wars are raging between the capitalist and socialist lines, the world-wide circulation of progressive ideas has become commonplace. It is not surprising therefore that even capitalism and neo-colonialism have to be wrapped up in socialist rhetoric and vocabulary. But more important is the fact that though material *class* forces may not immediately warrant it, a few progressive and revolutionary leaders manage to push through (officially) radical ideas and policies. The adoption of the Mwongozo by TANU, with its progressive features, was such an event."

But who are these "few progressive and revolutionary leaders"? As Shivji suggests, they do shape and crystallize, rather than merely reflect, popular consciousness; moreover, they seem to be cutting sharply against the interests of the bureaucratic bourgeoisie. It is precisely because Shivji's approach cannot fully illuminate such matters that other analysts have felt some other formulation than his to be necessary in order to explain, in class terms, the "socialist" dimensions of Tanzania's experiment.

Indeed, it is only because it is much too evocative and dismissive a phrase that one avoids applying to Shivji's analysis Murray's epithet: "pseudo-Marxist determinism". Nonetheless, Murray's critique of Fitch and Oppenheimer is in many respects the best approach to Shivji. And Murray's positive formulations can also serve to promise much the most effective alternative approach to Tanzanian reality. In this respect it is worth noting that even the definitional problem (which Murray himself approached somewhat too obliquely) has been faced, quite straightforwardly, by Micheala von Freyhold—working from what is in effect, a closely related viewpoint to that of Murray. Her solution, in a recent paper, is to use the term "nizers" for the "x" in our socio-political equation. As she explains it:

> " 'Nizers' or 'nizations' (from Africanization) is a term applied by Tanzanians to refer to that stratum or class which social scientists have called 'educated elite',

'labour aristocracy', or 'petty bourgeoisie'—those who took over important administrative and economic positions when colonialism was defeated.

" 'Educated elite' is an ideological term bound up with the elitist theories of dubious origin. 'Labour aristocracy' suggests a link between workers and 'nizers' which . . . does not exist. 'Petty bourgeoisie' has a double meaning: it refers to small capitalists on the one hand and all those who look to the bourgeoisie as their model on the other. As long as the educated stratum to which we refer is directly employed by colonialists or a national bourgeoisie it is necessarily a petty bourgeoisie in the second sense. In the absence of such direct employers the educated stratum can choose whether it wants to remain subservient to those by whom it has been created. Since the stratum in question may decide to become a petit bourgeoisie in both senses we would prefer to reserve the term for that particular situation.

" 'Nizers' is a precise and dialectical term. It refers firstly to the progressive aspect of Africanization, to the promise that those who take over the power would return this power to the people on whose behalf they took it away from the colonialists.

"It refers secondly to the fact that the 'nizers' have not created the existing economic and social structure but have taken it over, either adapting to it or changing the built in dependency on imperialism.

"It refers thirdly to the negative possibility that the original promises are not held, that the structure is not changed, that those who have taken the power will usurp it for themselves.

"Which of the connotations of the term 'nizers' will emerge as the decisive one is subject to the still on-going struggle among the nizers and the kind of support the different factions can mobilize among other classes—the workers and the peasants."[42]

It is precisely to this "still on-going struggle among the nizers" that Freyhold traces the socialist impulse in Tanzania: "In 1967 an enlightened political leadership had decided that Tanzania should not turn into a neo-colonial society. The Leadership Code was to cut the links between public office-holders and petty capitalism and nationalisations were to bring foreign capital under control. . . . Both measures were . . . a vital first step." And the direction of further steps also remains, in her eyes, a contested matter. "While the transformation of the nizers is an obvious prerequisite for the promised creation of a socialist society it is obvious that it will not proceed without a protracted struggle within that educated stratum itself. What the progressive parts of Tanzania's nizers envisage as their future is not yet reality. As long as the future is undecided there are still two ways in which one can look at the present educated stratum: as a nascent petty bourgeoisie which will not only be a faithful agent of international capital but which will eventually solidify into a class with petty capitalist connections and orientations or as the precursors of a socialist avantguarde." Of course, the general definitional problem has probably not been laid to rest by Freyhold's coinage, suggestive though it is; nor does she directly address herself to Shivji's prognosis of bureaucratic consolidation *without* "petty capitalist connections". But the emphasis seems to me to be basically correct.[43]

To argue so is not to ignore the contradictions which mitigate, and even undermine, the achievements of Tanzania's progressive "nizers".

Quite the reverse. In the essay cited above (footnote 43), I have stressed the extent to which various pressures—international and domestic—do play upon the system in such a way as to strengthen the least progressive elements in the "present educated stratum" and to "solidify" that stratum into a privileged class. It is quite true, as Shivji has demonstrated in another of his papers, that international capitalism can make adjustments and begin to shape to its own purposes the fact of nationalization. Corporations join with aid agencies and international economic institutions in reactivating "conventional wisdom" and coopting those "oligarchs" who are inclined to be so tempted. In addition, the expansion of the state sector has had the *result* (but, to repeat, not the primary purpose) of expanding the number who are prepared merely to feed off it, in the absence of countervailing tendencies.[44] If, unlike Ghana, some more real effort has been made to create a new base for the state among the workers and peasants, the pace of bureaucratic consolidation seems to be outstripping that attempt. In consequence, demobilization of the peasantry becomes the more likely result, while workers find themselves set not merely against the most conservative of managers but against the state itself and the increasingly homogeneous class which defends it.

The negative weight of "objective conditions" has been reinforced by subjective conditions. As Murray's analysis would suggest, ideological contestation in Tanzania has been a creative factor of great importance, with Nyerere's formulations in particular being crucial to facilitating a move to the left. But this ideology of the progressive "nizers" has also been marked by inadequacies which some might like to term "petty bourgeois" in nature: a hostility to Marxism, for example, and the consequent lack of a fully scientific analysis of imperialism and class struggle.[45] And this problem has been compounded by a much too sanguine reliance on existing institutions of the inherited state (Ministries and Cabinets, an untransformed party) which cannot easily be turned to purposes of Socialist construction.[46] As demonstrated in my earlier essay, these factors too have made it difficult for Nyerere and others to consolidate their original initiatives. The results are paradoxical (and not pre-ordained, à la Shivji). The conservative wing of the nizers now threatens to inherit a socialist initiative (and an even more "overdeveloped" state than existed at the moment of independence) in the creation of which it had little hand but which it has sought to warp to its own purposes from the moment of the policy's first being announced. All of which is to approach Shivji's conclusion, though not by Shivji's route:

"This marks the beginning of the political struggle and the rise of the proletarian line. There is bound to be increasing opposition to bureaucratic methods of work and 'management's' dominance, themselves a reflection of the neo-colonial structure of the economy and the corresponding class structure. The struggles of the workers and peasants against internal and external vested class interests will characterize the subsequent class struggles in Tanzania."[47]

For it is necessary to reaffirm that much about this continuing class struggle has been shaped by the reality of struggle within the stratum of the "nizers"—within the "oligarchy-in-the-making", if you like—during the first post-colonial decade.

*   *   *

The critique of Shivji is also a qualification of Alavi's approach. Apart from points made earlier concerning the important differences in context which East Africa presents, and some of the implications of these differences, it can now be argued that Alavi's approach is too rigid to fully comprehend the uncertainties which define the historical process in the immediate post-colonial period. In Tanzania, his "oligarchies" become such only more slowly and with much more ambiguous results than his model would lead one to expect. At the same time it can be firmly stated that the pressures which moves the situation towards such an unsavoury result as he seeks to theorize are indeed powerful. And, as noted, there is no doubt that these pressures have been, and are continually, making themselves felt upon Tanzania. As a result, "oligarchical" tendencies—the consolidation of Shivji's "bureaucratic bourgeoisie" (self-interested and ever more subservient to imperialism)—seem to have been the increasingly obvious result.

Has the further development of this trend altered perspectives on practice in Tanzania? Writing two years ago I felt confident to conclude a survey of Tanzania's efforts at socialist construction in the following terms: "Indigenous radicals will decide their own fates. Yet the fact that almost all have chosen to work within the established structures and upon the régime is no accident."[48] And there is still some significant contestation within the "petty bourgeoisie" and within the established institutions.[49] But where, for example, one could then argue, with some confidence, that the control of working-class organization by party and state had played, despite the costs, a positive role in curbing consumptionism and raising worker consciousness, there is now reason to be more sceptical about the logic of continuing control. Faced with "nizers" more bent than ever upon consolidating their power, independent organization of the working-class may seem an increasingly important goal.[50] Similarly, the time may be approaching when the independent political organization of progressive elements, already a (difficult) priority in most other one-party and military/administrative régimes in Africa, becomes a priority for Tanzania as well. Smash the post-colonial state or use it? But this is really a question which can only be asked, and answered, by those engaged in significant *praxis* within Tanzania itself.

NOTES

1. Hamza Alavi, "The State in Post-Colonial Societies—Pakistan and Bangladesh" in *New Left Review*, 74 (July–August 1972), pp. 59–81.
2. The most prominent of these is Issa Shivji, author of "Tanzania: The Silent Class Struggle" in *Cheche*, Special Issue (Dar es Salaam), September 1970, reprinted in L. Cliffe and J. S. Saul (eds.), *Socialism in Tanzania*, Vol. 2 (Nairobi, 1973), pp. 304–30; and "Tanzania: The Class Struggle Continues" (mimeo, Department of Development Studies, University of Dar es Salaam, 1973). The interesting work of Henry Mapolu (see footnotes 38 and 41 below) and Karim Hirji (footnote 37), among others, can also be cited in this connection.
3. This quotation and others in this section are from Alavi, op. cit., unless otherwise indicated.
4. Alavi may overstate this particular point. Ralph Miliband has recently paraphrased Poulantzas approvingly to the effect that "the political realm is not, in classical Marxism, the mere reflection of the economic realm, and that in relation to the state, the notion of the latter's 'relative autonomy' is central, not only in regard to 'exceptional circumstances', but in *all* circumstances". And Miliband concludes that "in fact, this notion may be taken as the starting point of Marxist political theory". Nonetheless, Alavi's formulation of the concept of autonomy with specific reference to the post-colonial state—his focus on the "overdevelopment" of the inherited colonial state, for example—is a crucial and distinctive one. See Ralph Miliband, "Poulantzas and the Capitalist State", *New Left Review*, 82 (November–December 1973), p. 85.
5. Nicos Poulantzas, *Political Power and Social Classes* (London, 1973), p. 191.
6. It must also be noted, though only in passing, that other attributes of the post-colonial state, and of the elements which control it, can work simultaneously to undermine this very kind of unity. See Richard Sklar, "Political Science and National Integration", *The Journal of Modern African Studies* (1967) and John S. Saul, "The Dialectic of Tribe and Class in Kenya and Uganda" (forthcoming).
7. The movement is "direct" but it can also be very slow, with the possibility of many of the newly-created "peasantry" being caught, under African conditions and in the absence of genuine mobilization, in a kind of limbo of underdevelopment. See, generally, John S. Saul and Roger Woods, "African Peasantries" in T. Shanin (ed.), *Peasants and Peasant Societies* (London, 1971), pp. 103–13, and for a striking, if controversial, East African case-study, Colin Leys, "Politics in Kenya: The Development of Peasant Society" in *British Journal of Political Science*, I, pp. 307–37.
8. Frantz Fanon, *The Wretched of the Earth* (London, 1967), p. 122.
9. Issa Shivji, "Tanzania: The Silent Class Struggle" (op. cit.).
10. Poulantzas, op. cit., p. 334.
11. Regis Debray, "Problems of Revolutionary Strategy in Latin America", *New Left Review*, 45 (September–October 1967), p. 35.
12. This does, of course, raise some questions—for East Africa—about Alavi's juxtaposition of oligarchy and indigenous bourgeoisie. In Kenya, these two elements—among the Africans—interpenetrate to a significant degree, rather than compete with one another, though the strategic position of the *Asian* "commercial bour-

geoisie" might be argued to have affected this pattern on the African side. This is, in any case, an area of inquiry to which we will return in subsequent sections.

13. Shivji, "Tanzania: The Class Struggle Continues", op. cit.

14. R. H. Green, "Economic Independence and Economic Cooperation" in D. P. Ghai (ed.), *Economic Independence in Africa* (Nairobi, 1973), p. 85. In fact Green's error lies in vastly *over-estimating* the progressive attributes of the Tanzanian situation—even as Shivji, in his turn, underestimates them (see below).

15. For summaries of such findings see John S. Saul, "African Socialism in One Country: Tanzania" in G. Arrighi and J. S. Saul, *Essays on the Political Economy of Africa* (New York, 1973), Ch. 6, and Uchumi Editorial Board, *Towards Socialist Planning*, Tanzanian Studies No. 1 (Dar es Salaam, 1972).

16. C. Meillassoux, "A Class Analysis of the Bureaucratic Process in Mali", *The Journal of Development Studies* (January 1970).

17. Interestingly, Meillassoux makes no distinction between party and administration in his analysis: "In this situation the only people able to take responsibility and power upon themselves were those with literate, administrative and managerial capabilities, equally necessary to handle a political party or to govern a State."

18. Thus "if the conflict with local business was a consequence of the necessity of the bureaucracy to provide itself with an economic base, the fight against the aristocratic class was a more direct competition for political power" (Meillassoux, p. 106).

19. It is worth noting that these extensions of the argument differ from Fanon's conclusion to what is otherwise a somewhat similar analysis, for Fanon seems to imply that such elements will infiltrate the national economy by moving in on the trading sector as entrepreneurs—viz., the very definition of this class as "an intellectual élite engaged in trade". Here is a very significant difference of opinion, as we shall see in examining Shivji's work more closely in Section III.

20. R. Fitch and M. Oppenheimer, *Ghana: End of an Illusion* (New York, 1966).

21. Roger Murray, "Second Thoughts on Ghana", *New Left Review*, 42 (March–April, 1967).

22. It should be noted that Murray tends to talk only of the members of the ruling political party when he discusses those who inherit the state; he does not really deal with the bureaucracy's role in all of this, despite his recognizing the need for "an appraisal of the politico-administrative role and weight of the *civil service* within the state apparatus". However, his characterization of the "autonomy and plasticity" of "the political class" would seem also to apply to the bureaucracy; under such circumstances they seem equally to be elements whose "partial and 'transitional' character . . . expresses itself in its absence of a determinate class standpoint grounded upon its site in the process of production". Interestingly, Meillassoux, from his different perspective, makes little distinction between bureaucrat and politician in identifying the state-based dominants in Mali (cf. footnote 17, above). This is also Shivji's approach; in Tanzania the civil service and political hierarchies interpenetrate and he is prepared to view members of both as candidates for his categories of "petty bourgeoisie" and "bureaucratic bourgeoisie".

23. On the problem of developing terms adequate to the task of dialectical analysis of real historical processes, see Bertil Ollman, *Alienation: Marx's Conception of Man in Capitalist Society* (Cambridge, 1971), especially Part I.

24. As Murray continues: "Socially, then, the picture we have is of a petty bourgeois group projected into the power vacuum caused by the lack of objective maturation of a nationalist capitalist class and the subjective errors of aspirant bourgeois politicians."

25. Thus, "the whole Nkrumahist ideological complex was undergoing profound

mutation in the 1960s. This process has two particularly striking features: the attempt to transcend the 'African Socialism' current of thought in favour of a more universal and scientific theory; and the related effort to institutionalize and accelerate the formation of an *ideological vanguard* of cadres who might then strive to make ideology a mass force (Winneba). This development, marked as it was by bizarre juxtapositions and unresolved contradictions, nevertheless acquires considerable significance . . ." All of which is not to deny that it was a "misconceived, contradictory 'socialism' " which emerged, characterized by (among other things) "the loss of any *integral commanding strategy*" (Murray, ibid.).

26. Actually this struggle can even be seen to take place *within* the individual members of this unformed "x" as they struggle with the "bizarre juxtapositions and unresolved contradictions" in their own lives, a reality which was dramatized for me during seven years of work with young recruits to the "petty bourgeoisie" at the University of Dar es Salaam.

27. Amilcar Cabral, "Brief Analysis of the Social Structure in Guinea" in his *Revolution in Guinea* (London, 1969), p. 59; the point is elaborated upon in his excellent essay "The Weapon of Theory" in the same volume.

28. Thus Murray (op. cit.) states that the "implicit positive model" offered by Fitch and Oppenheimer is "that of a political party which made the situation and demands of the most oppressed classes (urban and rural proletariat, sharecroppers, indebted tenant farmers) the absolute 'moral imperative' of its organization and action. This class-based party, acting for and through the oppressed but potentially revolutionary strata of society, could alone have provided the conscious support for a socialist path of development—with all its costs and risks." But he concludes of Ghana that "instead, the CPP demobilized these 'potential' forces".

29. Walter Rodney, "Some Implications of the Question of Disengagement from Imperialism" in *Majimaji* (Dar es Salaam, 1971), and reprinted in Cliffe and Saul, op. cit., volume II. The explicit reference to Shivji arises from the fact that Rodney is here reviewing the first of Shivji's two papers cited in footnote 2, above.

30. See, among other of his articles, Pratt's "The Cabinet and Presidential Leadership in Tanzania: 1960–66" in M. Lofchie (ed.), *The State of the Nations* (Berkeley and Los Angeles, 1971) and reprinted in Cliffe and Saul, ibid., volume II.

31. See footnote 2, above; succeeding quotations are from the second of Shivji's two papers, unless otherwise indicated.

32. Not crucial, but there is an ambiguity in the term "petty bourgeoisie" which is revealed here, one to which we will return in discussing Freyhold's attempt to conceptualize Tanzania's class structure.

33. Shivji gives no numerical basis to his argument, but I have elsewhere cited Resnick's argument that "out of 350,000 persons employed in wage and salaried jobs in 1968, only 44,000 fall into the 'privileged' class, . . . that is, are in occupations classified as 'high- and middle-level' by manpower definitions". See I. N. Resnick, "Class, Foreign Trade and Socialist Transformation in Tanzania", paper presented to the Economics Research Bureau Seminar, University of Dar es Salaam (mimeo, 1972).

34. As noted above (footnote 22), Shivji makes little distinction between party and civil service; nor do his critics who adhere, in effect, to the Murray line of analysis —although the latter might argue that rather more representatives of this progressive petty-bourgeoisie are to be found in the party (which has, however, a tendency to become itself bureaucratized).

35. Thus Nyerere has argued that "some Tanzanian leaders criticized the Arusha Declaration" because "they wished to use positions of power for private gain" and "almost the only way in which Africans could get capital to become landlords or capitalists was by virtue of their office or their seniority in the public service"; see

his "Introduction" to J. K. Nyerere, *Freedom and Socialism* (Nairobi, London, New York, 1968).

36. Such a conclusion with reference to the Tanzanian case, paralleling Murray's critique of Fitch and Oppenheimer's handling of Ghanaian developments, also raises some retrospective doubts about Meillassoux's discussion of Mali. Was the socialist assertion there as straightforwardly manipulative as Meillassoux suggests?

37. Shivji's model has been applied, with interesting results, to the educational sphere by Karim Hirji in his essay "School Education and Underdevelopment in Tanzania", *Majimaji*, 12 (September 1973). More alert to the ideological dimensions of Tanzanian development and very insightful, Hirji's analysis suffers, nonetheless, from some of the same rigidities as Shivji's. I intend to discuss his argument in more detail in a monograph on the University of Dar es Salaam, now in preparation.

38. Henry Mapolu, "The Workers' Movement in Tanzania", *Majimaji*, 12 (September 1973). See also Mapolu's "Labour unrest: irresponsibility or worker revolution", *Jenga* (Dar es Salaam), 12 (1972) and Nick Asili, "Strikes in Tanzania", *Majimaji*, 4 (September 1971).

39. For a subtle account which highlights the dialectic established in Tanzania between a committed section of the leadership and a working-class with steadily rising consciousness, see M. A. Bienefeld, "Workers, Unions and Development in Tanzania", paper delivered to a conference on "Trade Unions and the Working-Class in Africa", Toronto, 1973. Even NUTA, the official trade union ("that moribund organization", in Bienefeld's words) is seen to have played a role in this respect: "For its creation did forestall the creation of the self-centred, competitive unions, whose function and mentality is so well suited to the kind of interest group politics which the most powerful interests in an open economy find congenial, and who are so easily moulded into the business unions whose existence is defined by the capitalist economy. . . . (T)he worker was freed from the mesmerising spectacle of the perpetual competition for leadership by men who fight with promises for the spoils of office, while . . . the very bureaucratic nature of NUTA made it possible for the workers' allegiance to be transferred to the government more permanently."

40. Cf. footnote 28. Nyerere very early sounded the themes which were later to find expression in Mwongozo; thus, in 1967, he "called on the people of Tanzania to have great confidence in themselves and safeguard the nation's hard-won freedom. He warned the people against pinning all their hopes on the leadership who are apt to sell the people's freedom to meet their lusts. Mwalimu (i.e., Nyerere) warned that the people should not allow their freedom to be pawned as most of the leaders were purchasable" (*The Nationalist*, 5 September 1967).

41. On the very real and disturbing distortions in practice, however, see the striking analyses of Henry Mapolu, "The Organization and Participation of Workers in Tanzania", Economics Research Bureau Paper 72.1 (Dar es Salaam, 1972) and Phil Raikes, "Ujamaa Vijijini and Rural Socialist Development", paper delivered to the East African Universities Social Science Conference, Dar es Salaam, December 1973.

42. M. von Freyhold, "The Workers and the Nizers" (mimeo, University of Dar es Salaam, 1973). At the same time, it is also worth noting (as I am reminded by John Loxley) that in its popular usage the term "nizers" is generally applied by workers and peasants in a pejorative sense!

43. Indeed, it is quite close, in certain respects, to my account of the emergence of Tanzanian socialism in "African Socialism in One Country: Tanzania", op. cit. There, however, the prognosis of bureaucratic consolidation without petty capitalist connections *is* explored and one all too possible post-"socialist" system characterized as "the creation of a vicious circle within which a petty bourgeoisie,

on balance still relatively untransformed, demobilizes and instrumentalizes the mass of the population and guarantees, at best, a stagnant quasi-state capitalism, thereby checking further progress" (p. 298).

44. This is all the more likely to be the case precisely because this expansion of state activities into the economic sphere does expand the contact of the nizers with international corporations through management contracts, etc. and international economic agencies which are among the most co-optative of imperialism's many mechanisms.

45. Unfortunately, this tends (as again argued in my earlier paper) towards the same result as Murray noted in Ghana: "the loss of any *integral commanding strategy*".

46. This is the strongest point made in Haroub Othman, "The State in Tanzania: Who Controls It and Whose Interests does it Serve" (mimeo, Institute of Development Studies, University of Dar es Salaam, Tanzania, n.d.).

47. Shivji, op. cit., p. 107. Furthermore, if such a polarization of classes is indeed taking place in Tanzania, it can be predicted that an increased emphasis upon the *repressive* functions of the state will also serve to enhance that state's prominence in post-colonial Tanzania!

48. Saul, op. cit., p. 312.

49. An example is the passage of a quite progressive income tax bill in late 1973. Originally rejected by Parliament, it was passed without dissent by the same Parliament when it was reconvened for the purpose by an irate President Nyerere. The latter stated that "I am not prepared to accept that a Bill beneficial to the majority, should be rejected simply because it is not liked by a minority. If we agree to this, we will be setting a dangerous precedent whereby an entrenched minority can prevent measures aimed at promoting ujamaa from being taken. I reject this vehemently in the name of Tanu" (*The Daily News*, Tanzania, 29 November 1973). Paradoxically, this incident reveals both some of the strength and some of the weakness of the President's role in trying to lead a socialist transition. Moreover, the President's response to worker unrest has been rather more equivocal.

50. The place of popular forces in the Tanzanian socialist equation, although it has been somewhat slighted in this essay, has been discussed further in "African Socialism in One Country: Tanzania". Moreover, the possible role of the "peasants" in defining Tanzania's future raises even more complex questions than does the case of the workers. The range of variation of "peasantries" across so large and diverse a country is vast in any case, and expressions of peasant consciousness have not been so dramatic as those of the workers. But it seems likely that the experience of "nizer-socialism" has had some positive impact upon consciousness—and upon the future (despite the fact that bureaucratization, and World Bank "assistance", has undermined many officially-sponsored programmes). For a suggestive case-study see Adhu Awiti, *Class Struggle in Rural Society in Tanzania* (*Majimaji*, 7, October 1972) and, for a broader overview, my "African Peasantries and Revolutionary Change" in *Review of African Political Economy*, I, 1 (1974), especially Section V, "Tanzania".